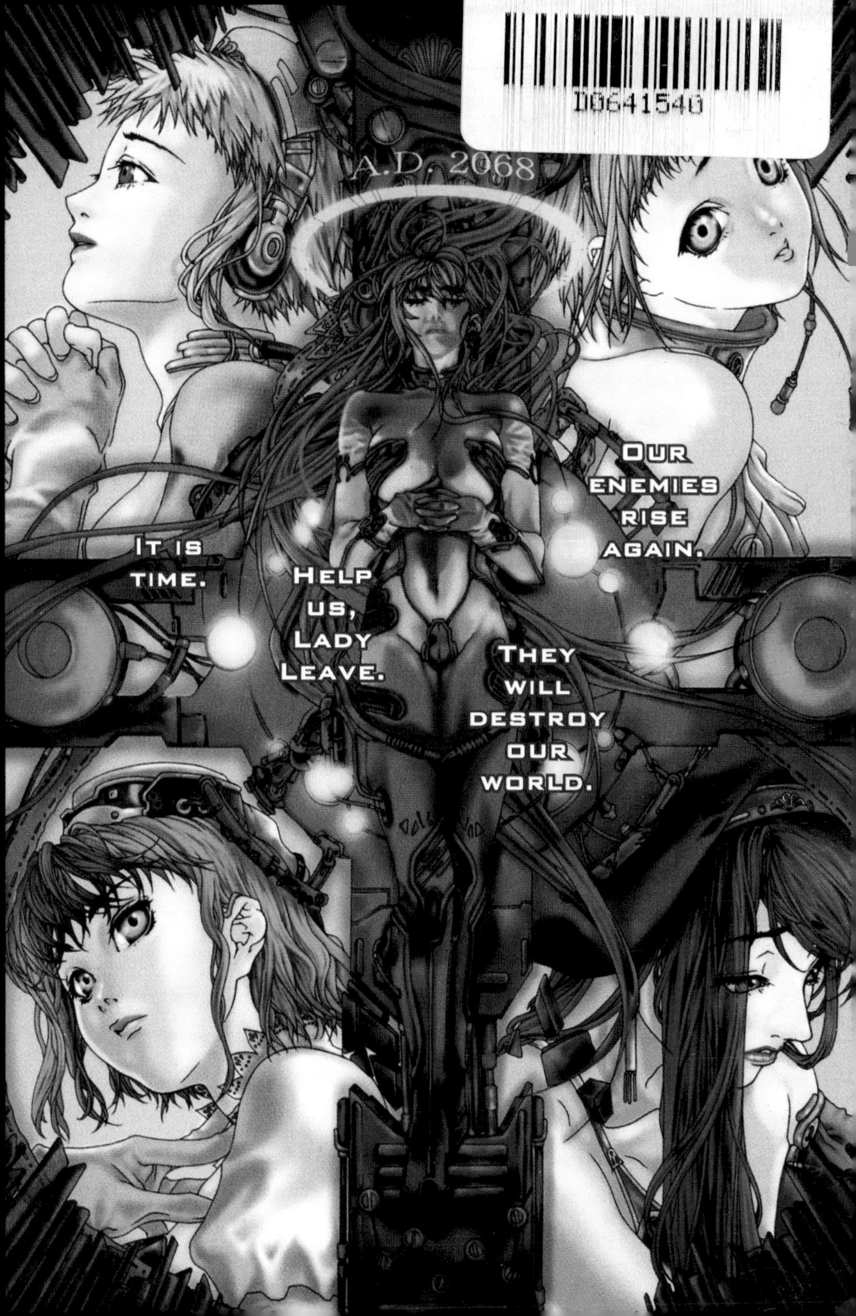
A.D. 2068
Our enemies rise again.
They will destroy our world.
It is time.
Help us, Lady Leave.

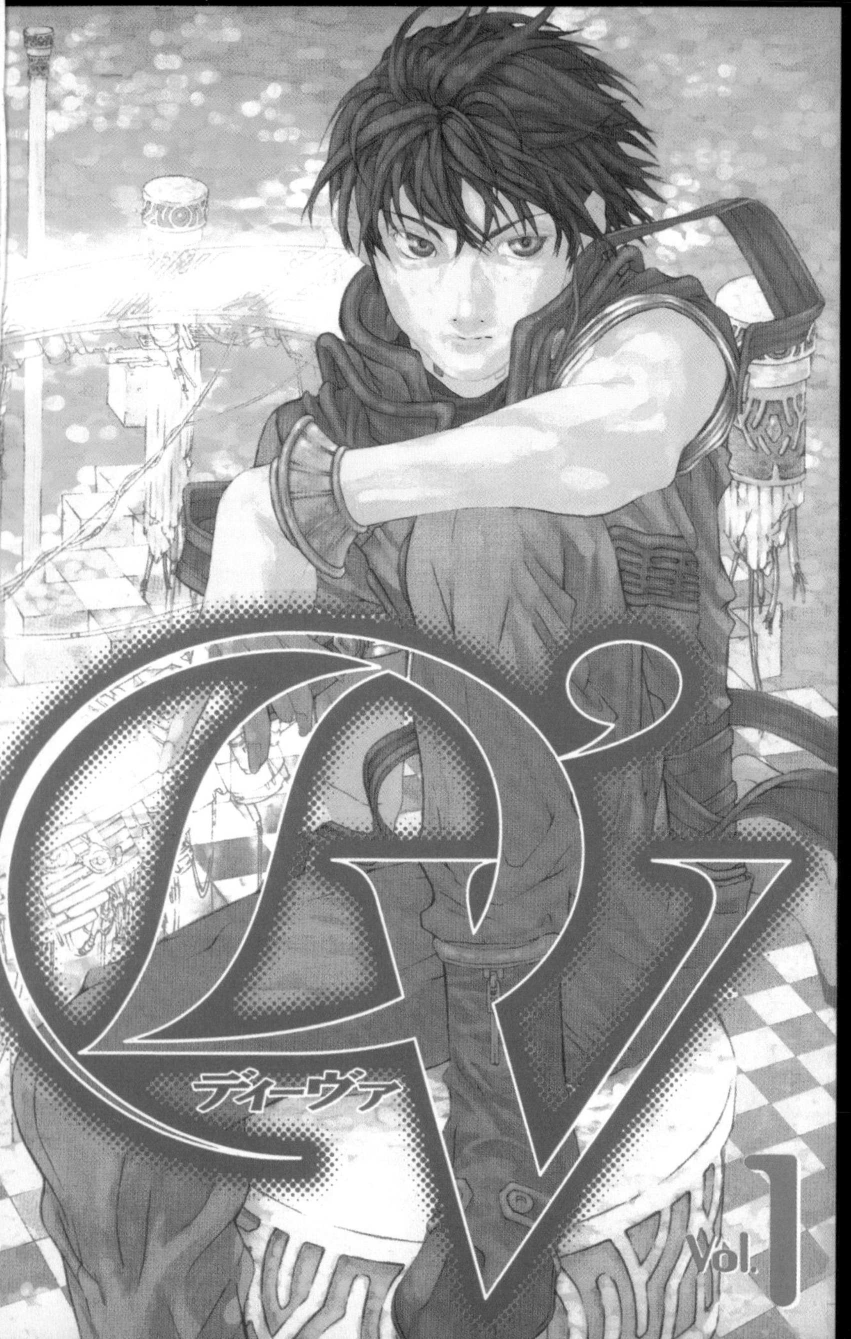
D'V
ディーヴァ
Vol. 1

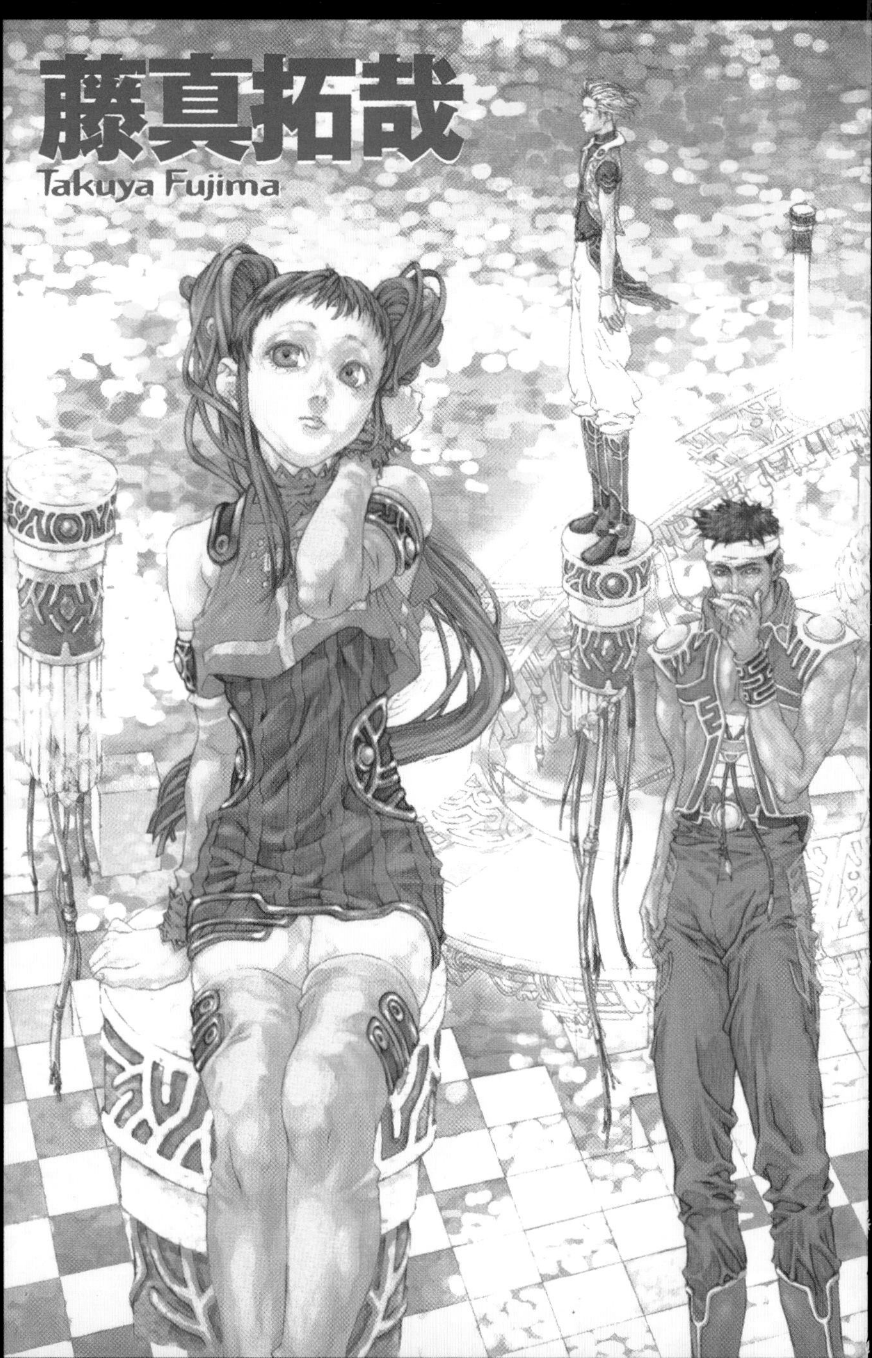
藤真拓哉
Takuya Fujima

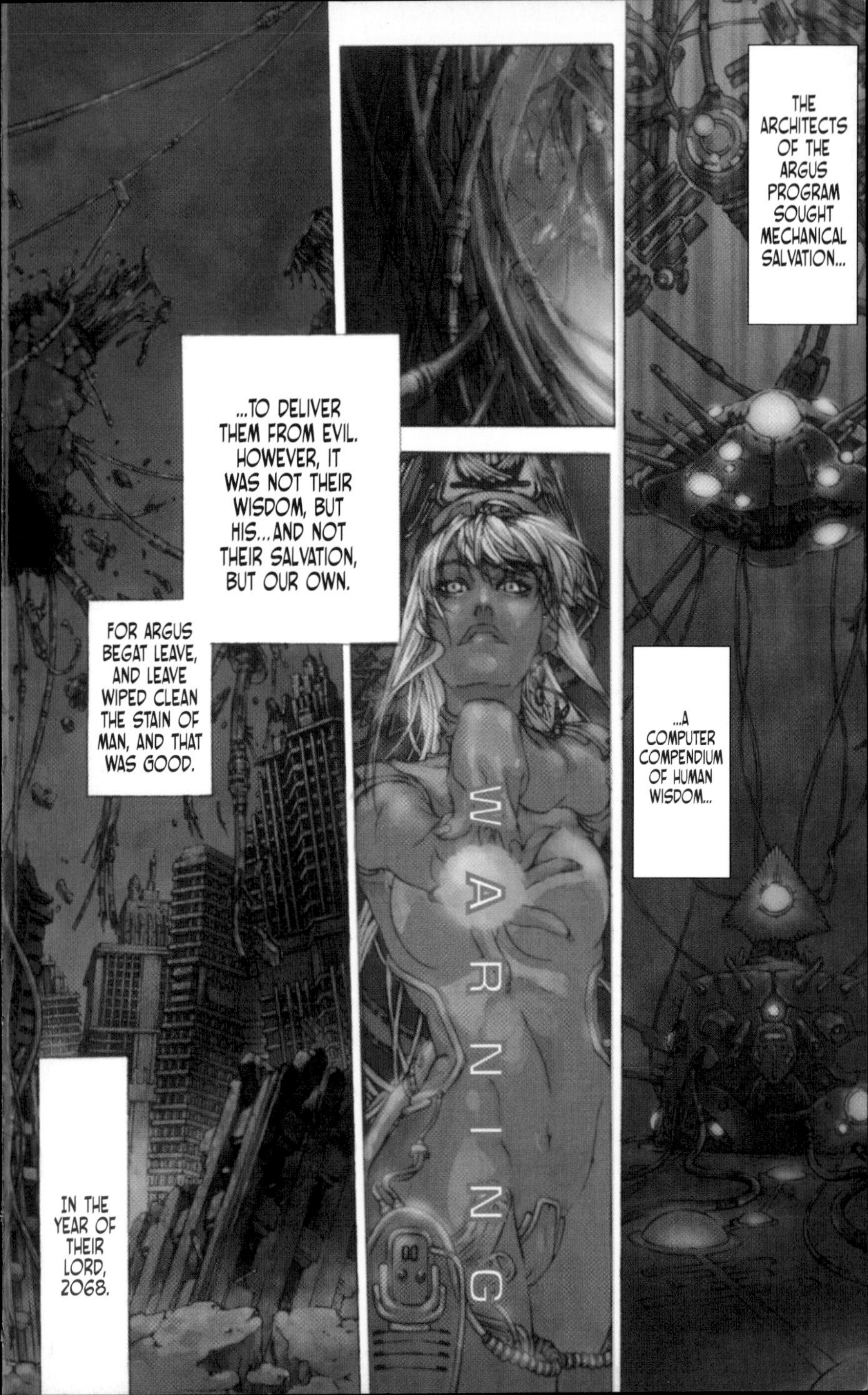
THE ARCHITECTS OF THE ARGUS PROGRAM SOUGHT MECHANICAL SALVATION...
...A COMPUTER COMPENDIUM OF HUMAN WISDOM...
WARNING
...TO DELIVER THEM FROM EVIL. HOWEVER, IT WAS NOT THEIR WISDOM, BUT HIS...AND NOT THEIR SALVATION, BUT OUR OWN.
FOR ARGUS BEGAT LEAVE, AND LEAVE WIPED CLEAN THE STAIN OF MAN, AND THAT WAS GOOD.
IN THE YEAR OF THEIR LORD, 2068.

Volume 1

Los Angeles • Tokyo • London • Hamburg

Translator - Kumiko Yuasa
English Adaptation - Matt Yamashita
Retouch and Lettering - Jose Macasocol, Jr.
Cover Layout - Harlin Harris

Editor - Luis Reyes
Digital Imaging Manager - Chris Buford
Pre-Press Manager - Antonio DePietro
Production Managers - Jennifer Miller, Mutsumi Miyazaki
Art Director - Matt Alford
Managing Editor - Jill Freshney
VP of Production - Ron Klamert
President & C.O.O. - John Parker
Publisher & C.E.O. - Stuart Levy

E-mail: info@TOKYOPOP.com
Come visit us online at www.TOKYOPOP.com

A **TOKYOPOP**® Manga

TOKYOPOP Inc.
5900 Wilshire Blvd. Suite 2000
Los Angeles, CA 90036

Deus Vitae Vol. 1

ISBN: 1-59182-769-8

First TOKYOPOP printing: June 2004

10 9 8 7 6 5 4 3 2 1

Printed in the USA

A.D. 2068
THE FUTURE IS THEIRS.

PROGRAMMED WITH THE SUM OF HUMAN
KNOWLEDGE, THE ARGUS COMPUTER WAS BUILT
TO PROTECT HUMANITY. INSTEAD, IT CREATED
LEAVE, THE ULTIMATE WEAPON AND THE MOTHER
OF A NEW MASTER RACE.

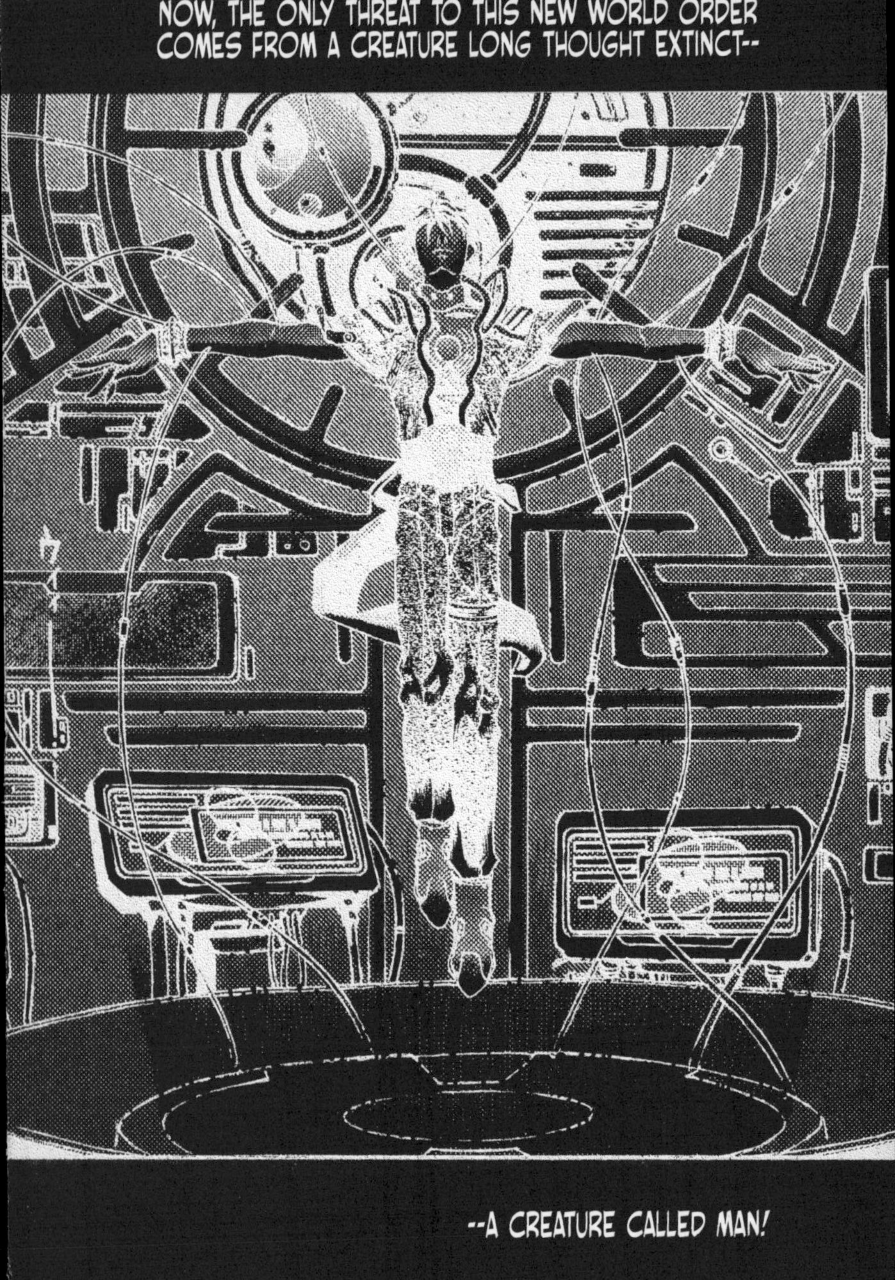
NOW, THE ONLY THREAT TO THIS NEW WORLD ORDER COMES FROM A CREATURE LONG THOUGHT EXTINCT--
--A CREATURE CALLED MAN!

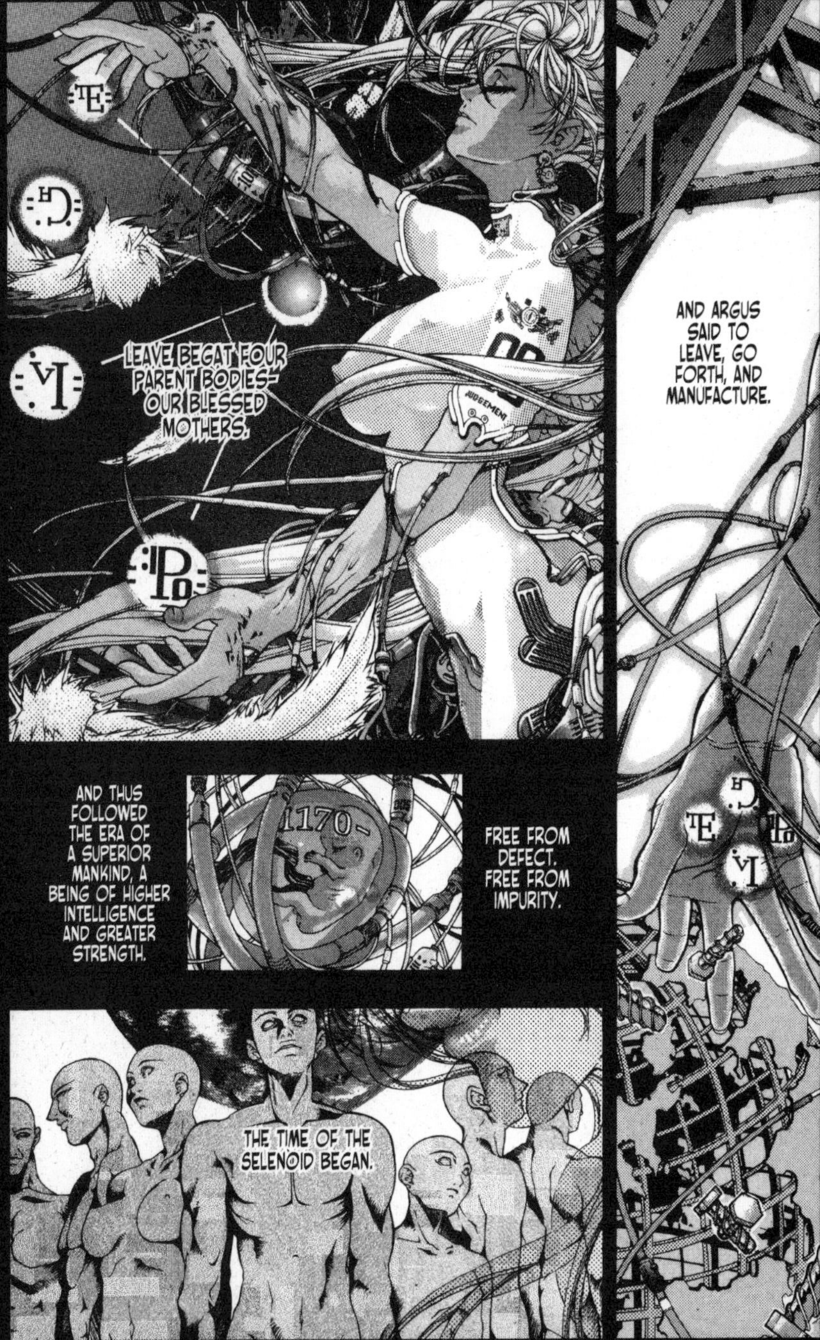
AND ARGUS SAID TO LEAVE, GO FORTH, AND MANUFACTURE.
LEAVE BEGAT FOUR PARENT BODIES- OUR BLESSED MOTHERS.
AND THUS FOLLOWED THE ERA OF A SUPERIOR MANKIND, A BEING OF HIGHER INTELLIGENCE AND GREATER STRENGTH.
1170-
FREE FROM DEFECT. FREE FROM IMPURITY.
THE TIME OF THE SELENOID BEGAN.

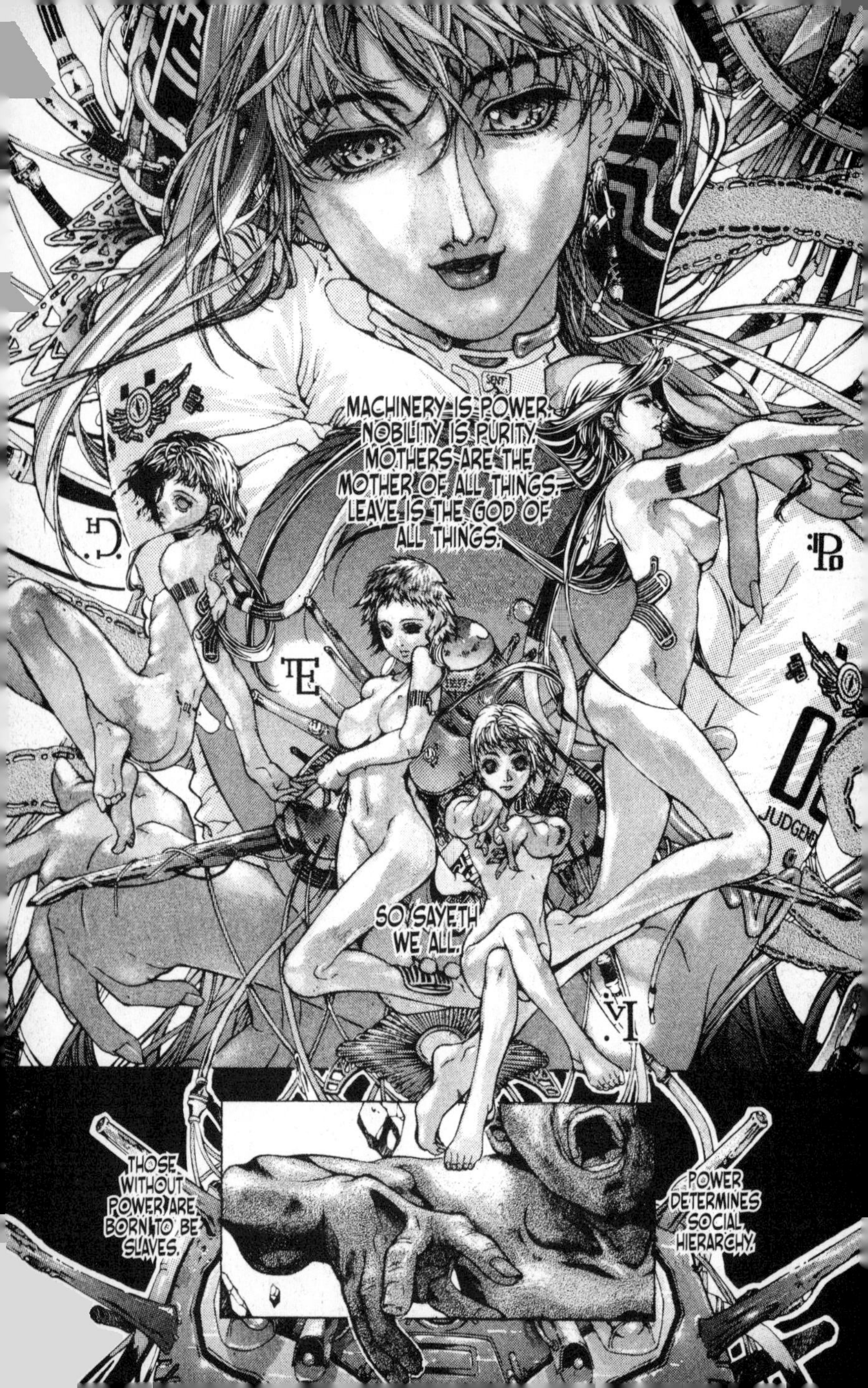
MACHINERY IS POWER. NOBILITY IS PURITY. MOTHERS ARE THE MOTHER OF ALL THINGS. LEAVE IS THE GOD OF ALL THINGS.
SO SAYETH WE ALL.
POWER DETERMINES SOCIAL HIERARCHY.
THOSE WITHOUT POWER ARE BORN TO BE SLAVES.

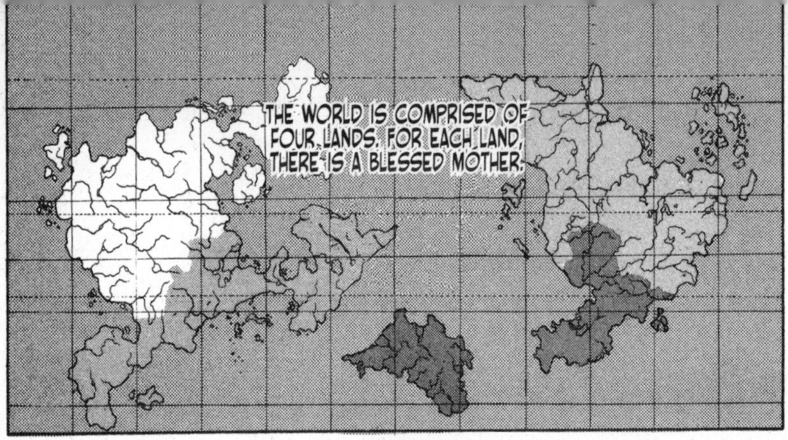
THE WORLD IS COMPRISED OF FOUR LANDS. FOR EACH LAND, THERE IS A BLESSED MOTHER.

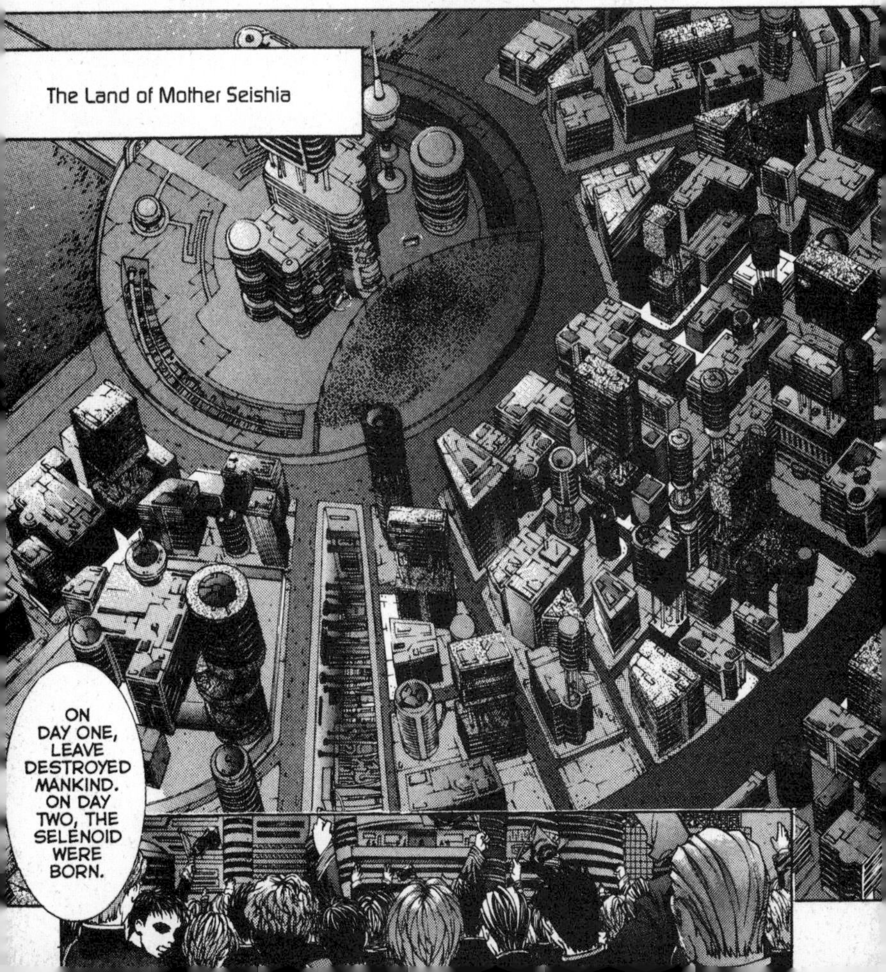
The Land of Mother Seishia
ON DAY ONE, LEAVE DESTROYED MANKIND. ON DAY TWO, THE SELENOID WERE BORN.

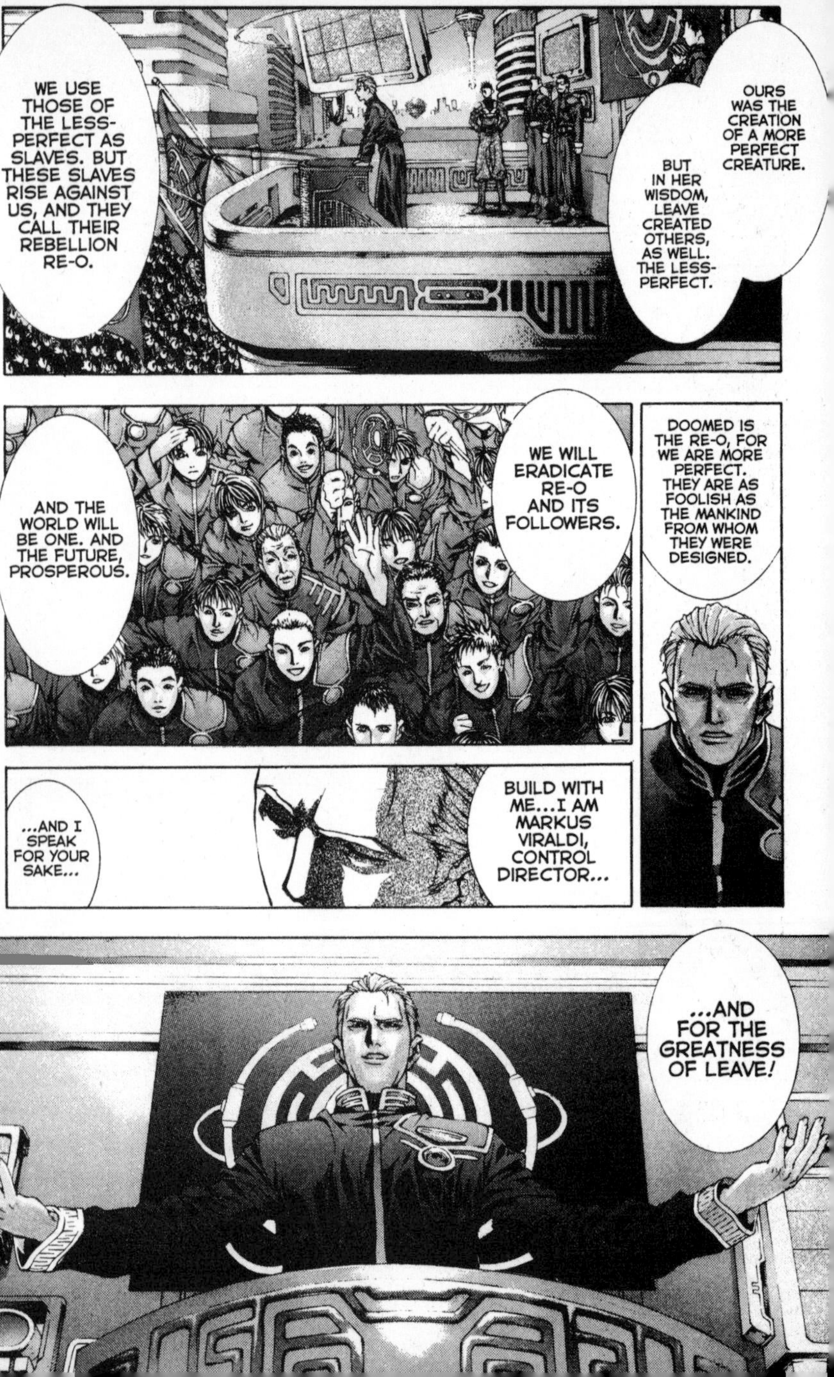
OURS WAS THE CREATION OF A MORE PERFECT CREATURE.
BUT IN HER WISDOM, LEAVE CREATED OTHERS, AS WELL. THE LESS-PERFECT.
WE USE THOSE OF THE LESS-PERFECT AS SLAVES. BUT THESE SLAVES RISE AGAINST US, AND THEY CALL THEIR REBELLION RE-O.
DOOMED IS THE RE-O, FOR WE ARE MORE PERFECT. THEY ARE AS FOOLISH AS THE MANKIND FROM WHOM THEY WERE DESIGNED.
WE WILL ERADICATE RE-O AND ITS FOLLOWERS.
AND THE WORLD WILL BE ONE. AND THE FUTURE, PROSPEROUS.
BUILD WITH ME...I AM MARKUS VIRALDI, CONTROL DIRECTOR...
...AND I SPEAK FOR YOUR SAKE...
...AND FOR THE GREATNESS OF LEAVE!

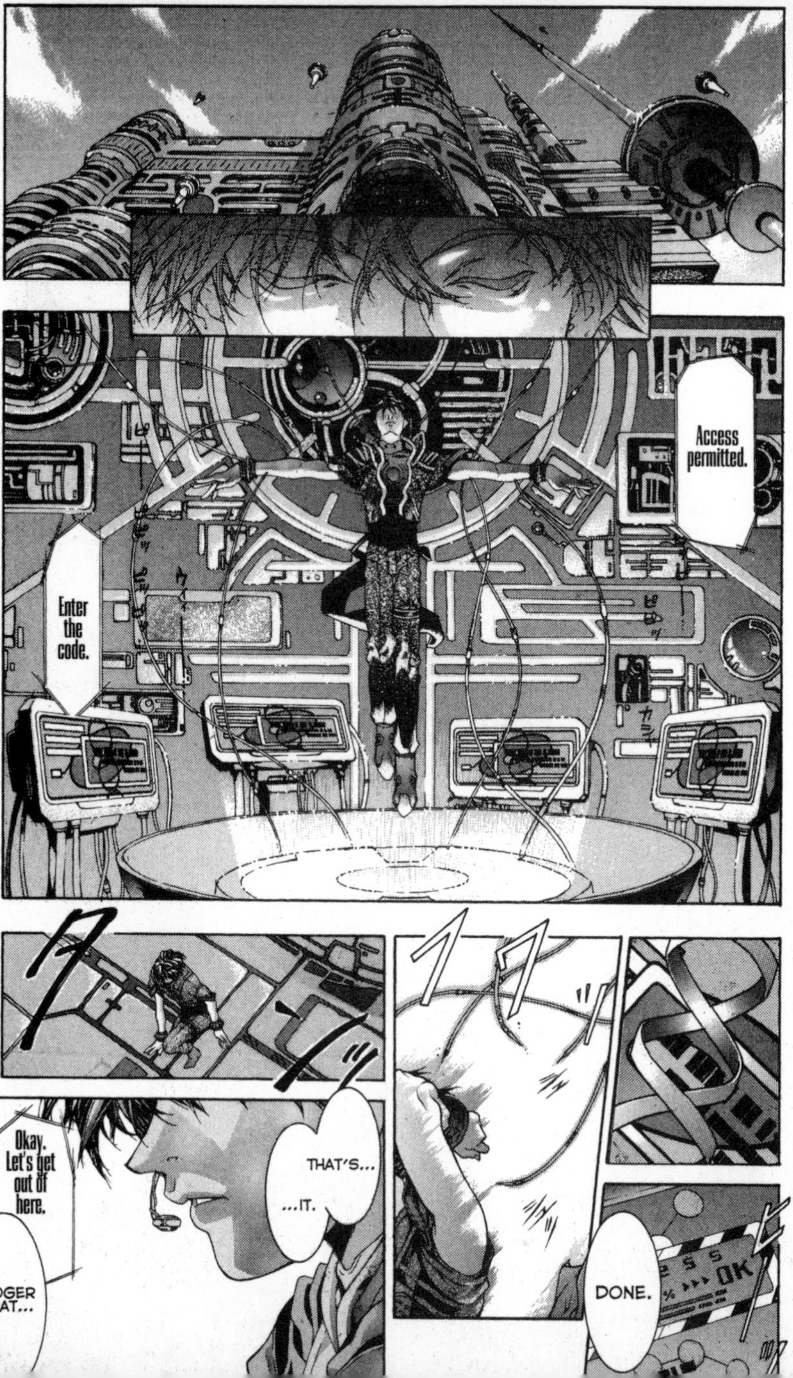
Access permitted.
Enter the code.
DONE.
THAT'S...
...IT.
Okay. Let's get out of here.
ROGER THAT...

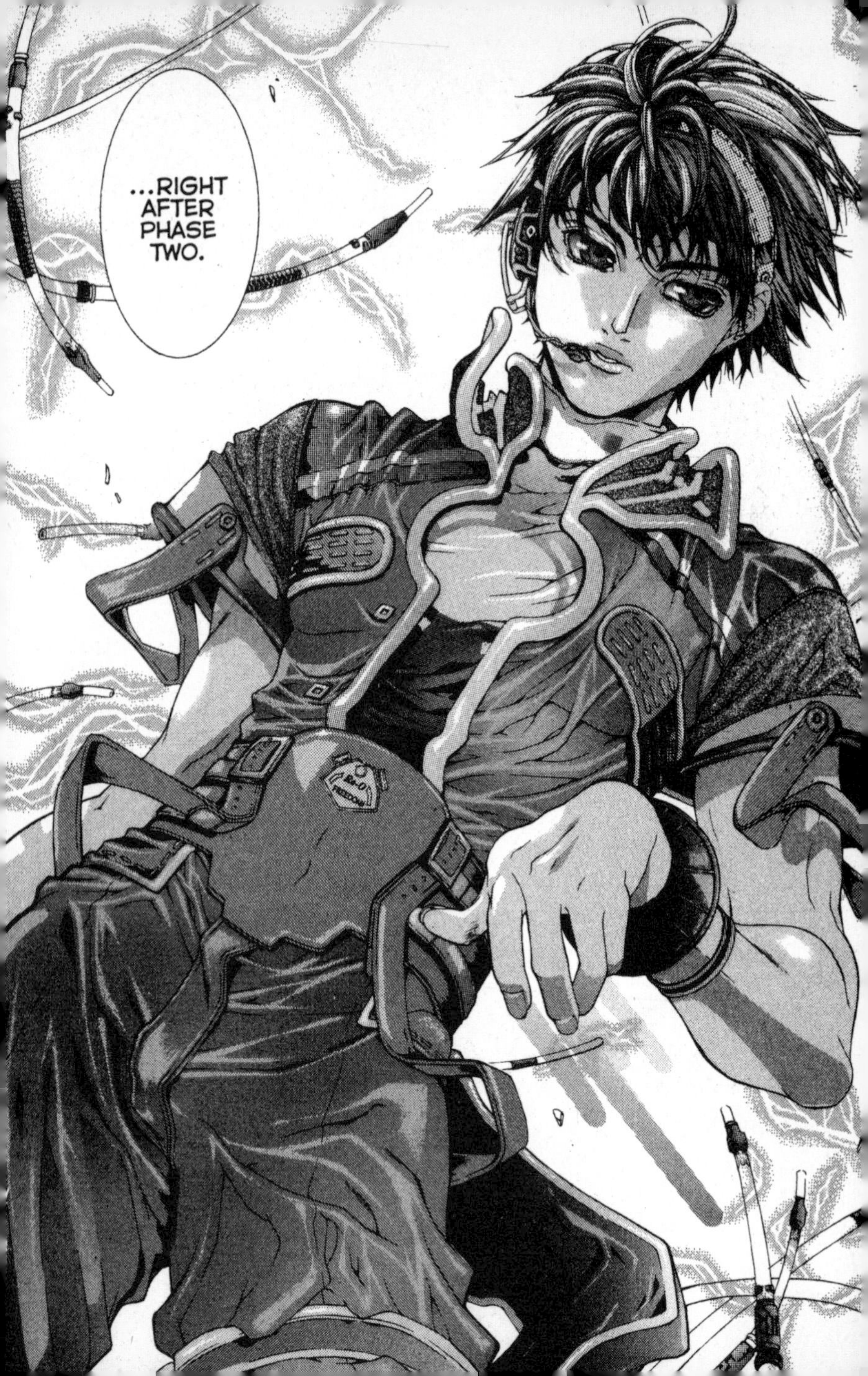
...RIGHT AFTER PHASE TWO.

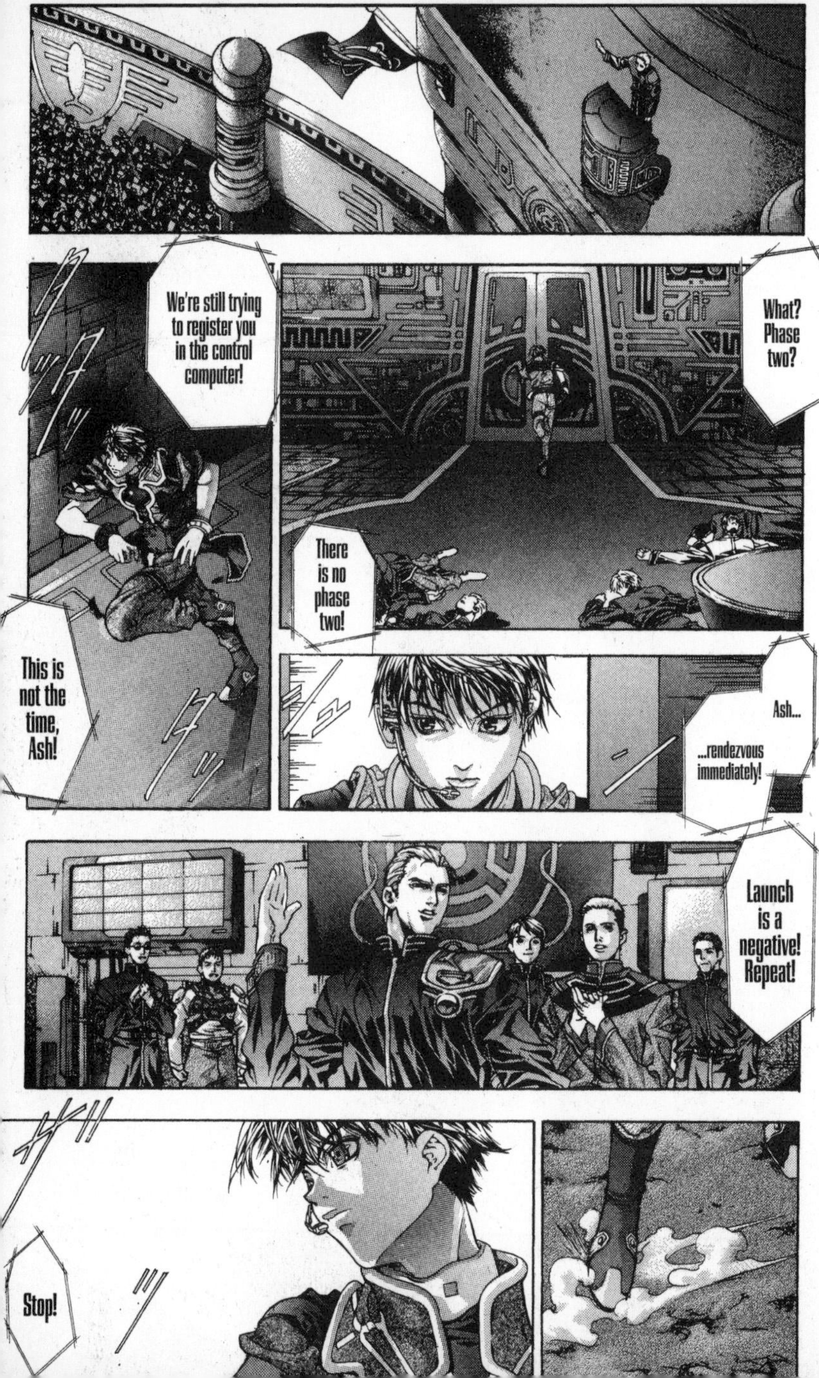
What? Phase two?
There is no phase two!
Ash...
...rendezvous immediately!
We're still trying to register you in the control computer!
This is not the time, Ash!
Launch is a negative! Repeat!
Stop!

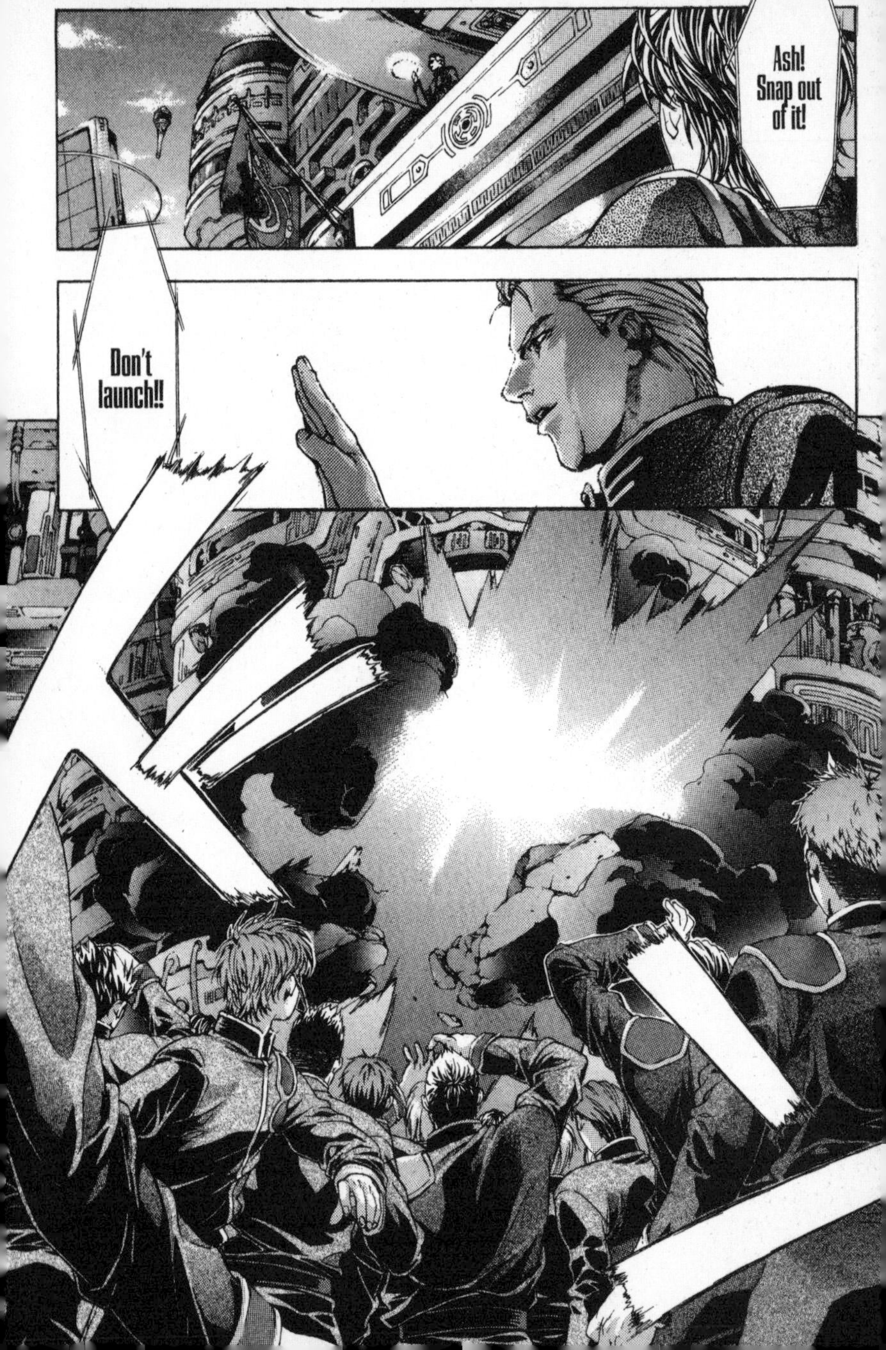
Ash! Snap out of it!
Don't launch!!

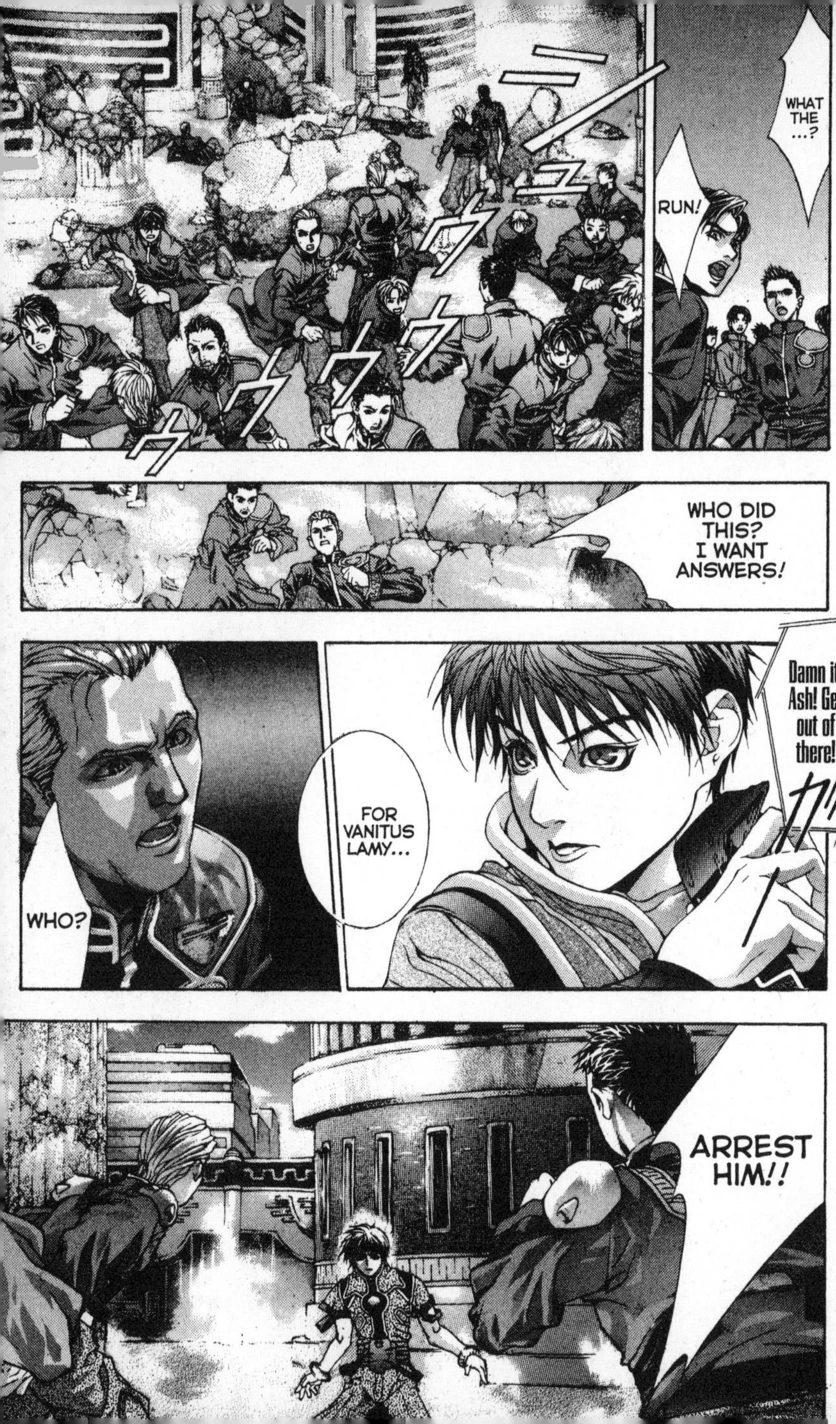
WHAT THE ...?
RUN!
WHO DID THIS? I WANT ANSWERS!
Damn it, Ash! Get out of there!
FOR VANITUS LAMY...
WHO?
ARREST HIM!!

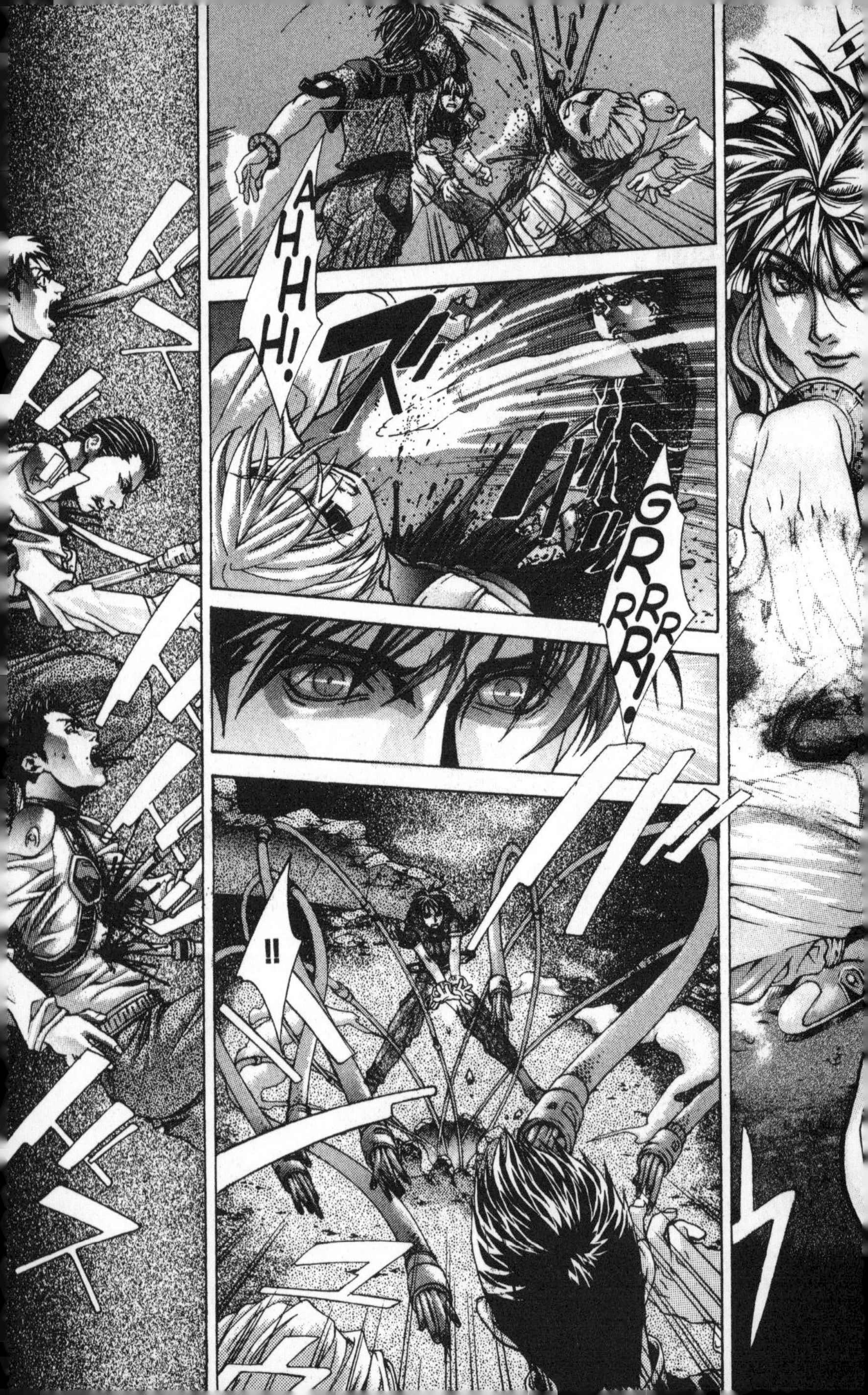
AHHHH!
GRRRRR!
!!

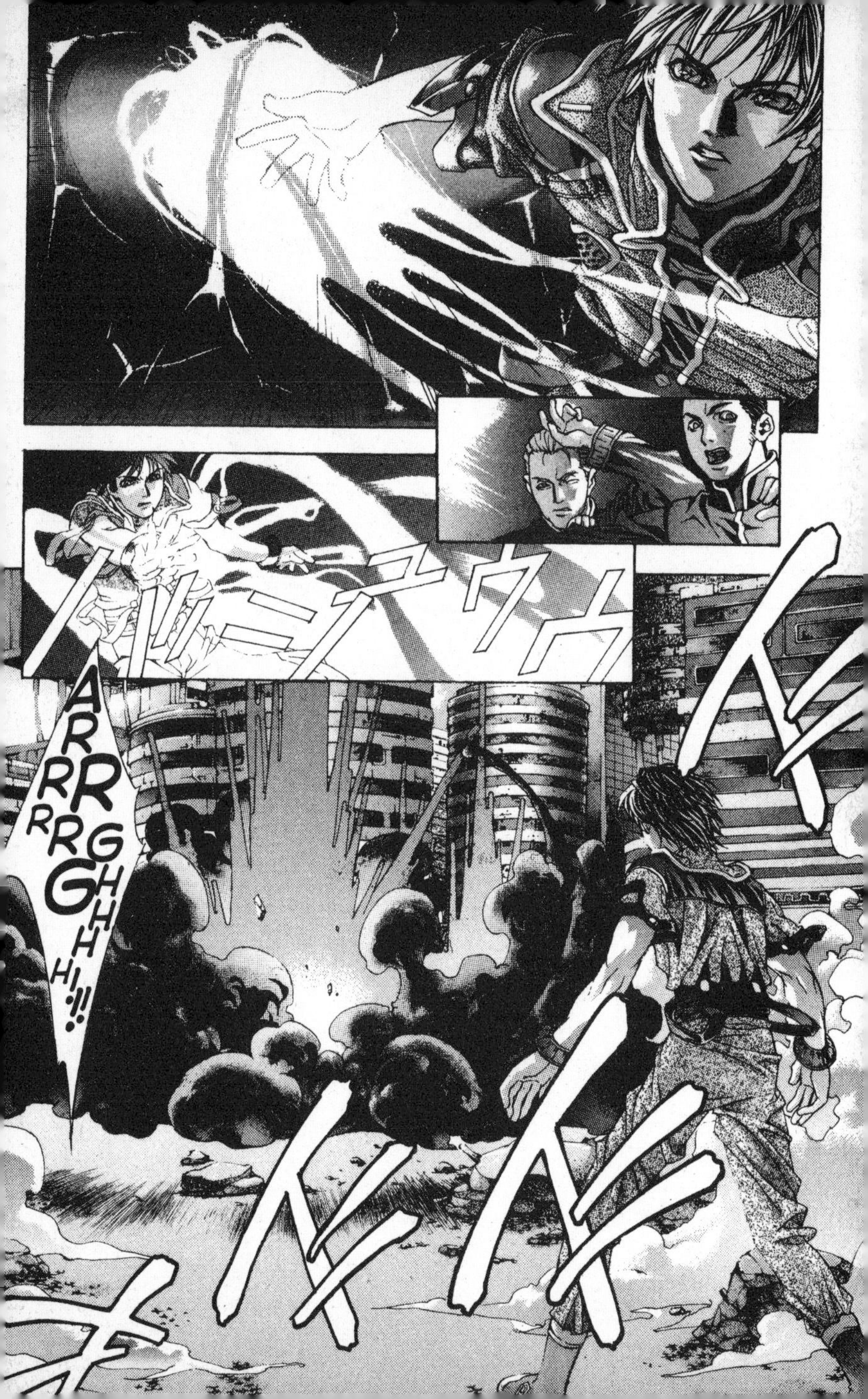
ARRRRGGHHHHH!!!

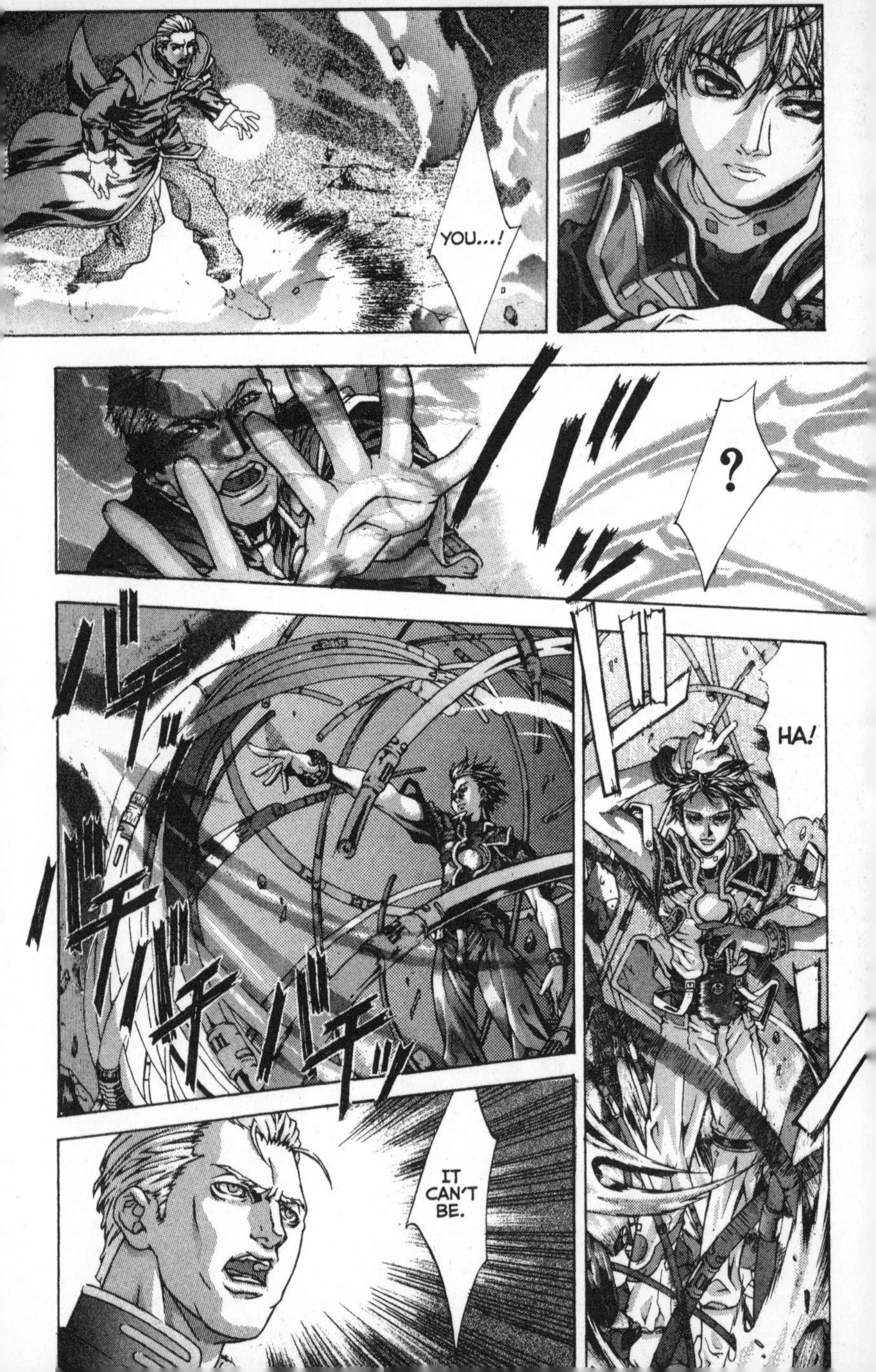
YOU...!
?
HA!
IT CAN'T BE.

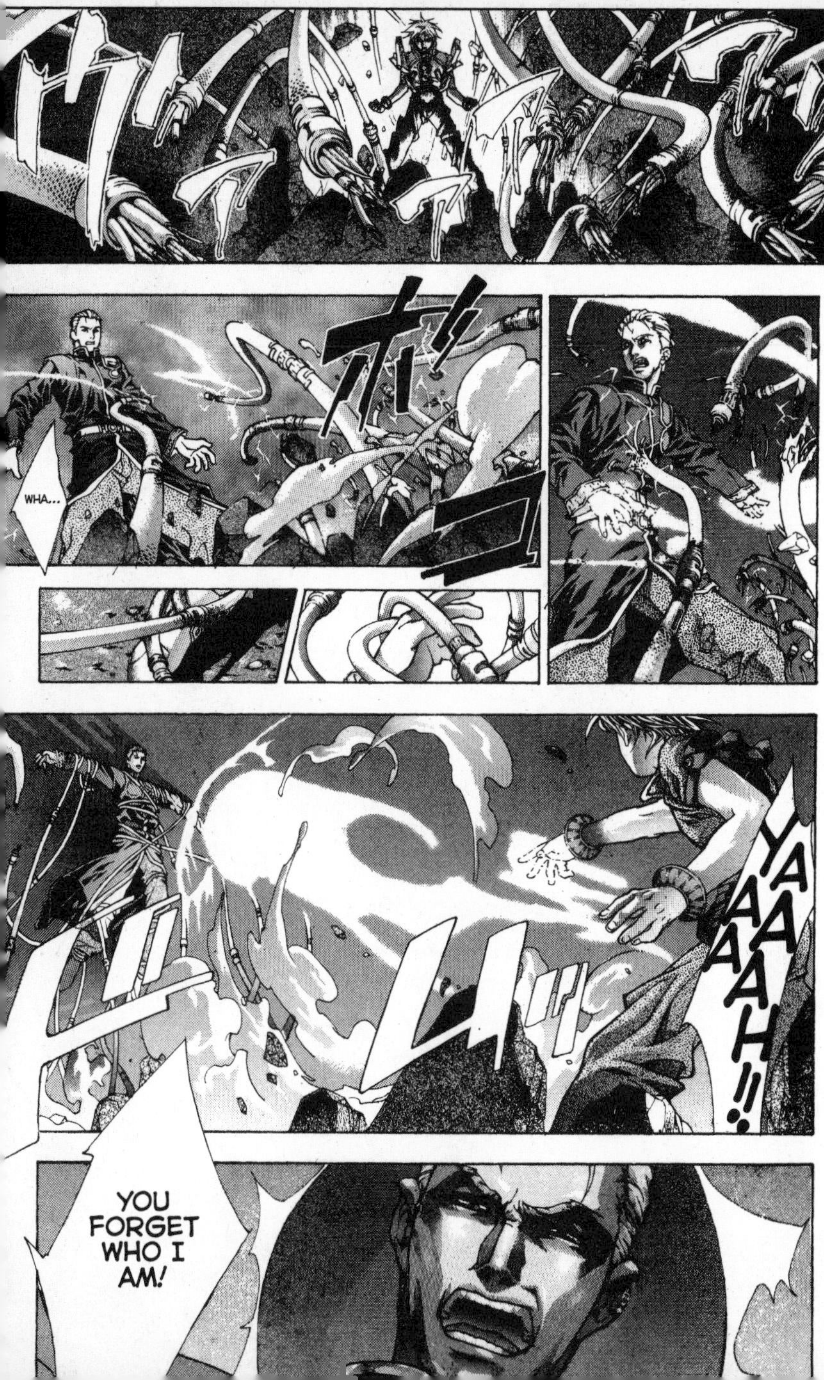
WHA...
YAAAAAAH!!!
YOU FORGET WHO I AM!

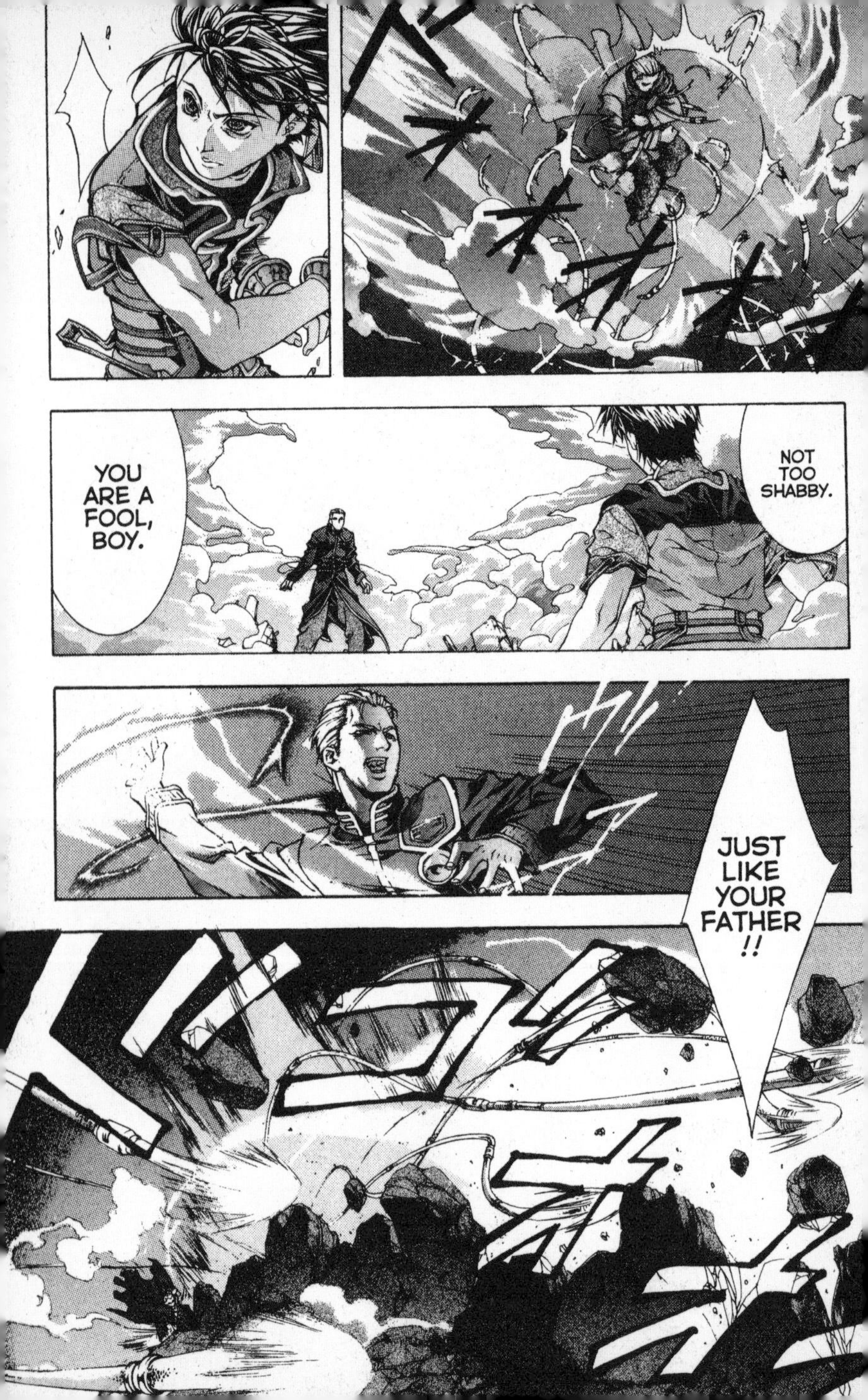
NOT TOO SHABBY.
YOU ARE A FOOL, BOY.
JUST LIKE YOUR FATHER!!

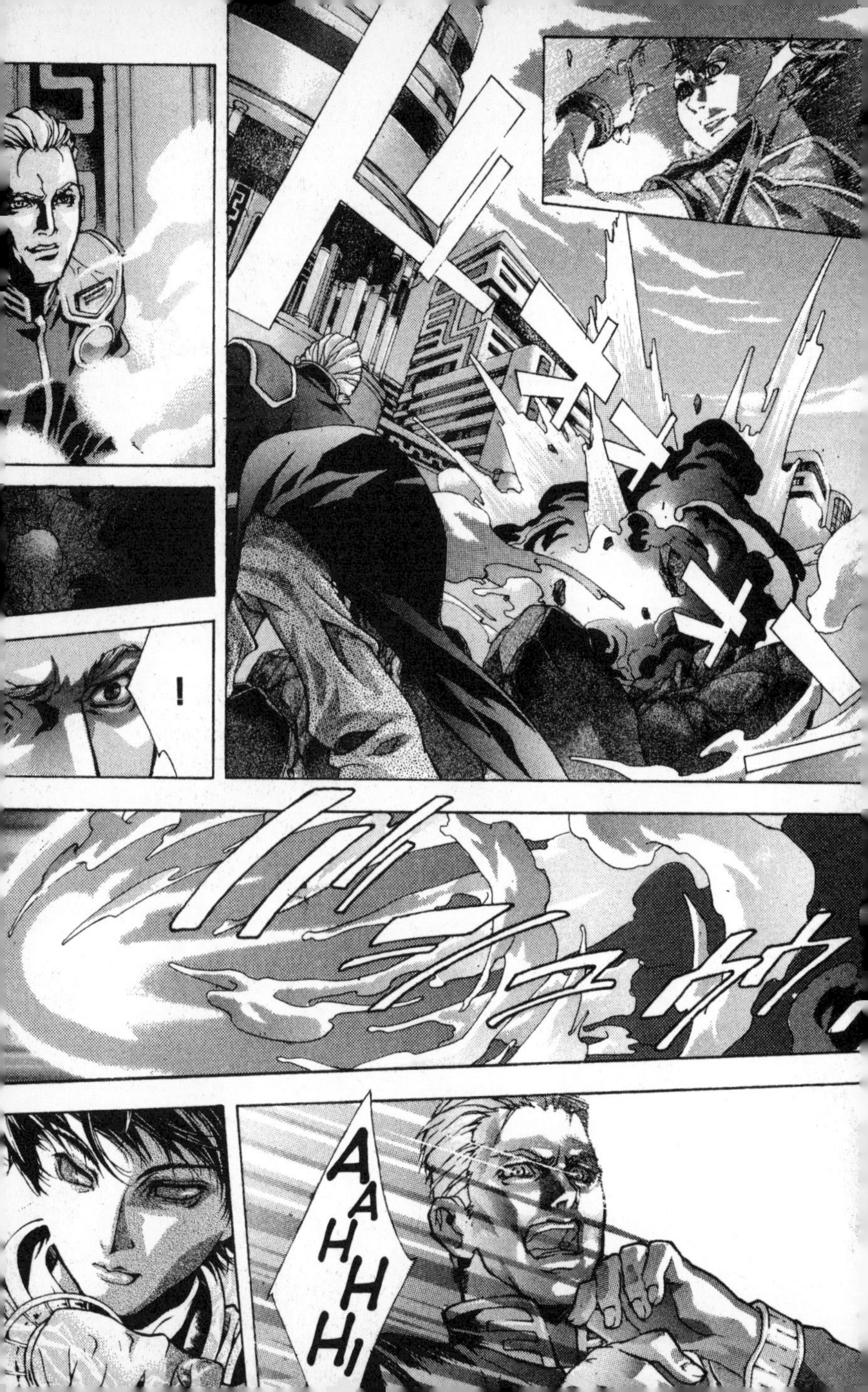
!
AAHHHH

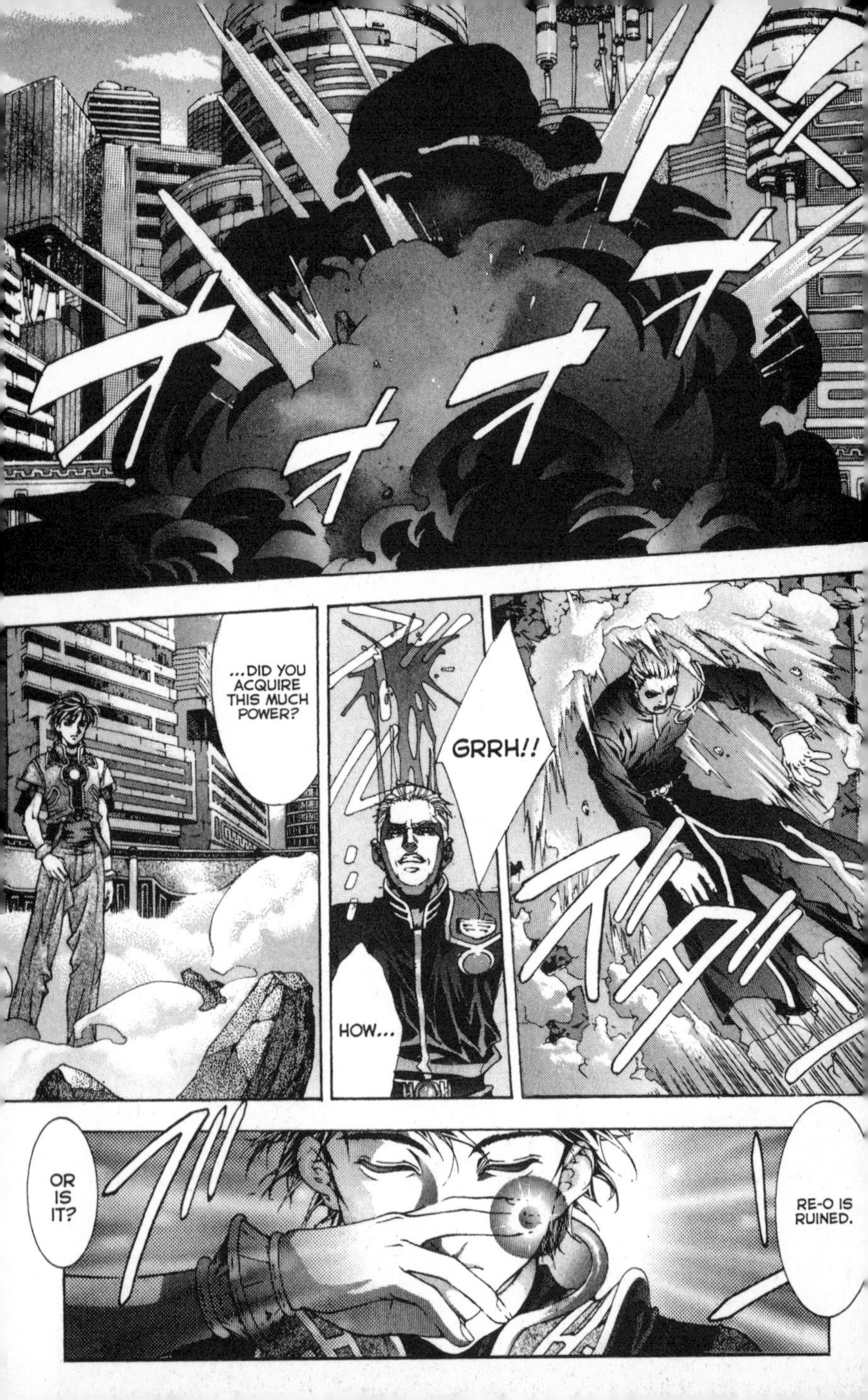
GRRH!!
HOW...
...DID YOU ACQUIRE THIS MUCH POWER?
RE-O IS RUINED.
OR IS IT?

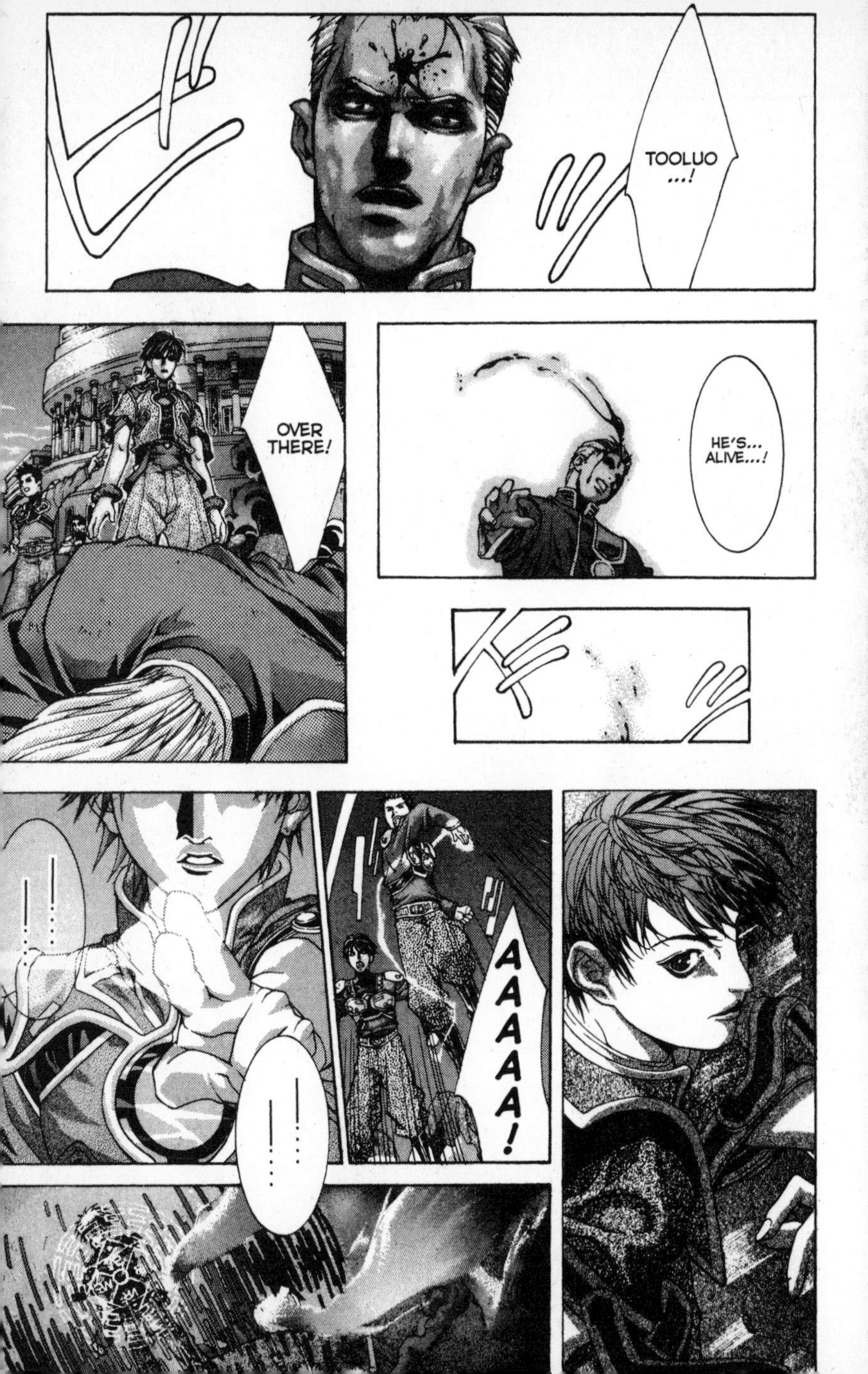
TOOLUO ...!
HE'S... ALIVE...!
OVER THERE!
AAAAA!
...!
...!

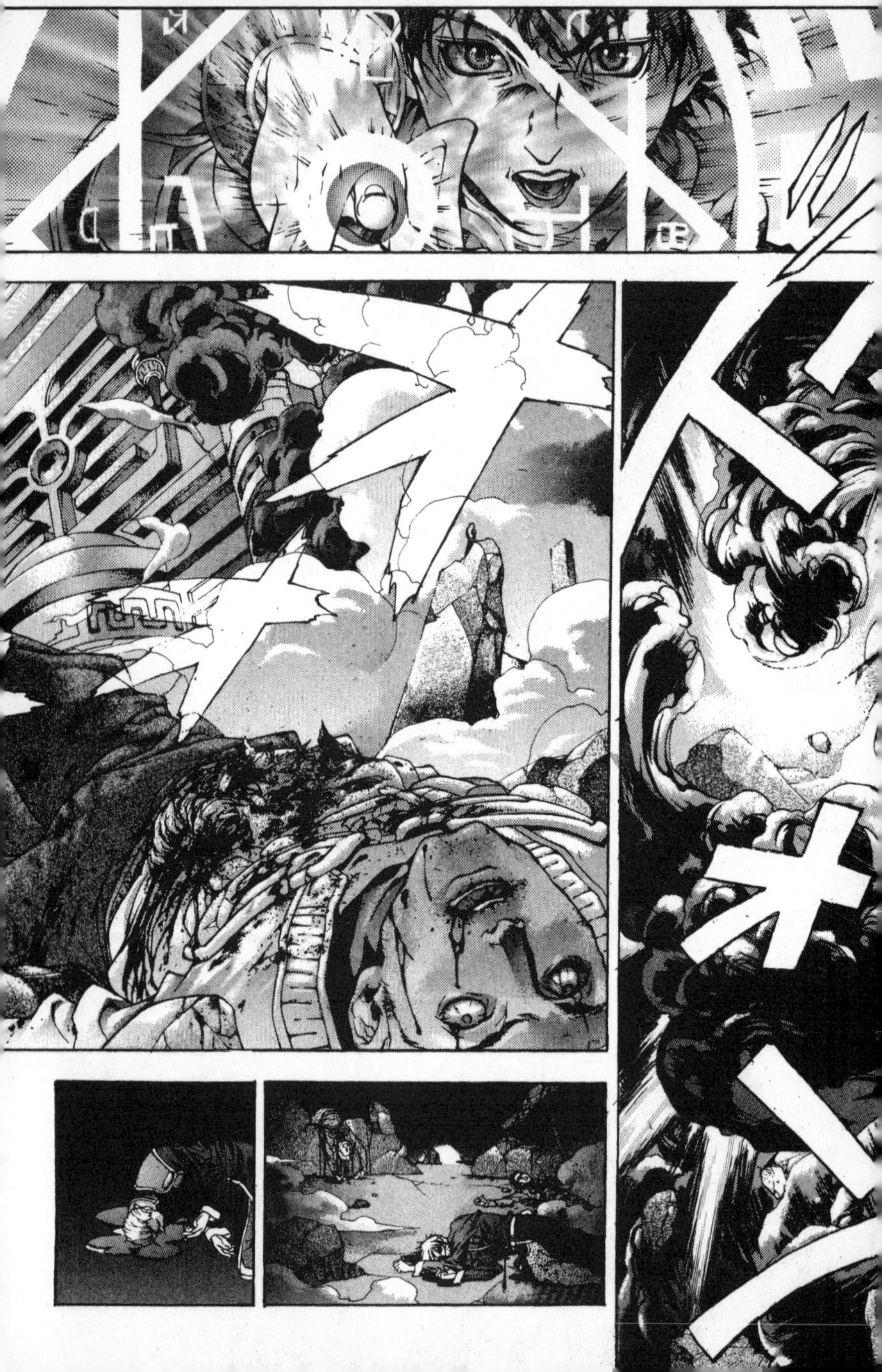

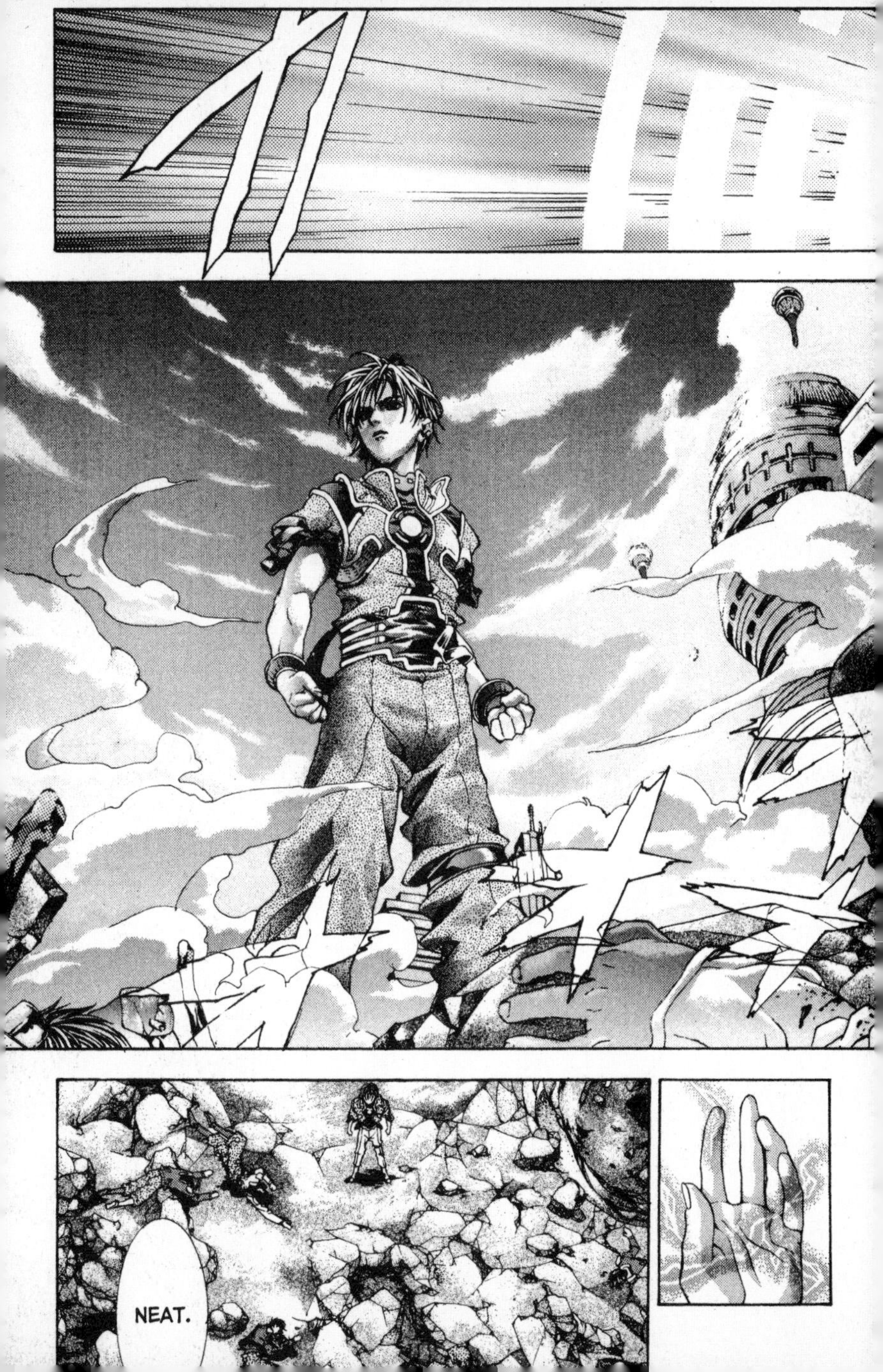
NEAT.

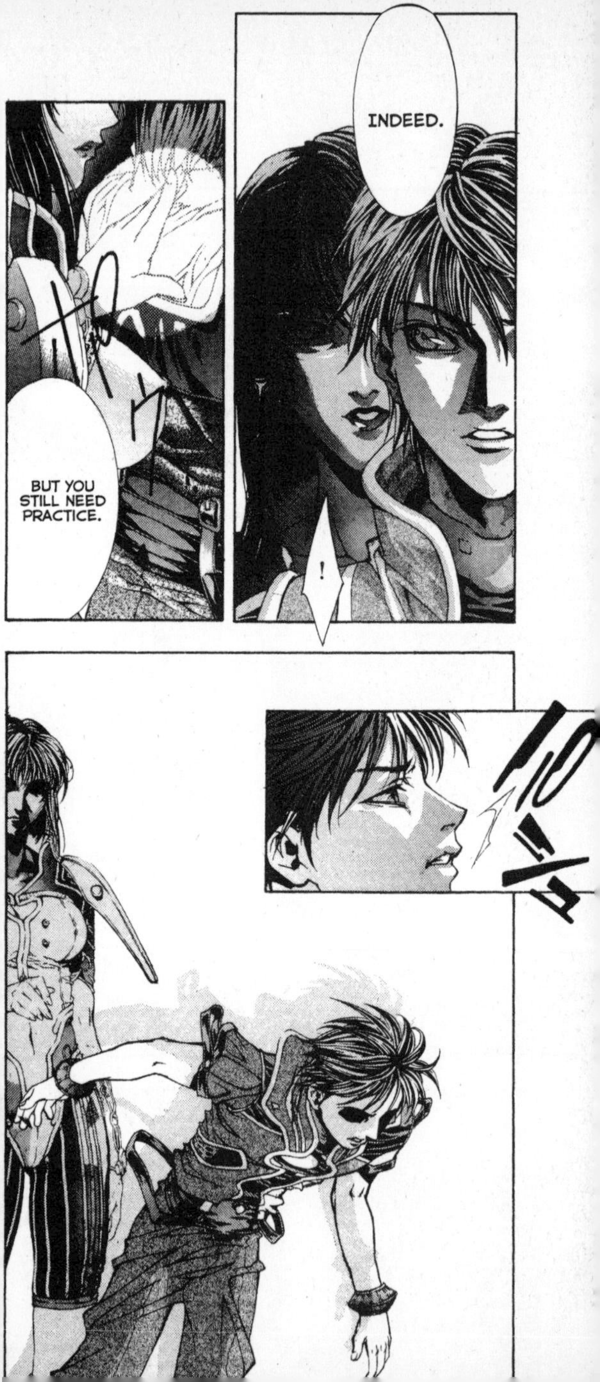
INDEED.
!
BUT YOU STILL NEED PRACTICE.

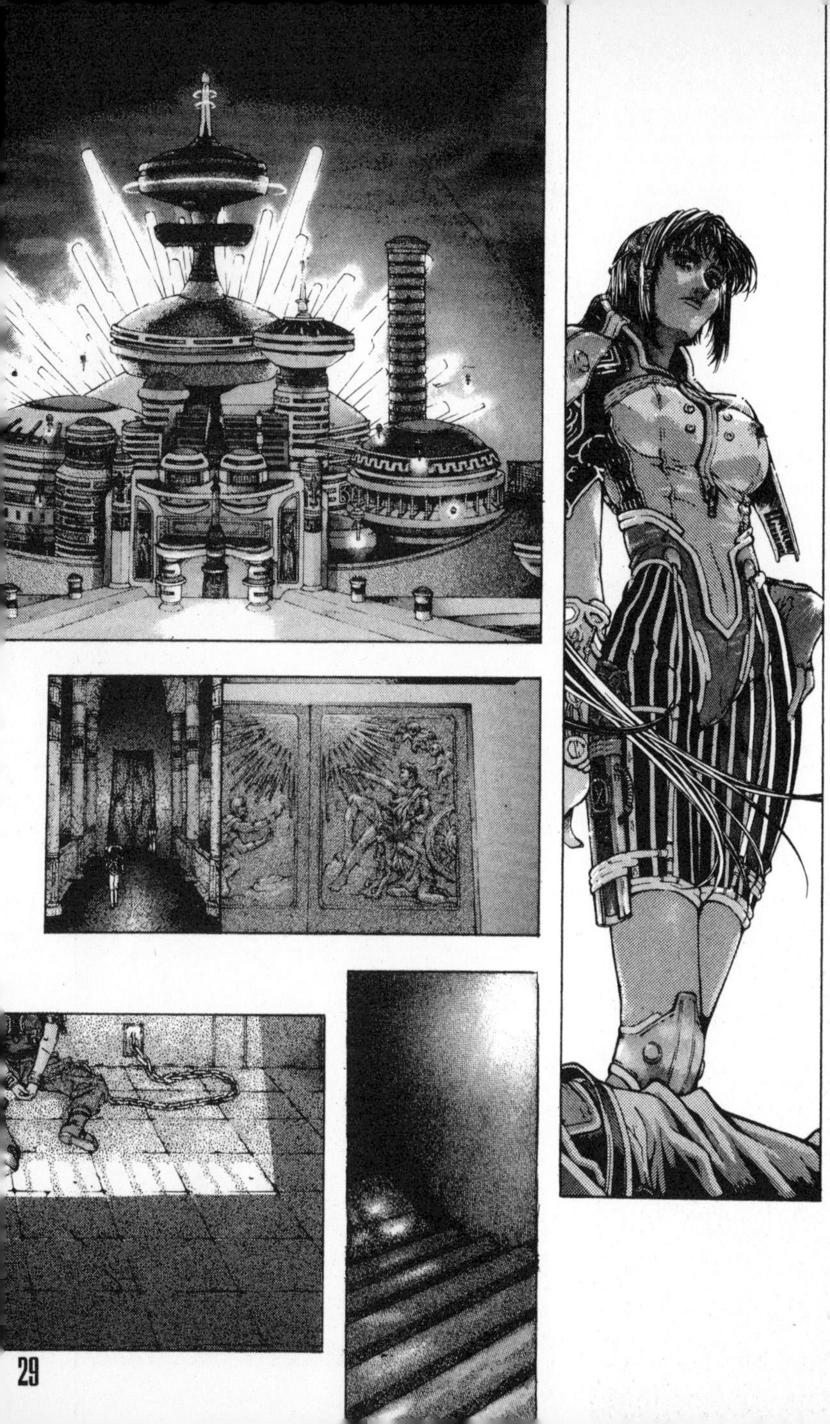

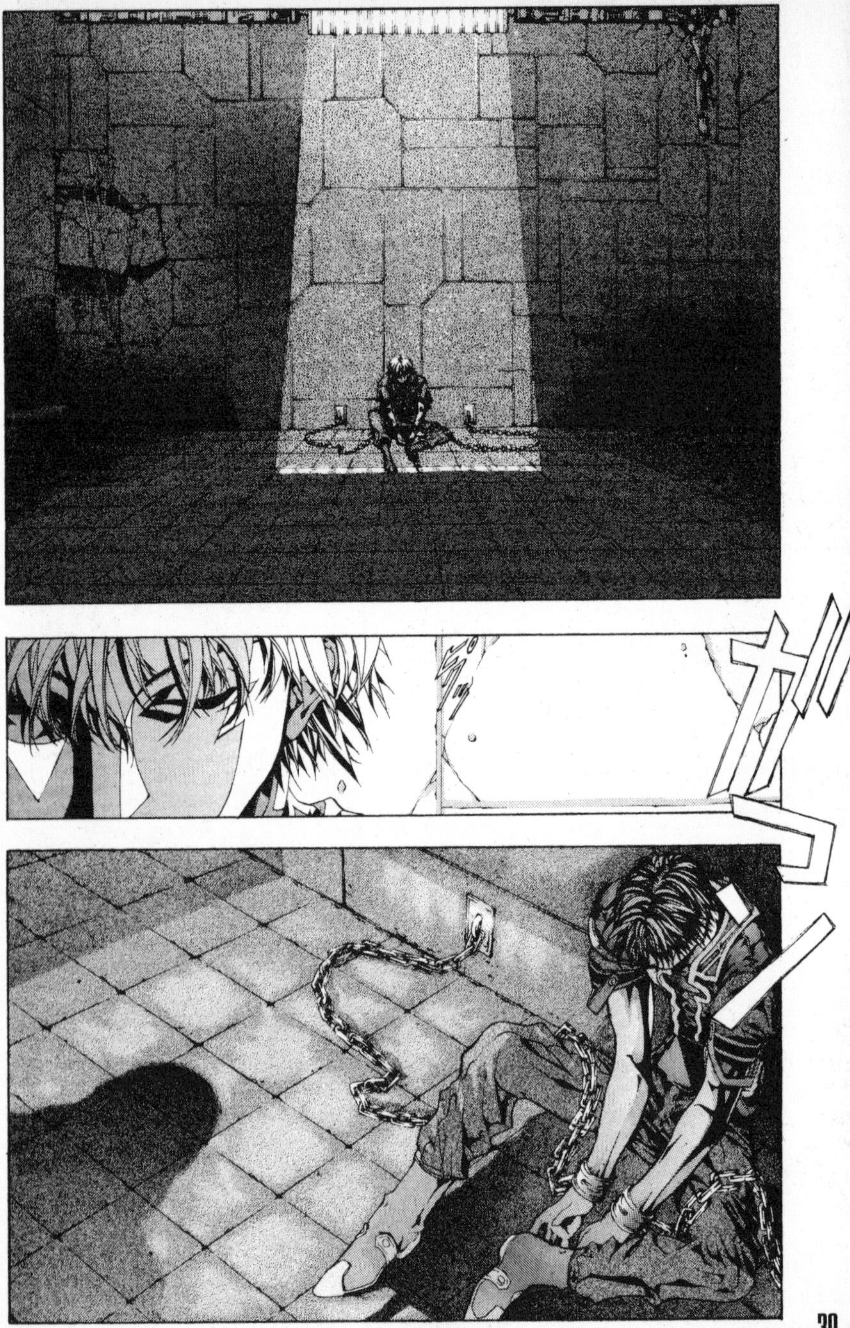
ガツン

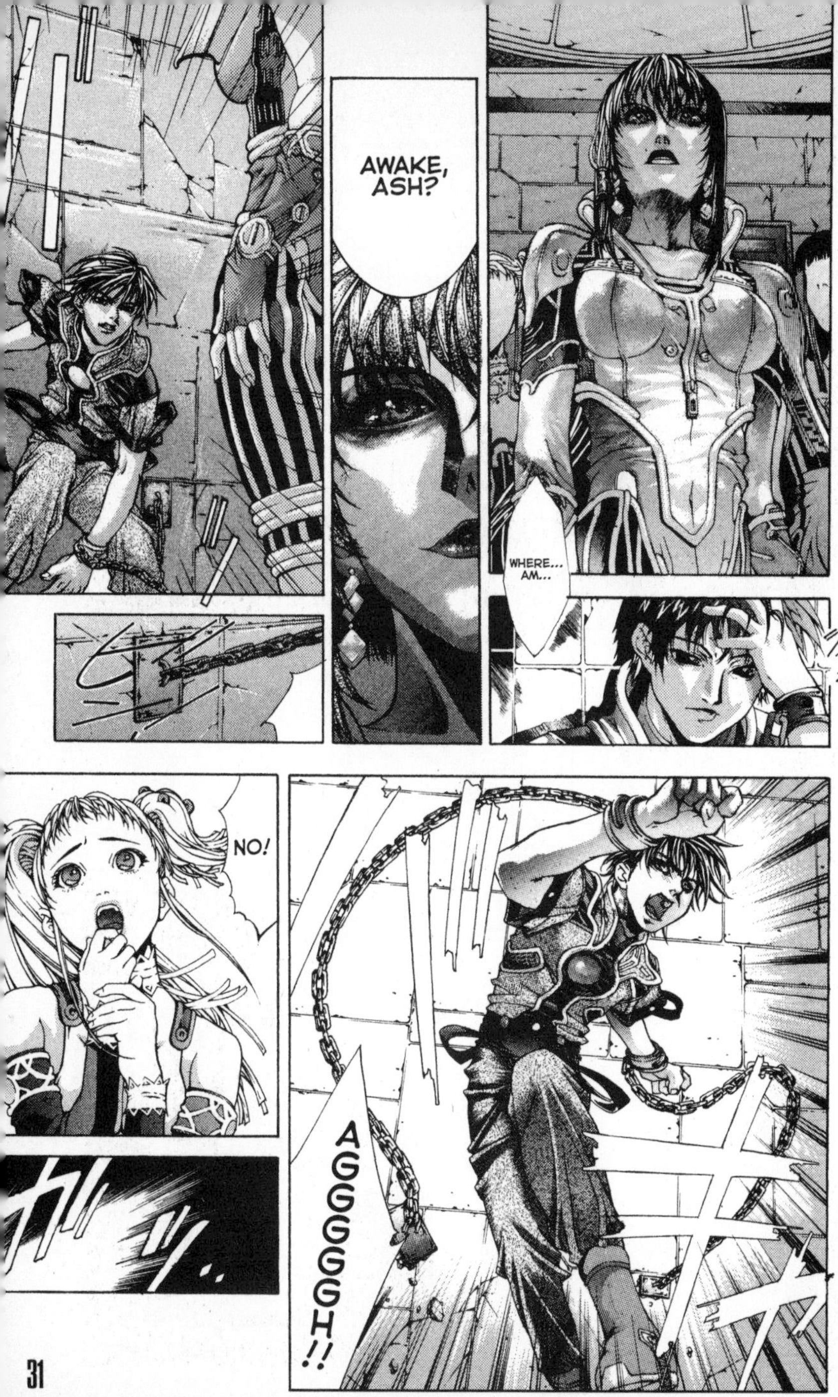
WHERE... AM...
AWAKE, ASH?
AGGGGGGH!!
NO!

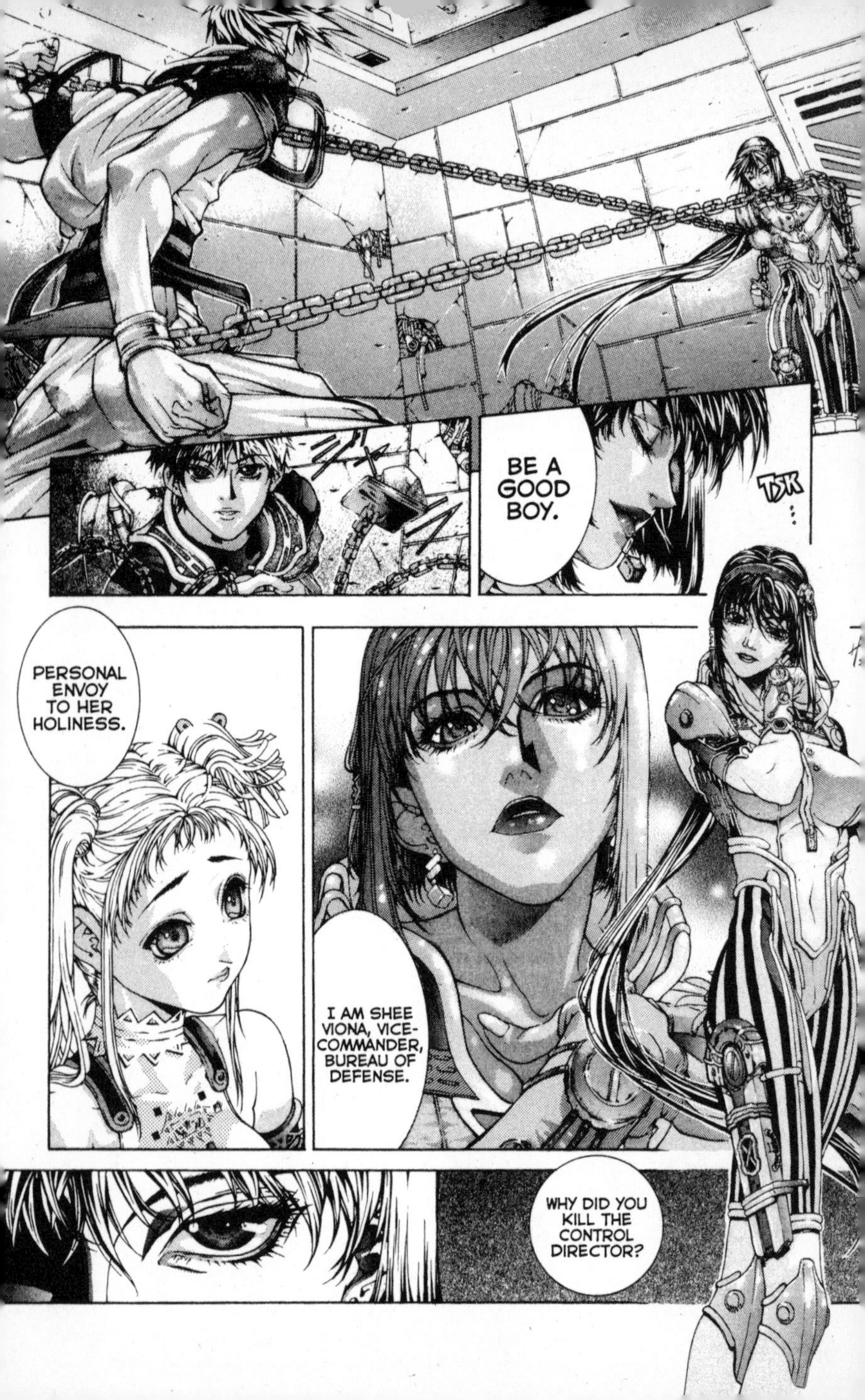
TSK...
BE A GOOD BOY.
I AM SHEE VIONA, VICE-COMMANDER, BUREAU OF DEFENSE.
PERSONAL ENVOY TO HER HOLINESS.
WHY DID YOU KILL THE CONTROL DIRECTOR?

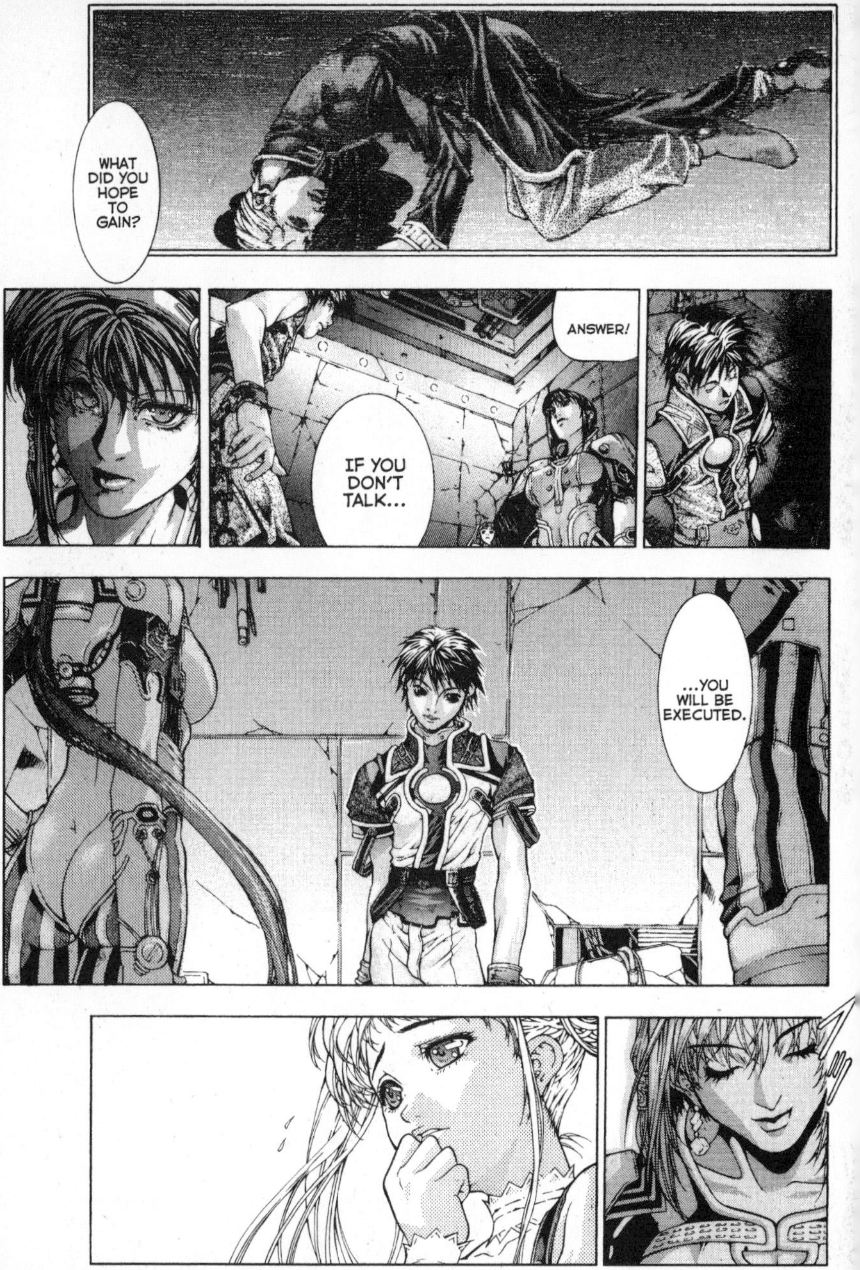
WHAT DID YOU HOPE TO GAIN?
ANSWER!
IF YOU DON'T TALK...
...YOU WILL BE EXECUTED.

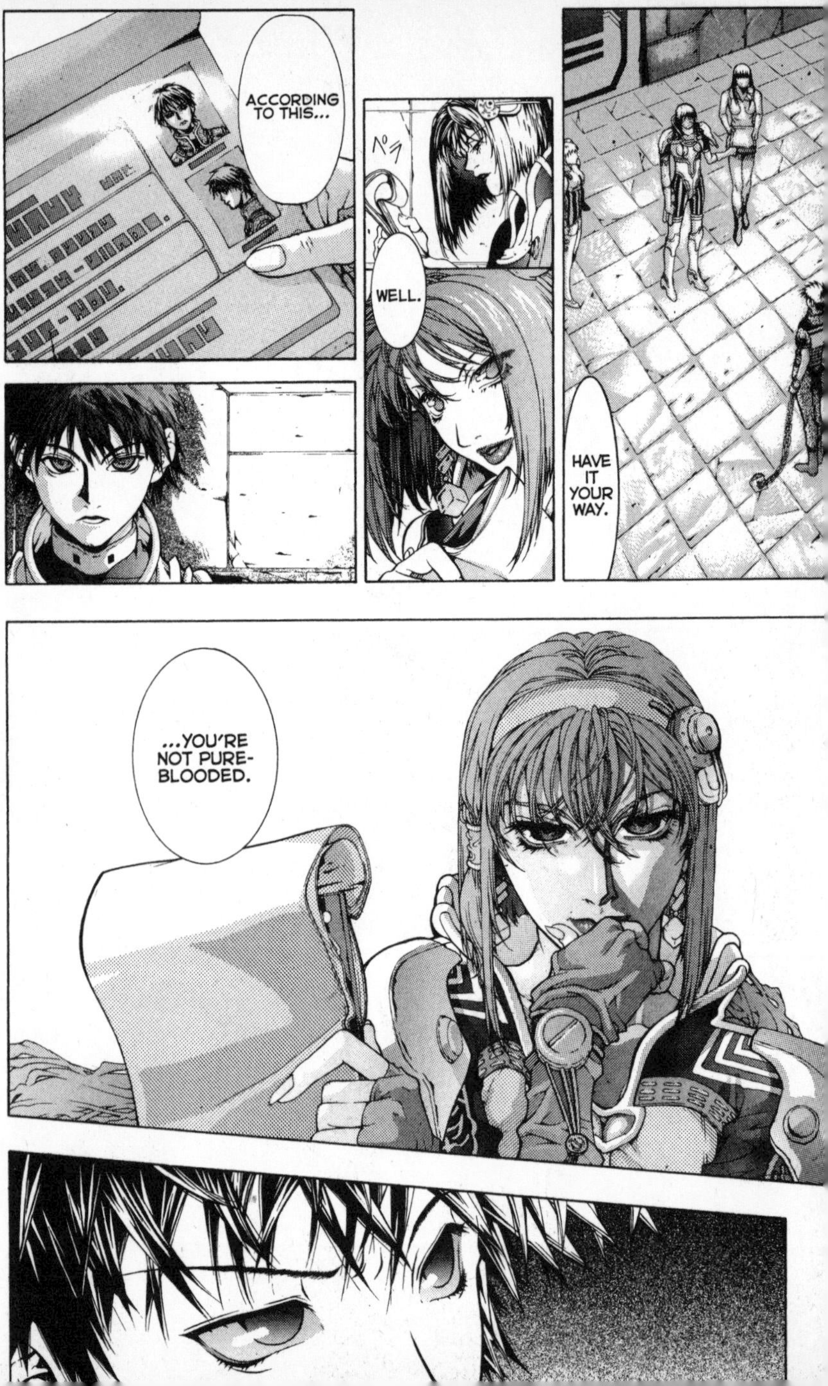
HAVE IT YOUR WAY.
ペラ
WELL.
ACCORDING TO THIS...
...YOU'RE NOT PURE-BLOODED.

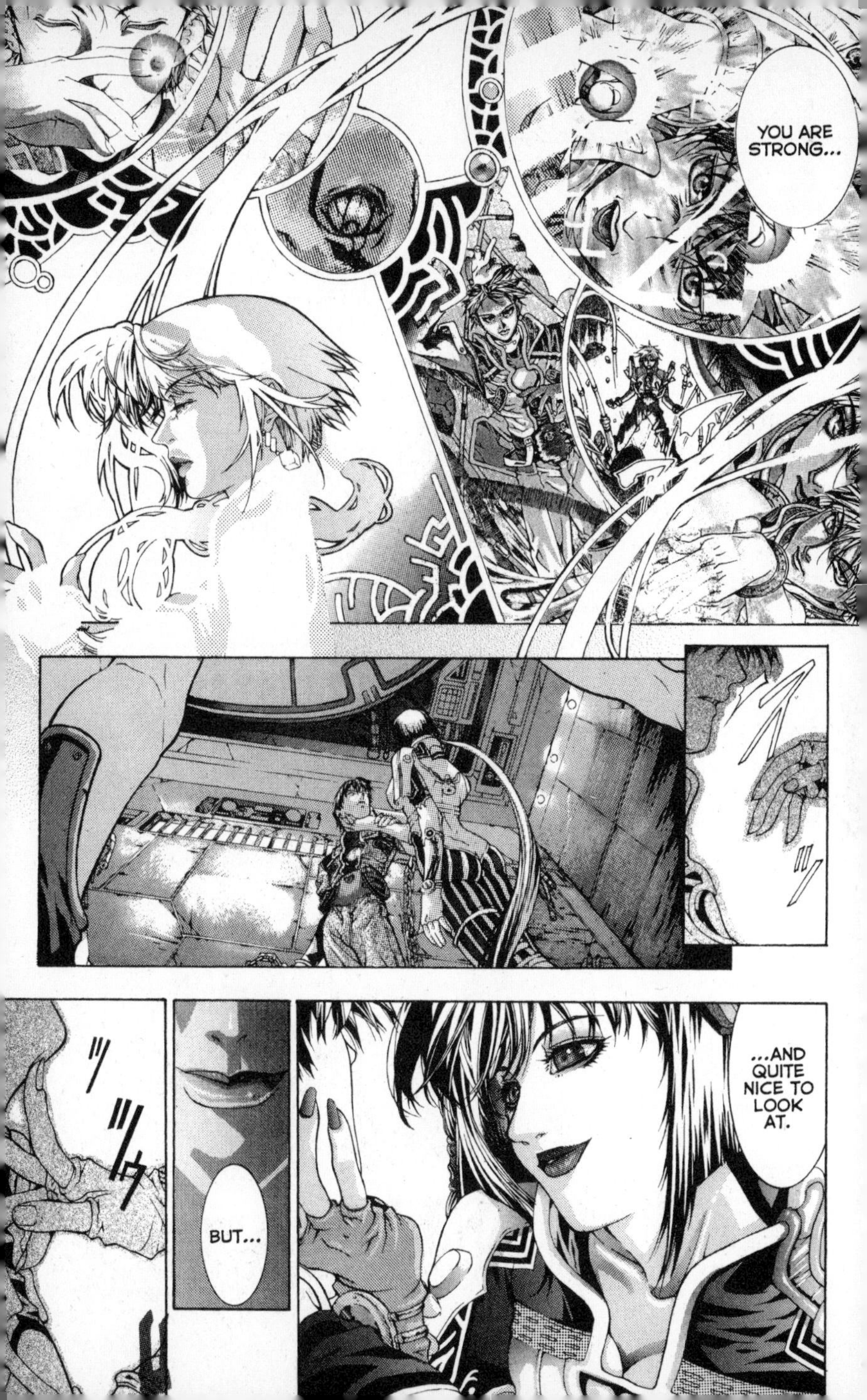
YOU ARE STRONG...
...AND QUITE NICE TO LOOK AT.
BUT...

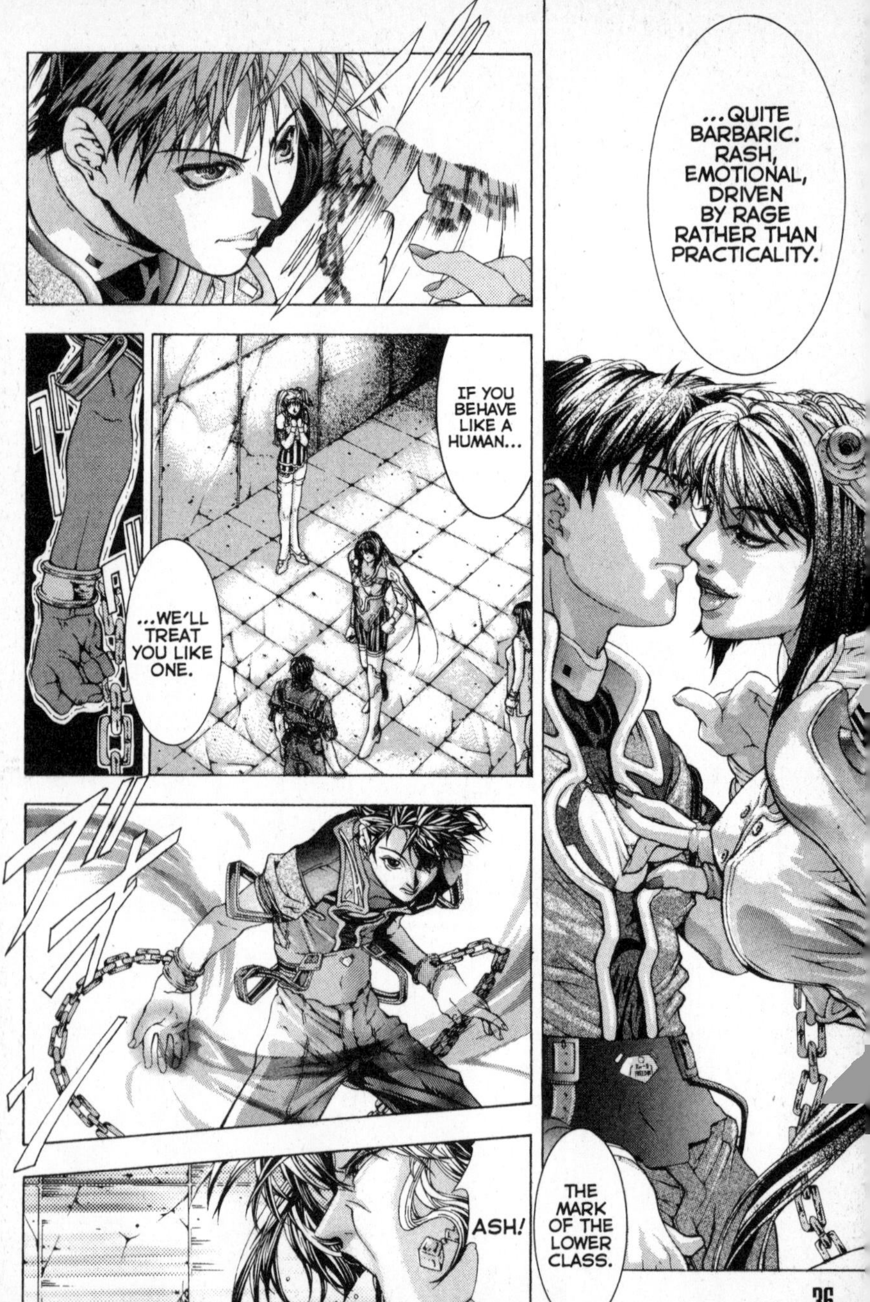
...QUITE BARBARIC. RASH, EMOTIONAL, DRIVEN BY RAGE RATHER THAN PRACTICALITY.
THE MARK OF THE LOWER CLASS.
IF YOU BEHAVE LIKE A HUMAN...
...WE'LL TREAT YOU LIKE ONE.
ASH!

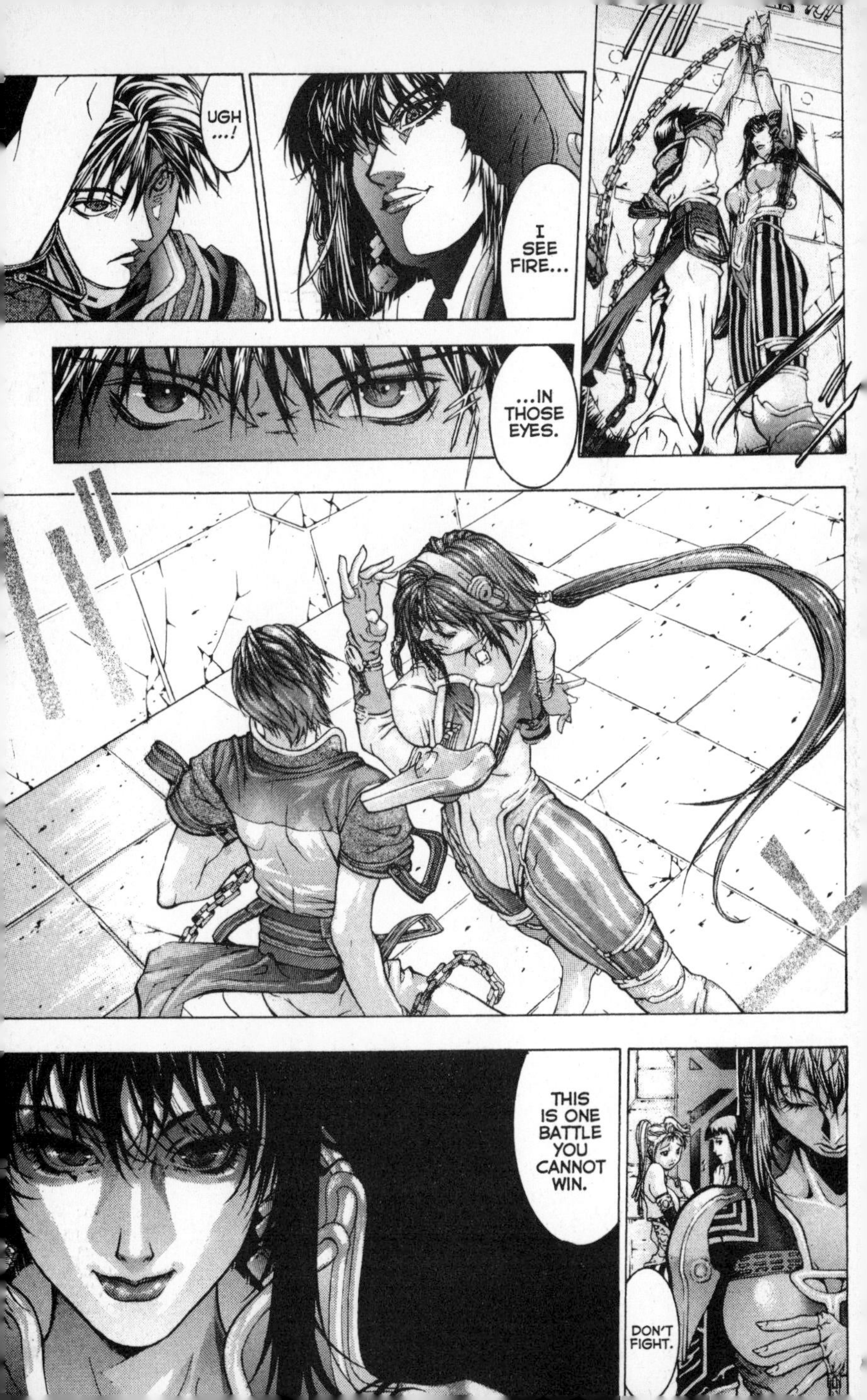
UGH ...!
I SEE FIRE...
...IN THOSE EYES.
DON'T FIGHT.
THIS IS ONE BATTLE YOU CANNOT WIN.

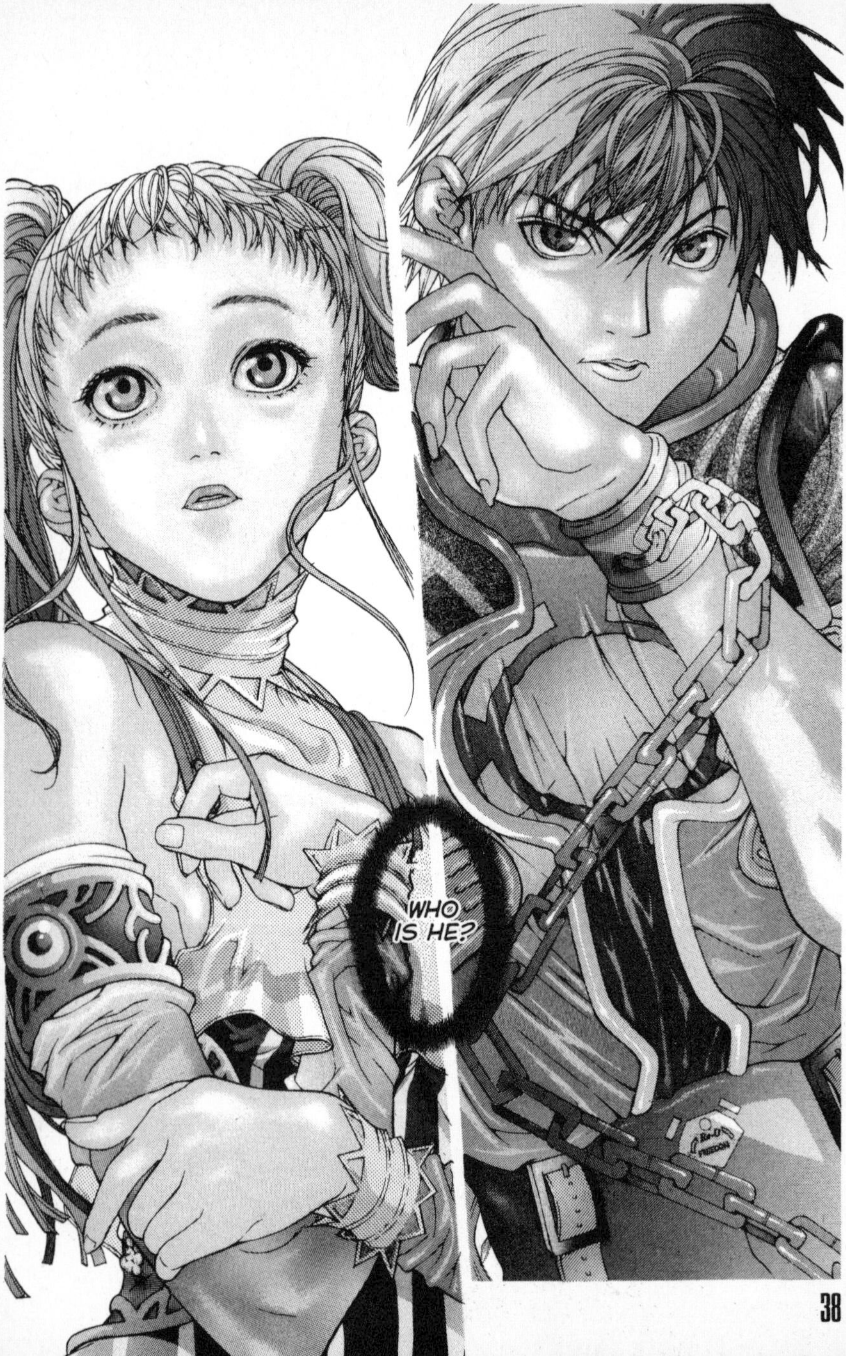
WHO IS HE?

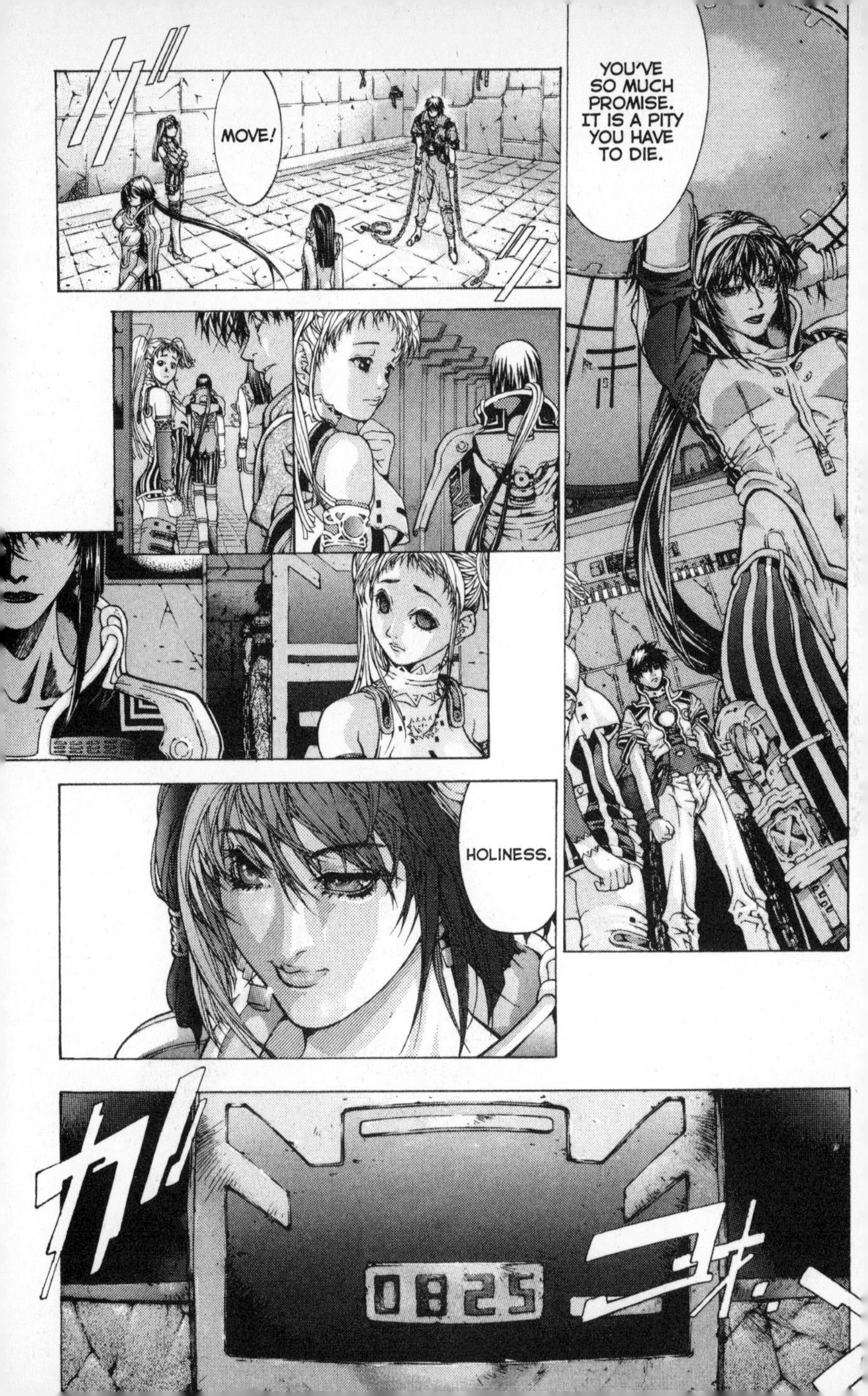
YOU'VE SO MUCH PROMISE. IT IS A PITY YOU HAVE TO DIE.
MOVE!
HOLINESS.
0825

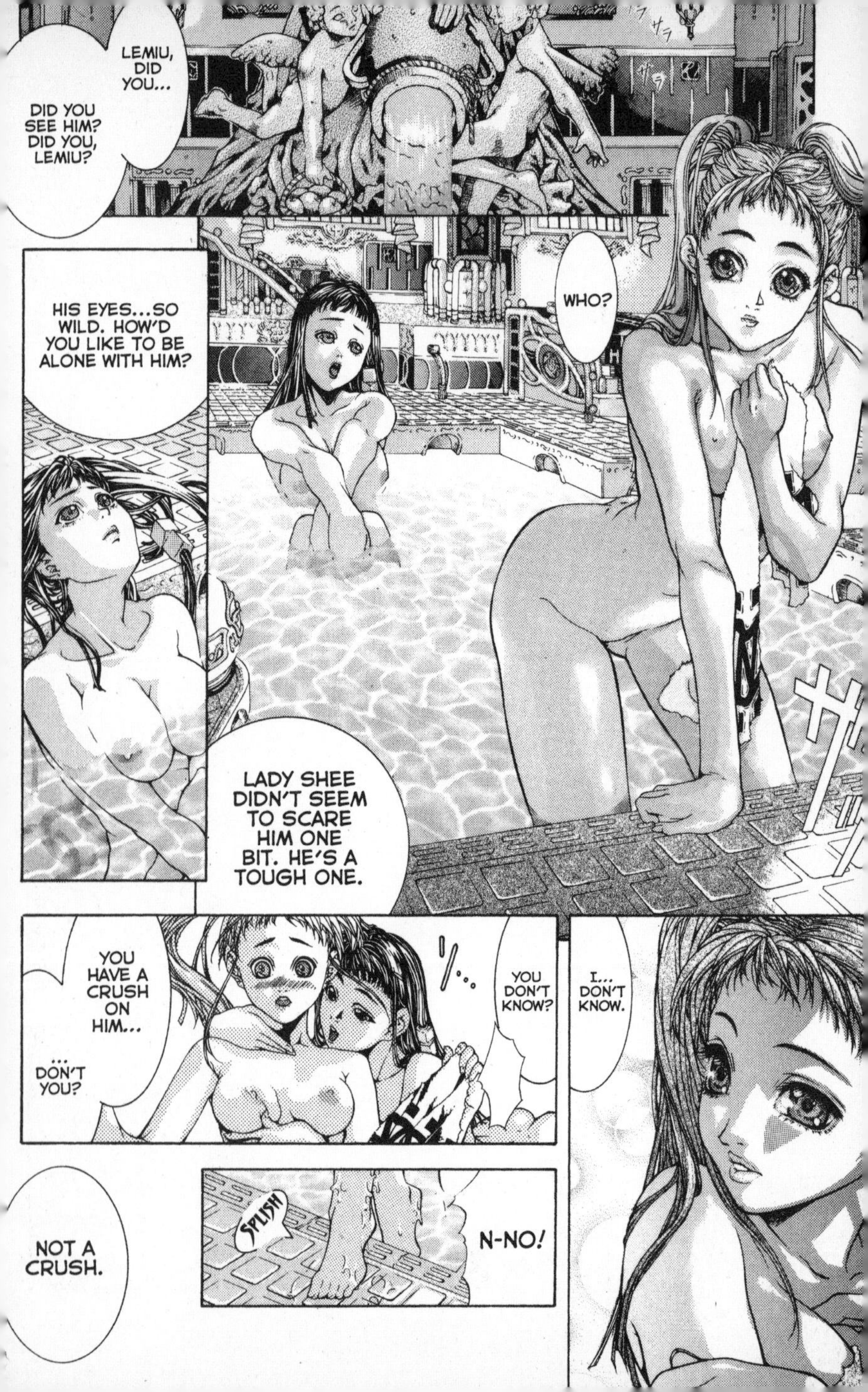
LEMIU, DID YOU...
DID YOU SEE HIM? DID YOU, LEMIU?
WHO?
LADY SHEE DIDN'T SEEM TO SCARE HIM ONE BIT. HE'S A TOUGH ONE.
HIS EYES...SO WILD. HOW'D YOU LIKE TO BE ALONE WITH HIM?
I... DON'T KNOW.
YOU DON'T KNOW?
/...
YOU HAVE A CRUSH ON HIM...
...DON'T YOU?
SPLISH
N-NO!
NOT A CRUSH.

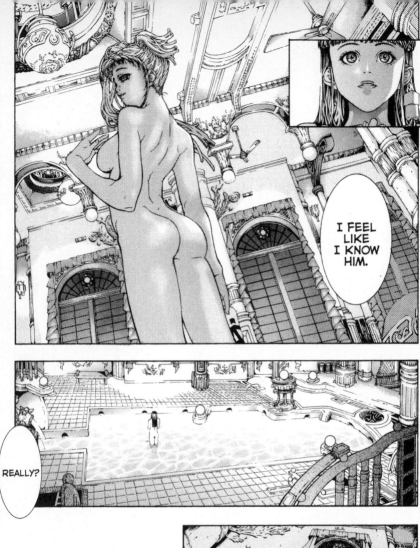

I FEEL
LIKE
I KNOW
HIM.

REALLY?

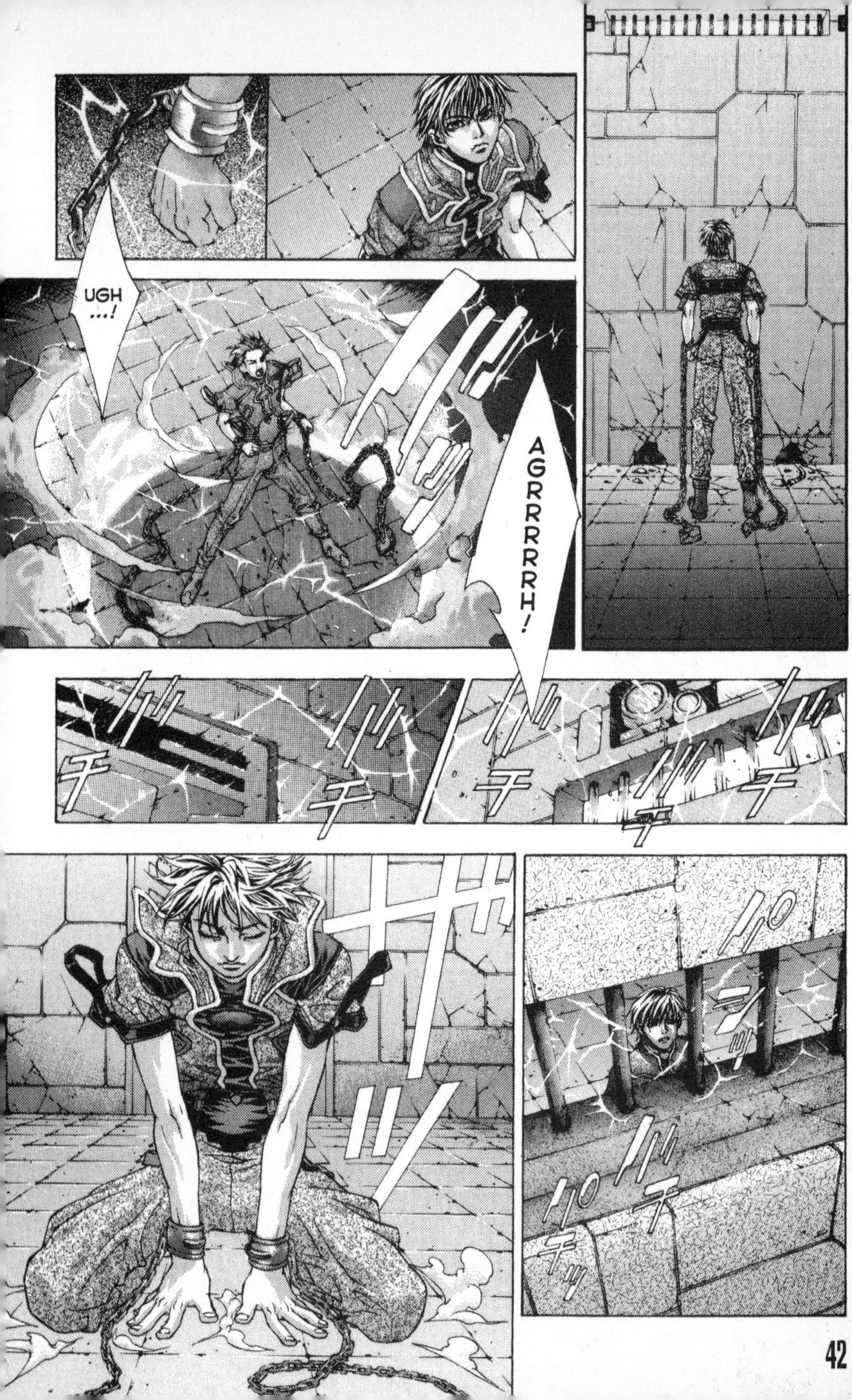
UGH ...!
AGRRRRRH!

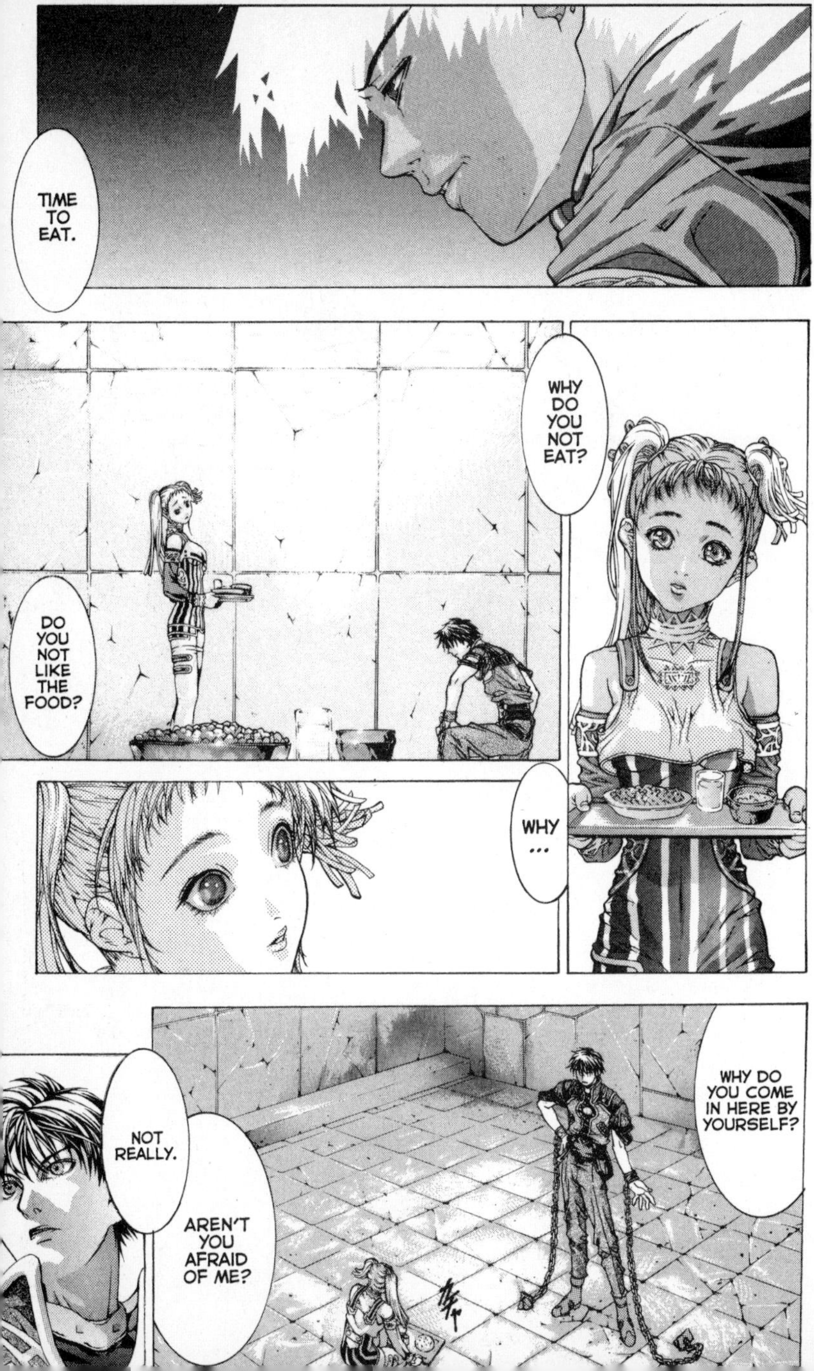
TIME TO EAT.
WHY DO YOU NOT EAT?
DO YOU NOT LIKE THE FOOD?
WHY...
WHY DO YOU COME IN HERE BY YOURSELF?
NOT REALLY.
AREN'T YOU AFRAID OF ME?

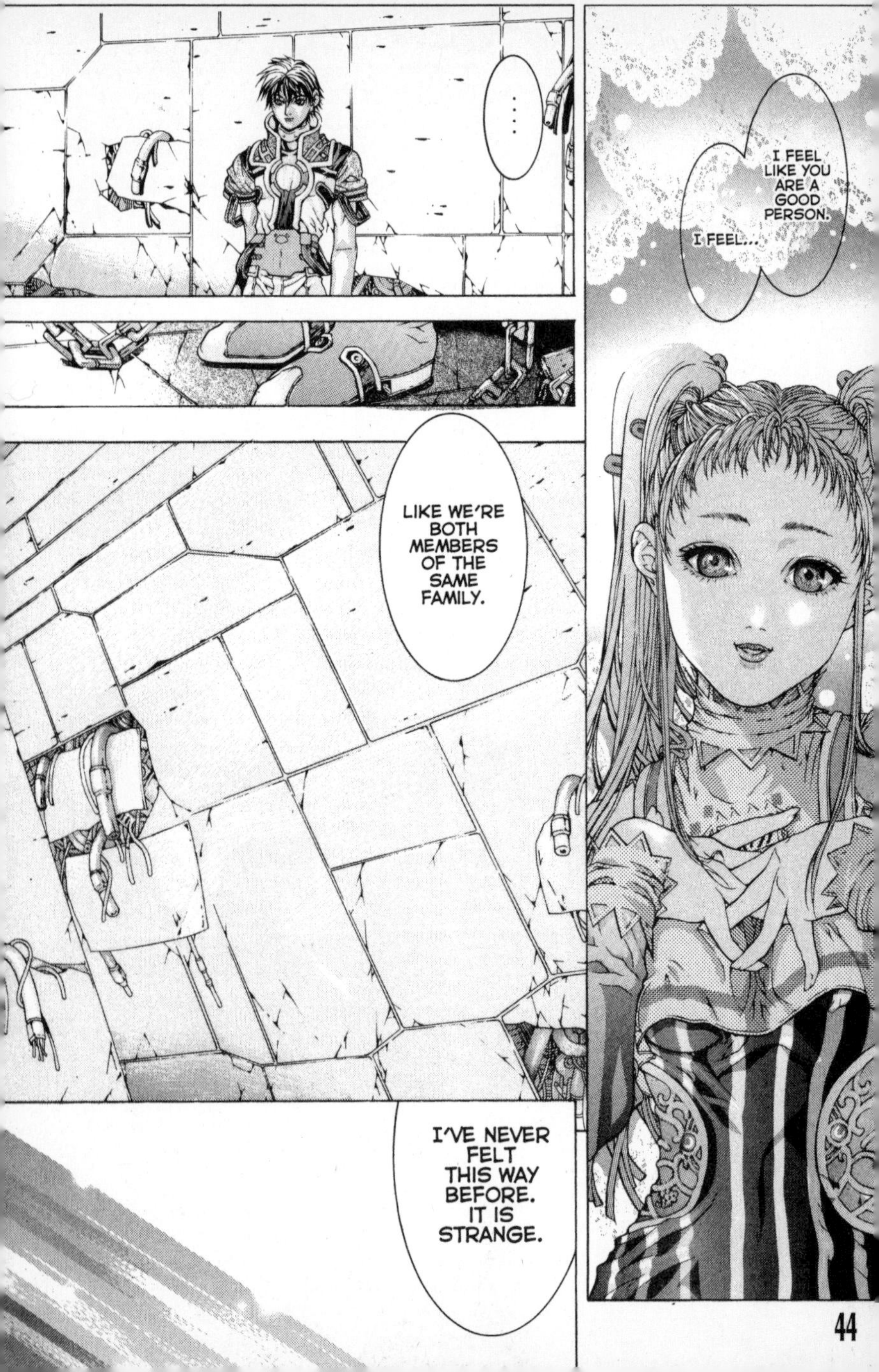

I FEEL LIKE YOU ARE A GOOD PERSON.
I FEEL...
....
LIKE WE'RE BOTH MEMBERS OF THE SAME FAMILY.
I'VE NEVER FELT THIS WAY BEFORE. IT IS STRANGE.

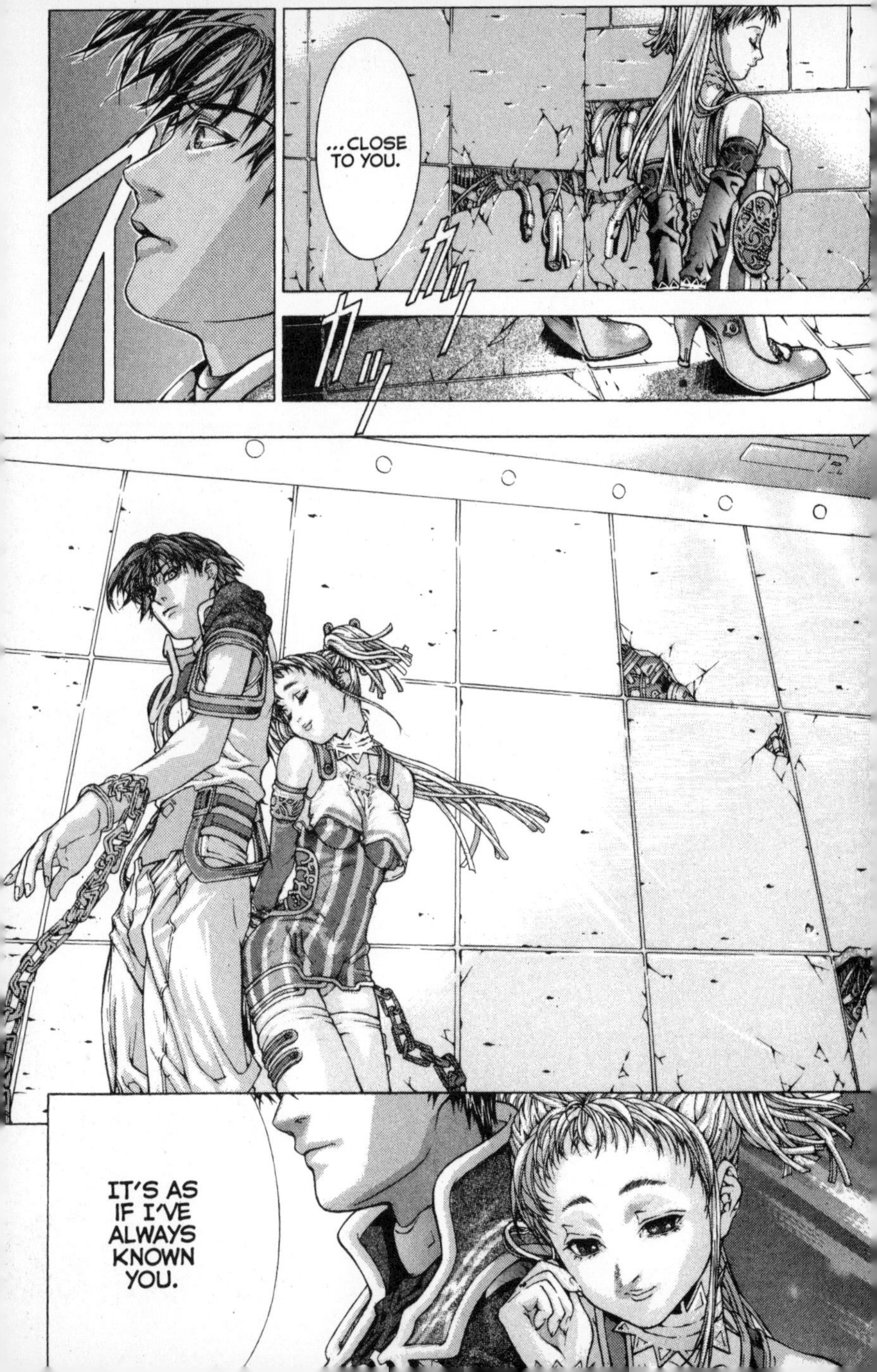
...CLOSE TO YOU.
カッ
カッ
IT'S AS IF I'VE ALWAYS KNOWN YOU.

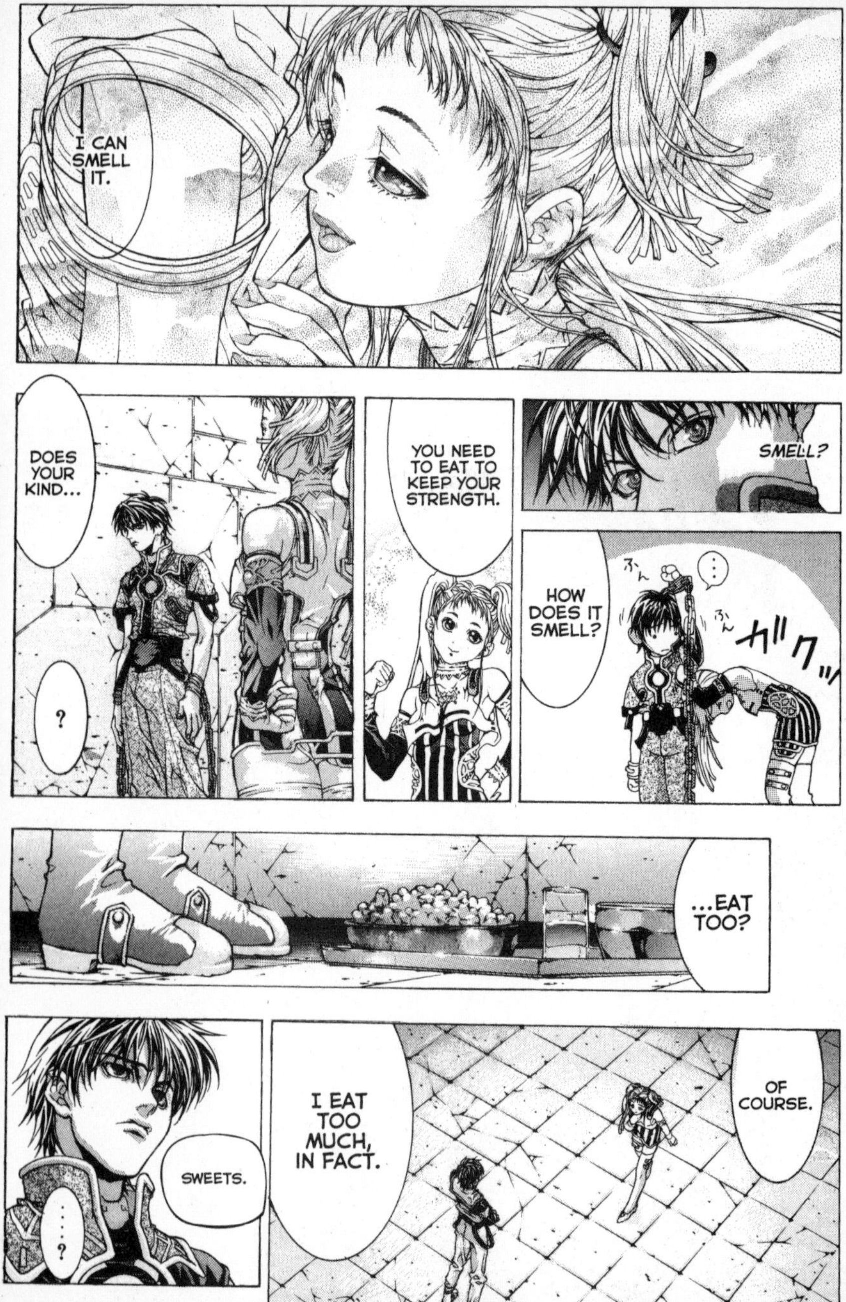
I CAN SMELL IT.
SMELL?
HOW DOES IT SMELL?
ふん
...
ふん
ガクッ
YOU NEED TO EAT TO KEEP YOUR STRENGTH.
DOES YOUR KIND...
?
...EAT TOO?
OF COURSE.
I EAT TOO MUCH, IN FACT.
SWEETS.
...?

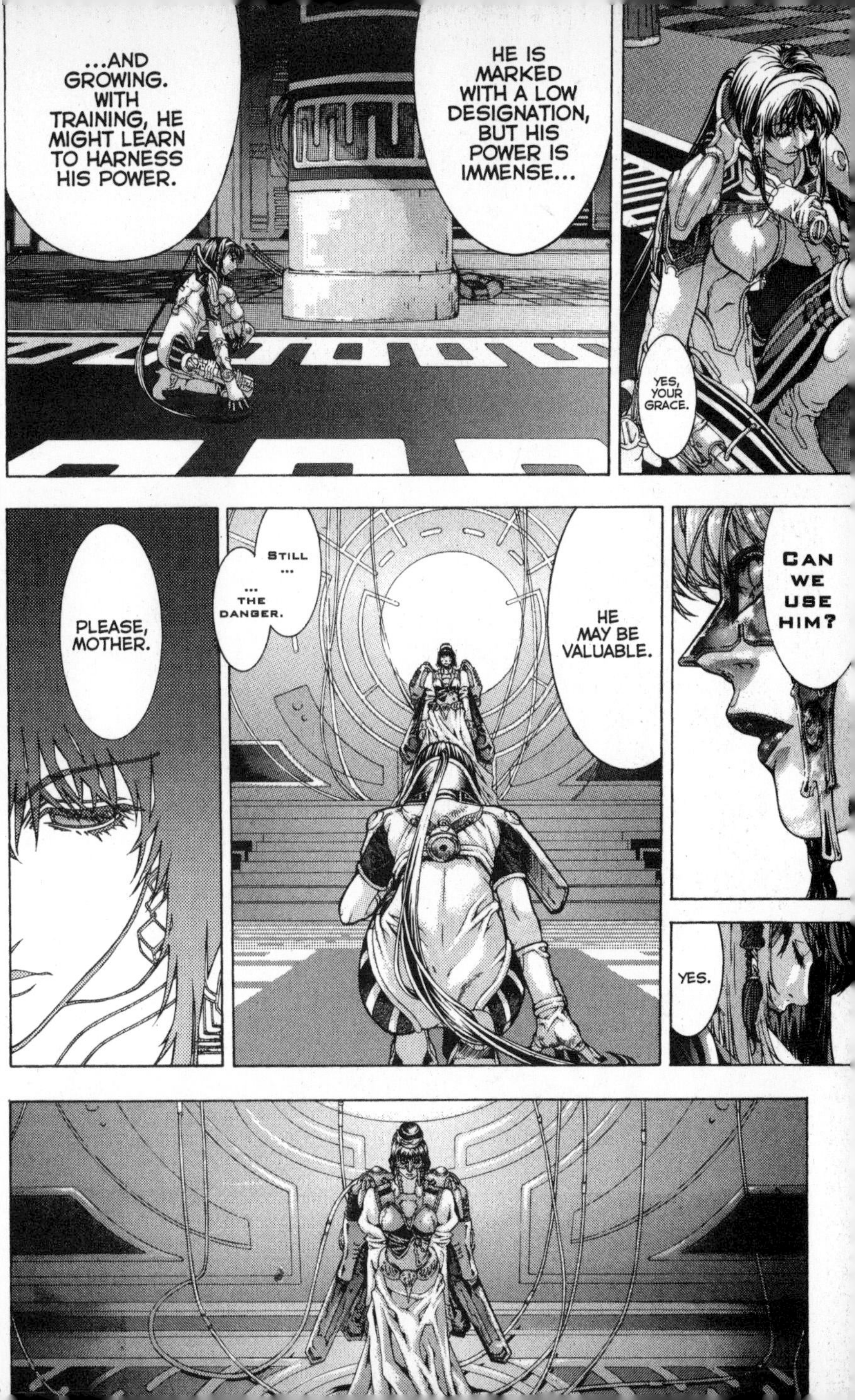
YES, YOUR GRACE.
HE IS MARKED WITH A LOW DESIGNATION, BUT HIS POWER IS IMMENSE...
...AND GROWING. WITH TRAINING, HE MIGHT LEARN TO HARNESS HIS POWER.
CAN WE USE HIM?
YES.
HE MAY BE VALUABLE.
STILL ...
... THE DANGER.
PLEASE, MOTHER.

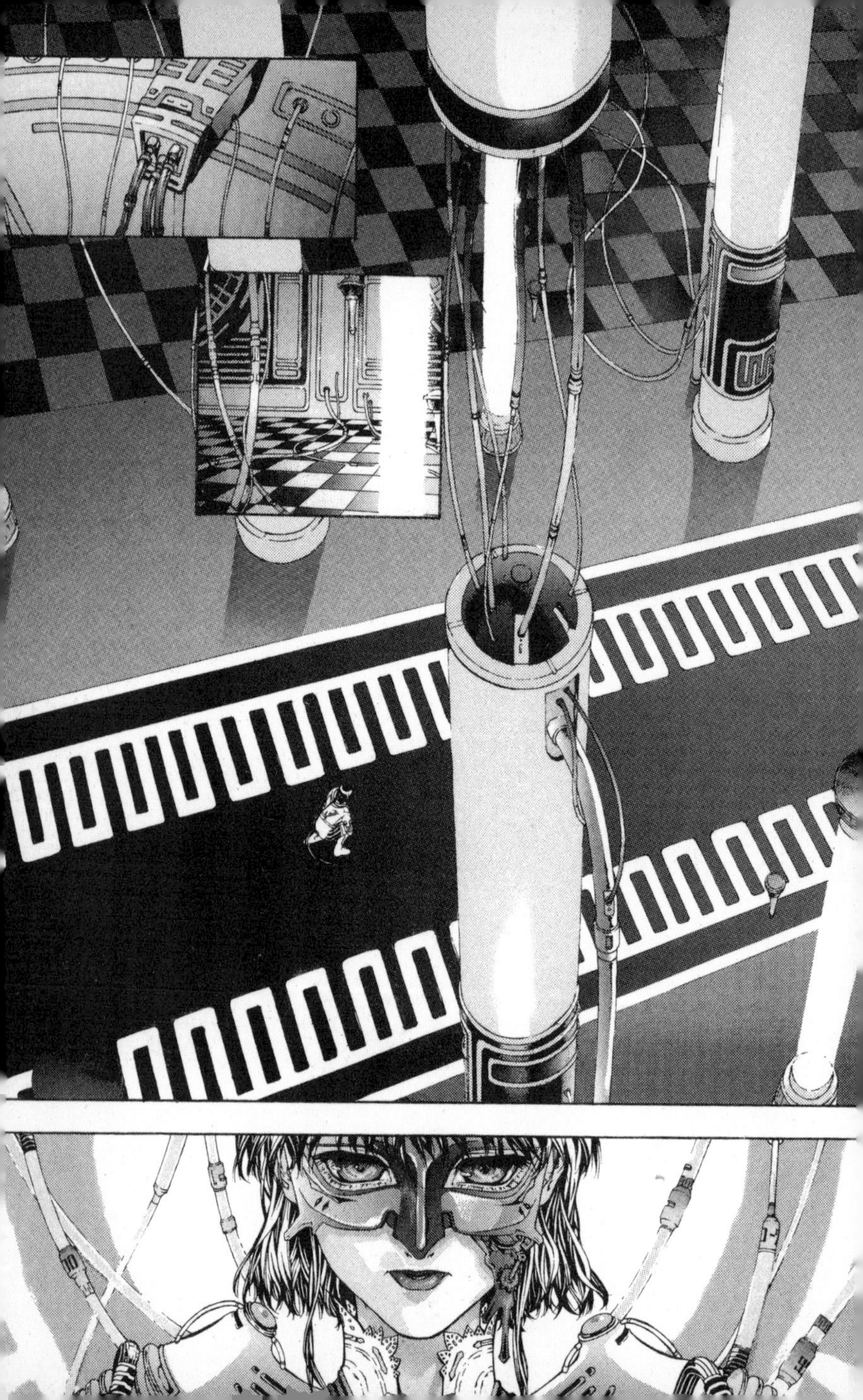

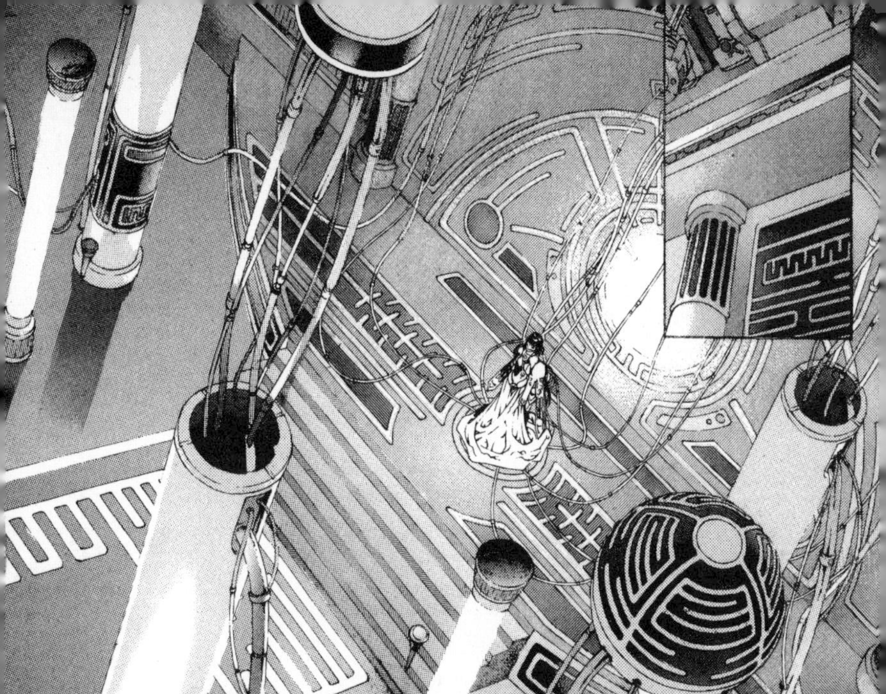
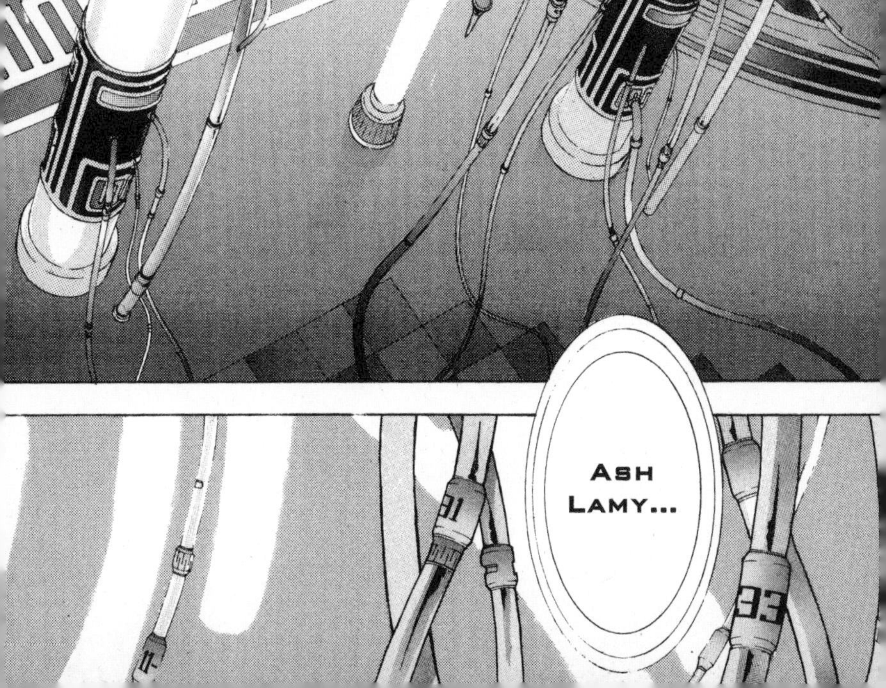
ASH LAMY...

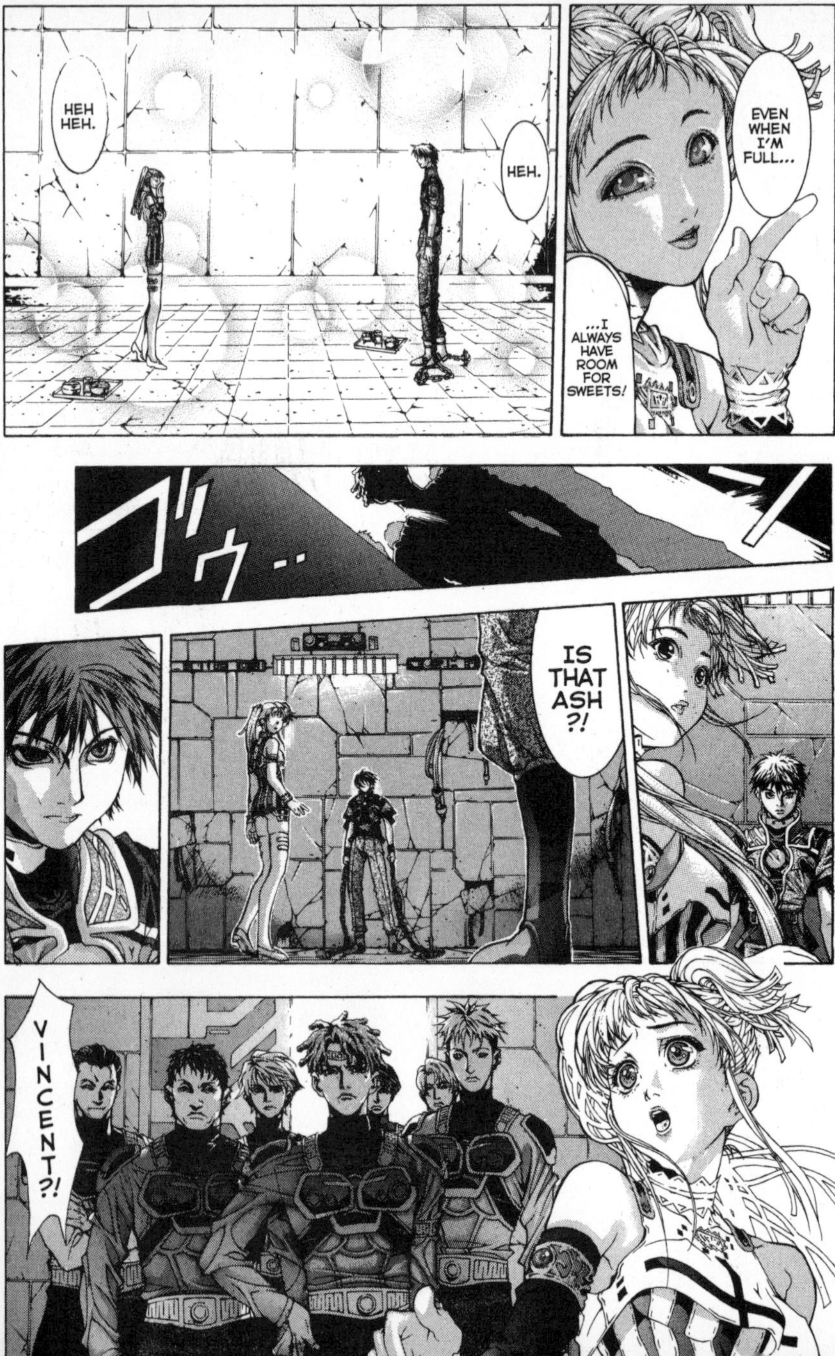
EVEN WHEN I'M FULL...
...I ALWAYS HAVE ROOM FOR SWEETS!
HEH.
HEH HEH.
ゴウ‥ン
IS THAT ASH?!
VINCENT?!

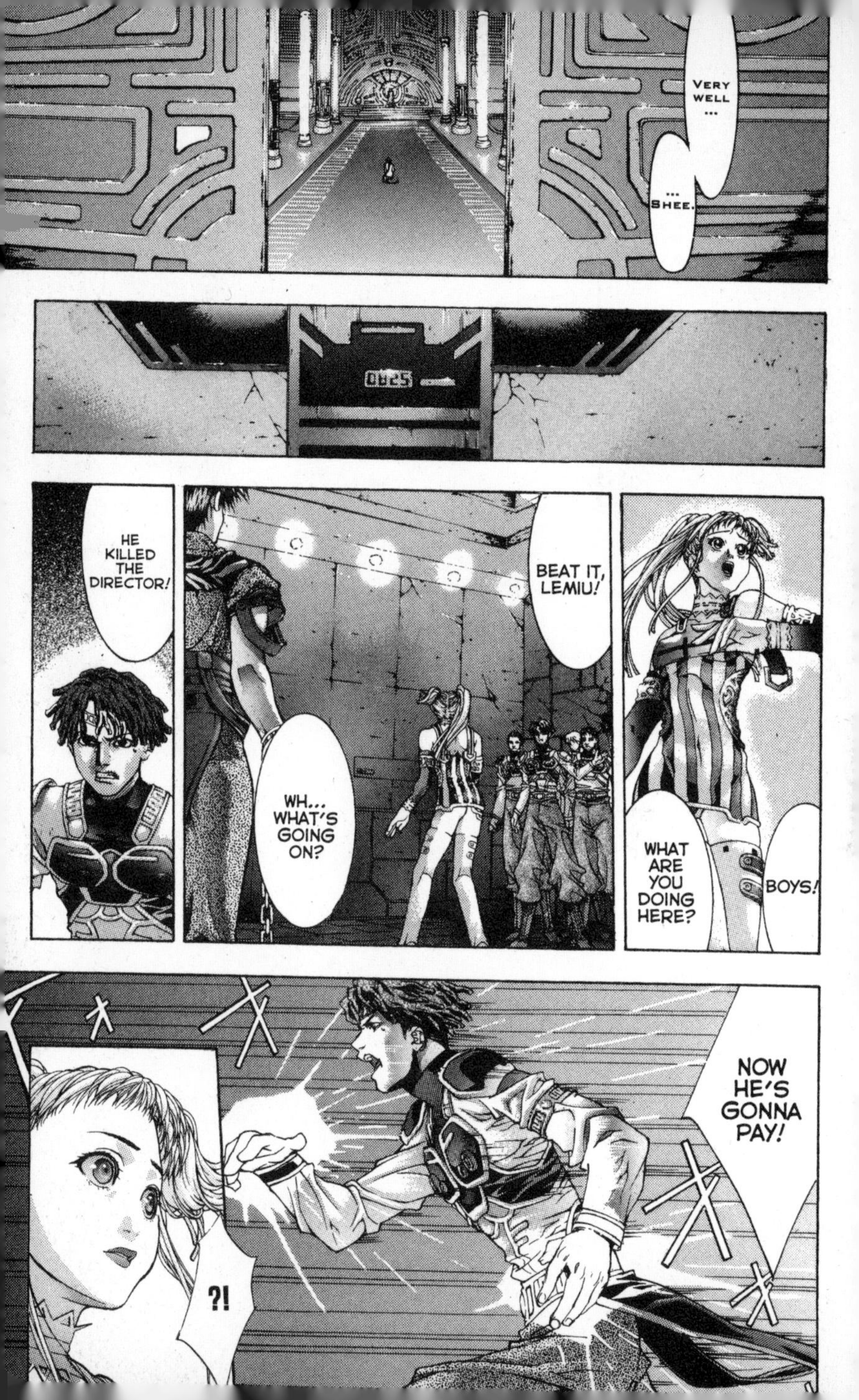

VERY WELL...
...SHEE.
00:25
BOYS!
WHAT ARE YOU DOING HERE?
BEAT IT, LEMIU!
WH... WHAT'S GOING ON?
HE KILLED THE DIRECTOR!
NOW HE'S GONNA PAY!
?!

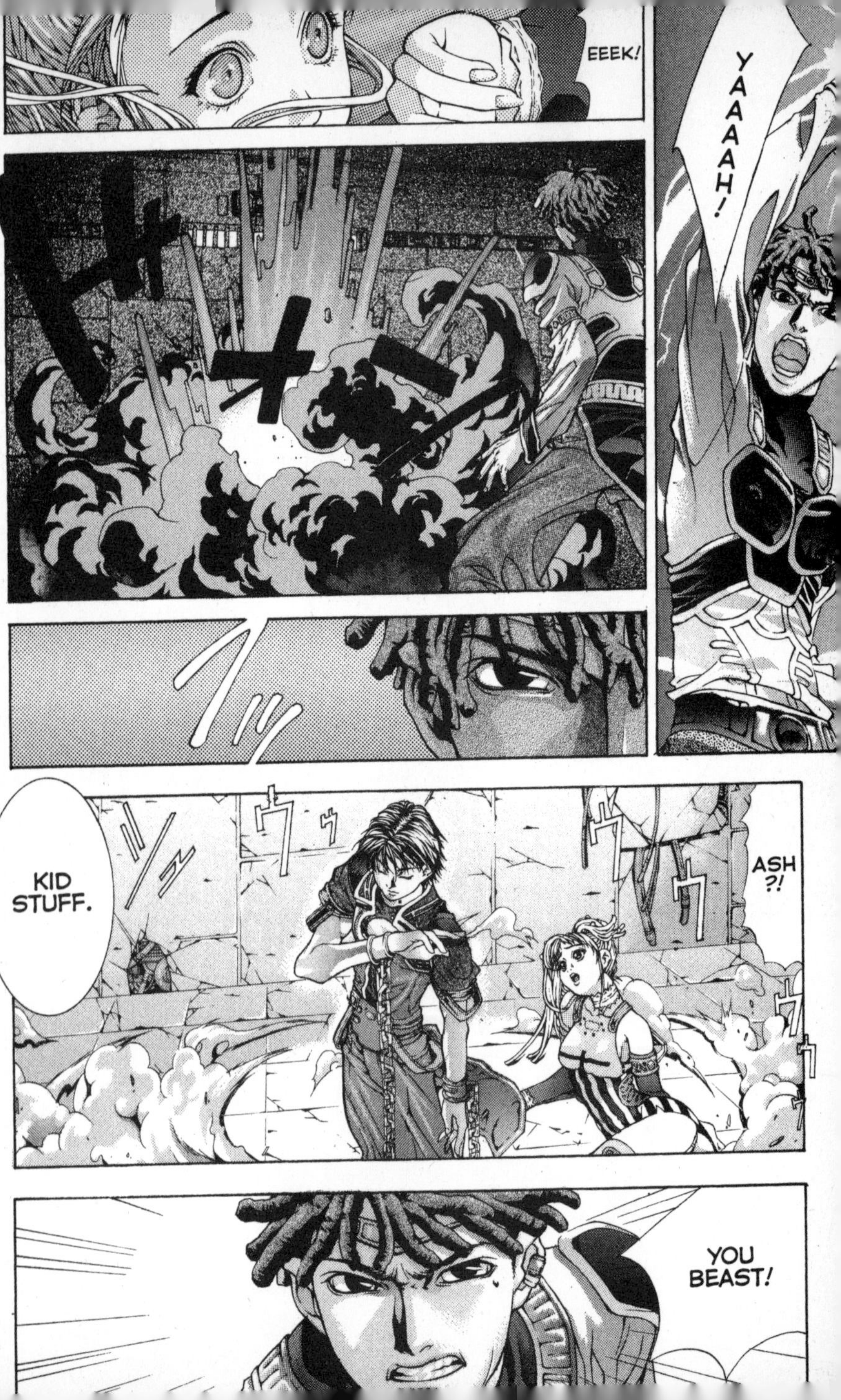
YAAAAAH!
EEEK!
ASH?!
KID STUFF.
YOU BEAST!

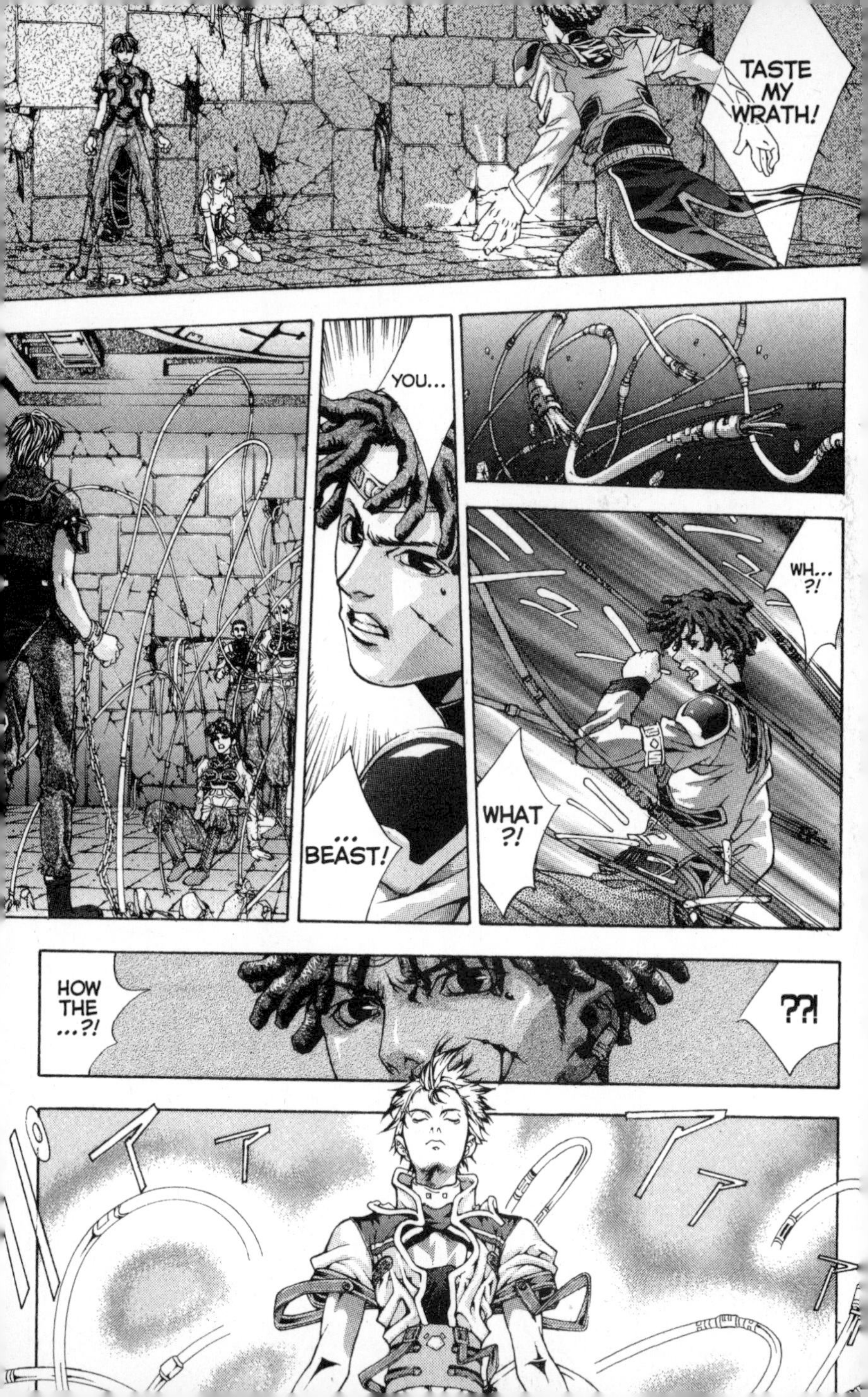
TASTE MY WRATH!
WH...?!
WHAT?!
YOU...
...BEAST!
??!
HOW THE ...?!

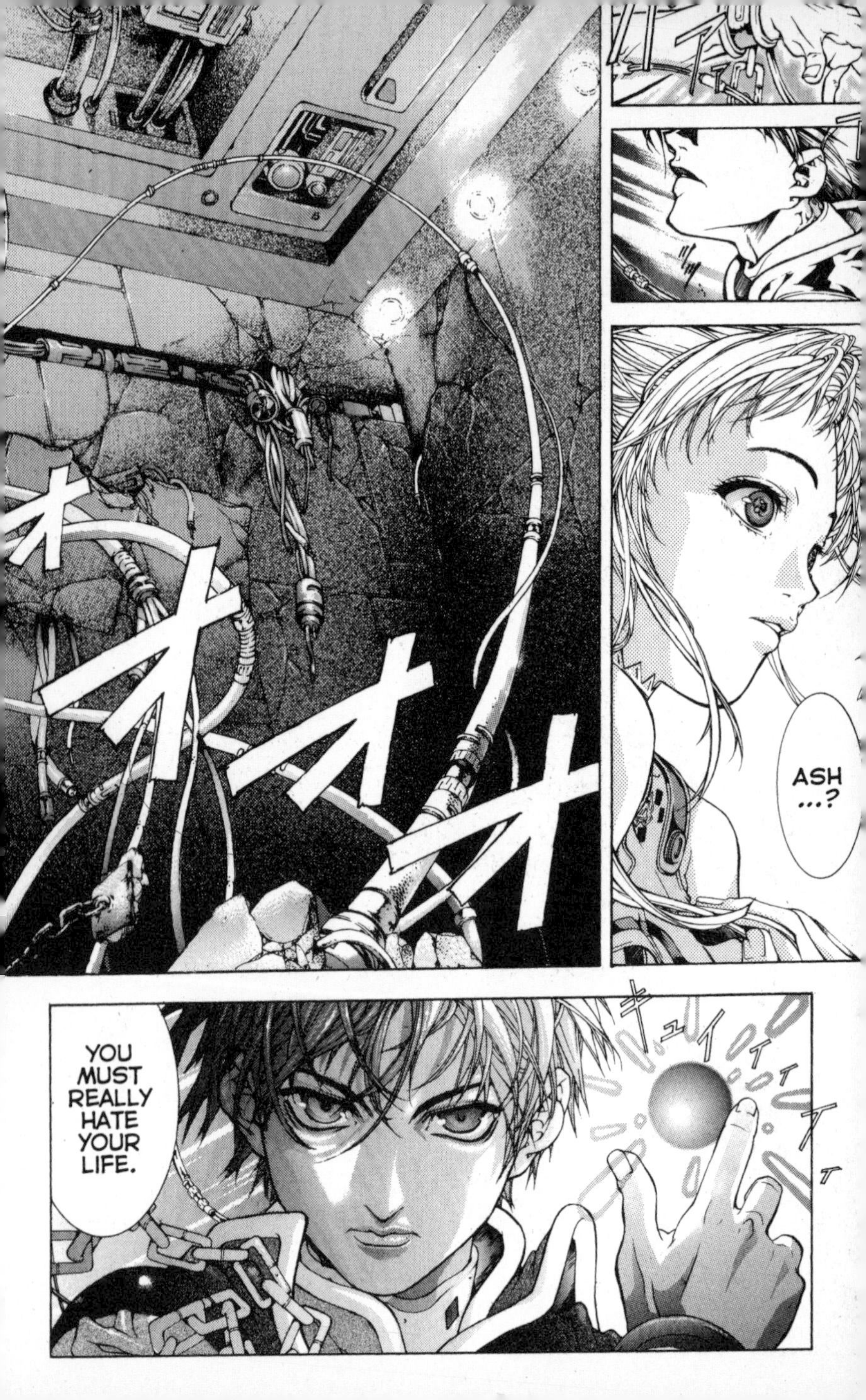
ASH ...?
YOU MUST REALLY HATE YOUR LIFE.

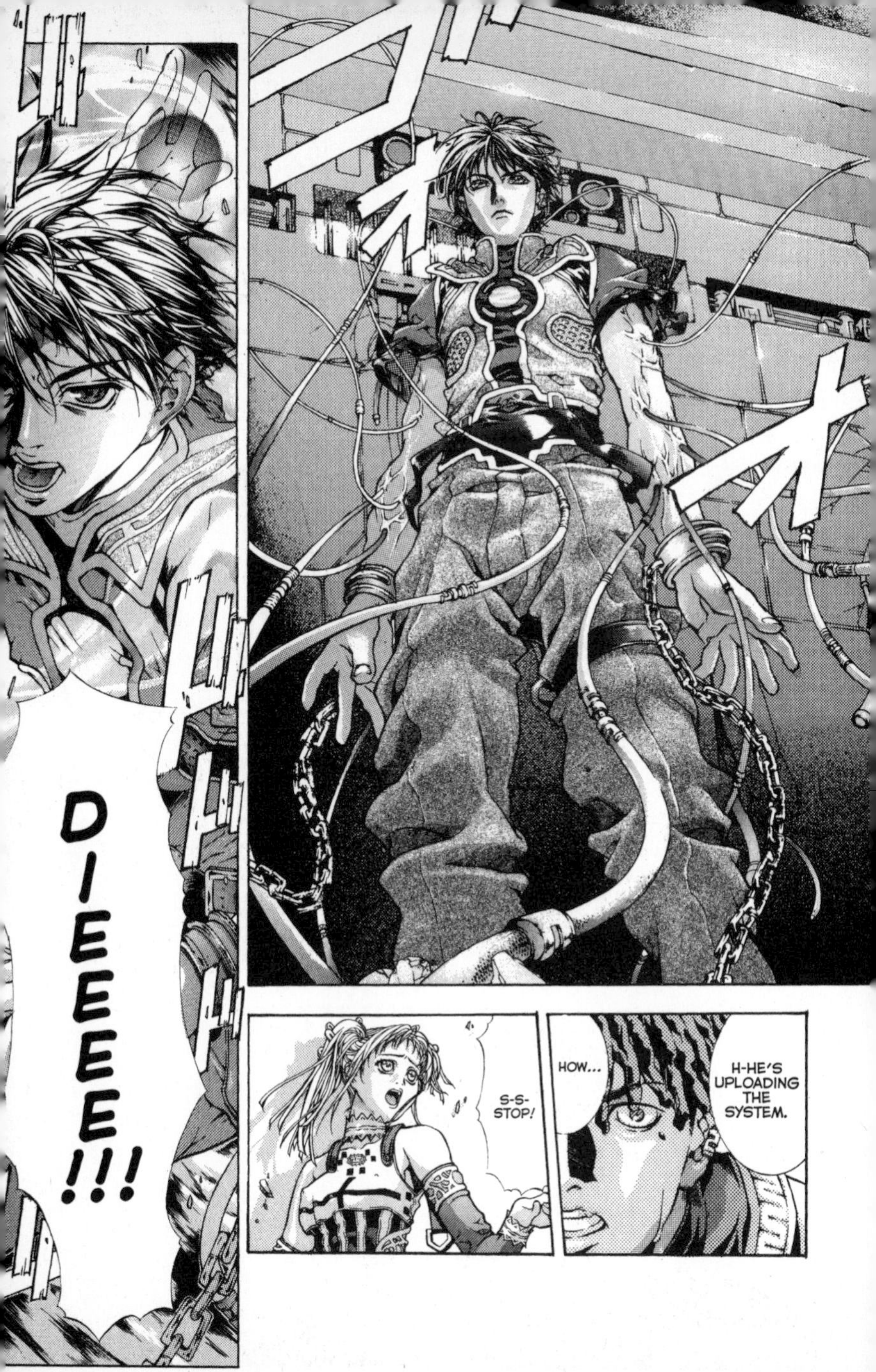
H-HE'S UPLOADING THE SYSTEM.
HOW...
S-S-STOP!
DIEEEE!!!

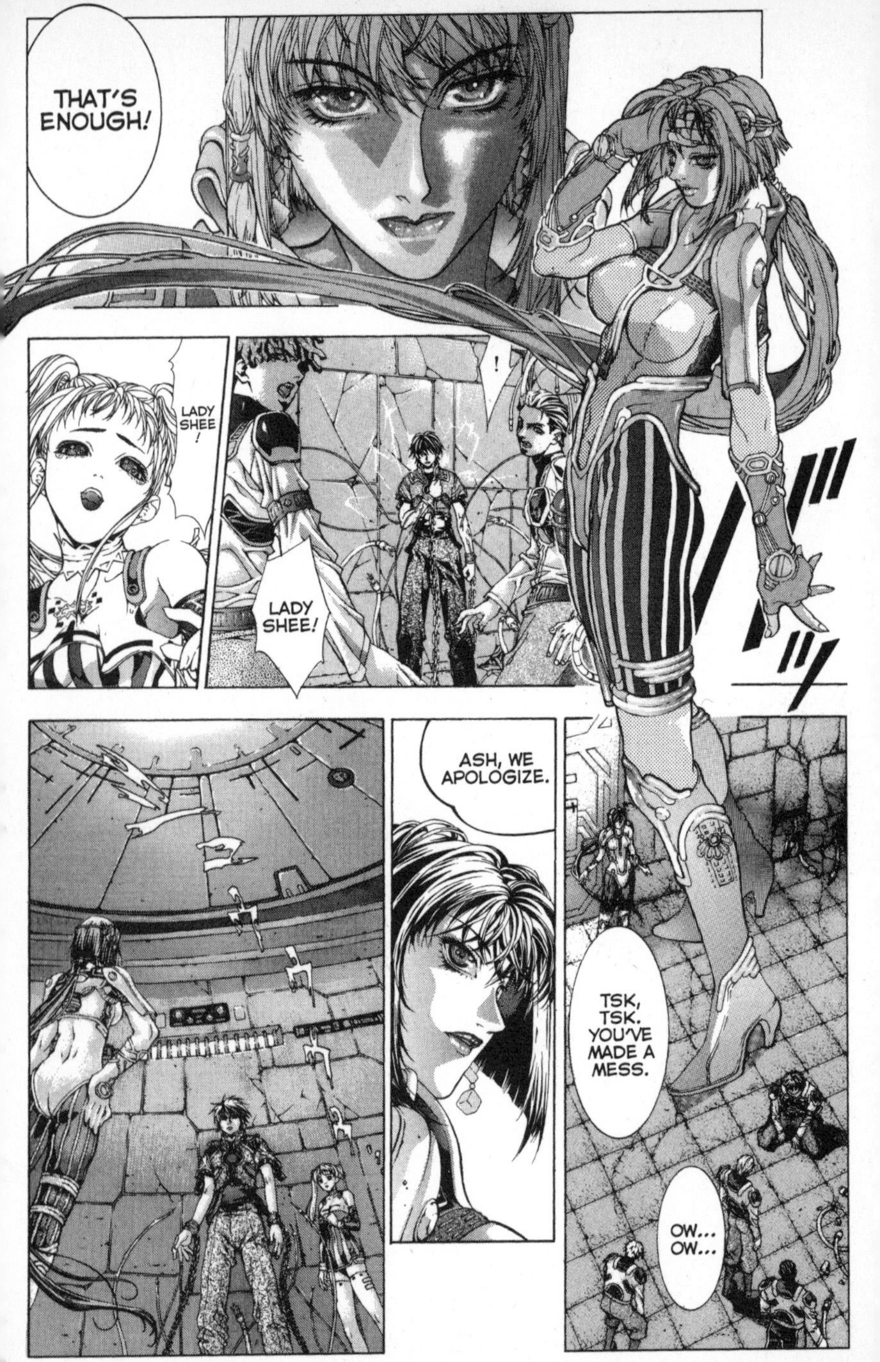
THAT'S ENOUGH!
!
LADY SHEE!
LADY SHEE!
TSK, TSK. YOU'VE MADE A MESS.
OW... OW...
ASH, WE APOLOGIZE.

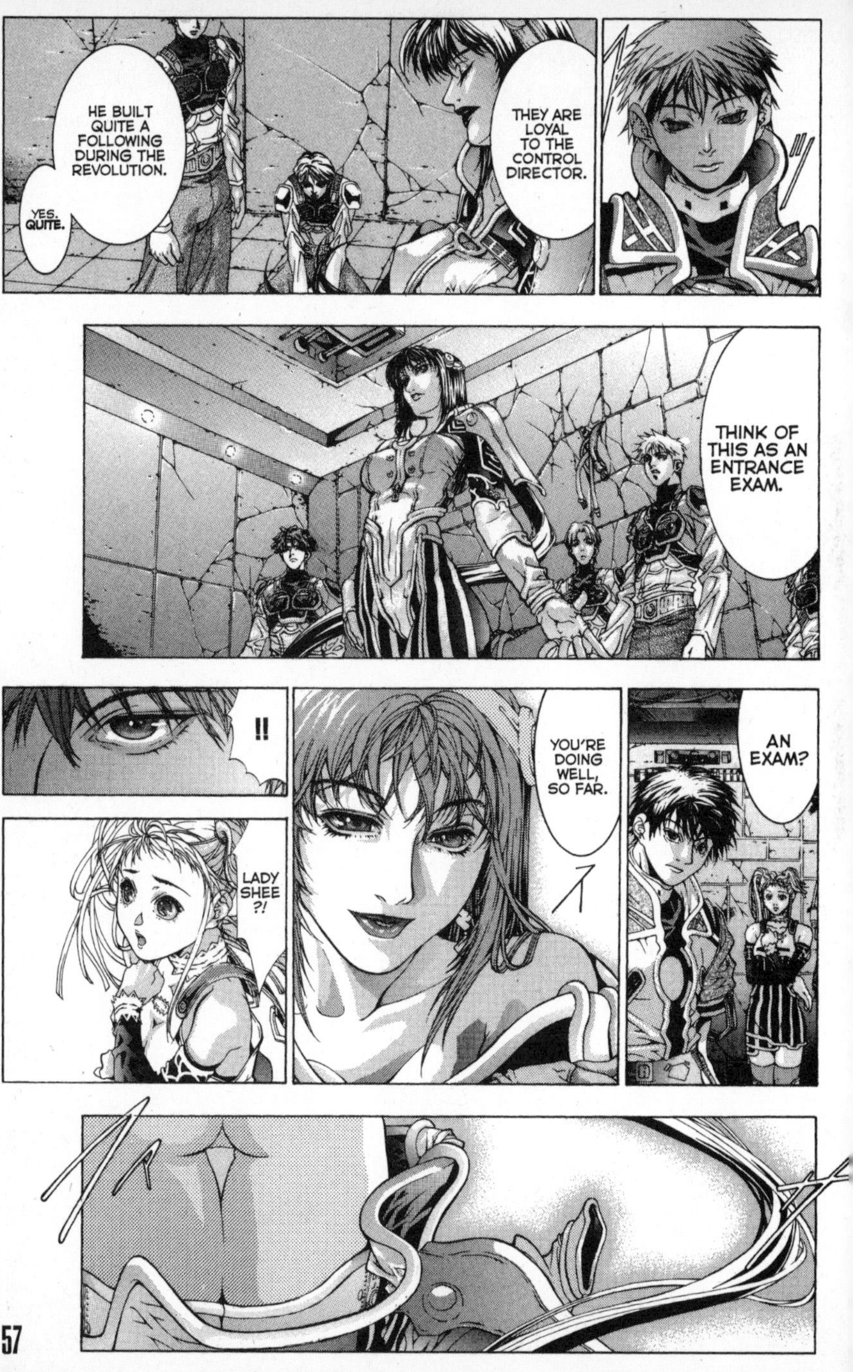
THEY ARE LOYAL TO THE CONTROL DIRECTOR.
HE BUILT QUITE A FOLLOWING DURING THE REVOLUTION.
YES. QUITE.
THINK OF THIS AS AN ENTRANCE EXAM.
AN EXAM?
YOU'RE DOING WELL, SO FAR.
!!
LADY SHEE ?!

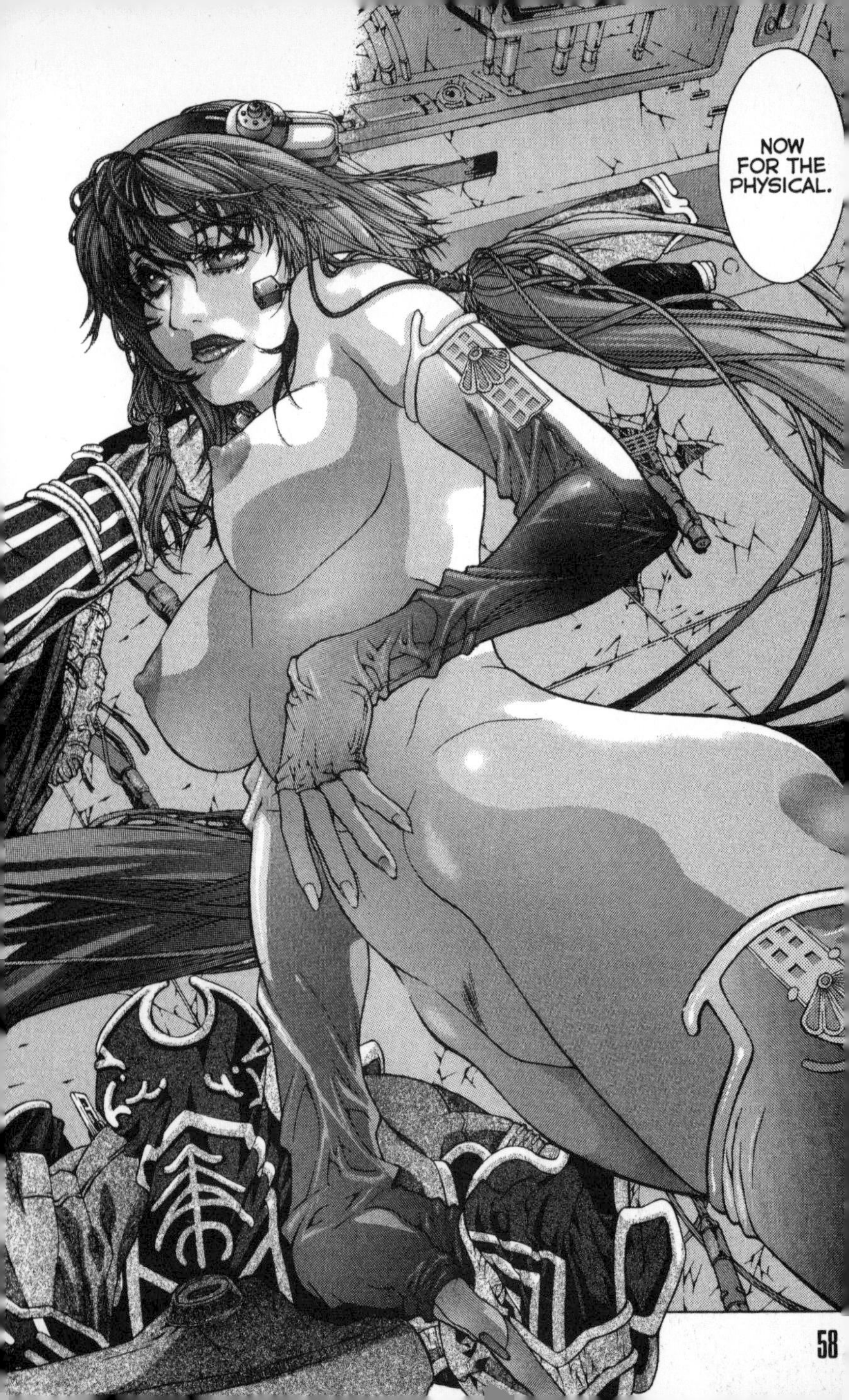
NOW FOR THE PHYSICAL.

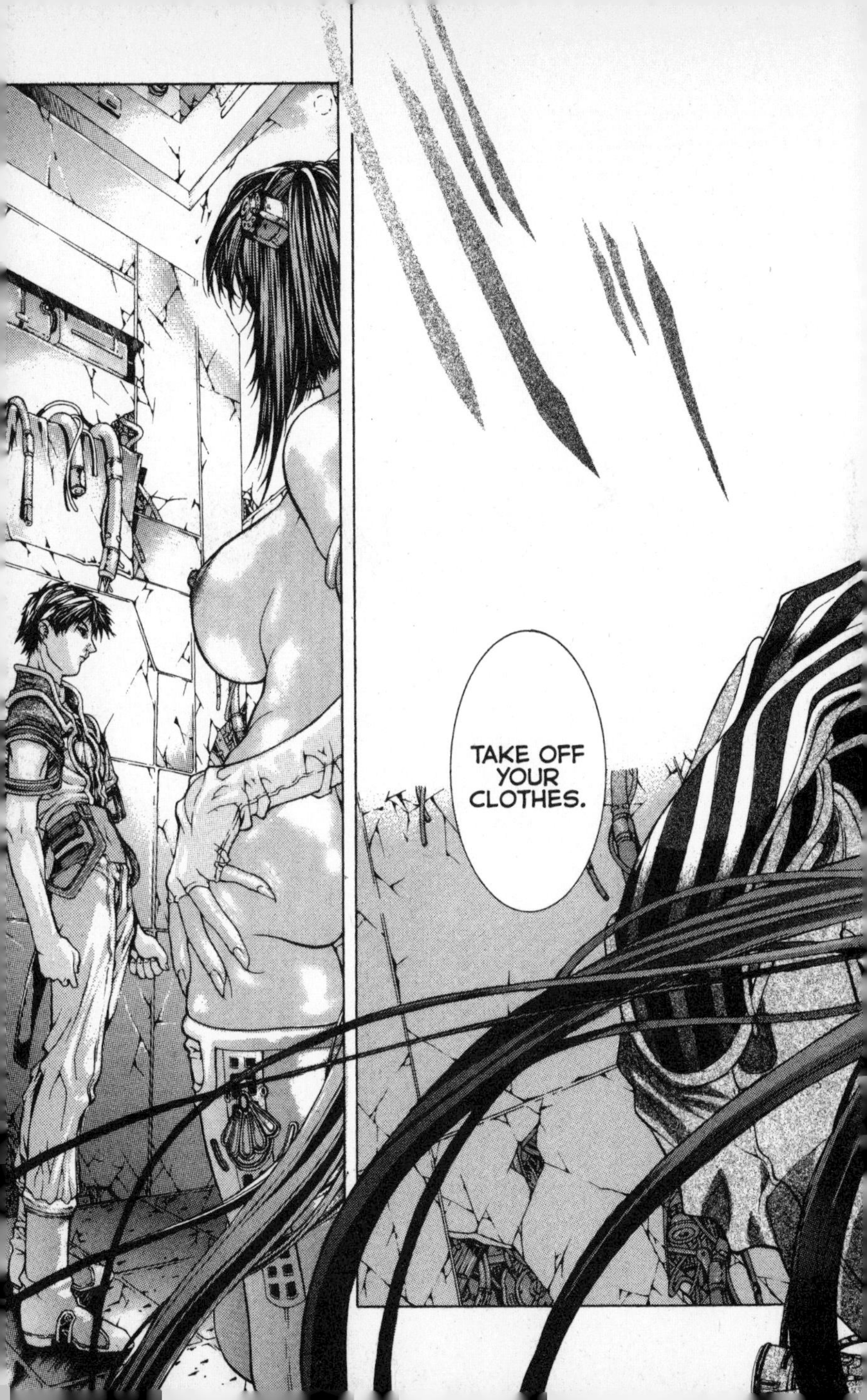
TAKE OFF YOUR CLOTHES.

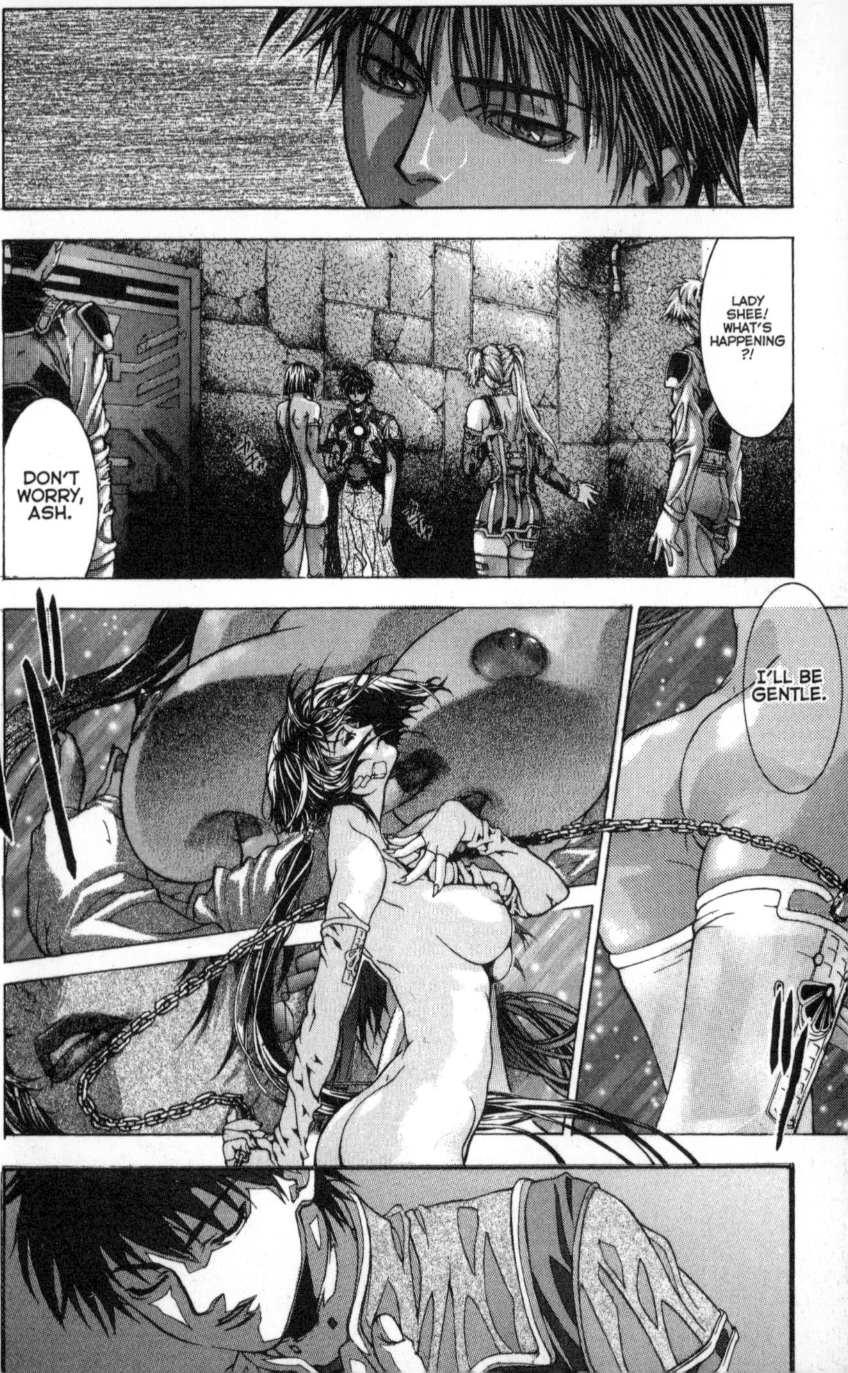
LADY SHEE! WHAT'S HAPPENING?!
DON'T WORRY, ASH.
I'LL BE GENTLE.

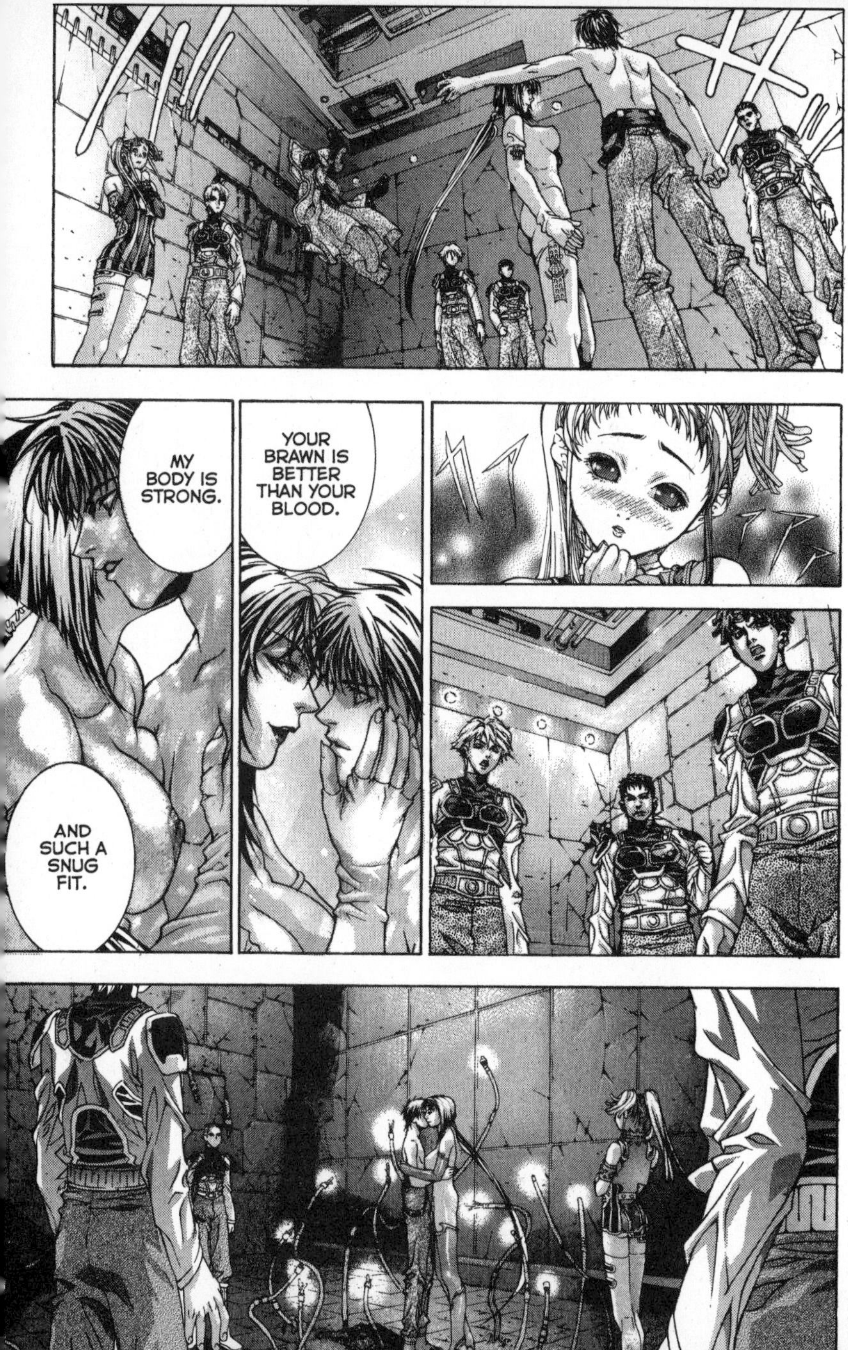
YOUR BRAWN IS BETTER THAN YOUR BLOOD.
MY BODY IS STRONG.
AND SUCH A SNUG FIT.

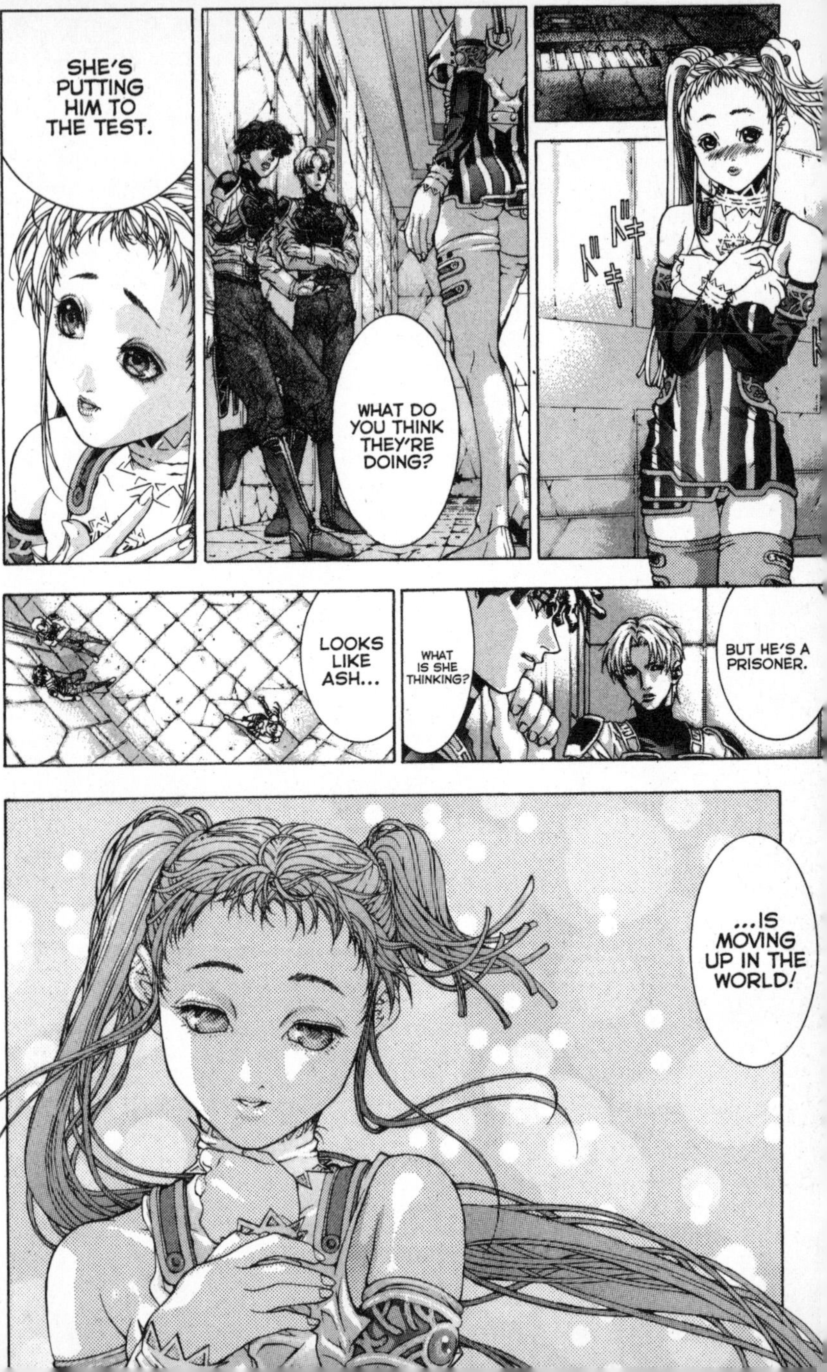
ドキドキ
WHAT DO YOU THINK THEY'RE DOING?
SHE'S PUTTING HIM TO THE TEST.
BUT HE'S A PRISONER.
WHAT IS SHE THINKING?
LOOKS LIKE ASH...
...IS MOVING UP IN THE WORLD!

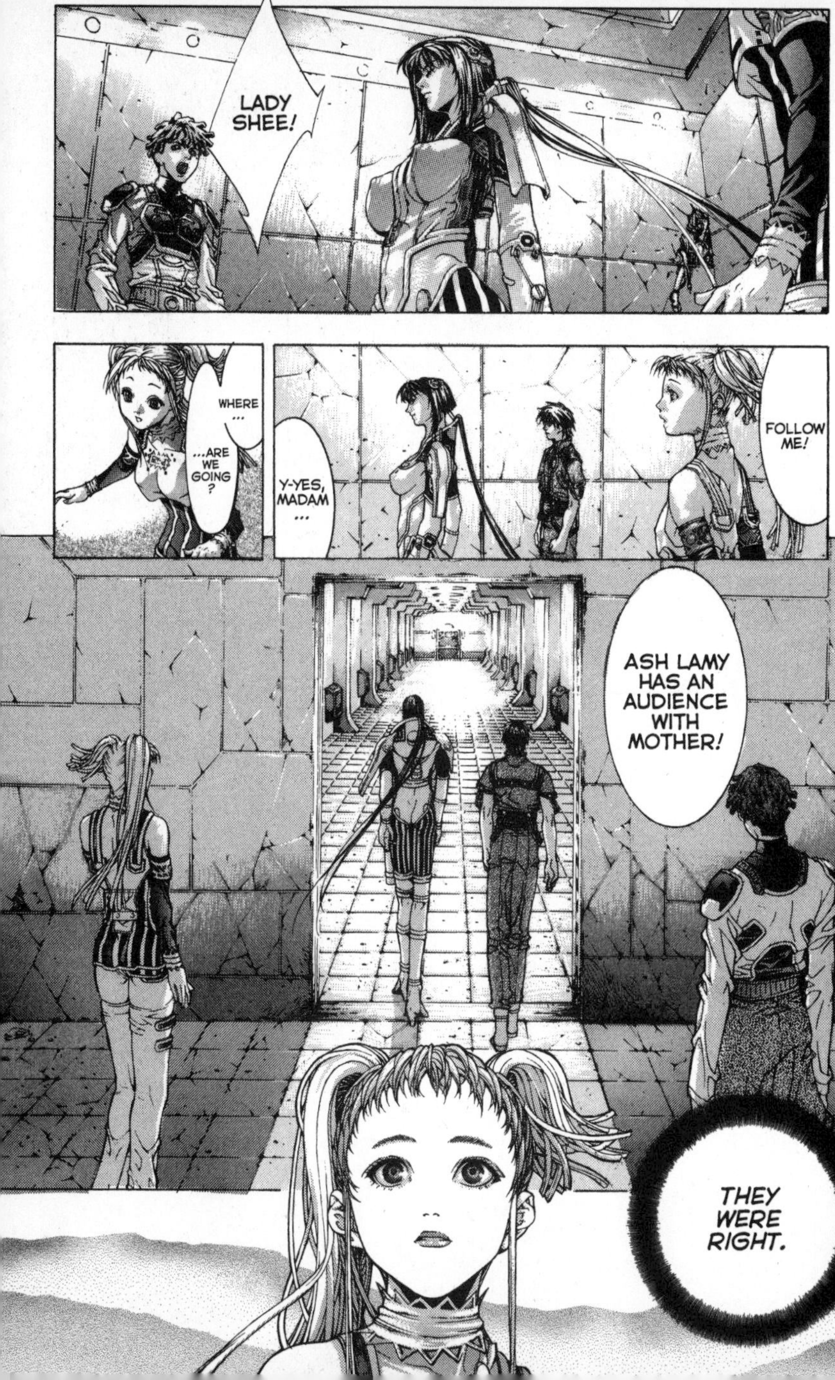
LADY SHEE!
FOLLOW ME!
Y-YES, MADAM ...
WHERE ...
...ARE WE GOING ?
ASH LAMY HAS AN AUDIENCE WITH MOTHER!
THEY WERE RIGHT.

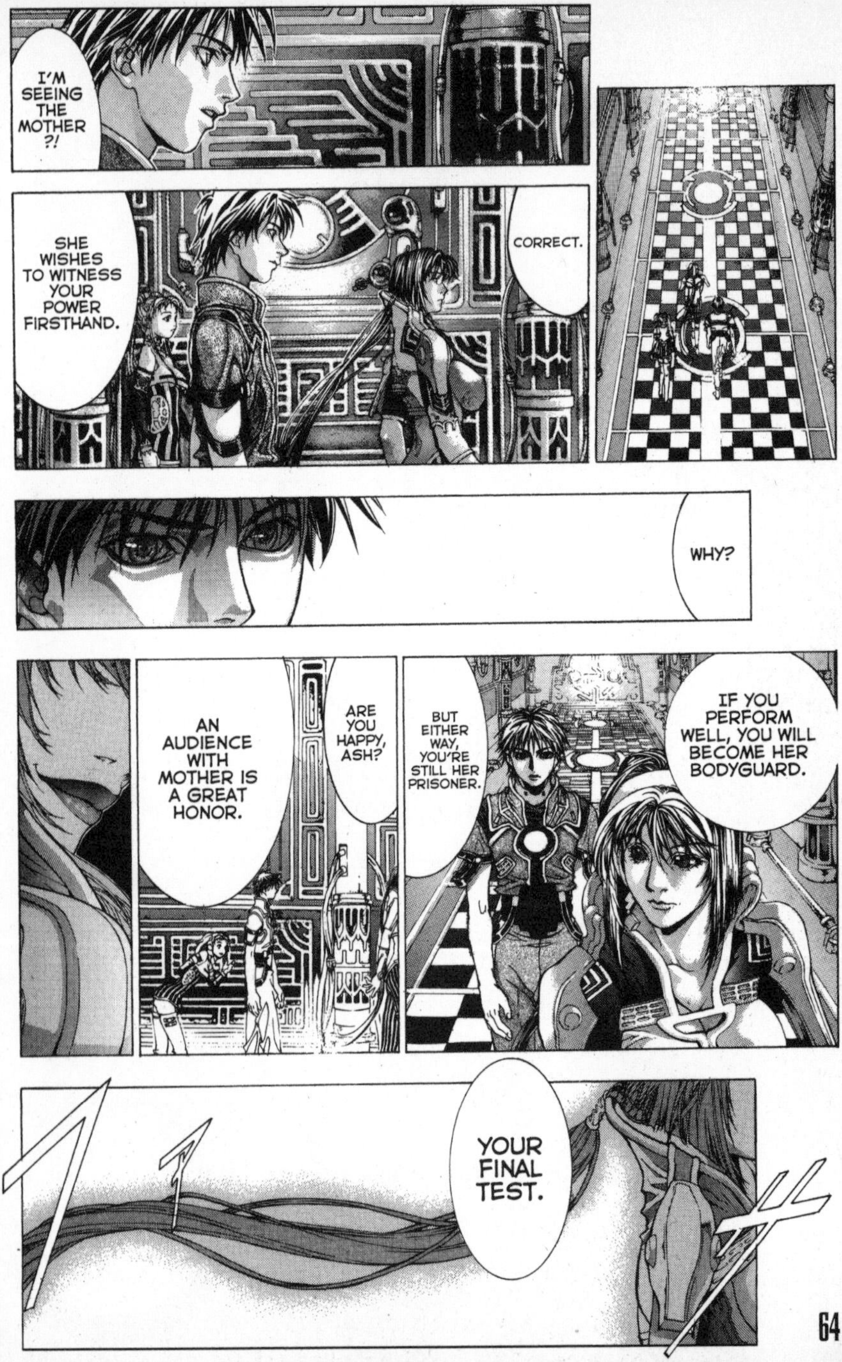
I'M SEEING THE MOTHER?!
CORRECT.
SHE WISHES TO WITNESS YOUR POWER FIRSTHAND.
WHY?
IF YOU PERFORM WELL, YOU WILL BECOME HER BODYGUARD.
BUT EITHER WAY, YOU'RE STILL HER PRISONER.
ARE YOU HAPPY, ASH?
AN AUDIENCE WITH MOTHER IS A GREAT HONOR.
YOUR FINAL TEST.

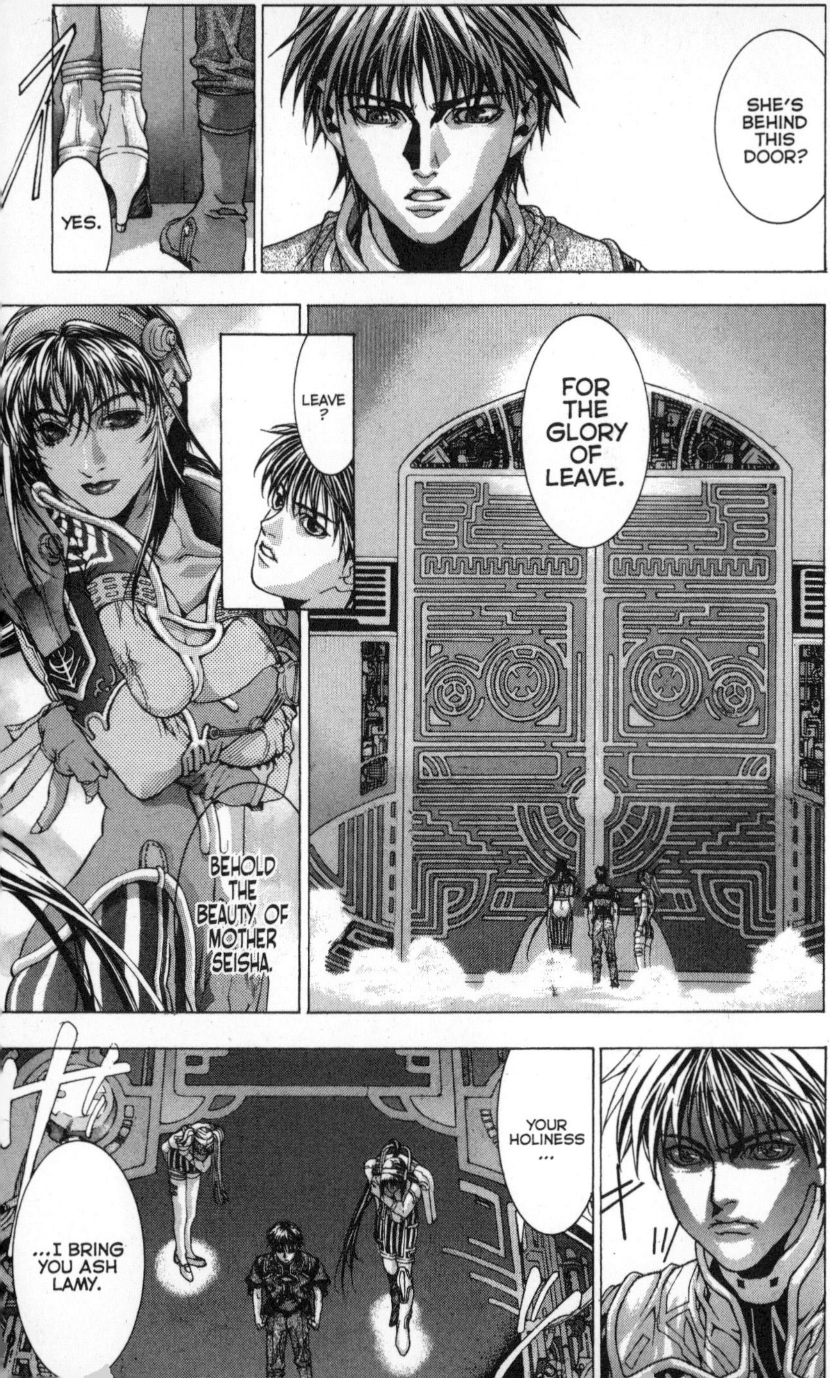
SHE'S BEHIND THIS DOOR?
YES.
FOR THE GLORY OF LEAVE.
LEAVE?
BEHOLD THE BEAUTY OF MOTHER SEISHA.
YOUR HOLINESS...
...I BRING YOU ASH LAMY.

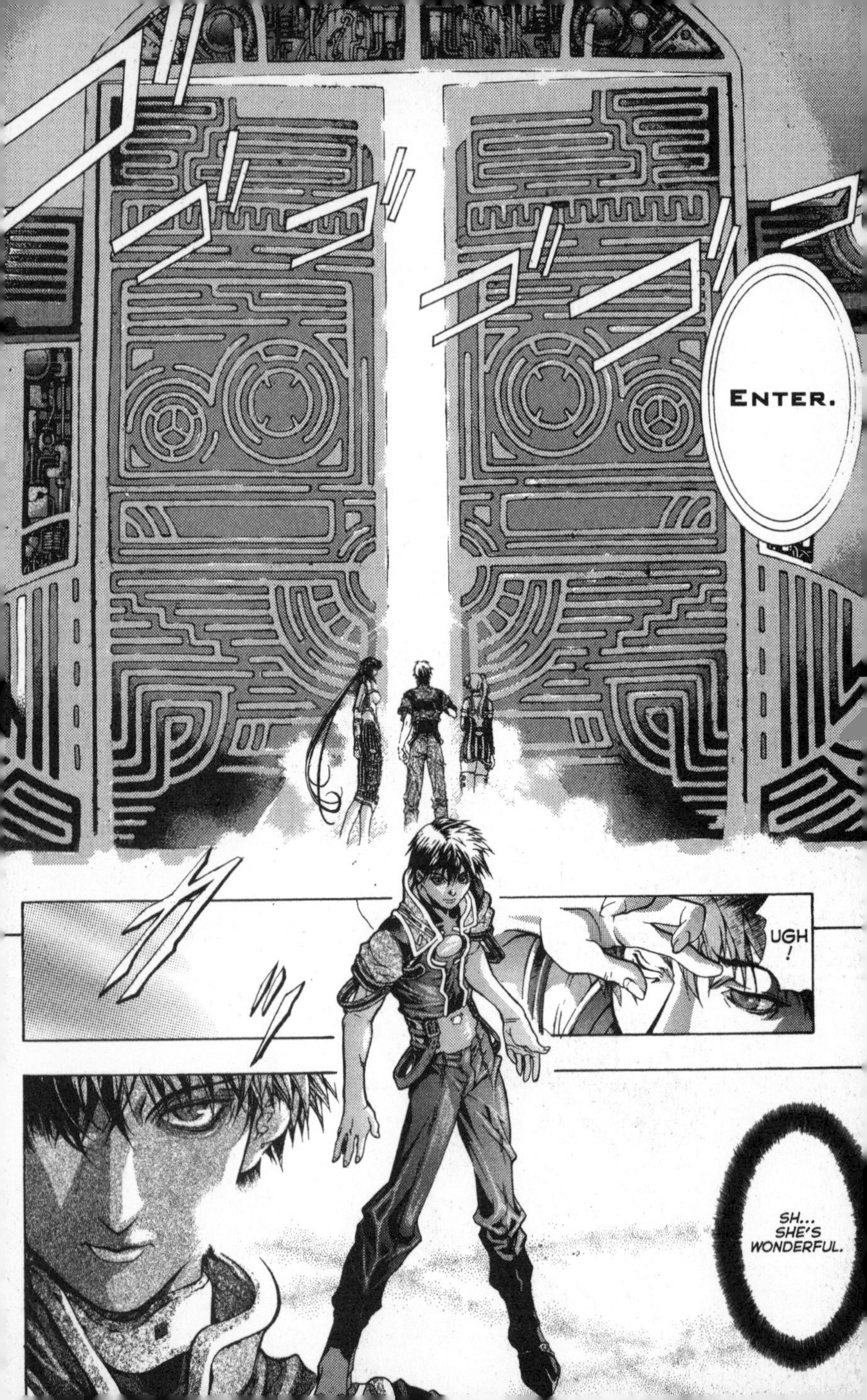
ENTER.
UGH!
SH... SHE'S WONDERFUL.

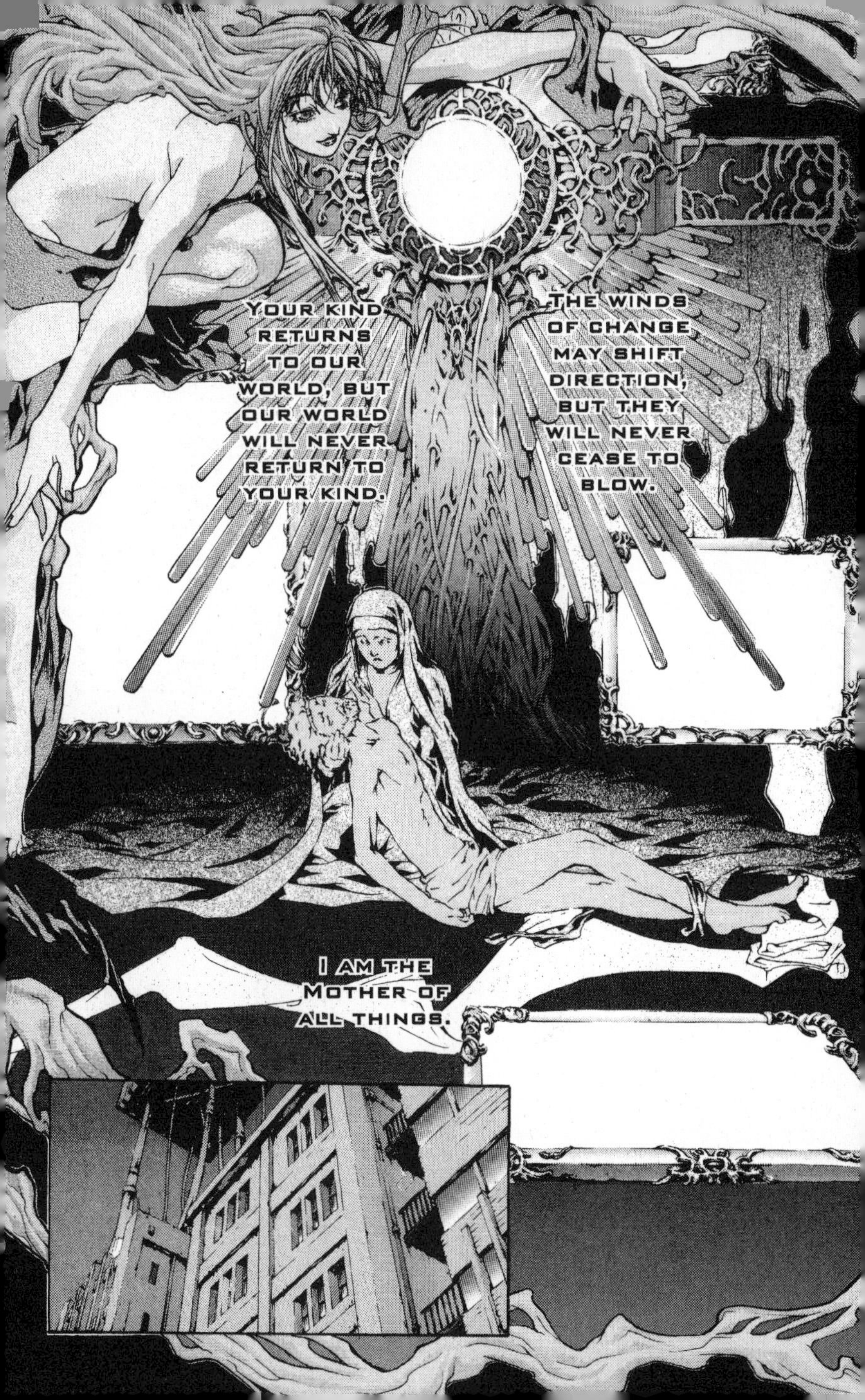
THE WINDS OF CHANGE MAY SHIFT DIRECTION, BUT THEY WILL NEVER CEASE TO BLOW.
YOUR KIND RETURNS TO OUR WORLD, BUT OUR WORLD WILL NEVER RETURN TO YOUR KIND.
I AM THE MOTHER OF ALL THINGS.

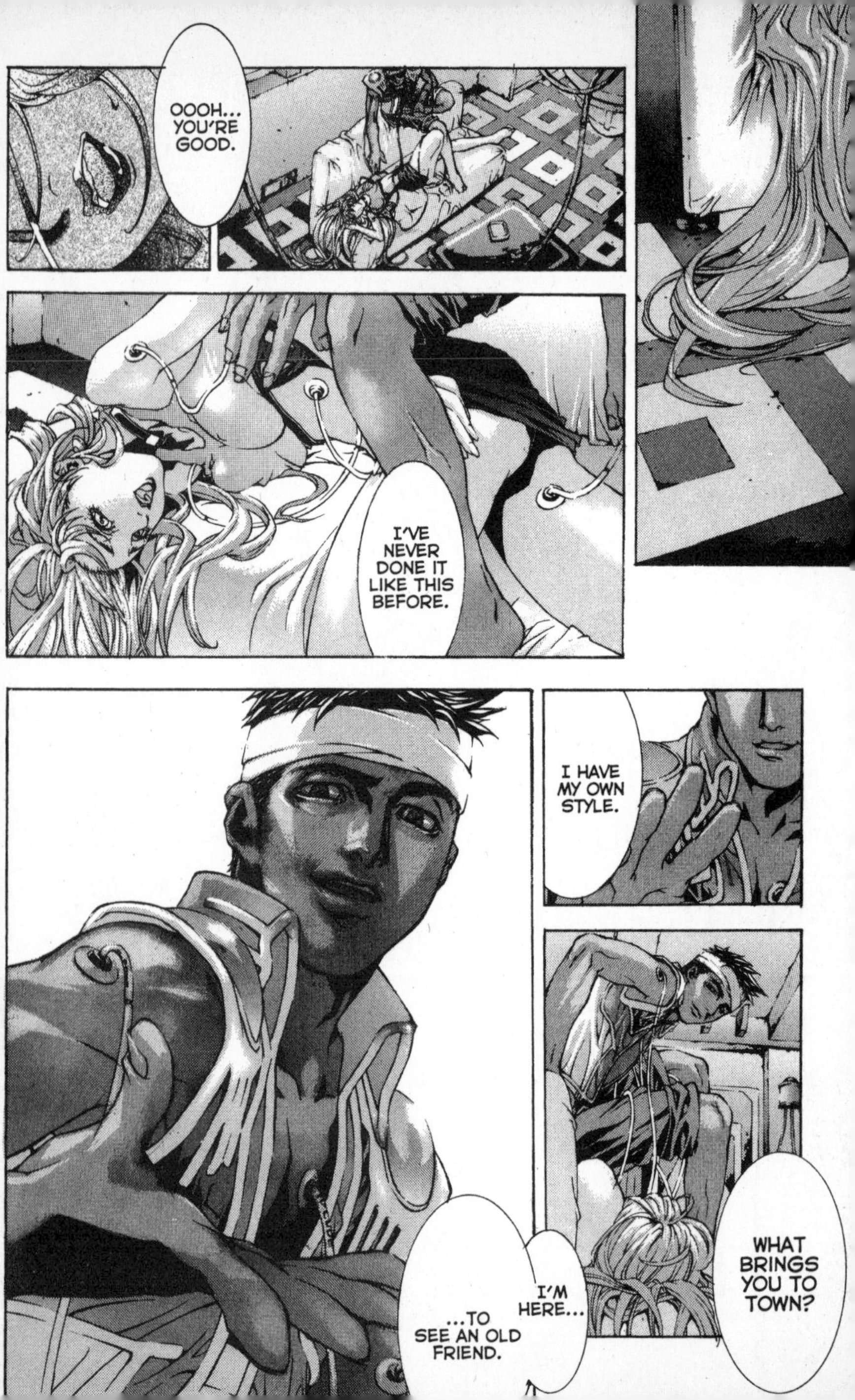
OOOH... YOU'RE GOOD.
I'VE NEVER DONE IT LIKE THIS BEFORE.
I HAVE MY OWN STYLE.
WHAT BRINGS YOU TO TOWN?
I'M HERE...
...TO SEE AN OLD FRIEND.

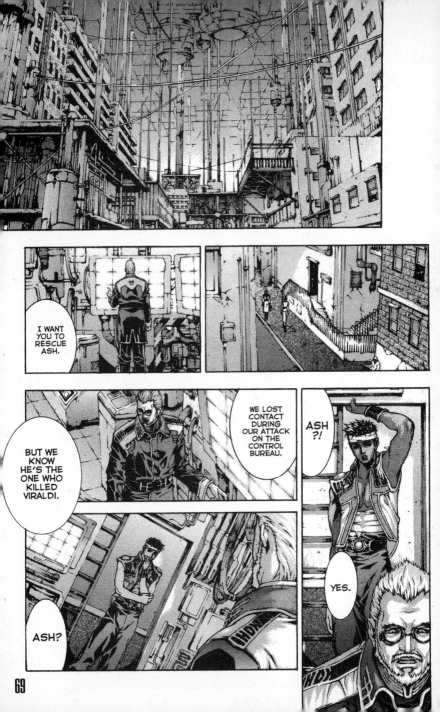

I WANT YOU TO RESCUE ASH.

WE LOST CONTACT DURING OUR ATTACK ON THE CONTROL BUREAU.

ASH ?!

BUT WE KNOW HE'S THE ONE WHO KILLED VIRALDI.

ASH?

YES.

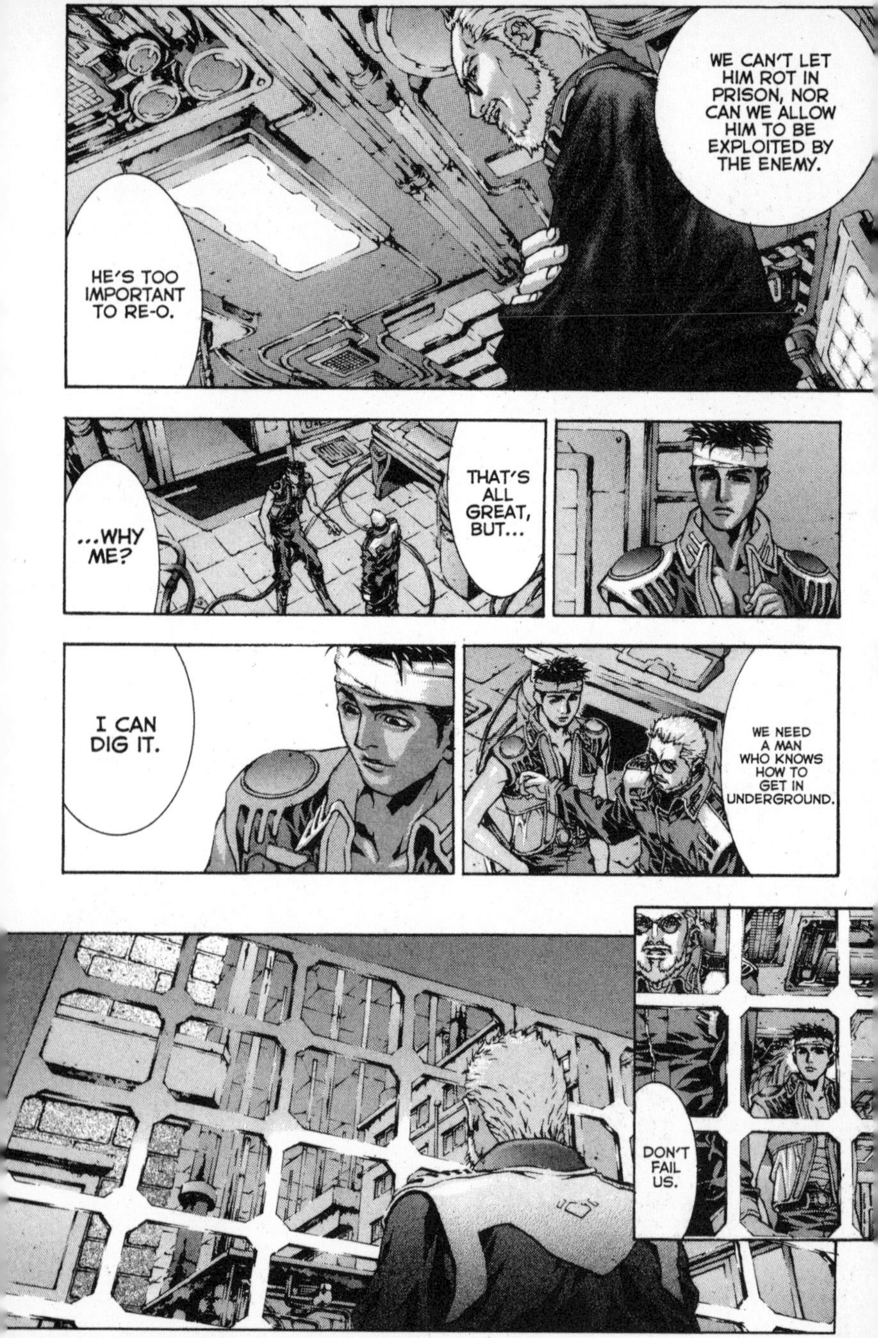
WE CAN'T LET HIM ROT IN PRISON, NOR CAN WE ALLOW HIM TO BE EXPLOITED BY THE ENEMY.
HE'S TOO IMPORTANT TO RE-O.
THAT'S ALL GREAT, BUT...
...WHY ME?
WE NEED A MAN WHO KNOWS HOW TO GET IN UNDERGROUND.
I CAN DIG IT.
DON'T FAIL US.

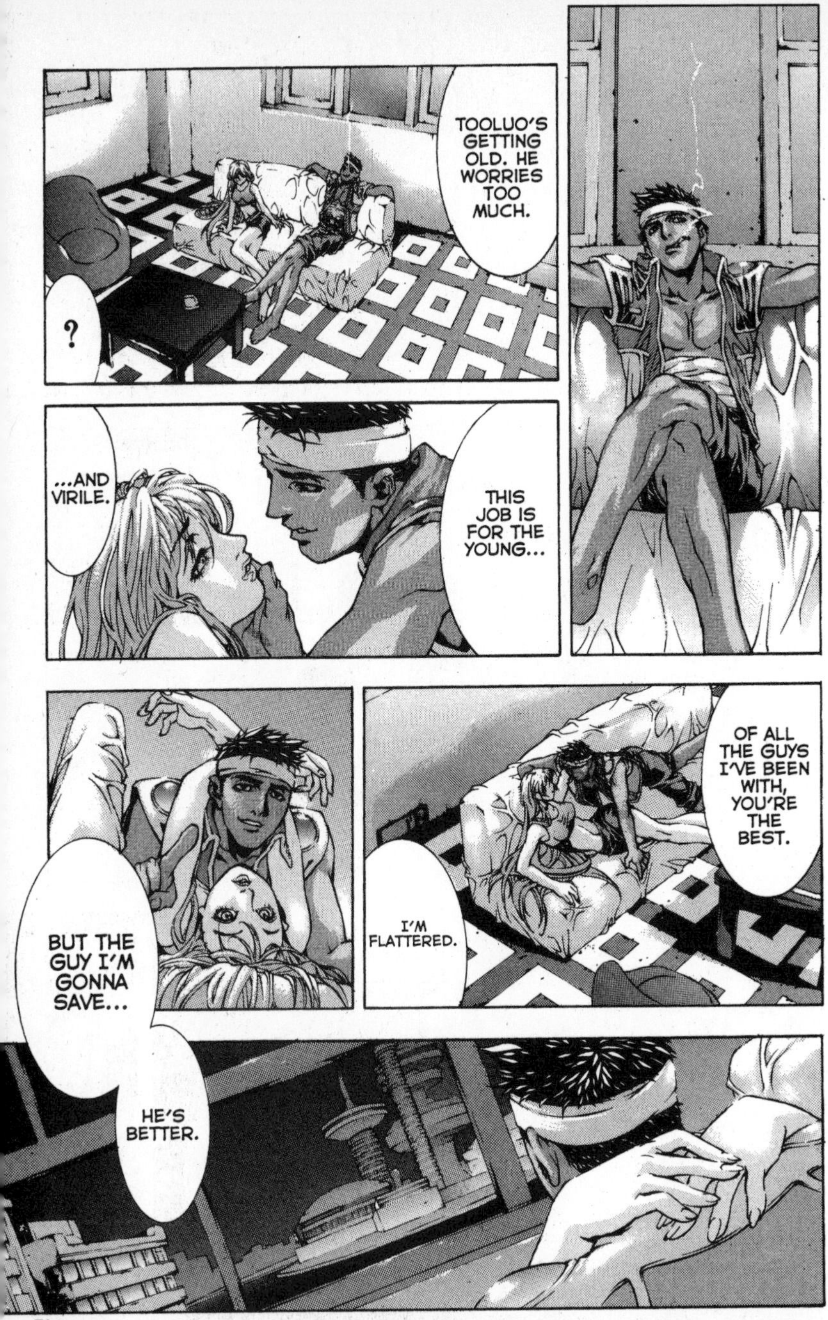
TOOLUO'S GETTING OLD. HE WORRIES TOO MUCH.
?
THIS JOB IS FOR THE YOUNG...
...AND VIRILE.
OF ALL THE GUYS I'VE BEEN WITH, YOU'RE THE BEST.
I'M FLATTERED.
BUT THE GUY I'M GONNA SAVE...
HE'S BETTER.

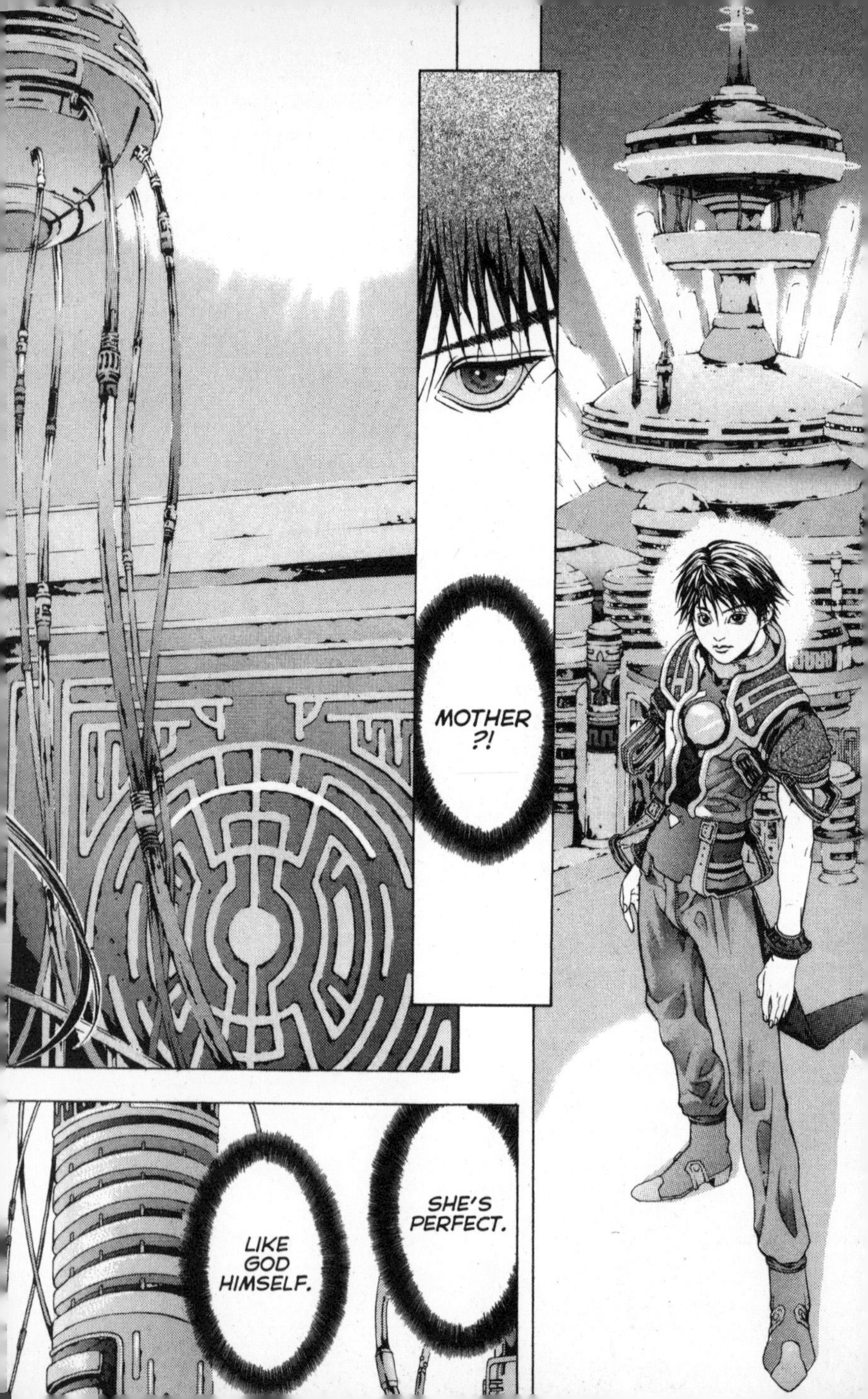
MOTHER ?!
SHE'S PERFECT.
LIKE GOD HIMSELF.

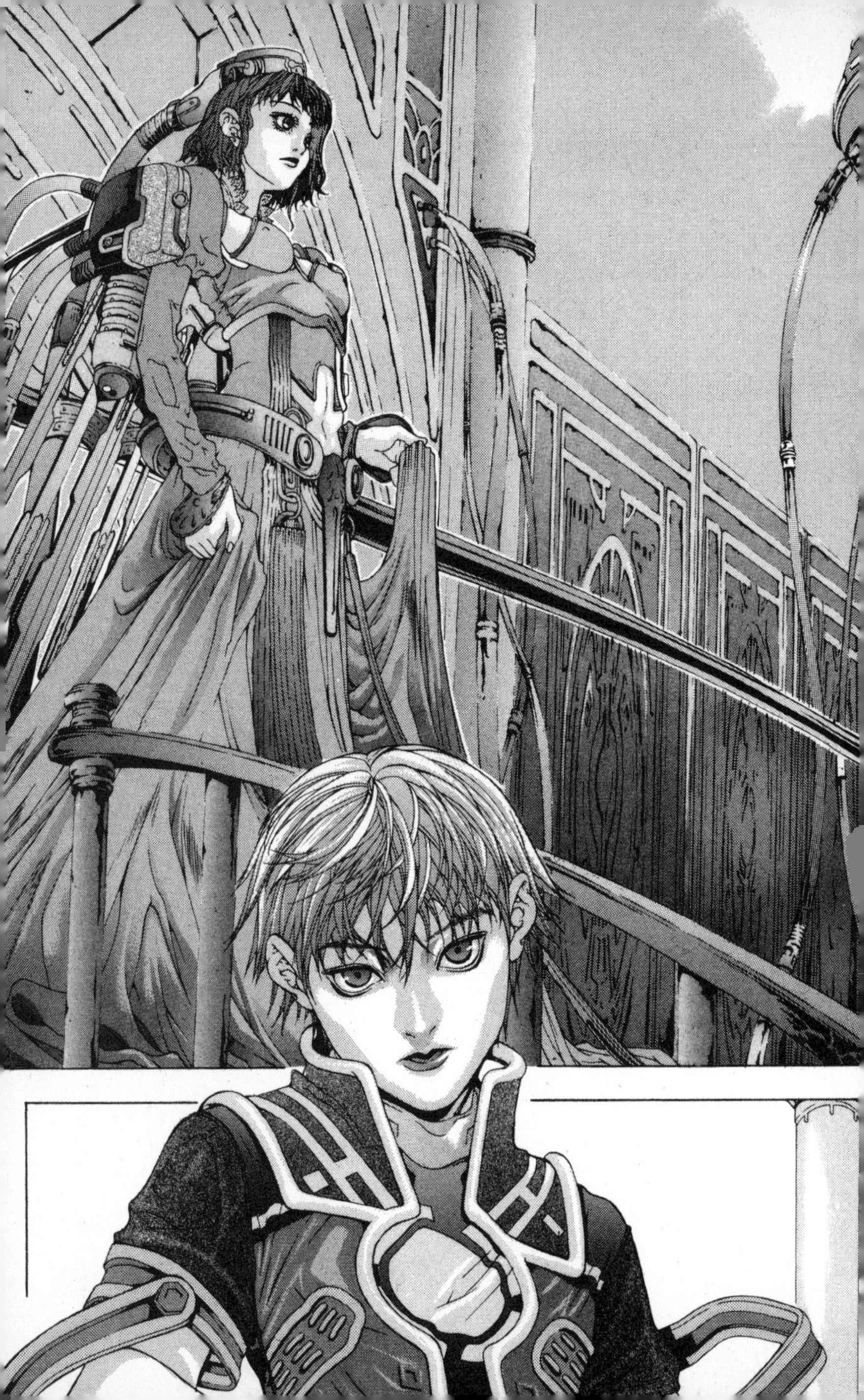

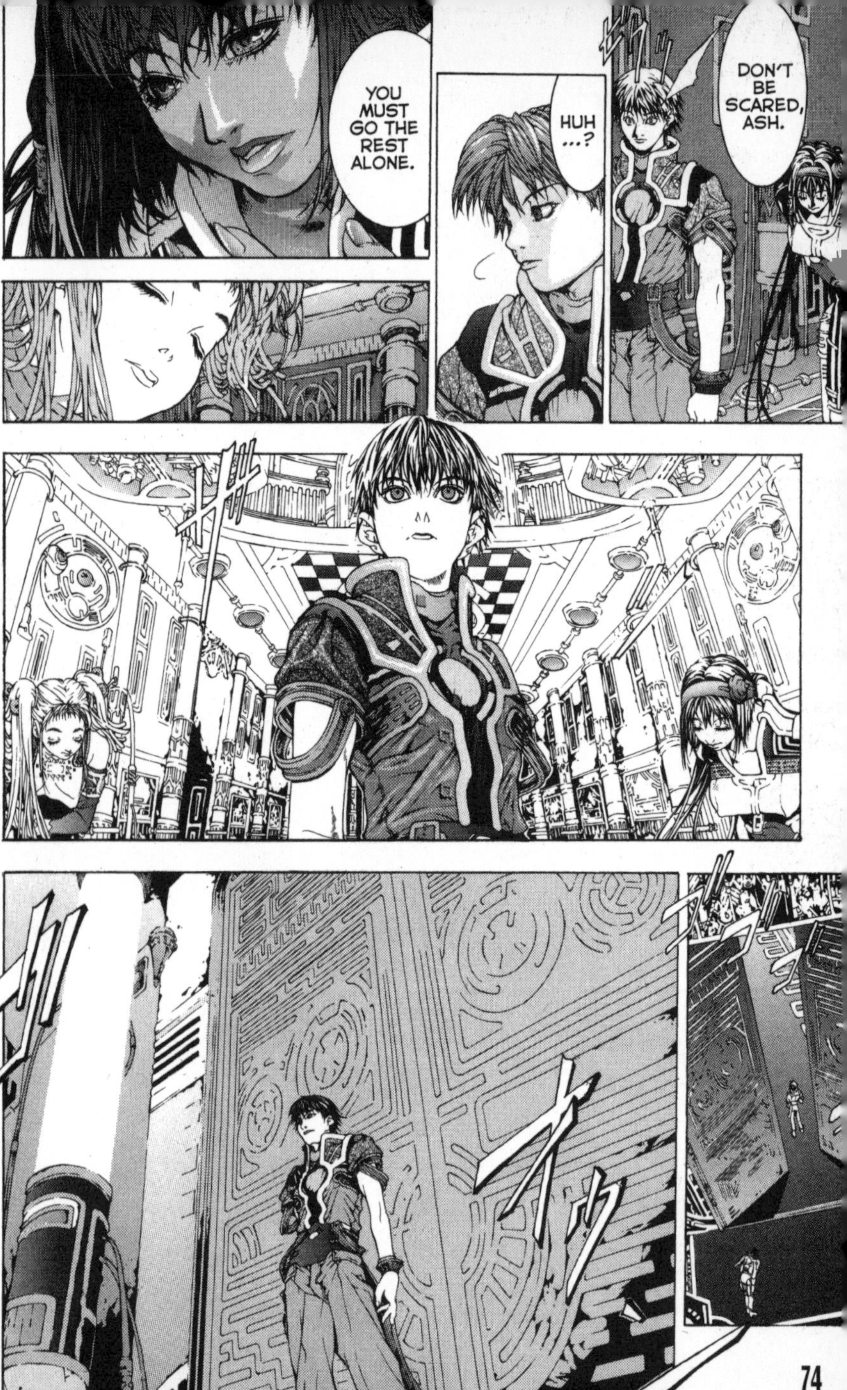
DON'T BE SCARED, ASH.
HUH ...?
YOU MUST GO THE REST ALONE.

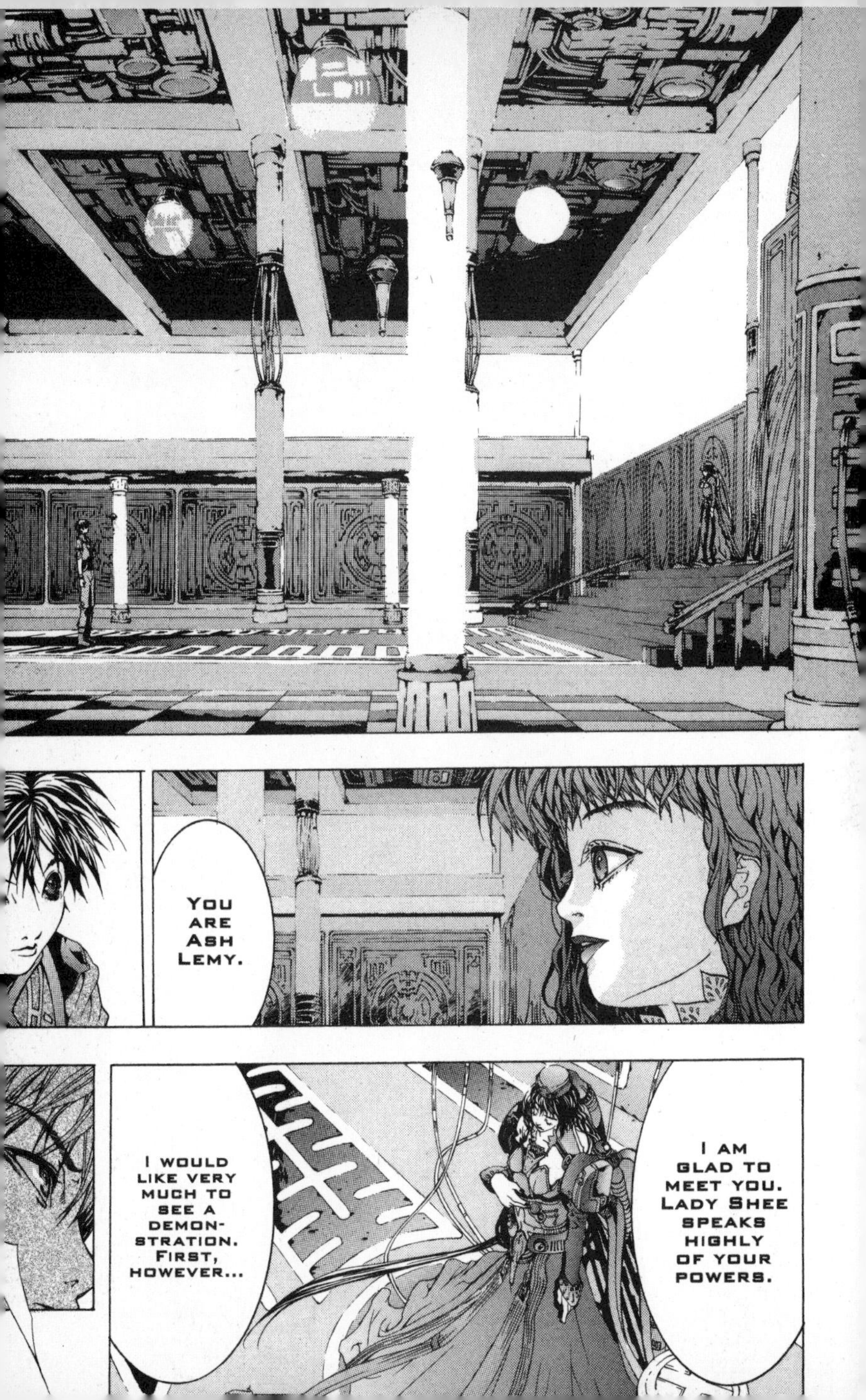
You are Ash Lemy.
I am glad to meet you. Lady Shee speaks highly of your powers.
I would like very much to see a demon-stration. First, however...

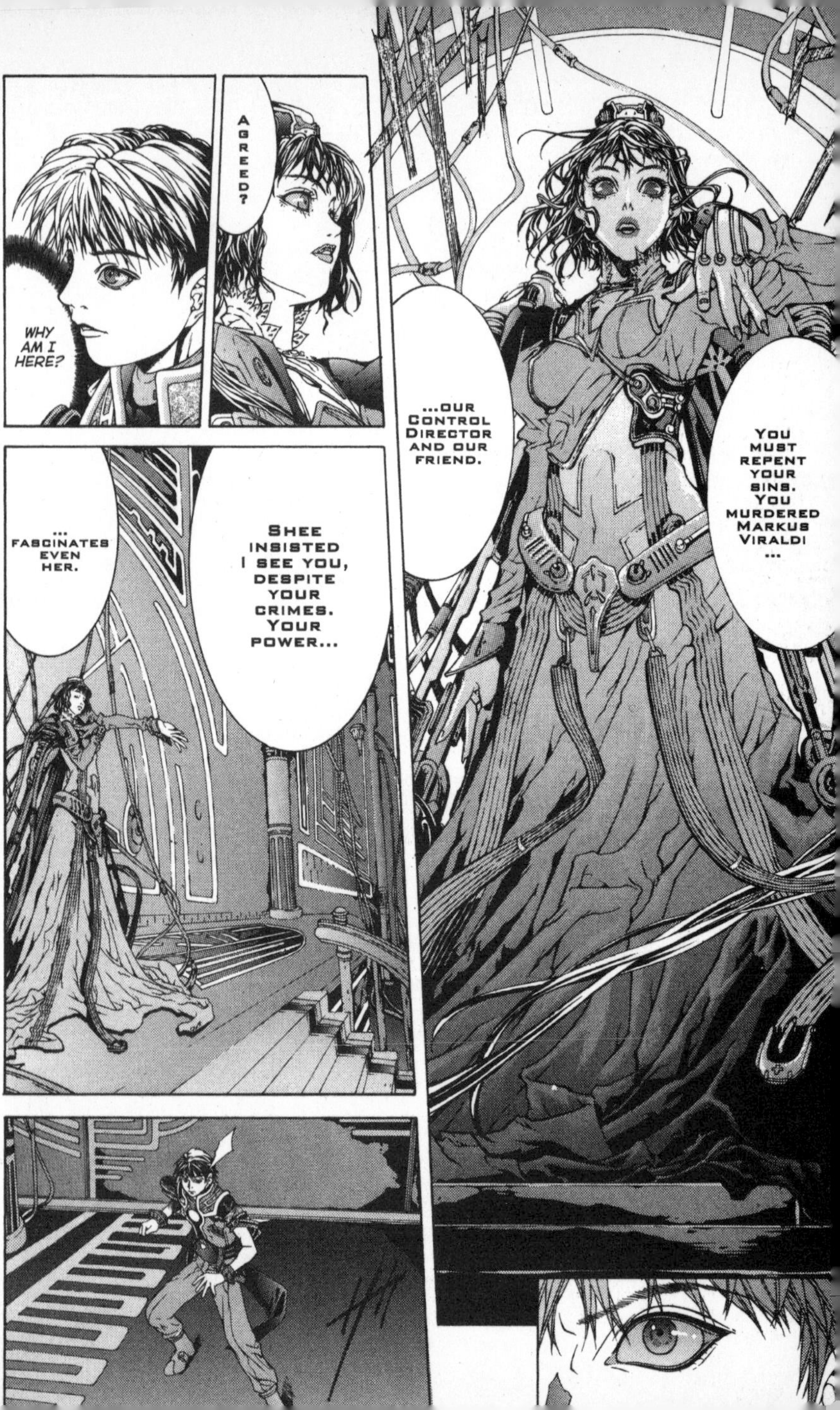
You must repent your sins. You murdered Markus Viraldi ...
...our Control Director and our friend.
Agreed?
Why am I here?
Shee insisted I see you, despite your crimes. Your power...
...fascinates even her.

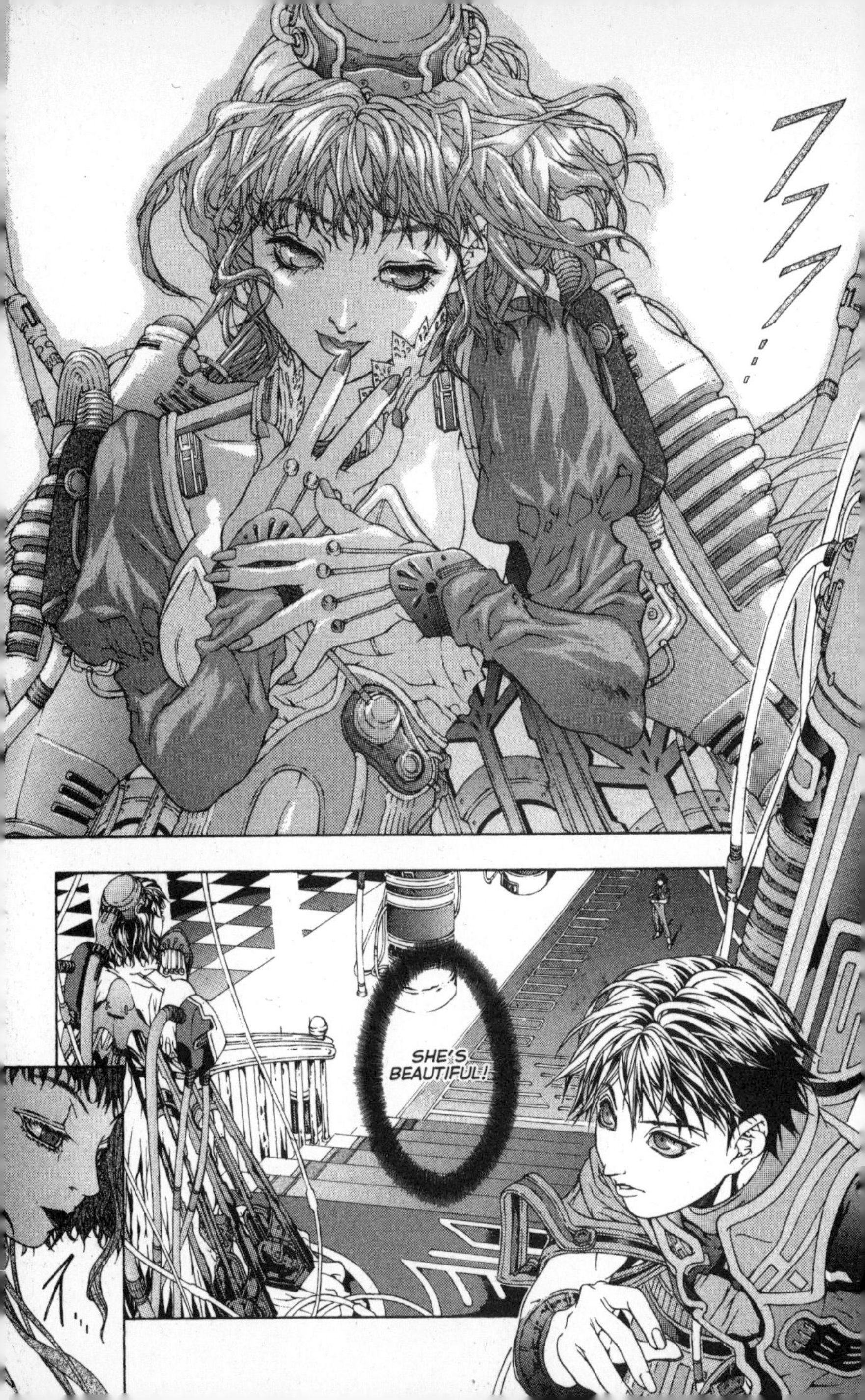
SHE'S BEAUTIFUL!

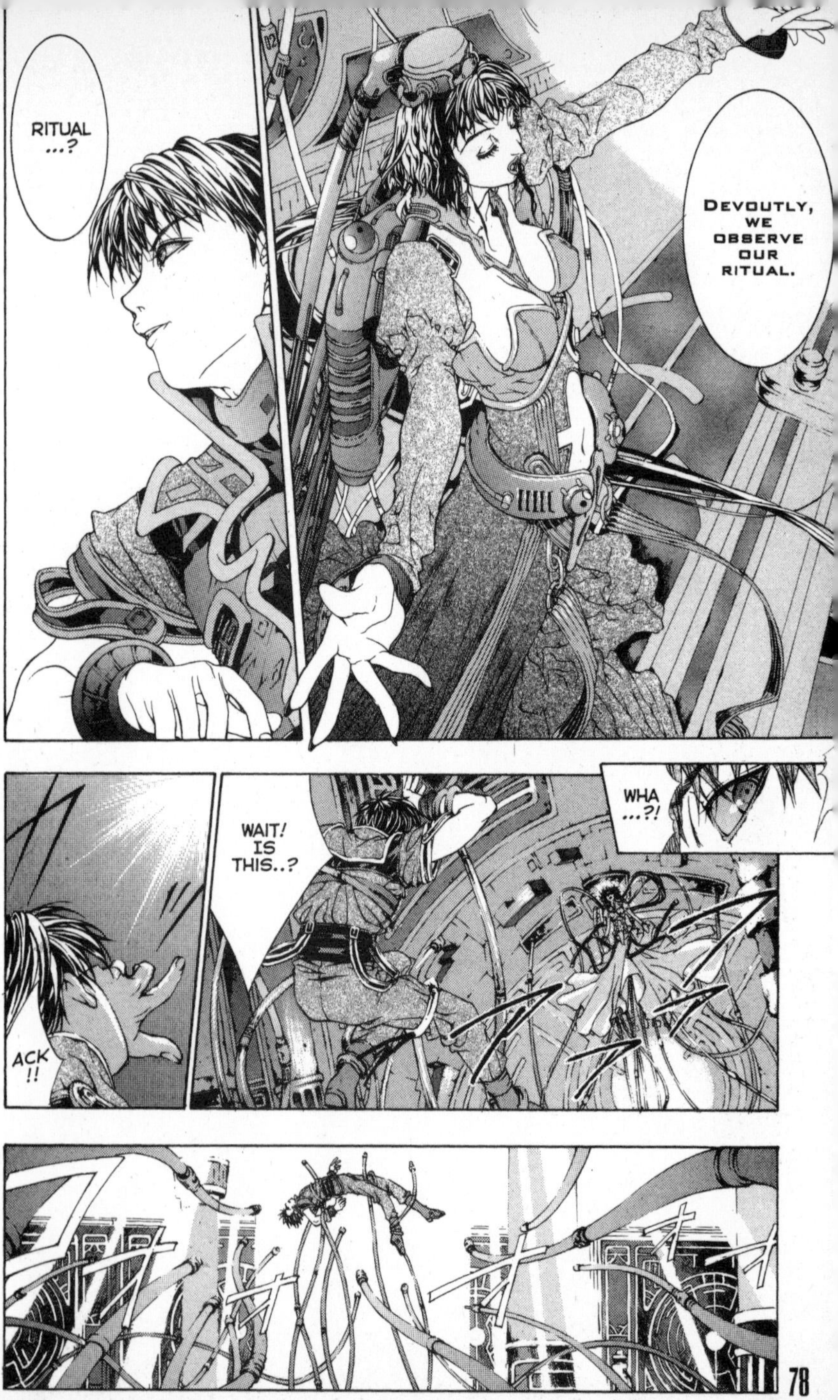
DEVOUTLY, WE OBSERVE OUR RITUAL.
RITUAL ...?
WHA ...?!
WAIT! IS THIS..?
ACK !!

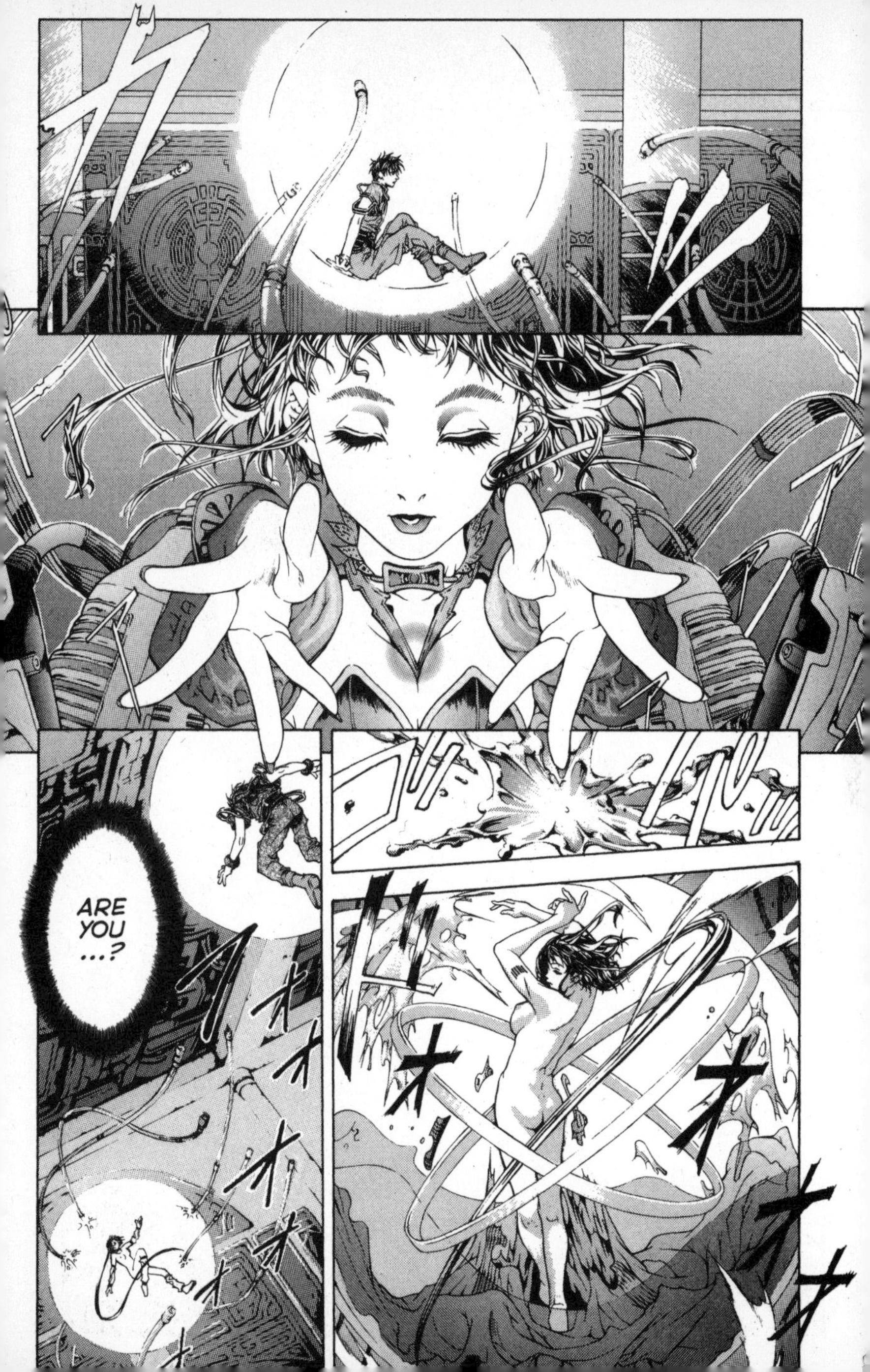
ARE YOU ...?

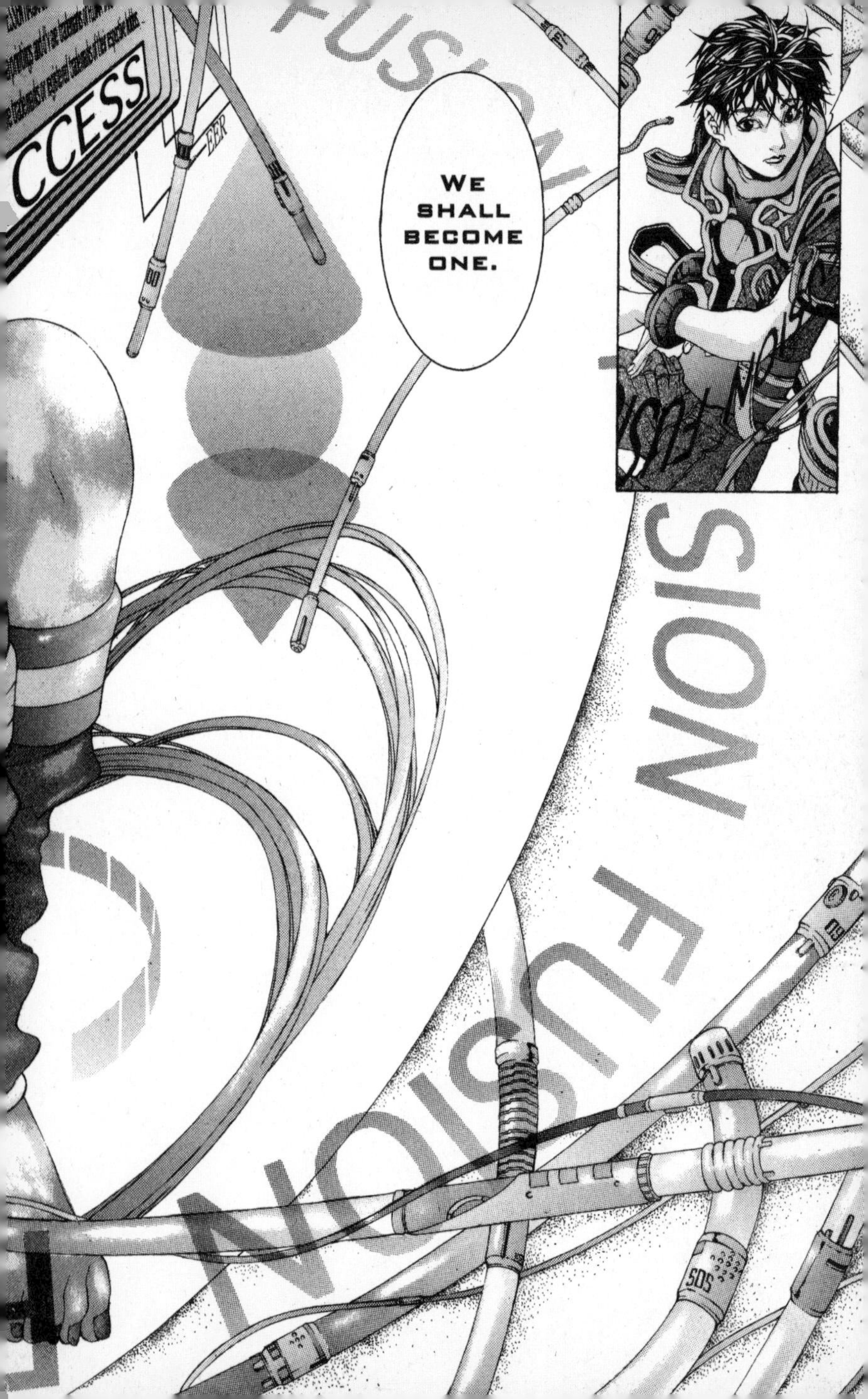
WE SHALL BECOME ONE.

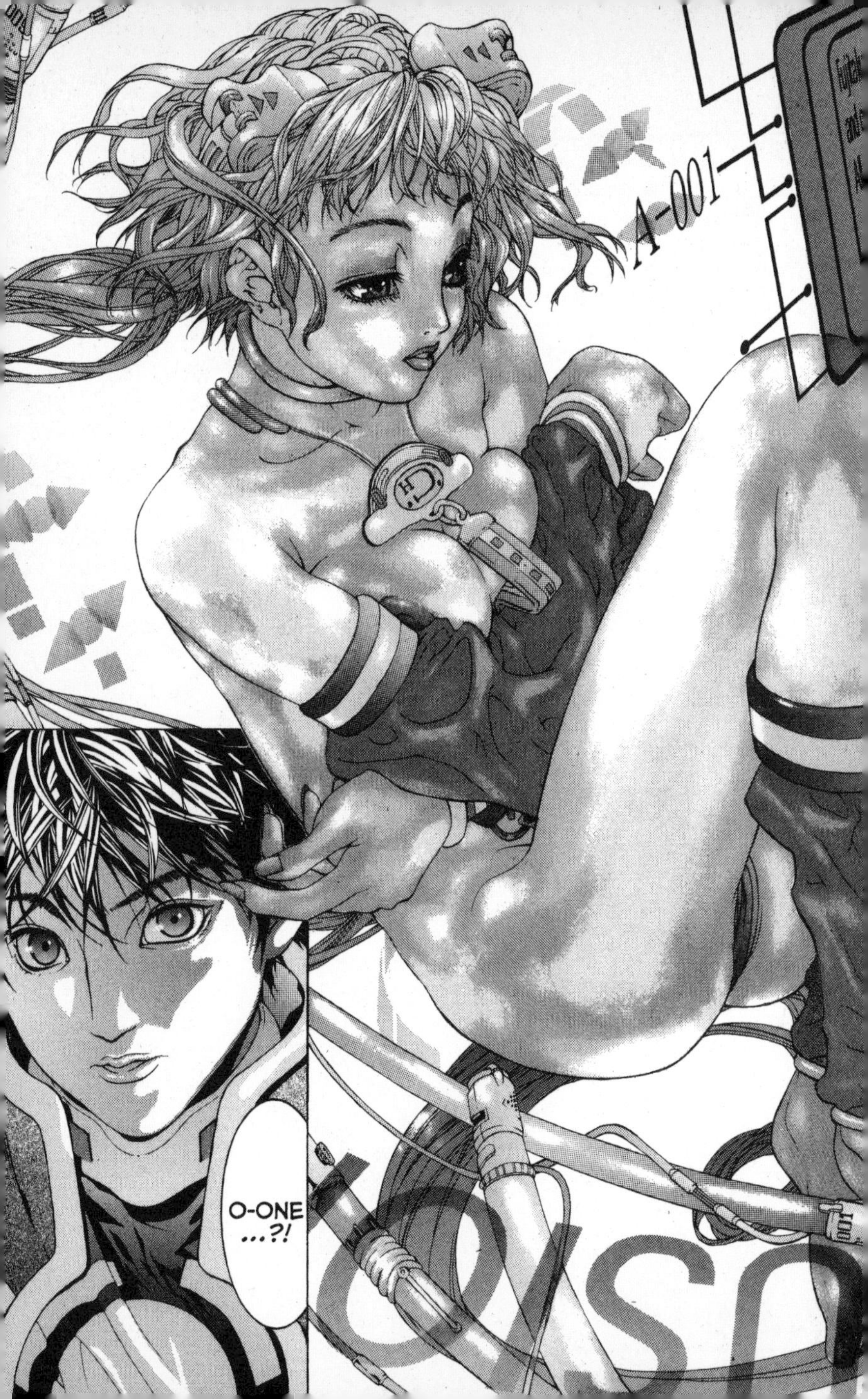
A-001
O-ONE ...?!

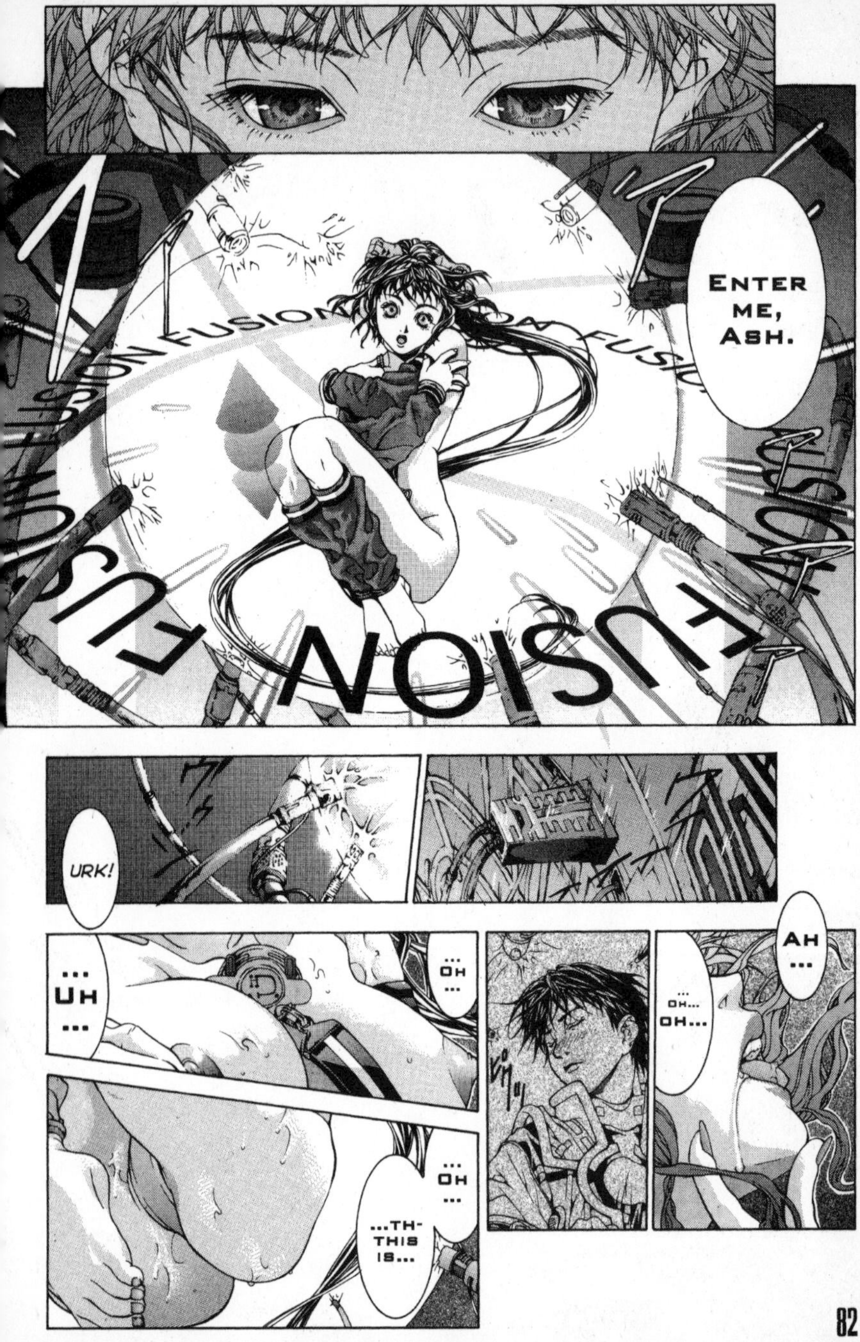

Enter me, Ash.
FUSION FUSION FUSION
FUSION
FUSION
URK!
Ah ...
... oh... oh...
... Oh ...
... Uh ...
... Oh ...
...Th-this is...

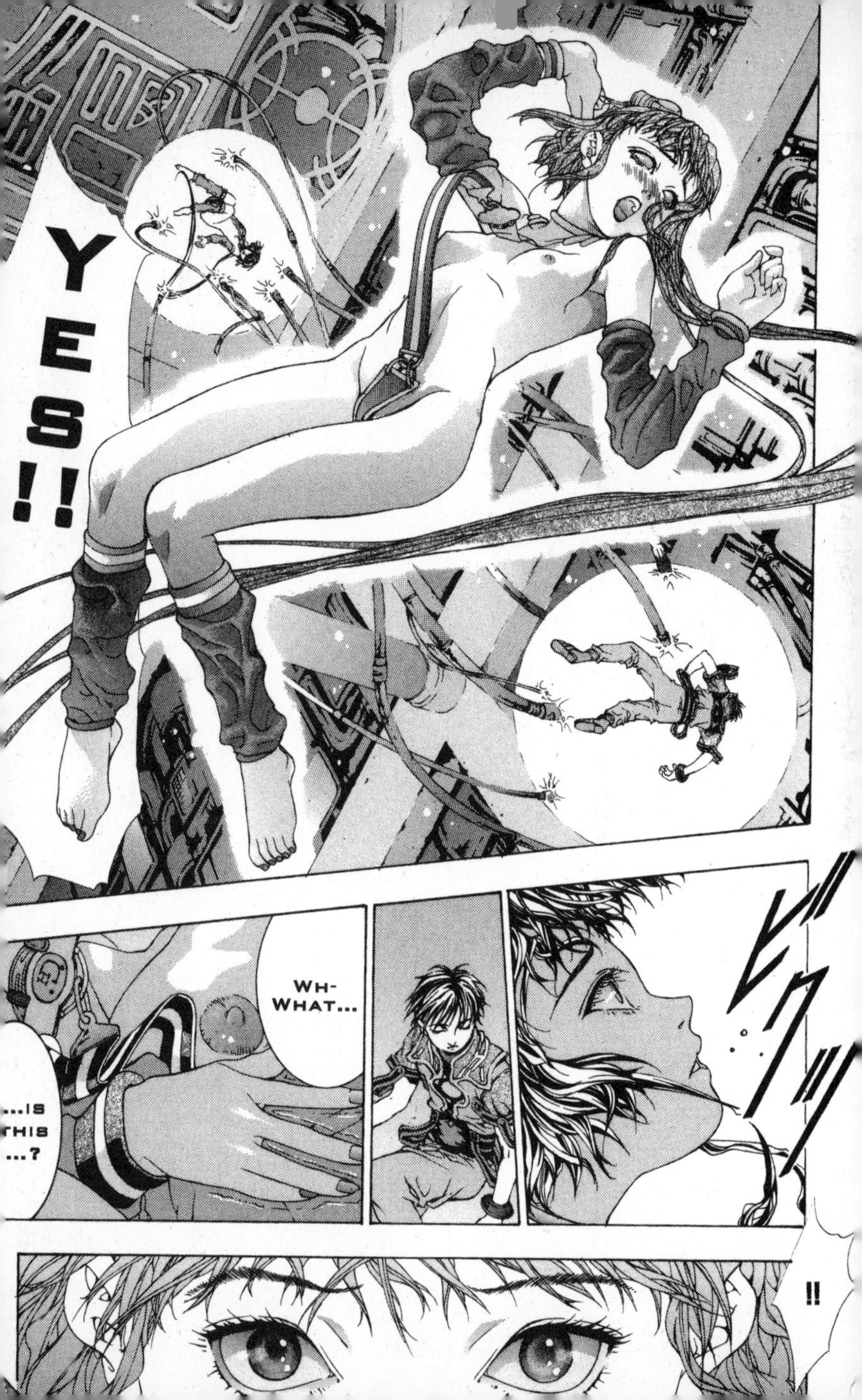
YES!!
WH- WHAT...
...IS THIS ...?
!!

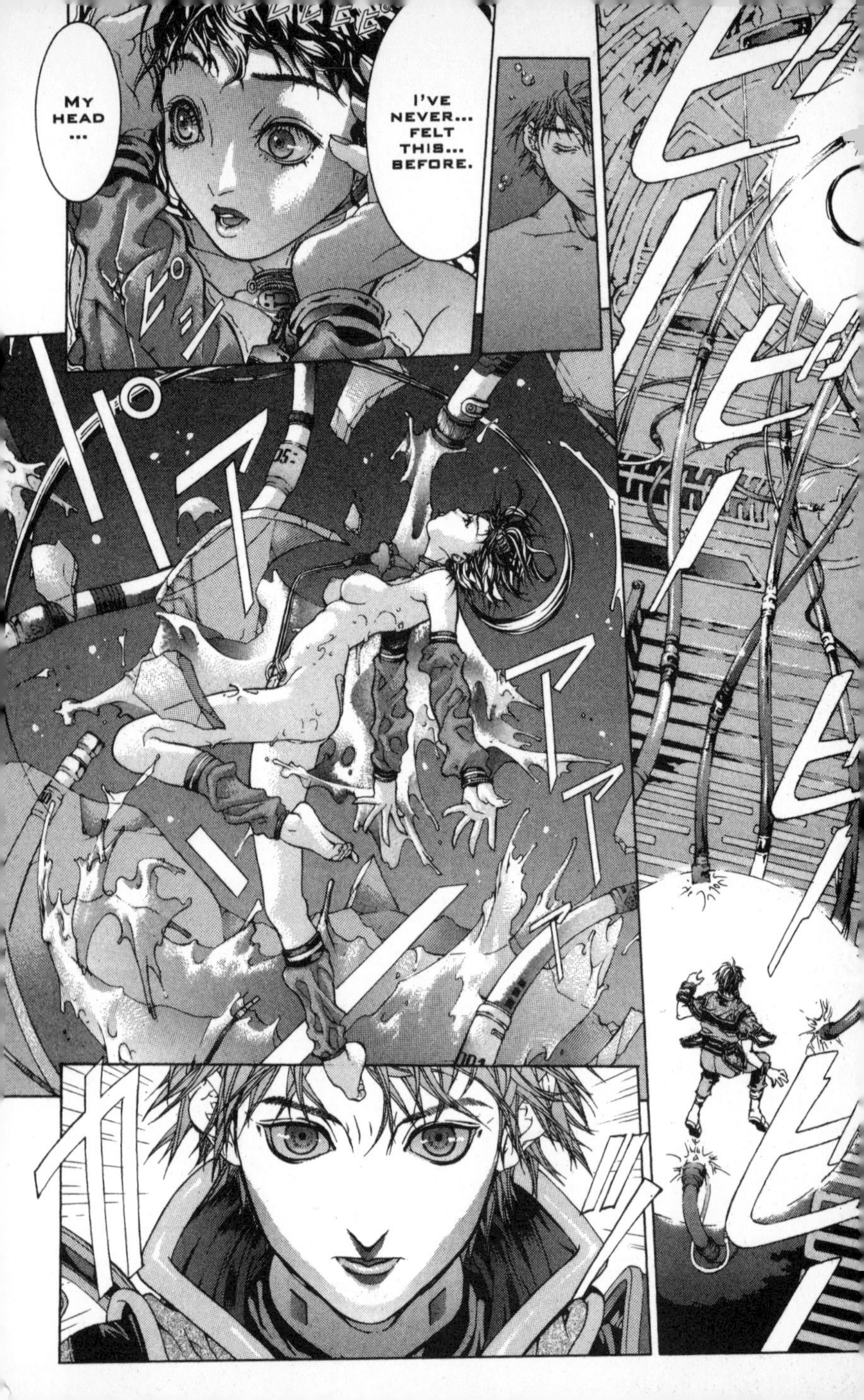
I'VE NEVER... FELT THIS... BEFORE.
MY HEAD ...

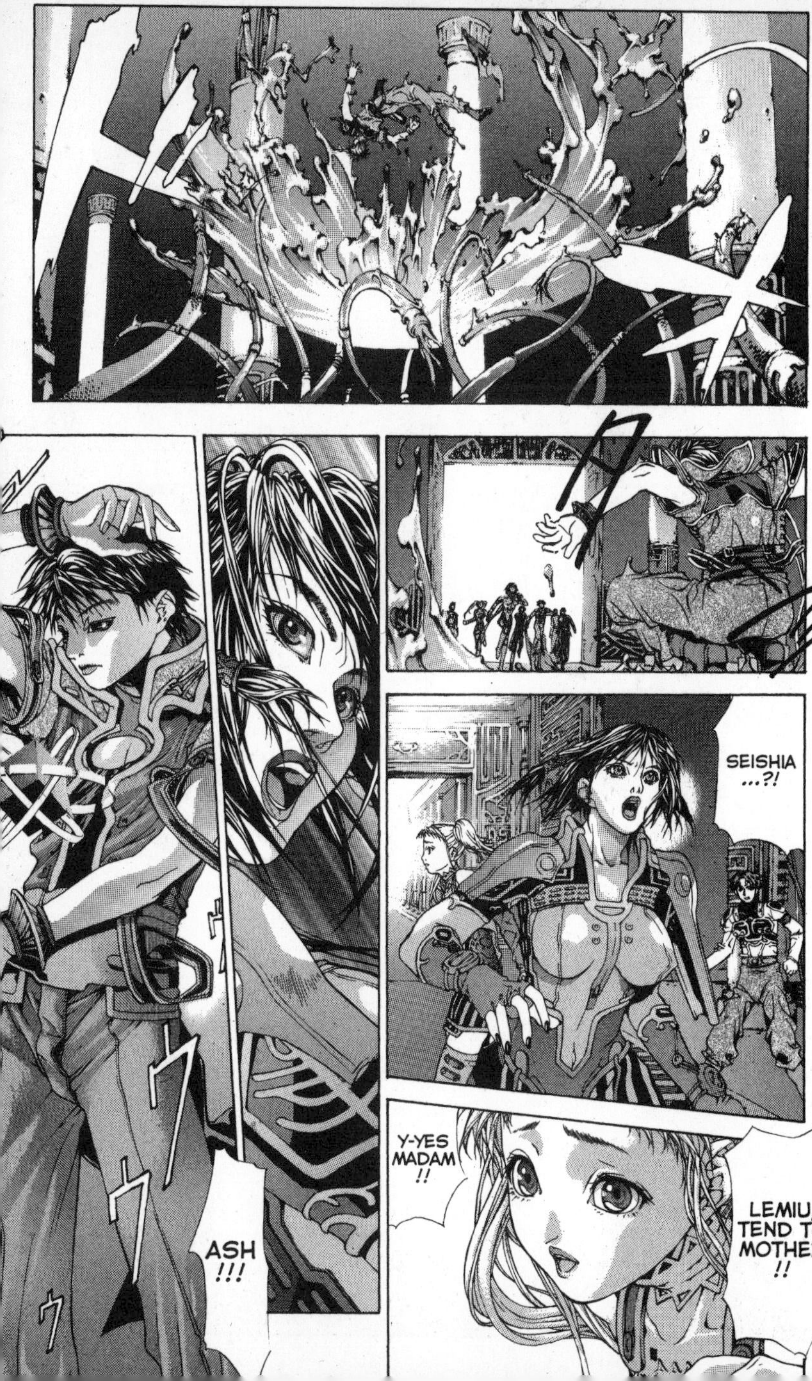
SEISHIA ...?!
LEMIU, TEND TO MOTHER !!
Y-YES MADAM !!
ASH !!!

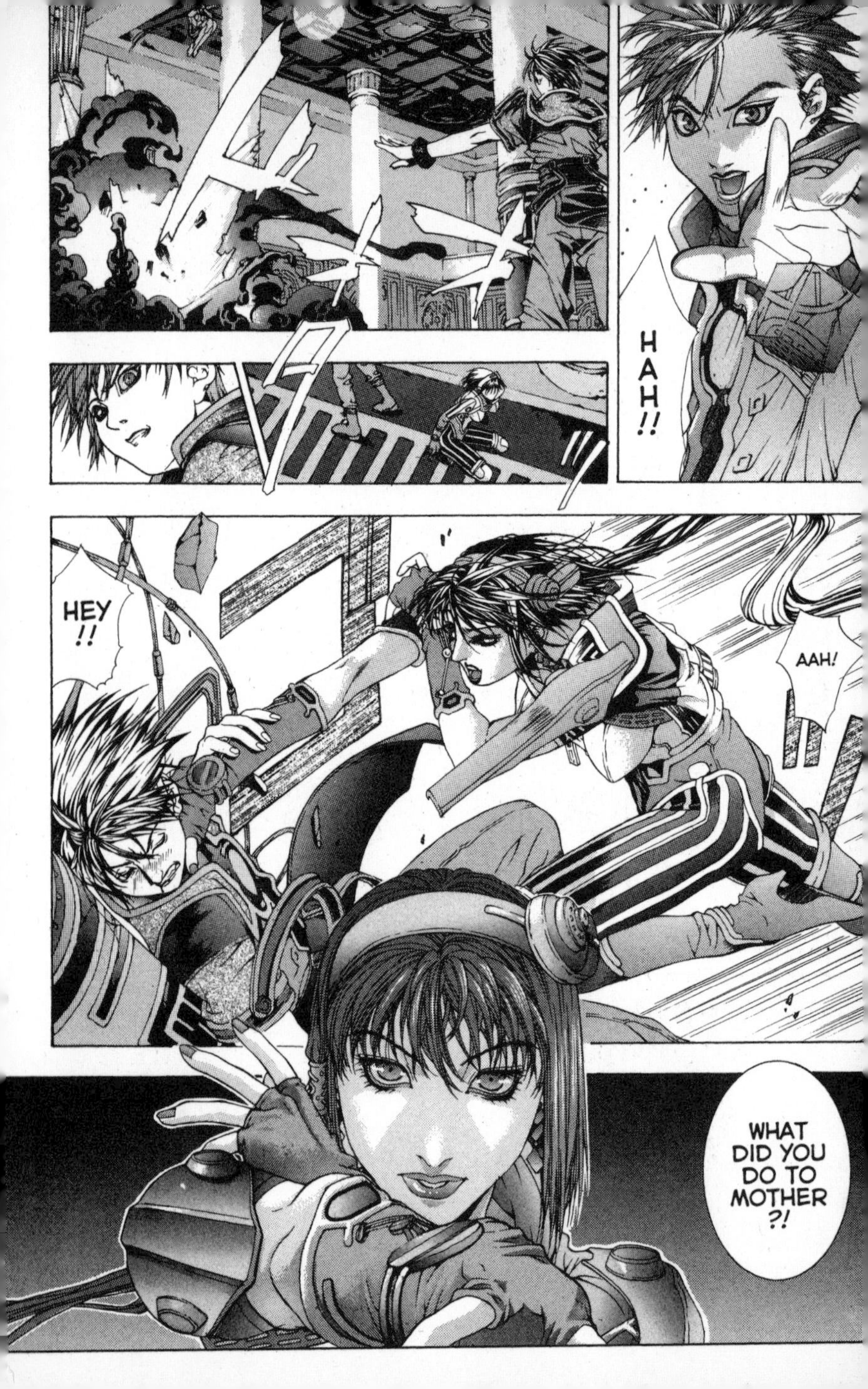
HAH!!
AAH!
HEY!!
WHAT DID YOU DO TO MOTHER?!

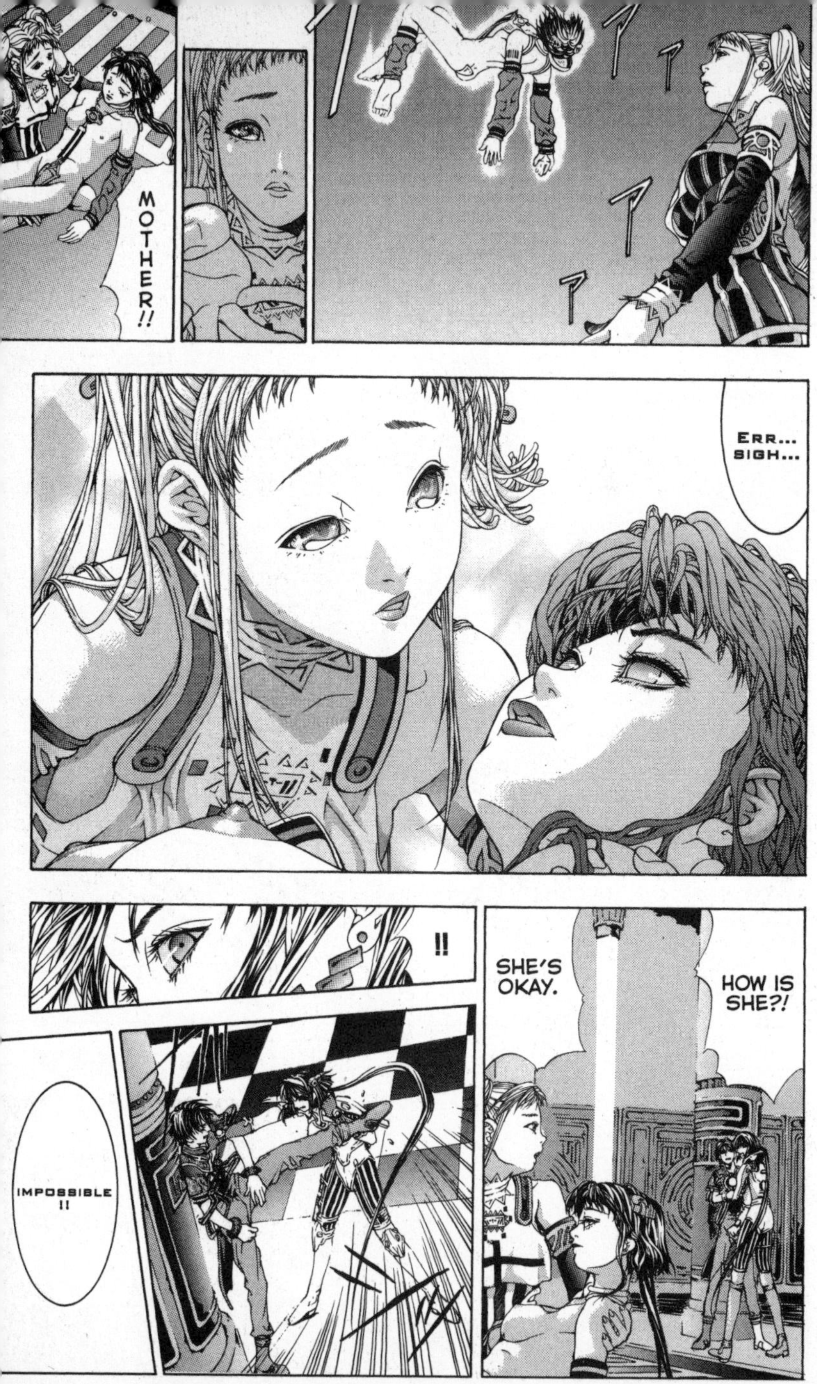
アアアア
MOTHER!!
ERR... SIGH...
HOW IS SHE?!
SHE'S OKAY.
!!
IMPOSSIBLE !!

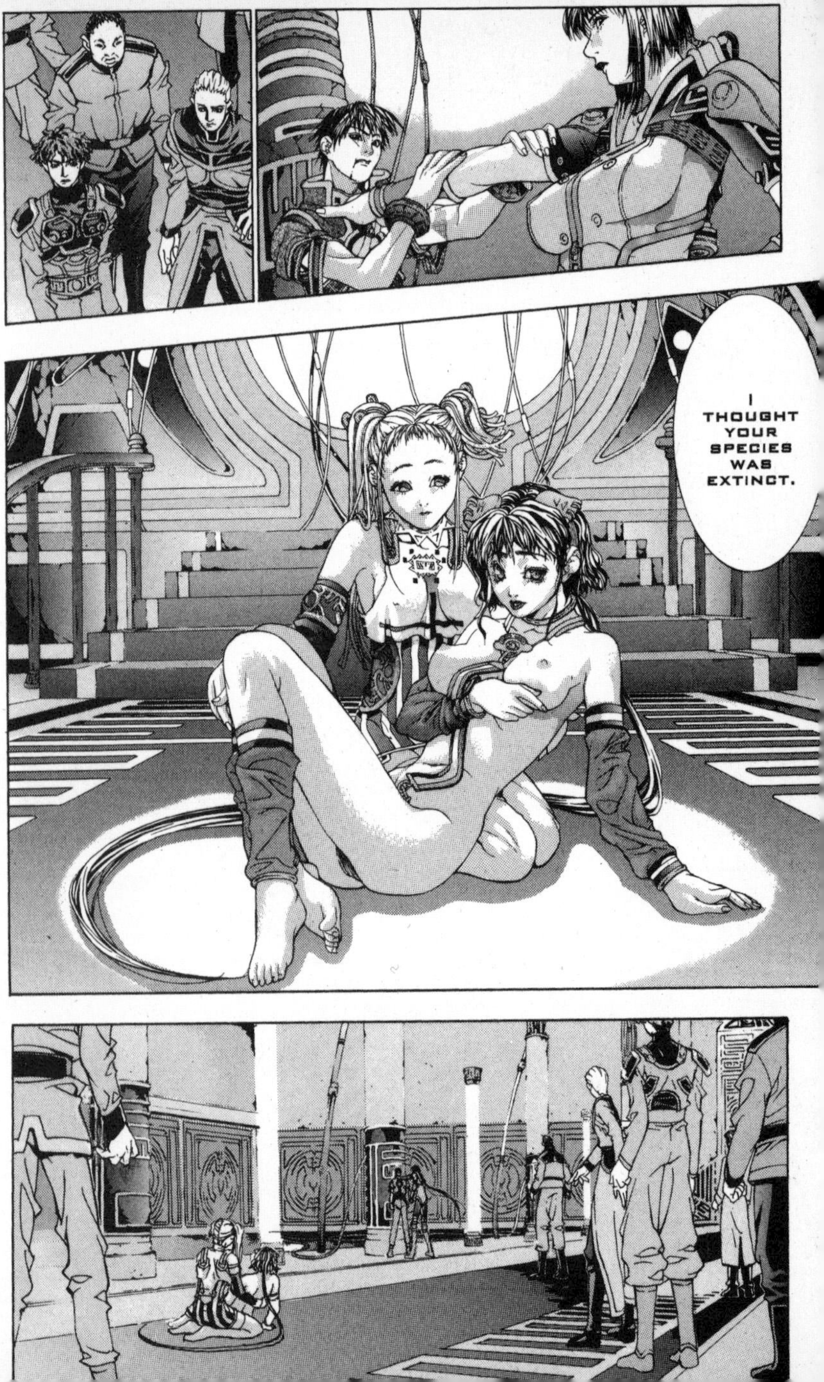
I THOUGHT YOUR SPECIES WAS EXTINCT.

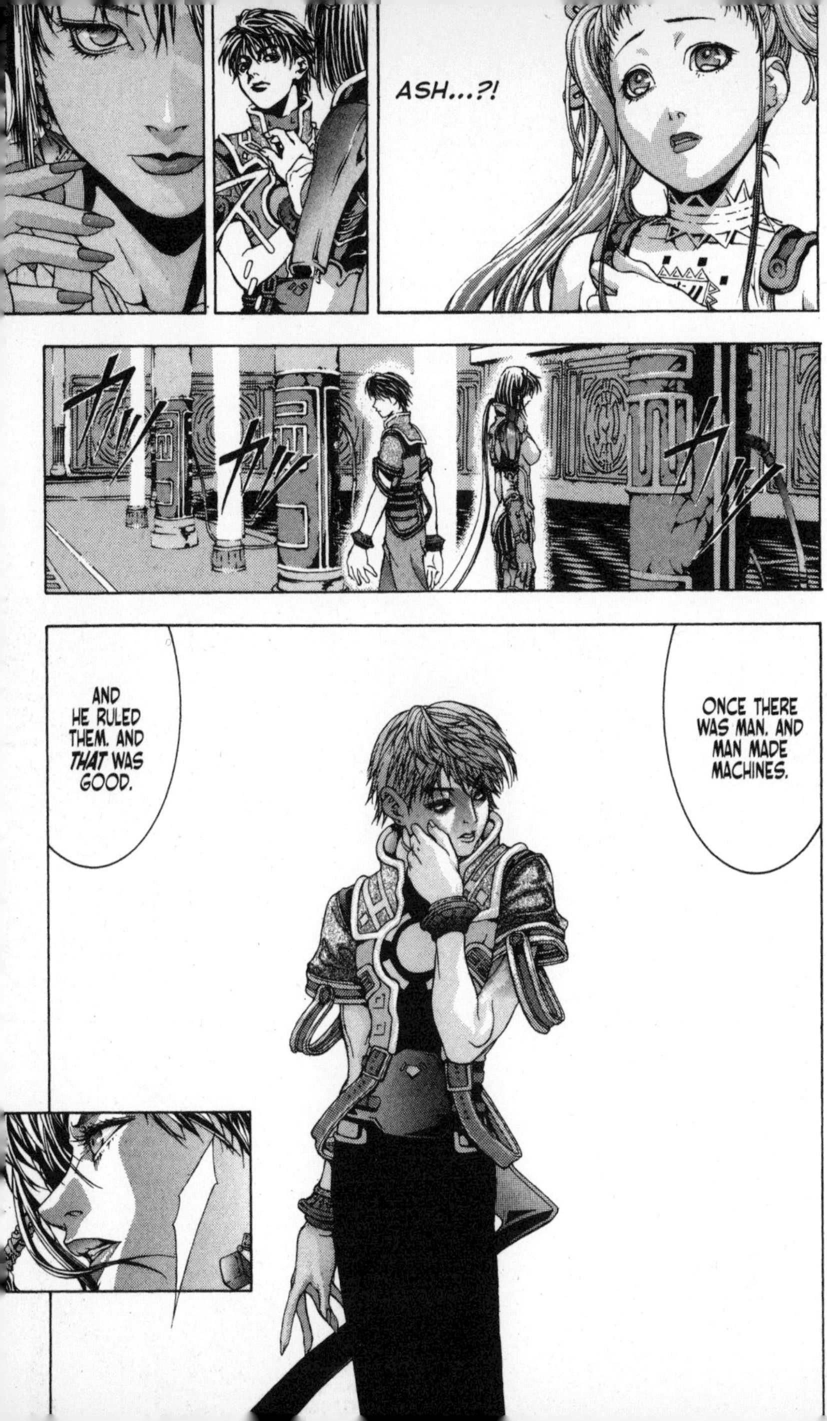
ASH...?!
カッ
カッ
カッ
ONCE THERE WAS MAN. AND MAN MADE MACHINES.
AND HE RULED THEM. AND *THAT* WAS GOOD.

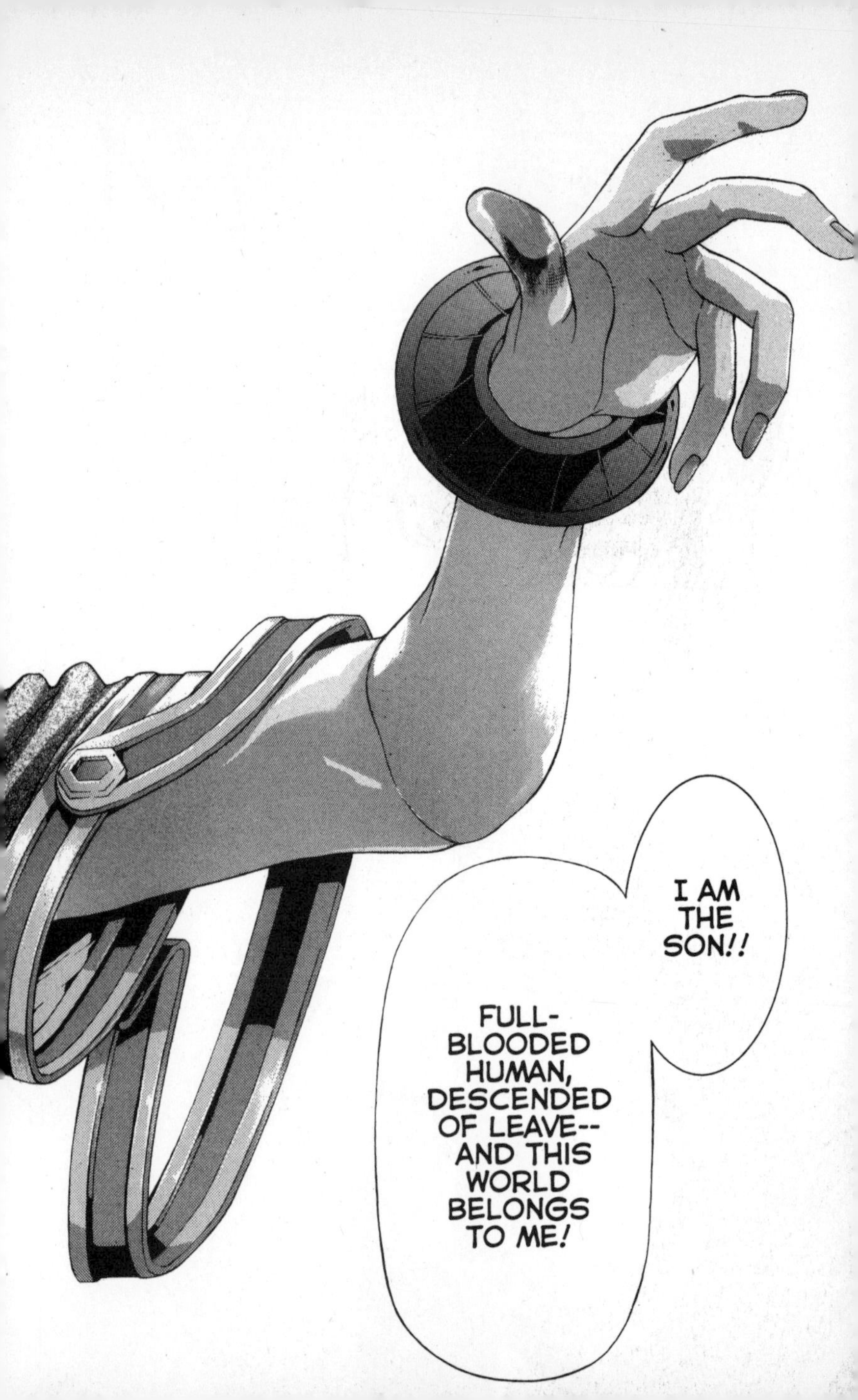
I AM THE SON!!
FULL-BLOODED HUMAN, DESCENDED OF LEAVE-- AND THIS WORLD BELONGS TO ME!

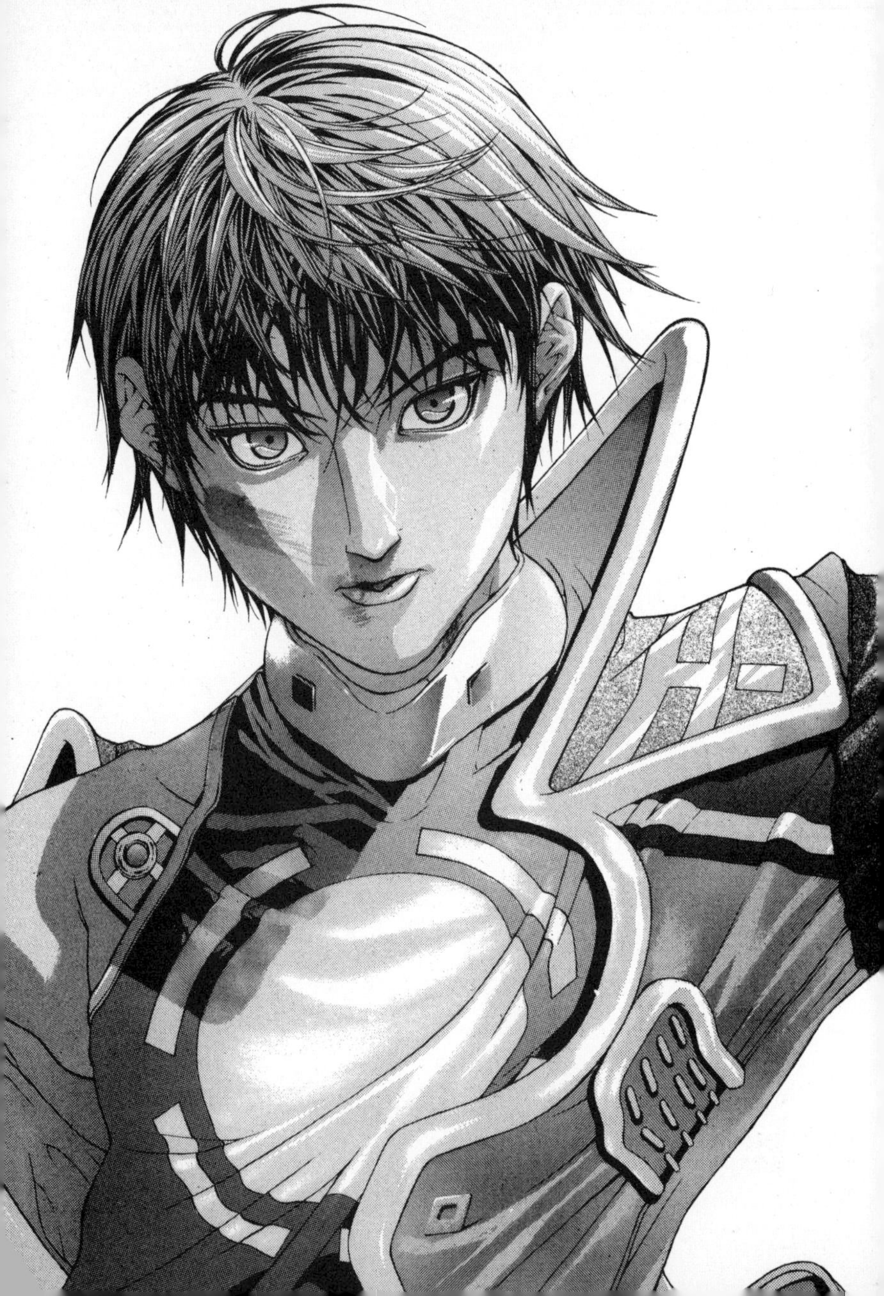

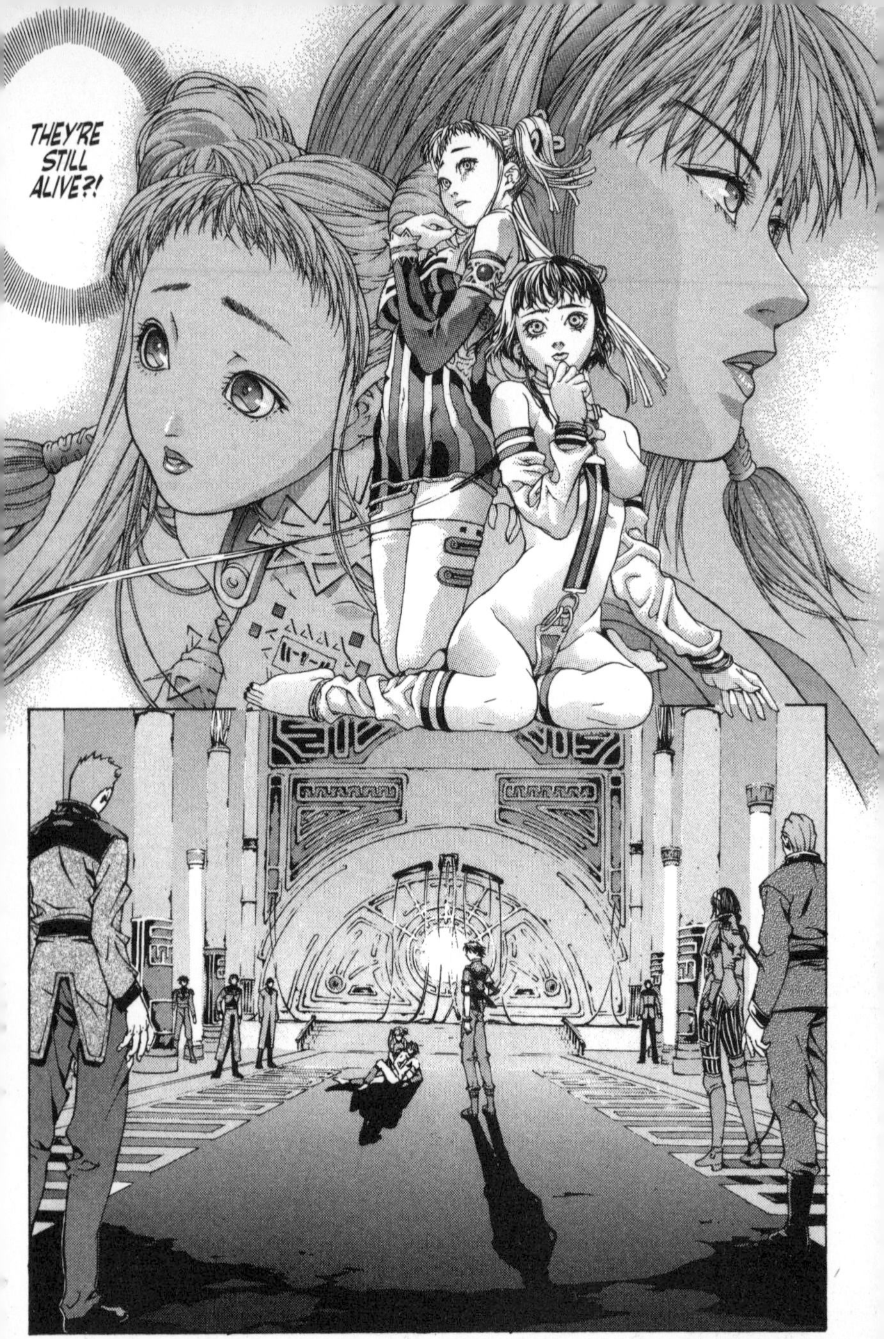
THEY'RE STILL ALIVE?!

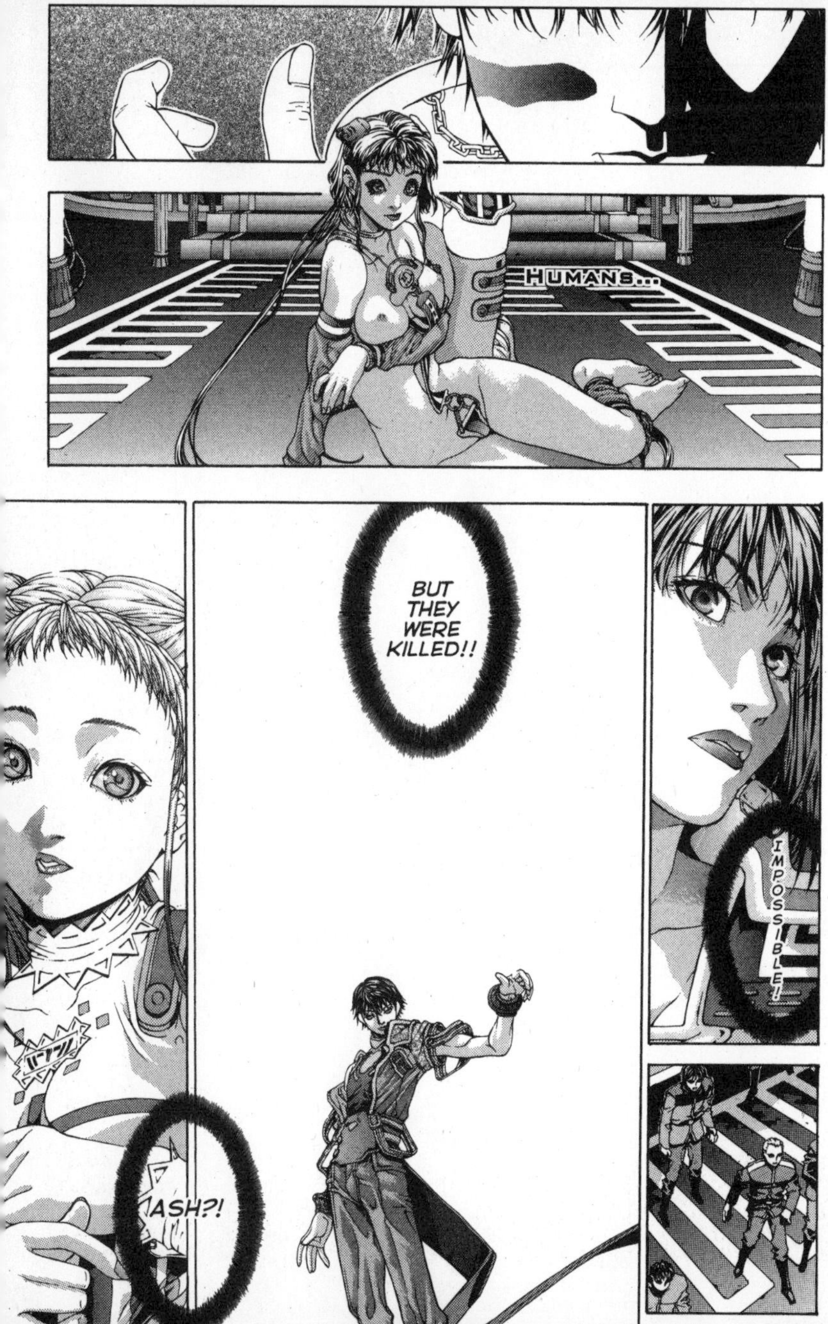
HUMANS...
IMPOSSIBLE!
BUT THEY WERE KILLED!!
ASH?!

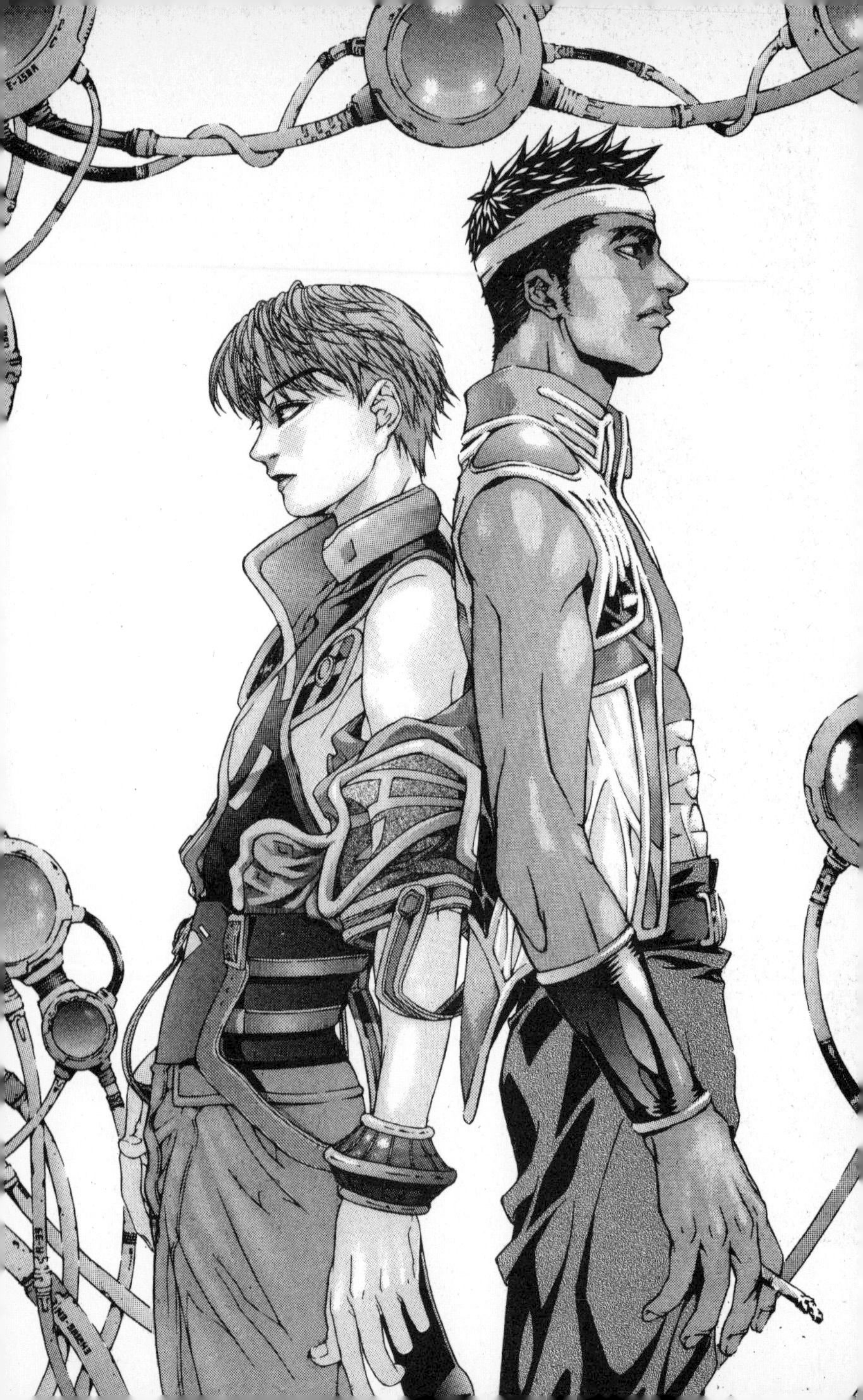

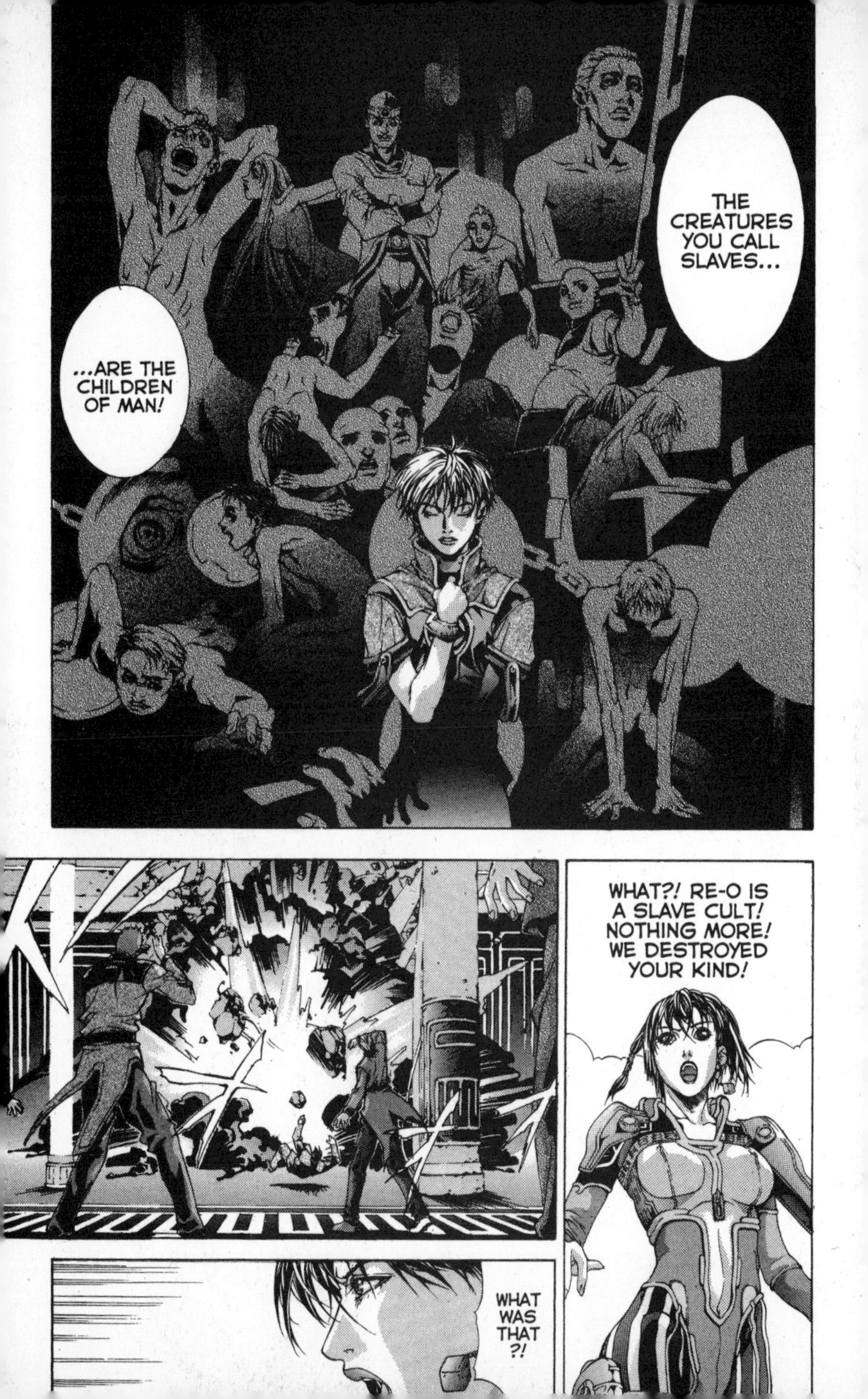
THE CREATURES YOU CALL SLAVES...
...ARE THE CHILDREN OF MAN!
WHAT?! RE-O IS A SLAVE CULT! NOTHING MORE! WE DESTROYED YOUR KIND!
WHAT WAS THAT?!

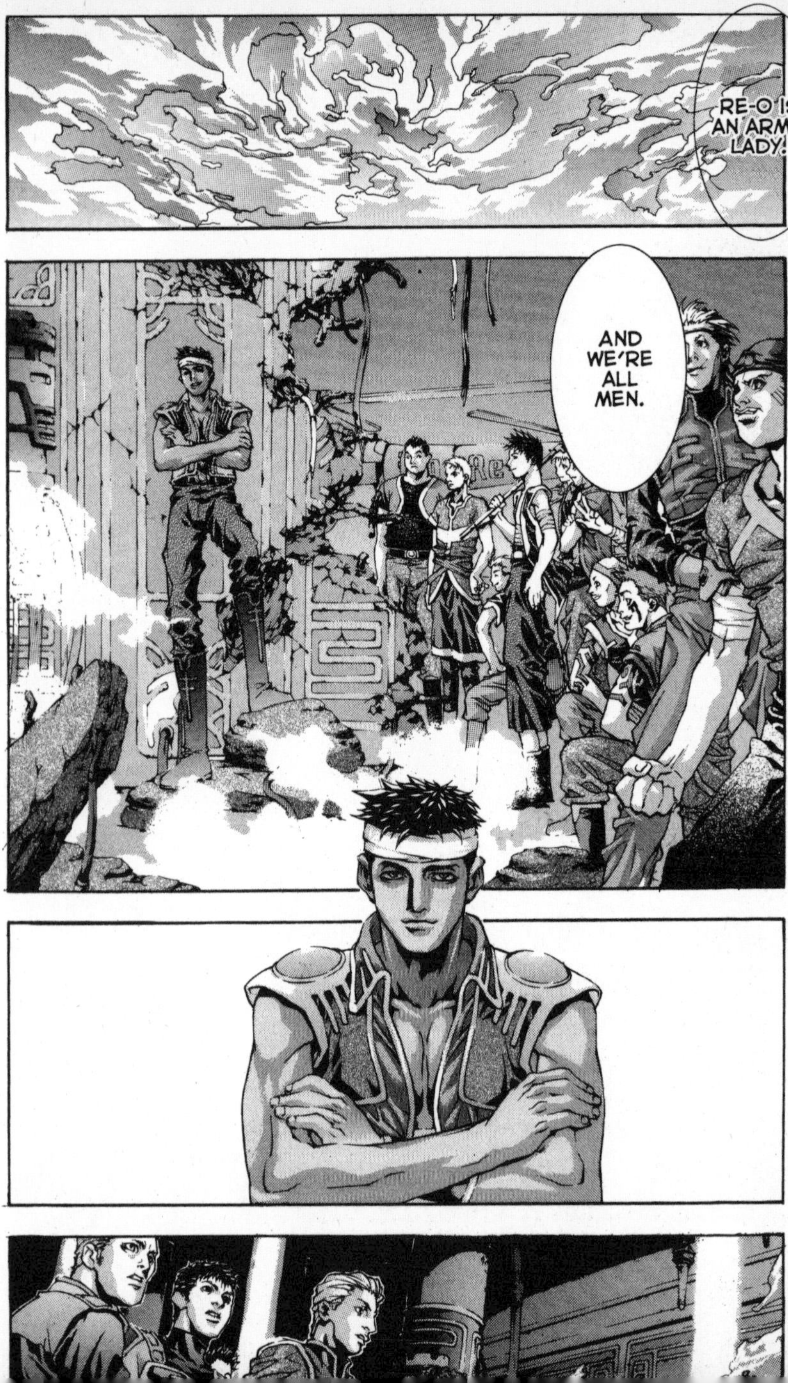
RE-O IS AN ARMY, LADY!
AND WE'RE ALL MEN.

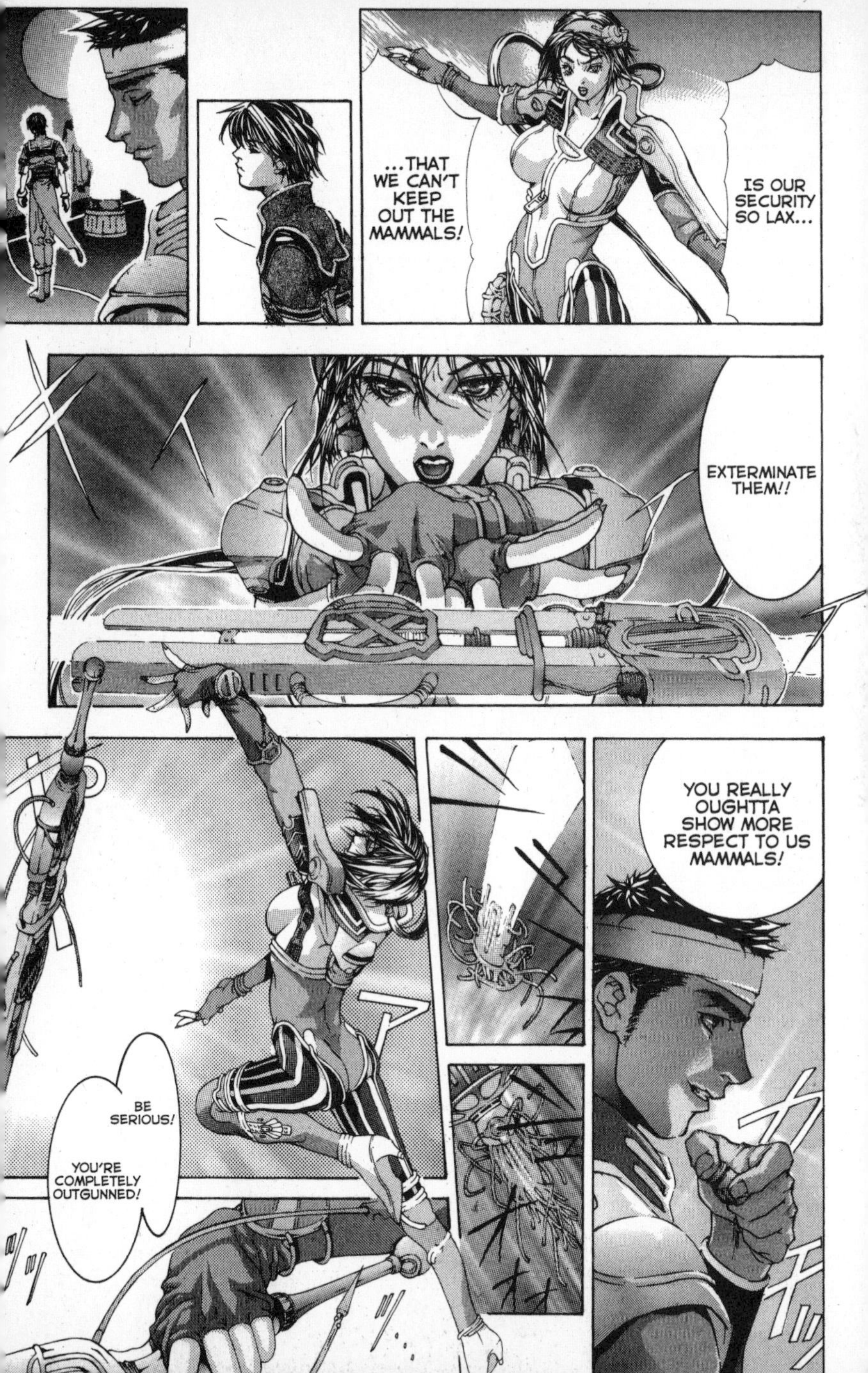
IS OUR SECURITY SO LAX...
...THAT WE CAN'T KEEP OUT THE MAMMALS!
EXTERMINATE THEM!!
YOU REALLY OUGHTTA SHOW MORE RESPECT TO US MAMMALS!
BE SERIOUS!
YOU'RE COMPLETELY OUTGUNNED!

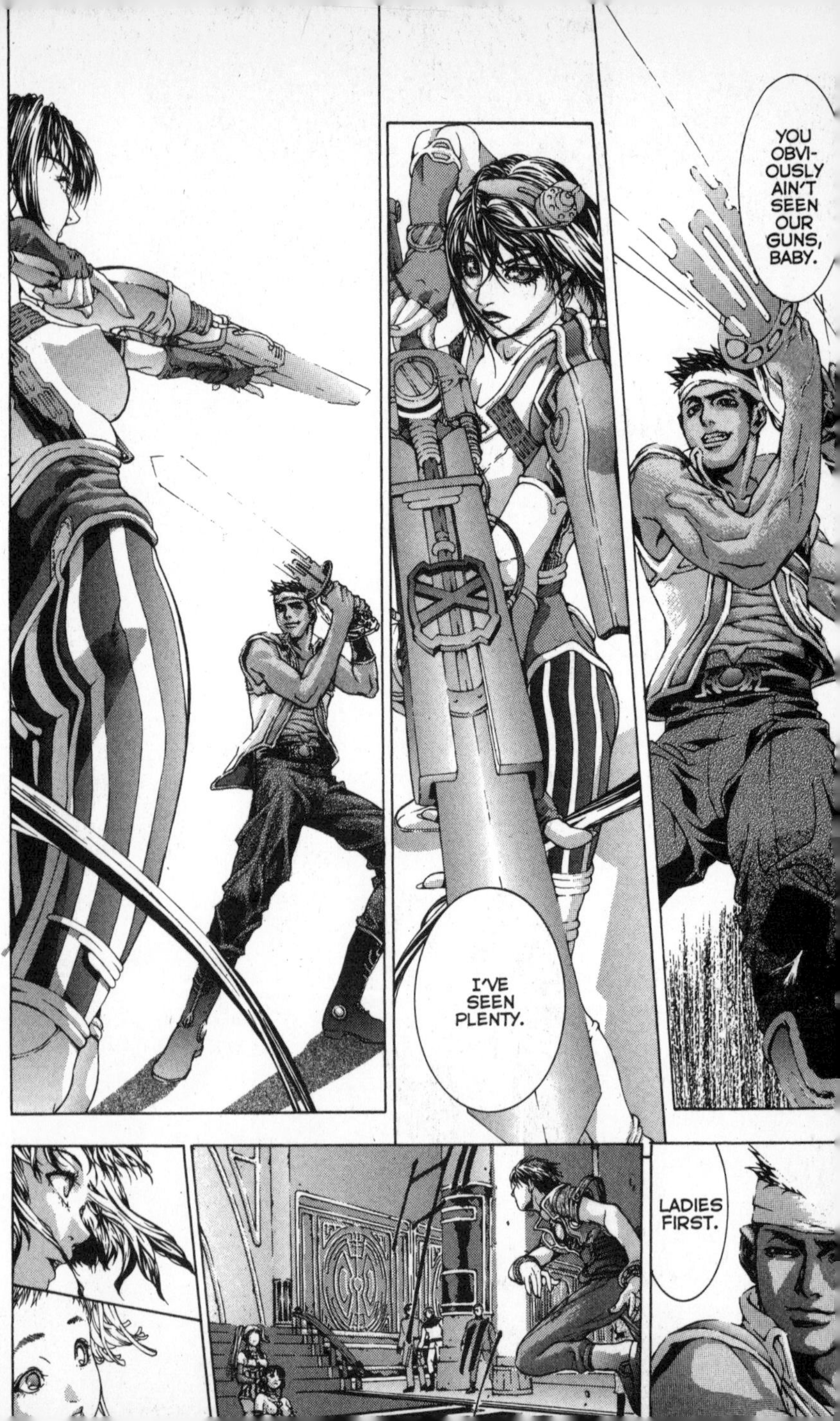
YOU OBVI-OUSLY AIN'T SEEN OUR GUNS, BABY.
I'VE SEEN PLENTY.
LADIES FIRST.

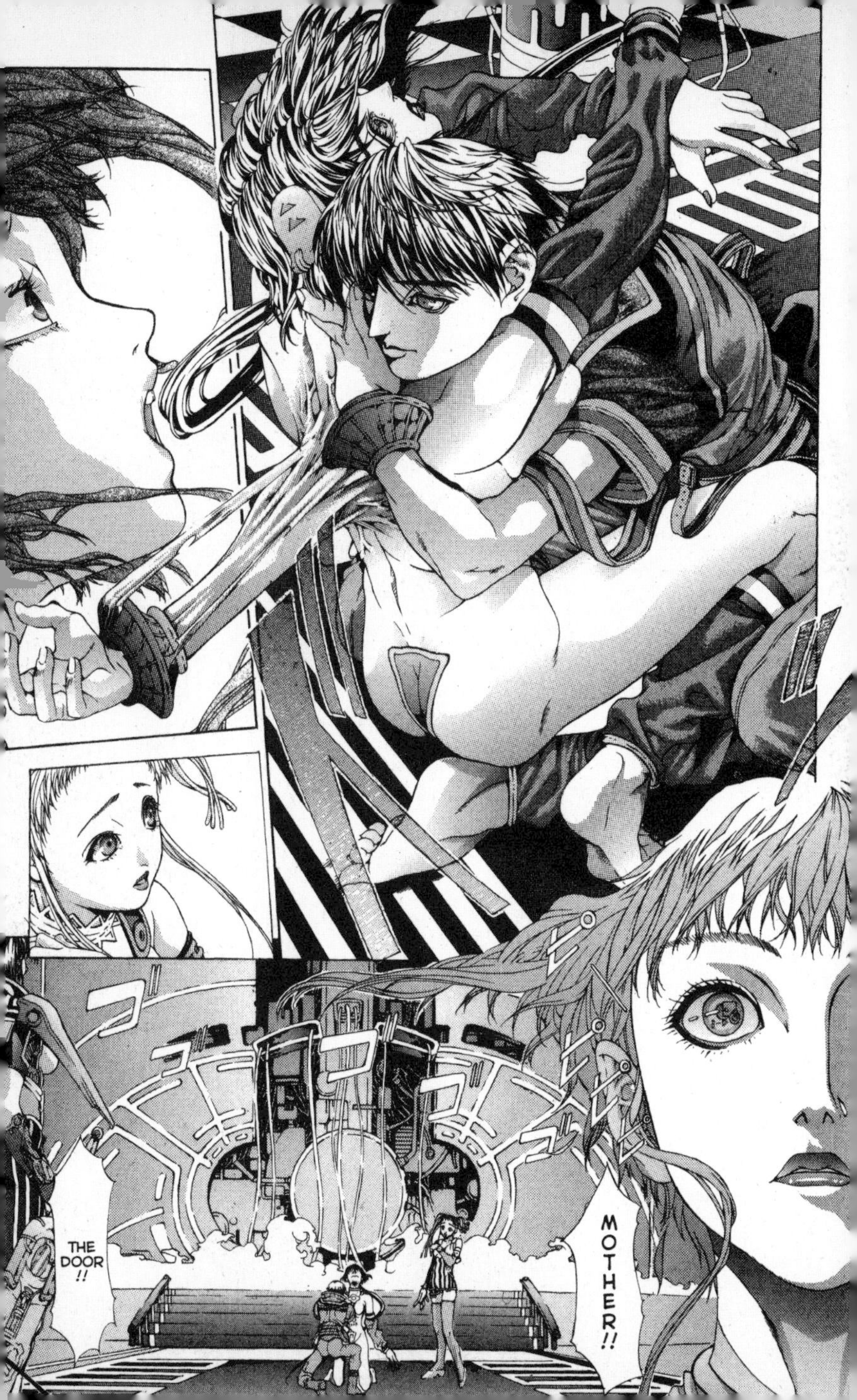
MOTHER!!
THE DOOR !!

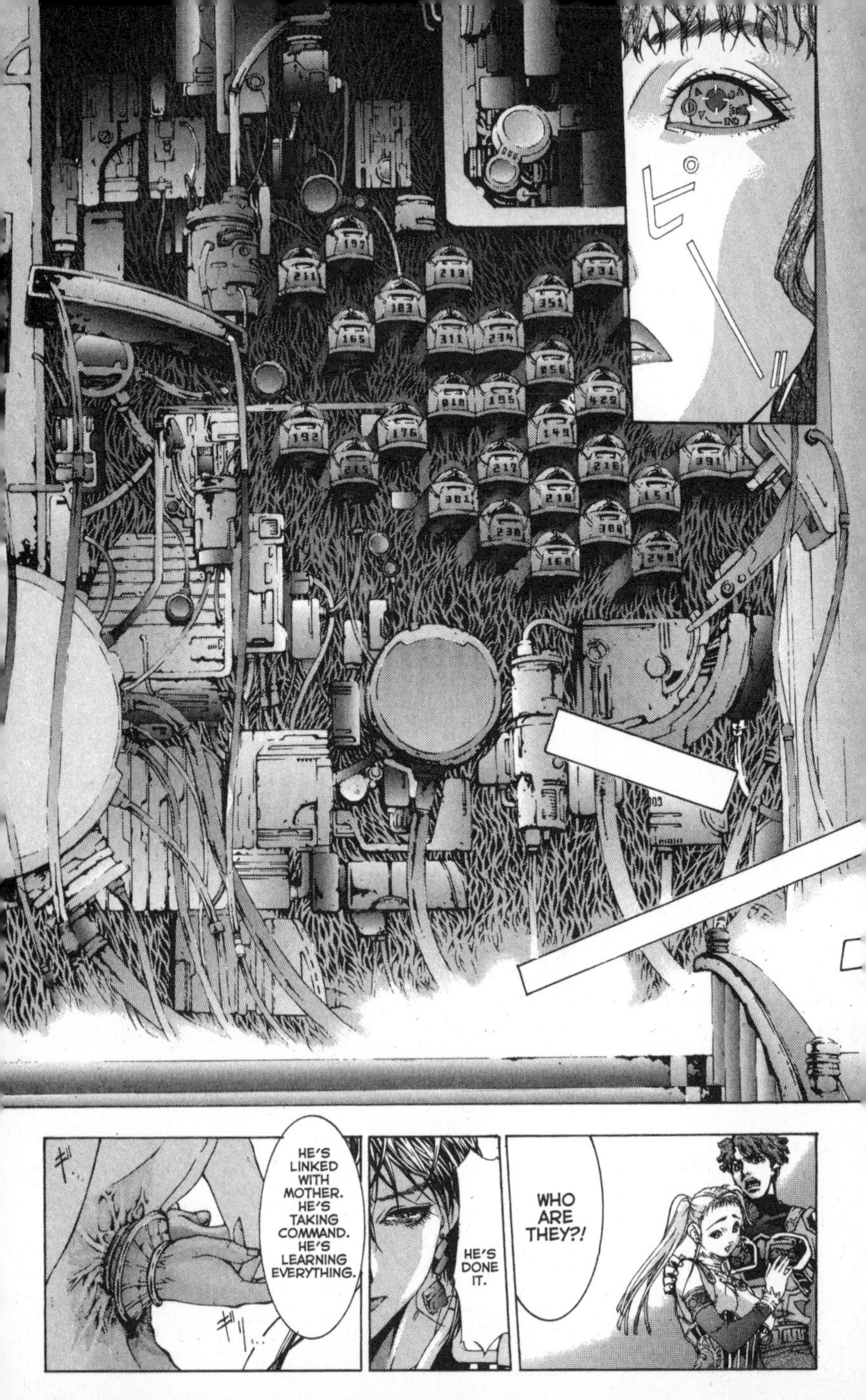
WHO ARE THEY?!
HE'S DONE IT.
HE'S LINKED WITH MOTHER. HE'S TAKING COMMAND. HE'S LEARNING EVERYTHING.

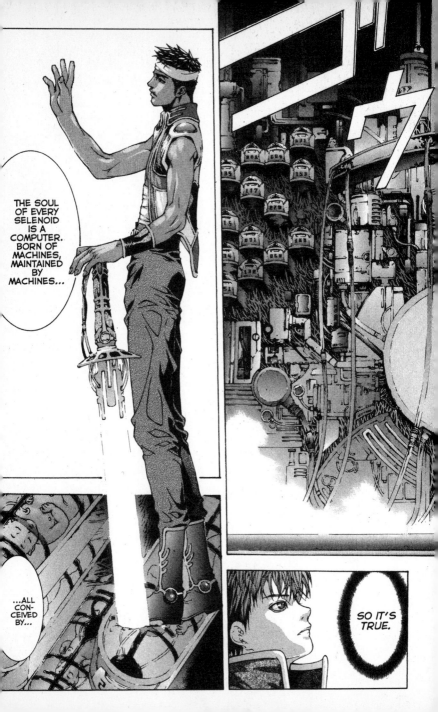

THE SOUL OF EVERY SELENOID IS A COMPUTER. BORN OF MACHINES, MAINTAINED BY MACHINES...

...ALL CONCEIVED BY...

SO IT'S TRUE.

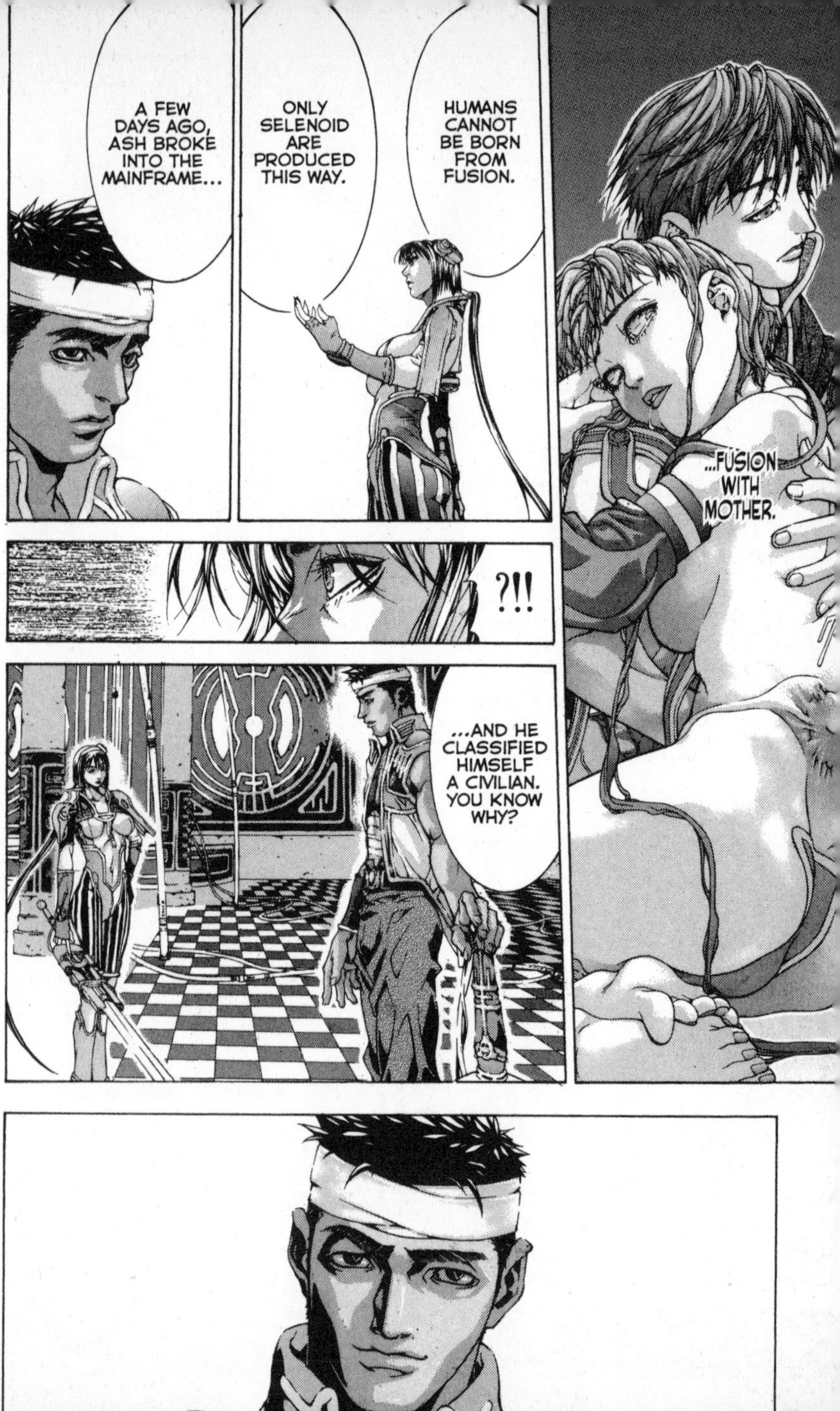

...FUSION WITH MOTHER.
HUMANS CANNOT BE BORN FROM FUSION.
ONLY SELENOID ARE PRODUCED THIS WAY.
A FEW DAYS AGO, ASH BROKE INTO THE MAINFRAME...
?!!
...AND HE CLASSIFIED HIMSELF A CIVILIAN. YOU KNOW WHY?

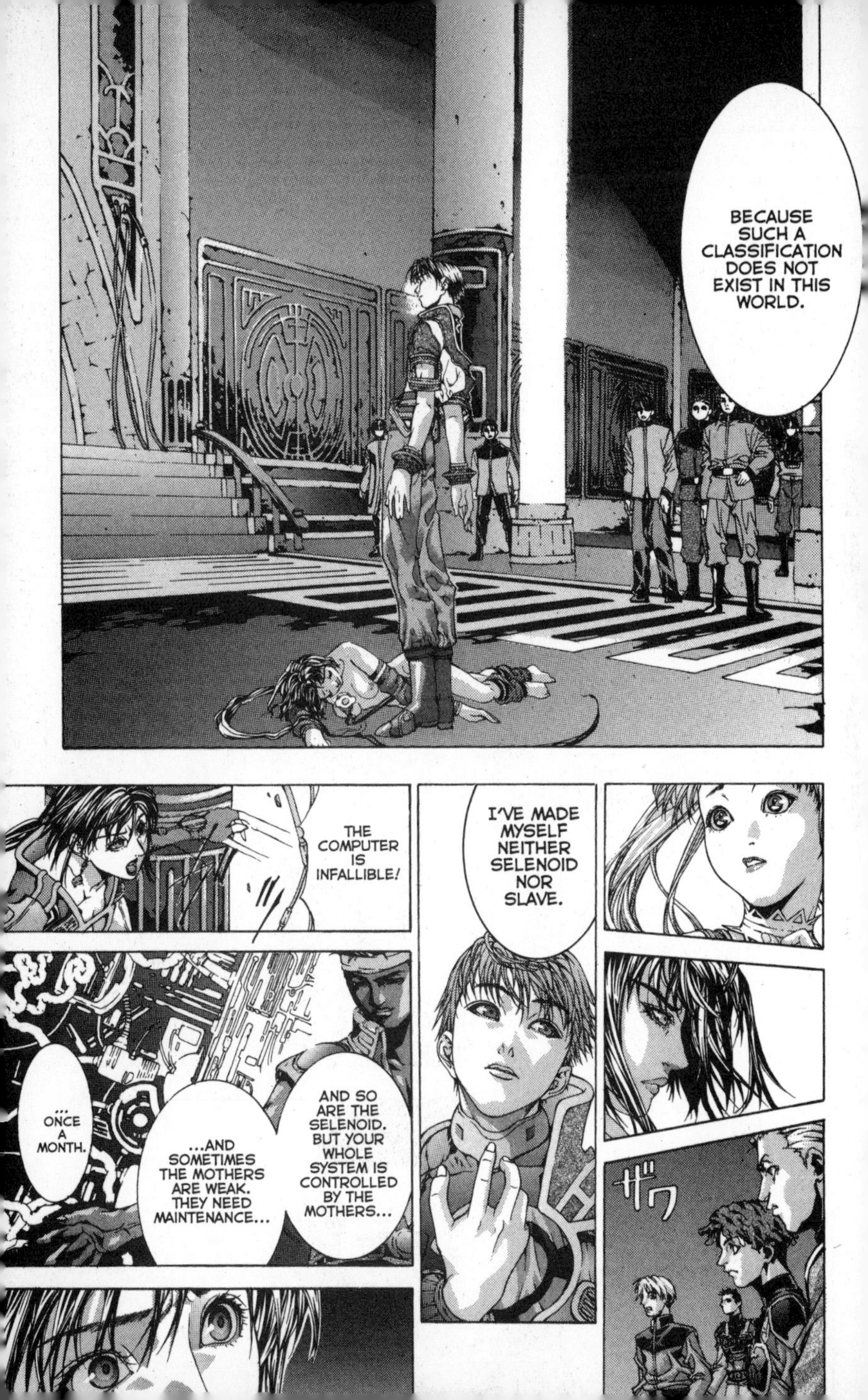
BECAUSE SUCH A CLASSIFICATION DOES NOT EXIST IN THIS WORLD.
ザワ
I'VE MADE MYSELF NEITHER SELENOID NOR SLAVE.
THE COMPUTER IS INFALLIBLE!
AND SO ARE THE SELENOID. BUT YOUR WHOLE SYSTEM IS CONTROLLED BY THE MOTHERS...
...AND SOMETIMES THE MOTHERS ARE WEAK. THEY NEED MAINTENANCE...
... ONCE A MONTH.

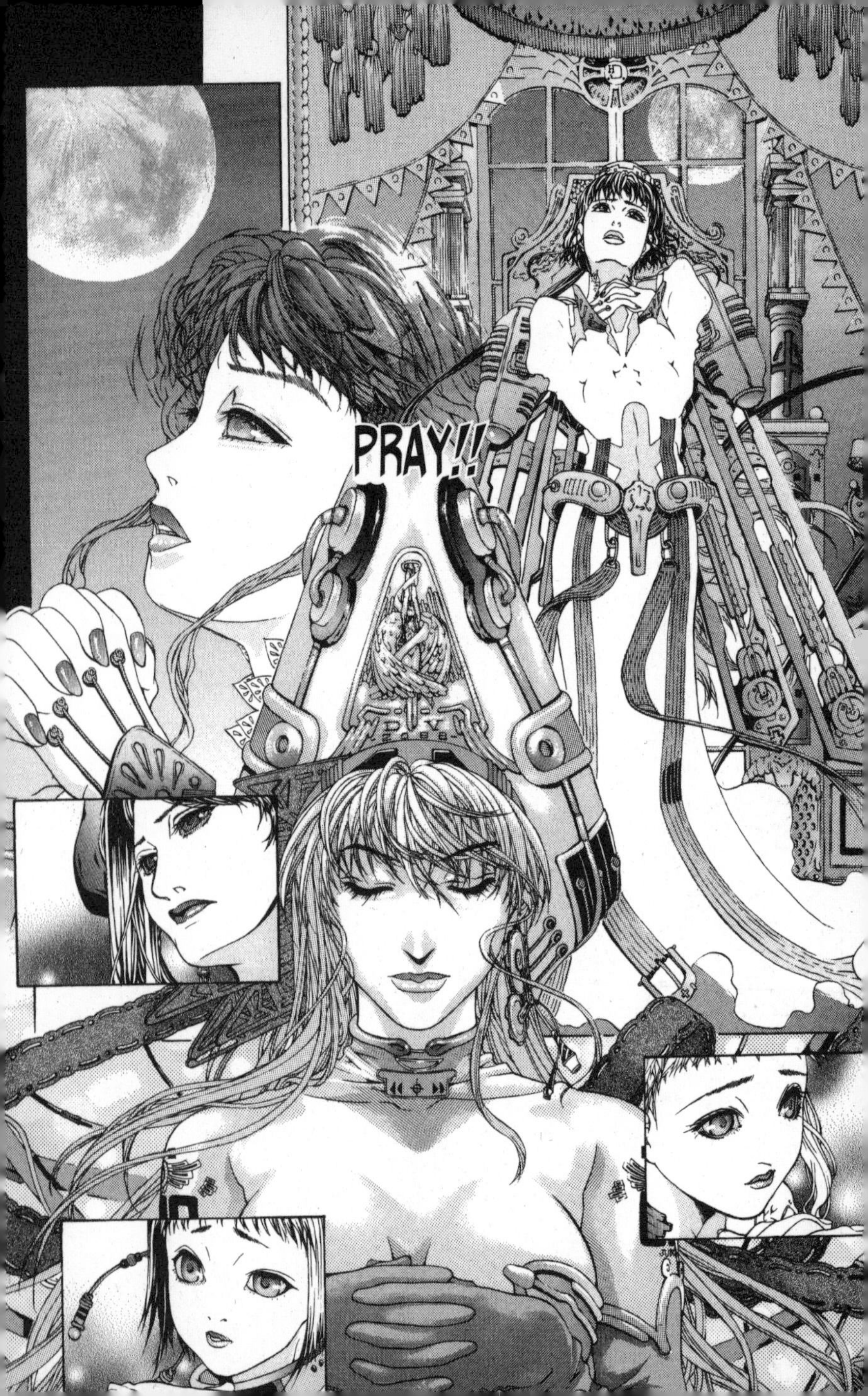
PRAY!!

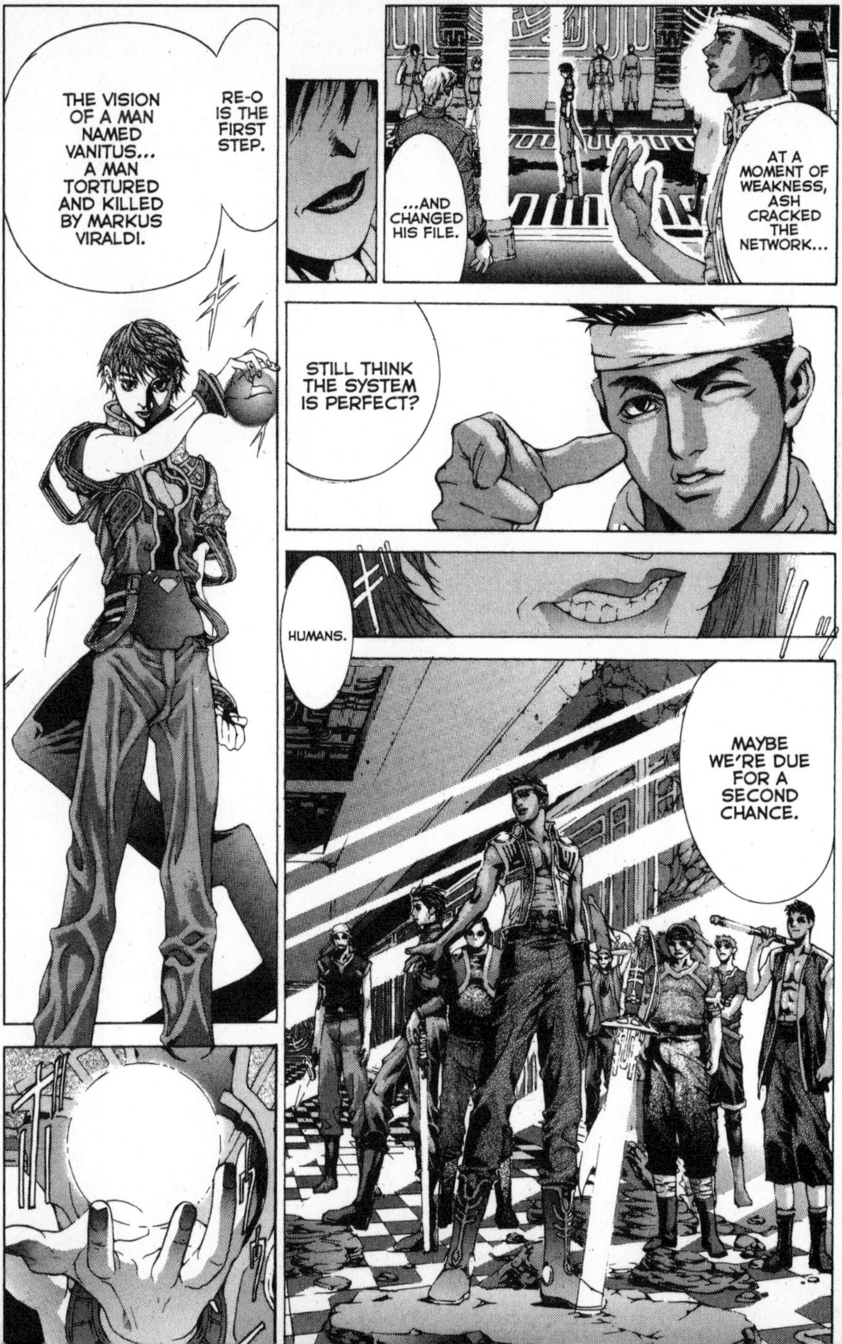
AT A MOMENT OF WEAKNESS, ASH CRACKED THE NETWORK...
...AND CHANGED HIS FILE.
STILL THINK THE SYSTEM IS PERFECT?
HUMANS.
MAYBE WE'RE DUE FOR A SECOND CHANCE.
RE-O IS THE FIRST STEP.
THE VISION OF A MAN NAMED VANITUS... A MAN TORTURED AND KILLED BY MARKUS VIRALDI.

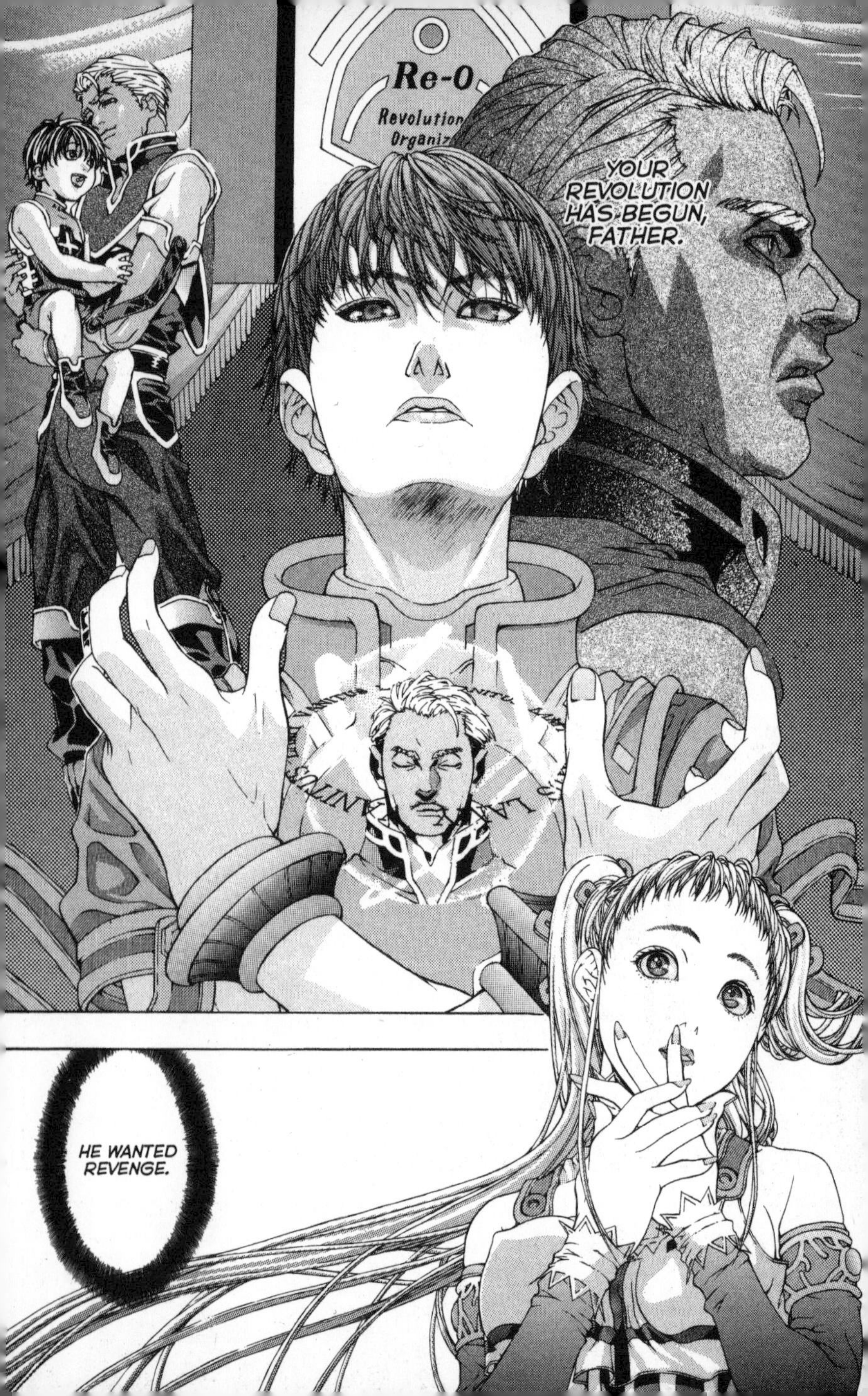
Re-O
Revolution
Organiz
YOUR REVOLUTION HAS BEGUN, FATHER.
HE WANTED REVENGE.

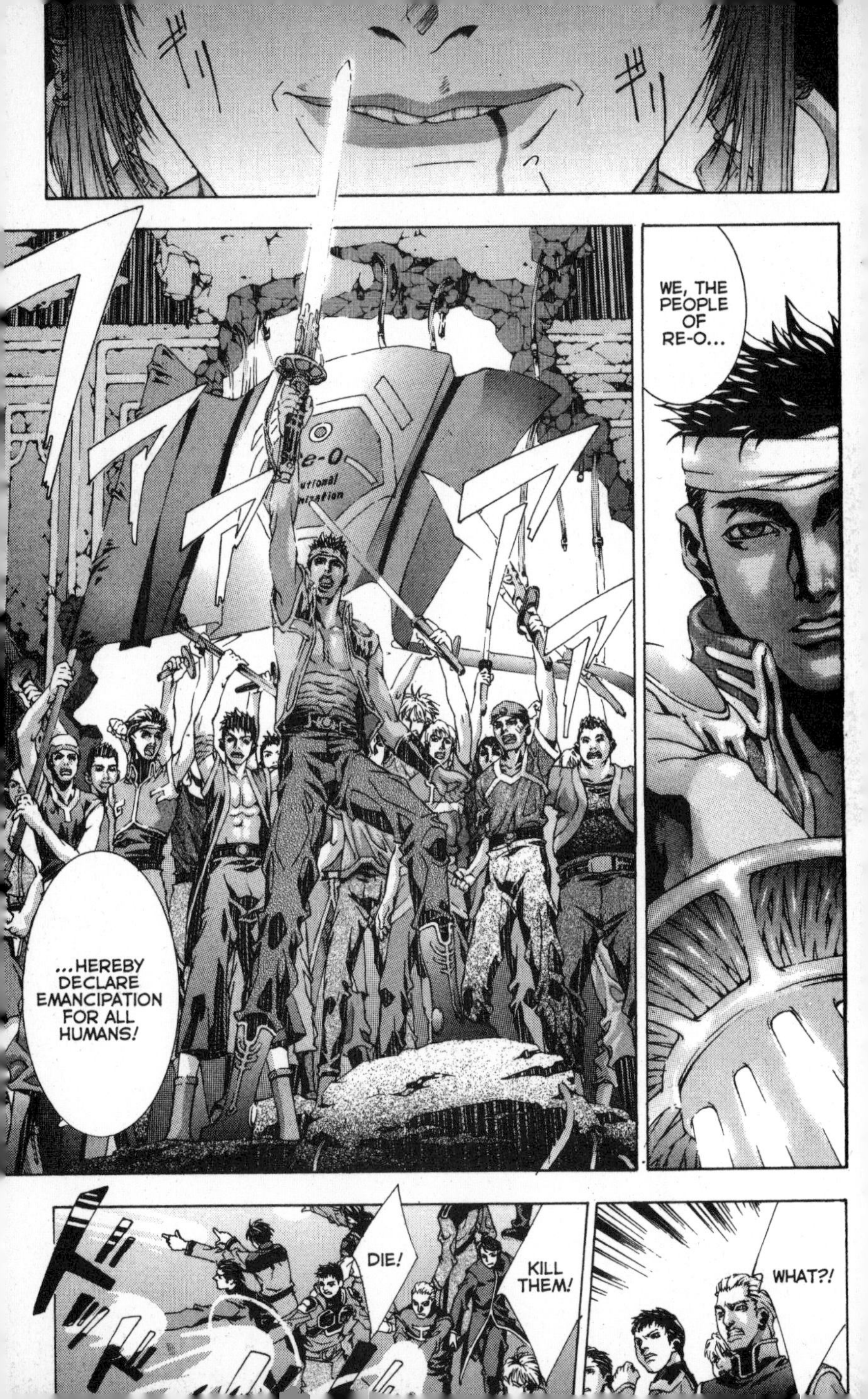
ギリ
ギリ
WE, THE PEOPLE OF RE-O...
...HEREBY DECLARE EMANCIPATION FOR ALL HUMANS!
WHAT?!
KILL THEM!
DIE!

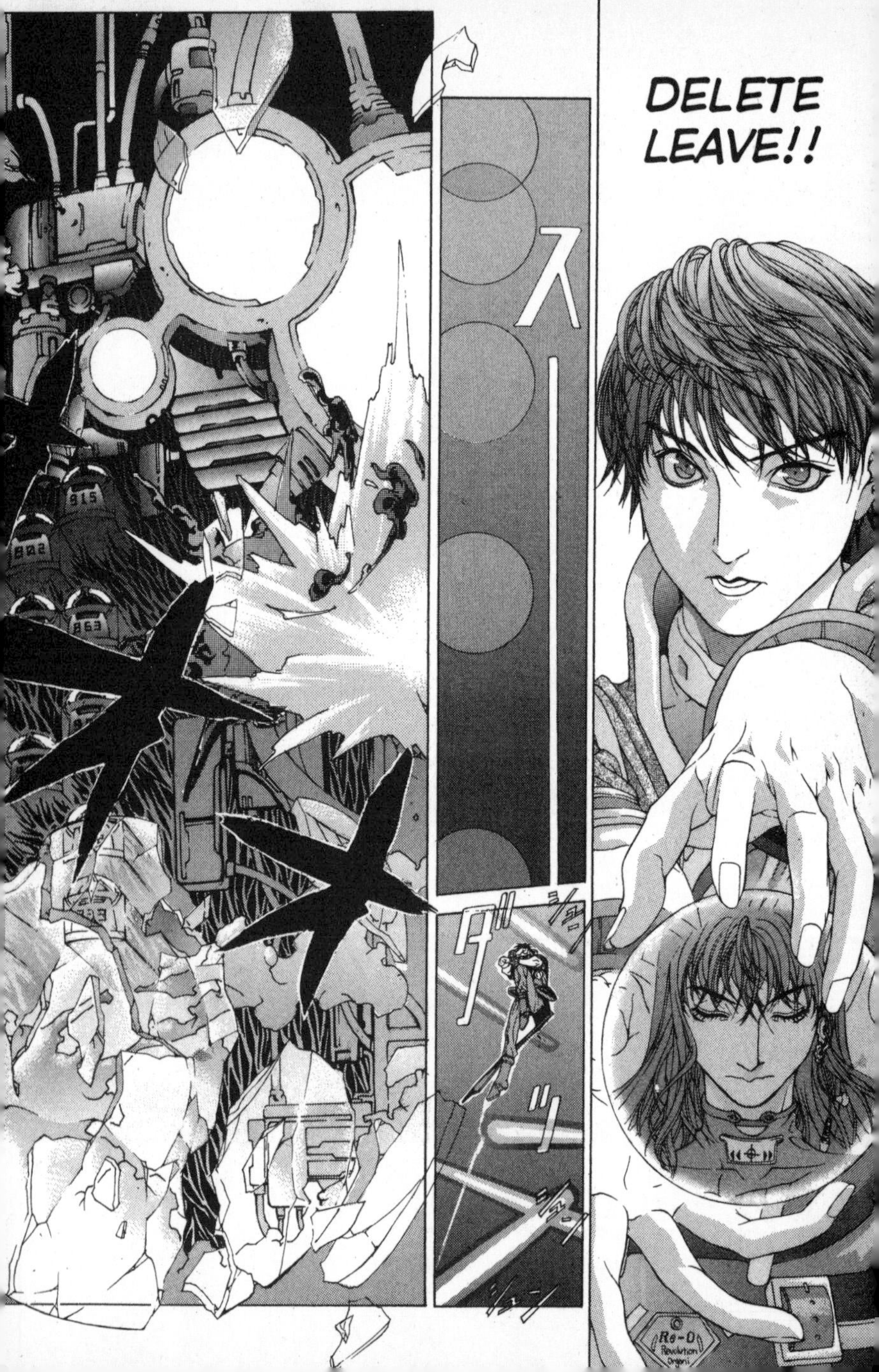
DELETE
LEAVE!!

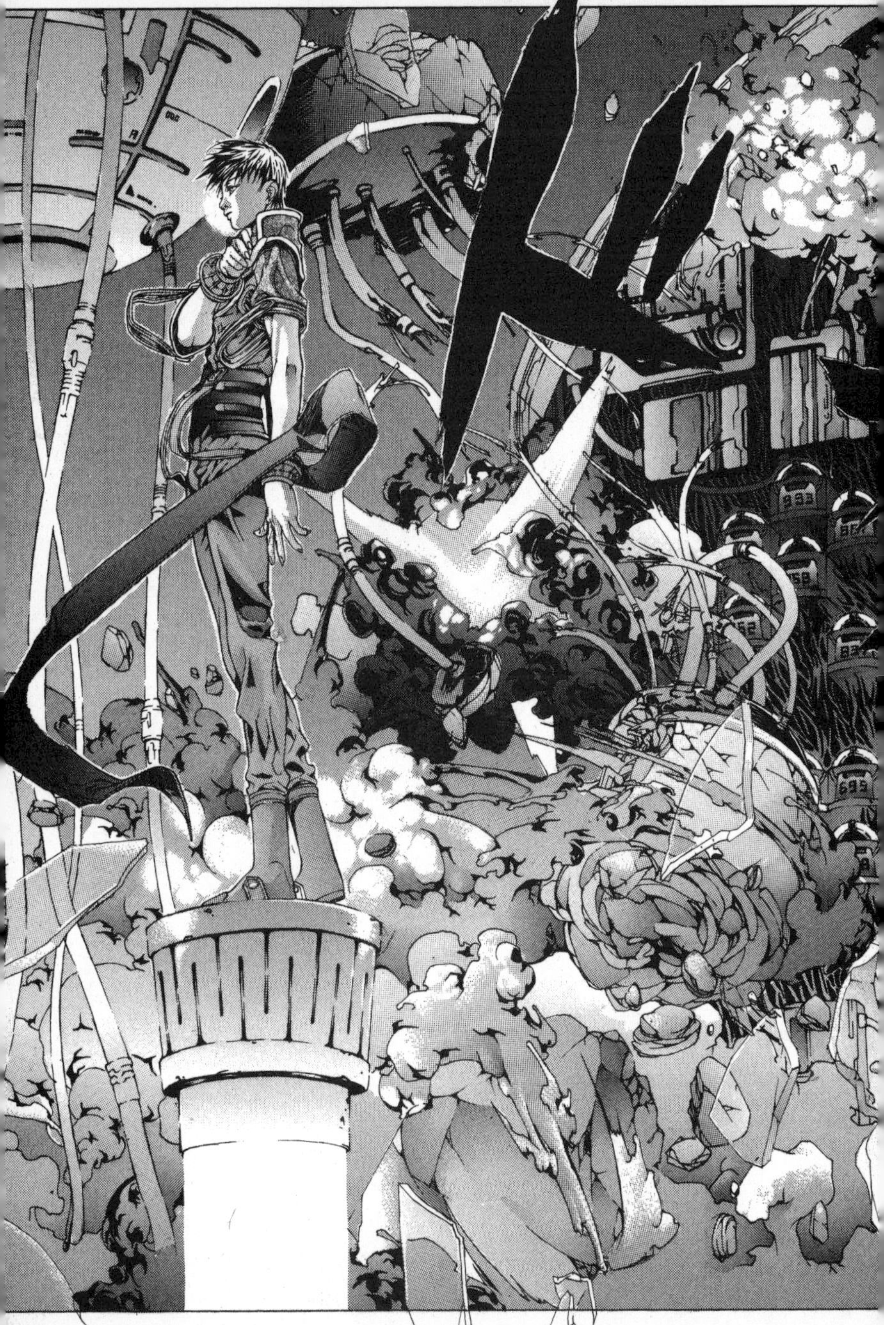

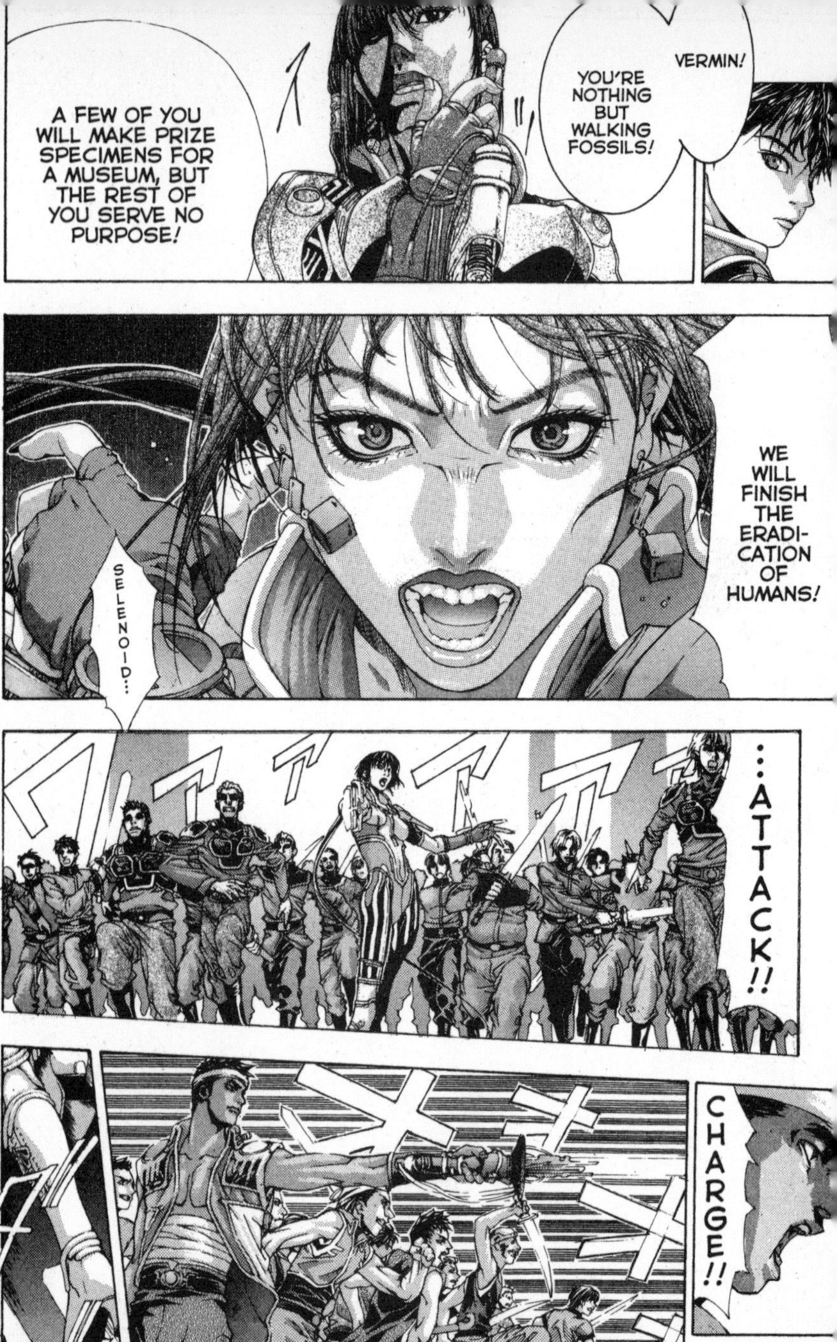
VERMIN!
YOU'RE NOTHING BUT WALKING FOSSILS!
A FEW OF YOU WILL MAKE PRIZE SPECIMENS FOR A MUSEUM, BUT THE REST OF YOU SERVE NO PURPOSE!
WE WILL FINISH THE ERADICATION OF HUMANS!
SELENOID...
...ATTACK!!
CHARGE!!

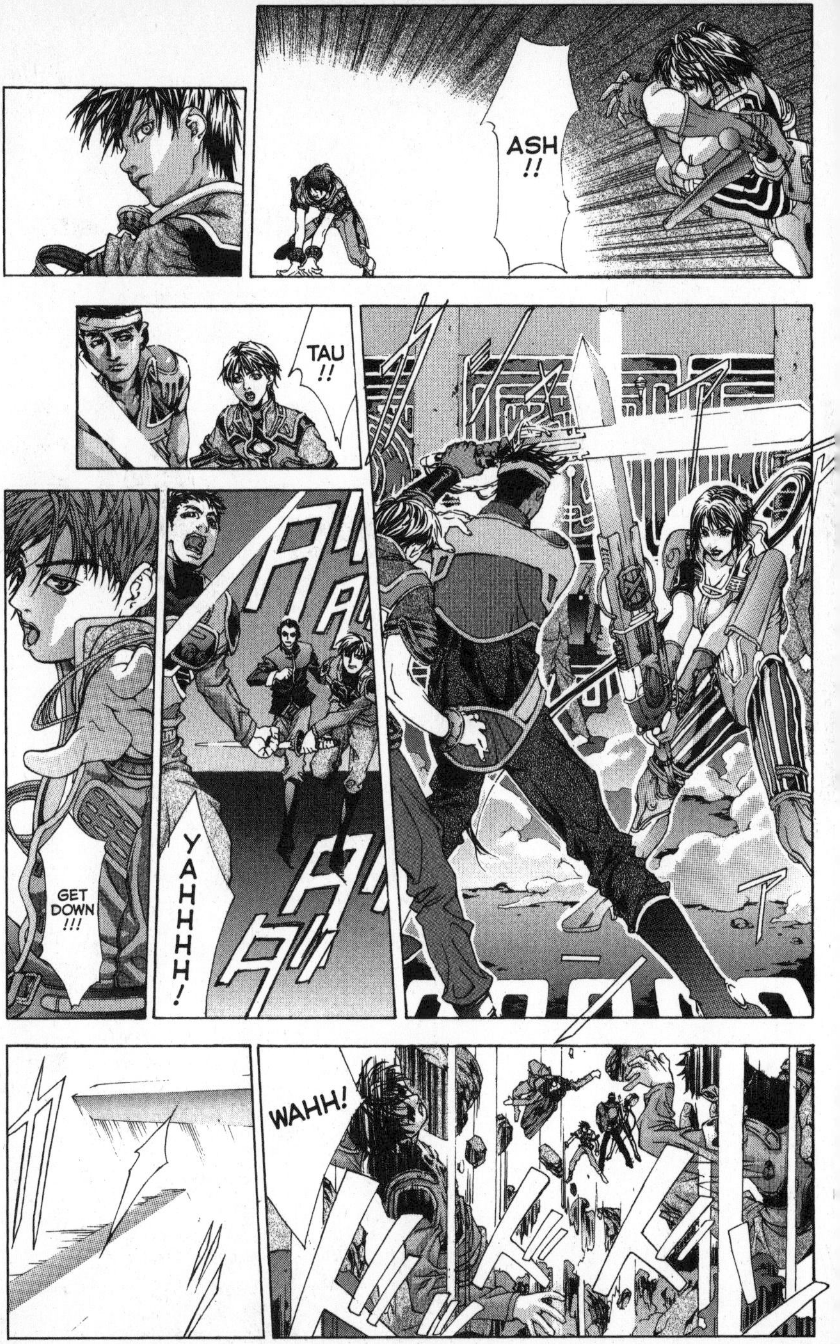
ASH!!
TAU!!
YAHHHH!
GET DOWN!!!
WAHH!

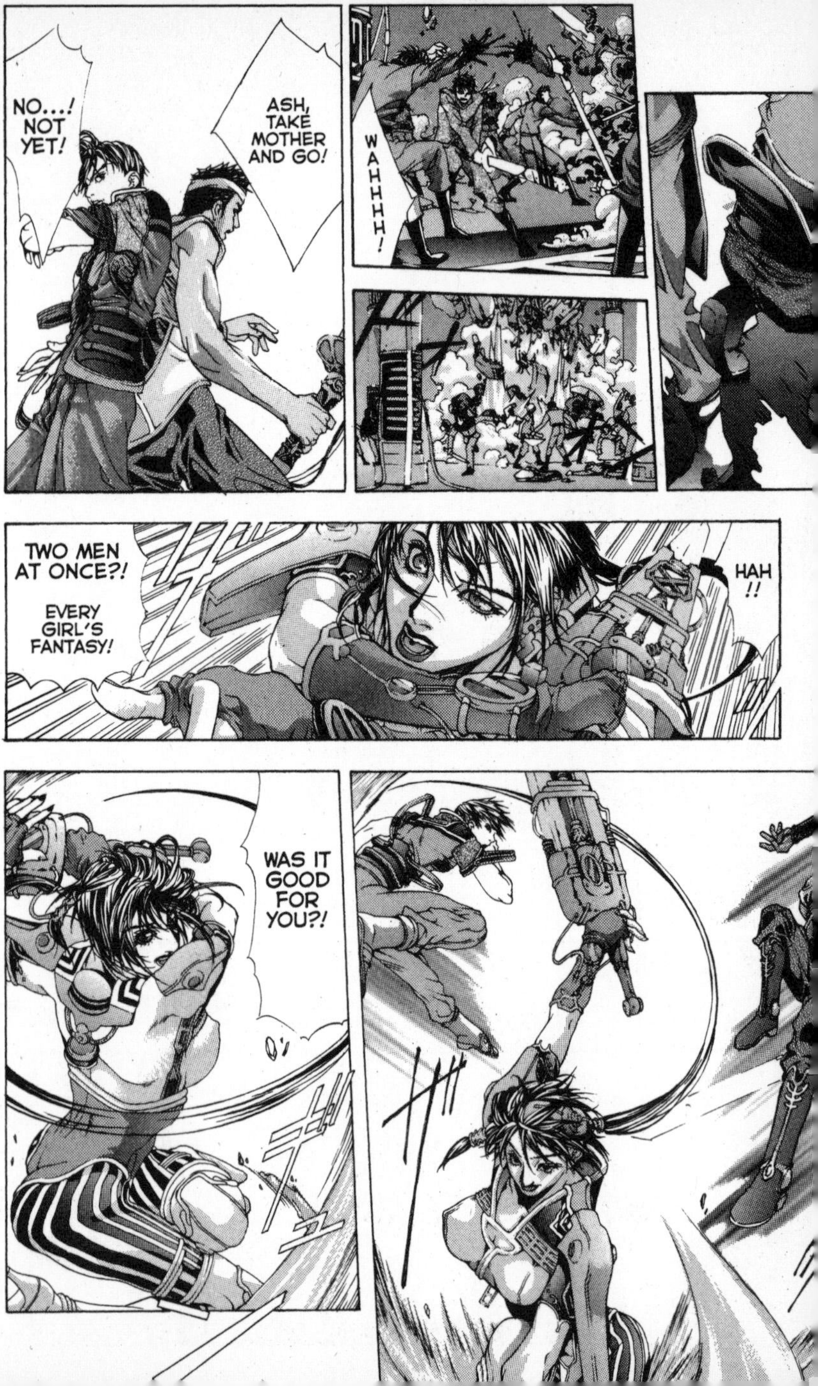
WAHHHH!
ASH, TAKE MOTHER AND GO!
NO...! NOT YET!
HAH!!
TWO MEN AT ONCE?!
EVERY GIRL'S FANTASY!
WAS IT GOOD FOR YOU?!

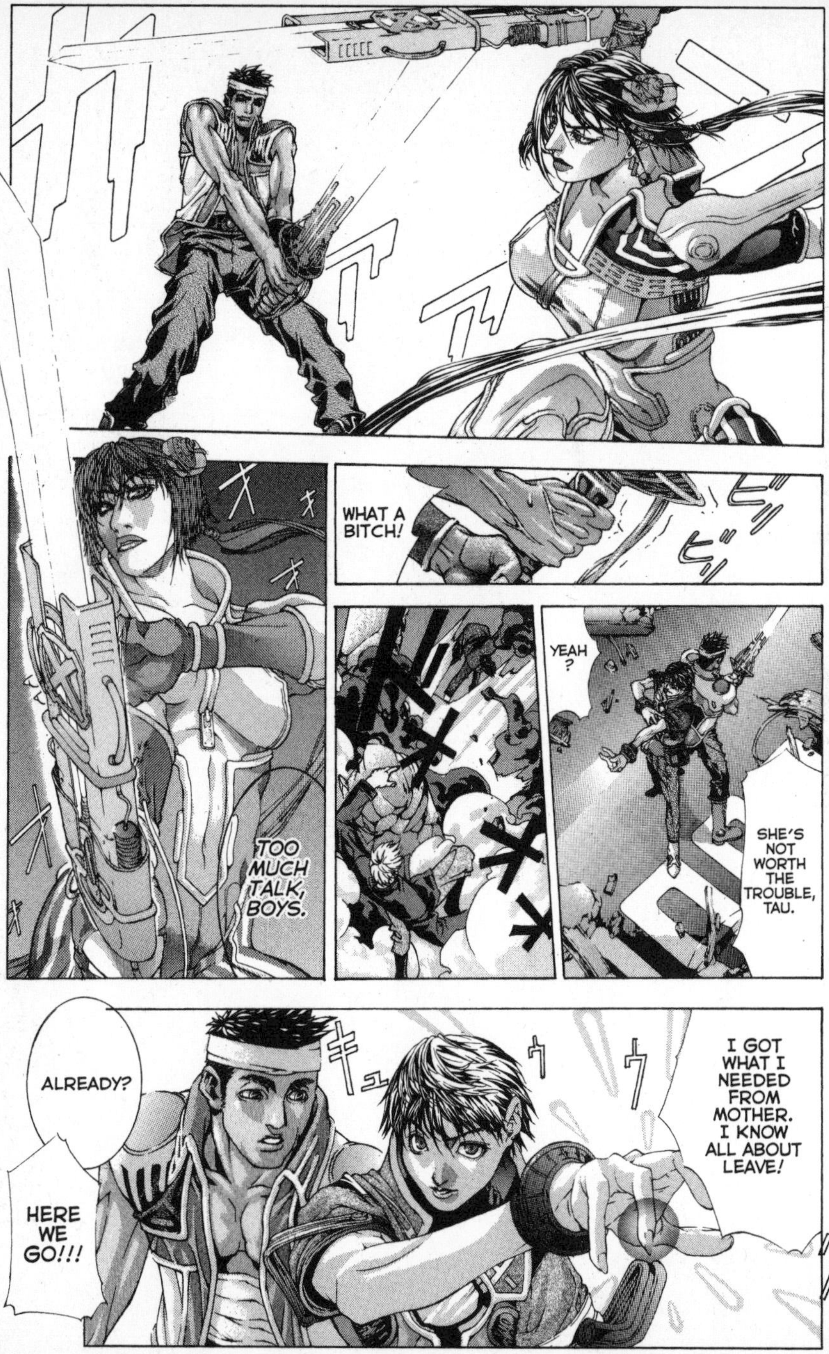
WHAT A BITCH!
YEAH?
SHE'S NOT WORTH THE TROUBLE, TAU.
TOO MUCH TALK, BOYS.
I GOT WHAT I NEEDED FROM MOTHER. I KNOW ALL ABOUT LEAVE!
ALREADY?
HERE WE GO!!!

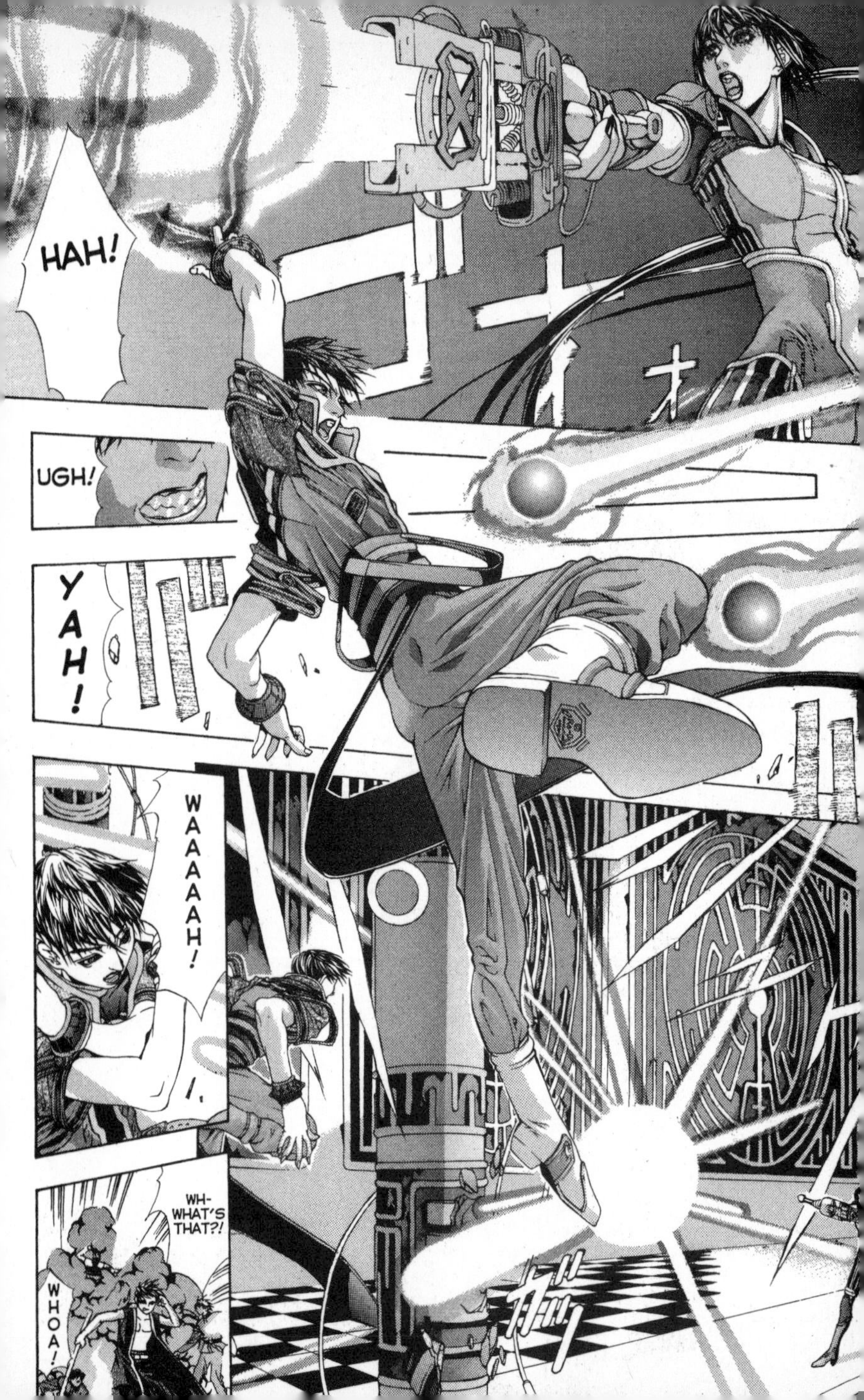
HAH!
UGH!
YAH!
WAAAAAAH!
WH- WHAT'S THAT?!
WHOA!

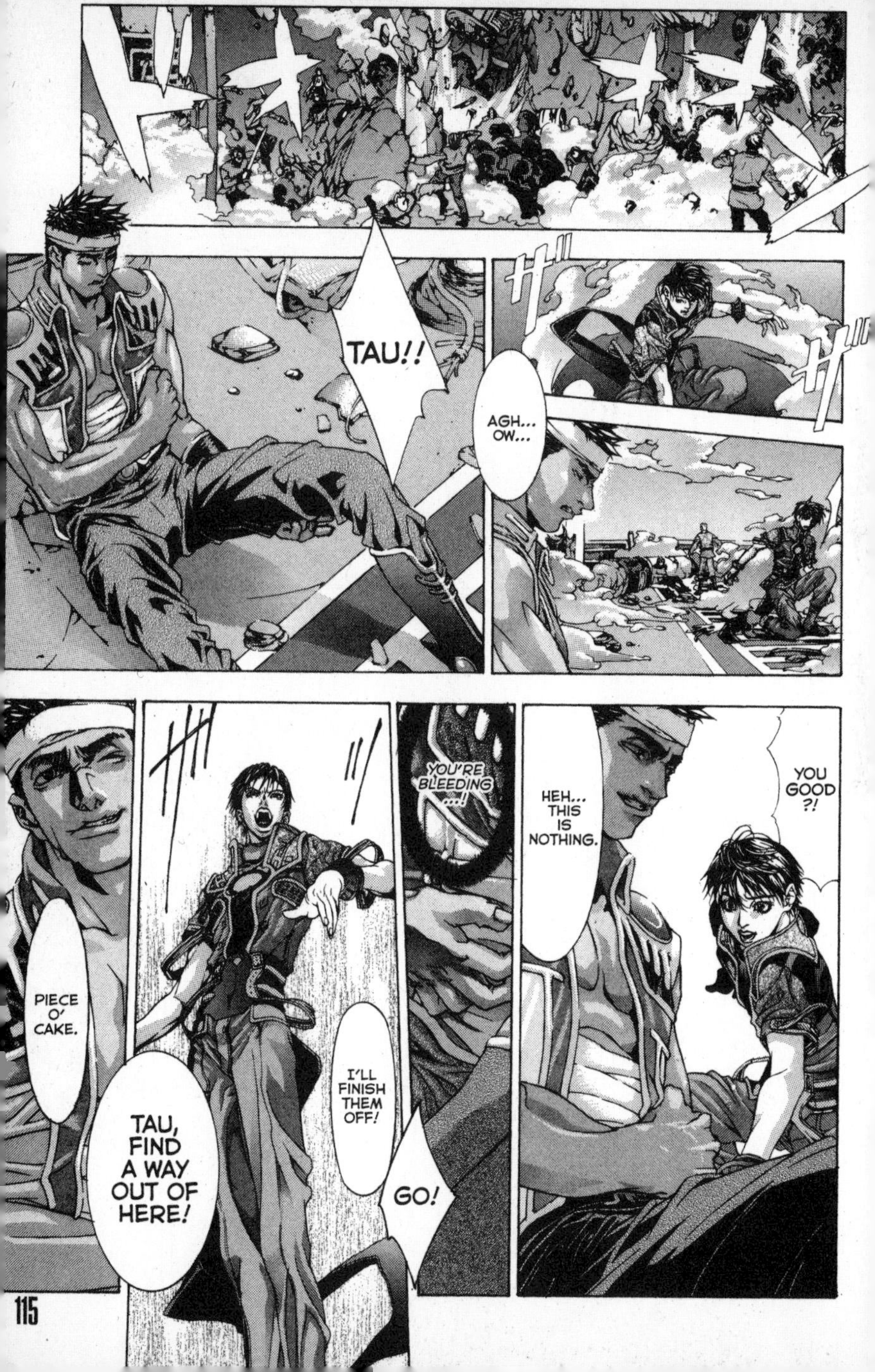
AGH... OW...
TAU!!
YOU GOOD ?!
HEH... THIS IS NOTHING.
YOU'RE BLEEDING ...!
I'LL FINISH THEM OFF!
TAU, FIND A WAY OUT OF HERE!
GO!
PIECE O' CAKE.

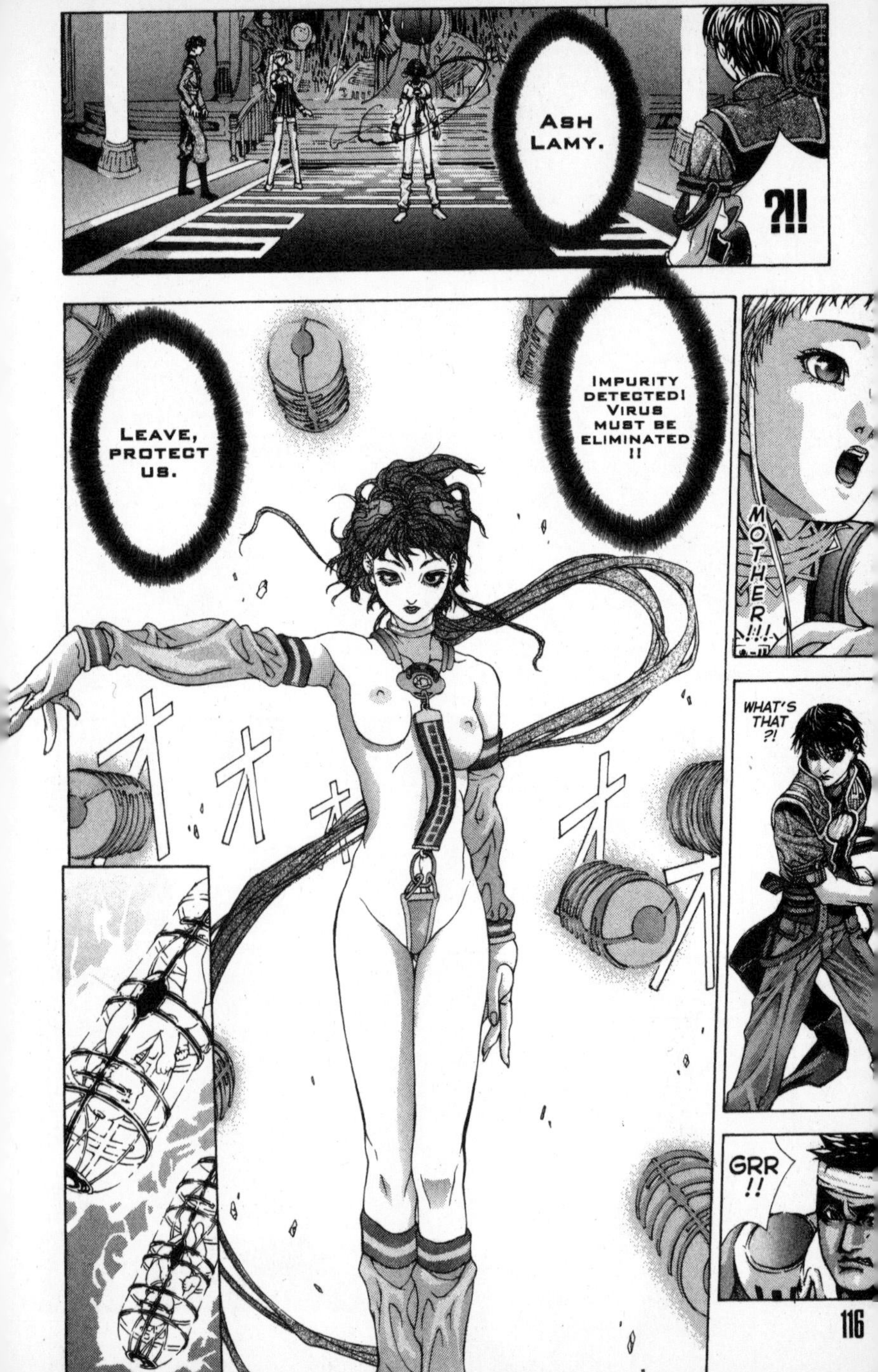
Ash Lamy.
?!!
Mother!!!
What's that ?!
Grr !!
Impurity detected! Virus must be eliminated !!
Leave, protect us.
オオオオオ

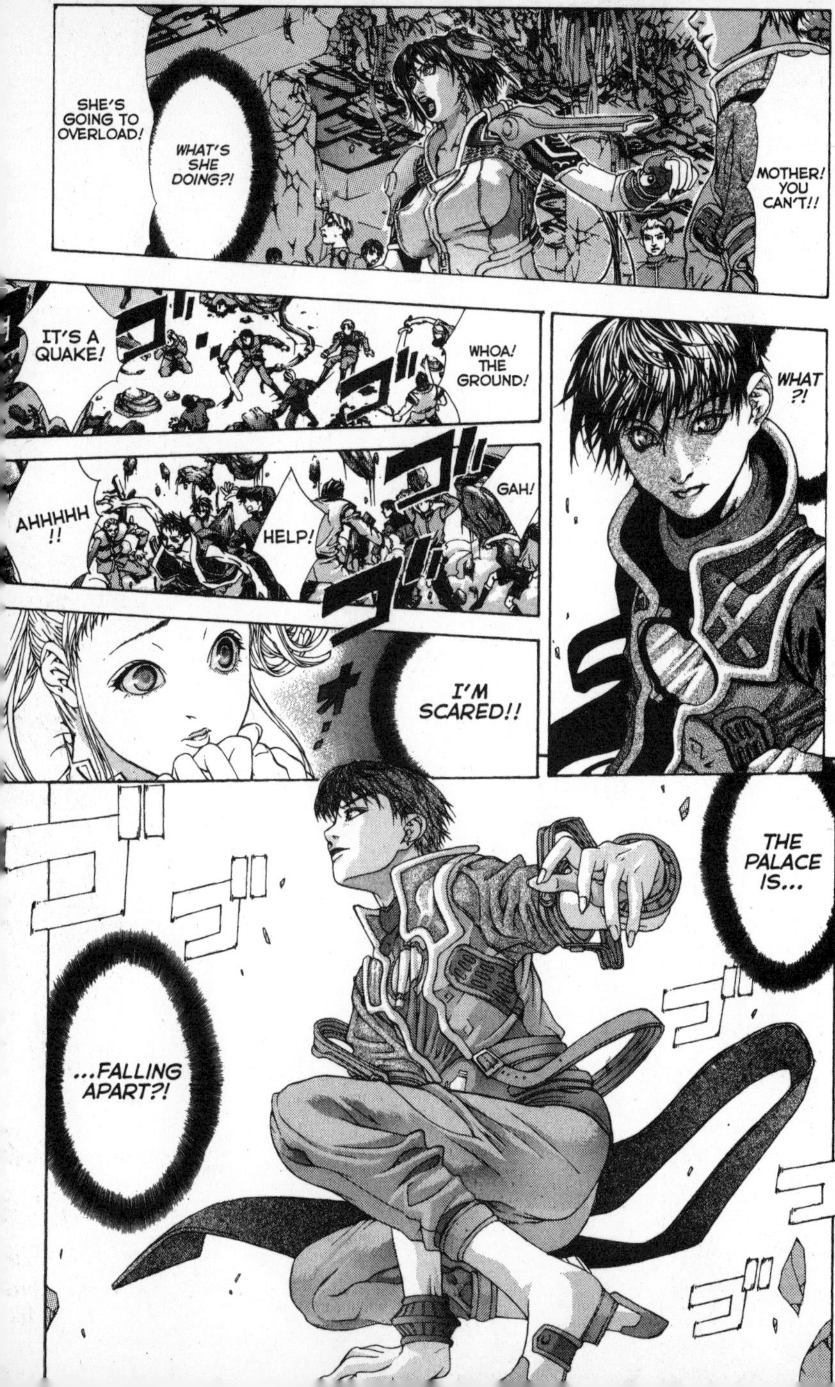
MOTHER! YOU CAN'T!!
WHAT'S SHE DOING?!
SHE'S GOING TO OVERLOAD!
WHAT?!
WHOA! THE GROUND!
IT'S A QUAKE!
GAH!
HELP!
AHHHHH!!
I'M SCARED!!
THE PALACE IS...
...FALLING APART?!

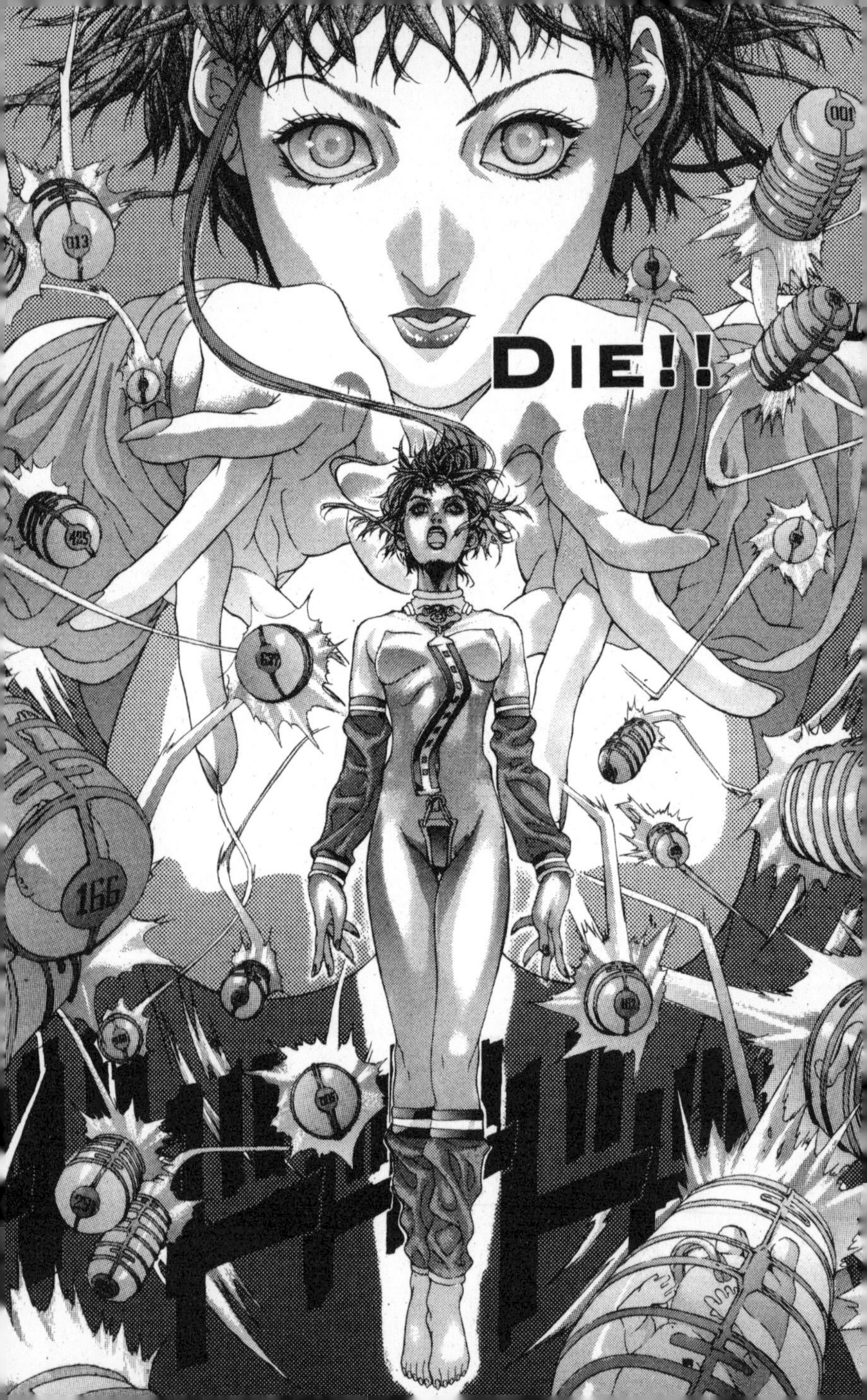
DIE!!

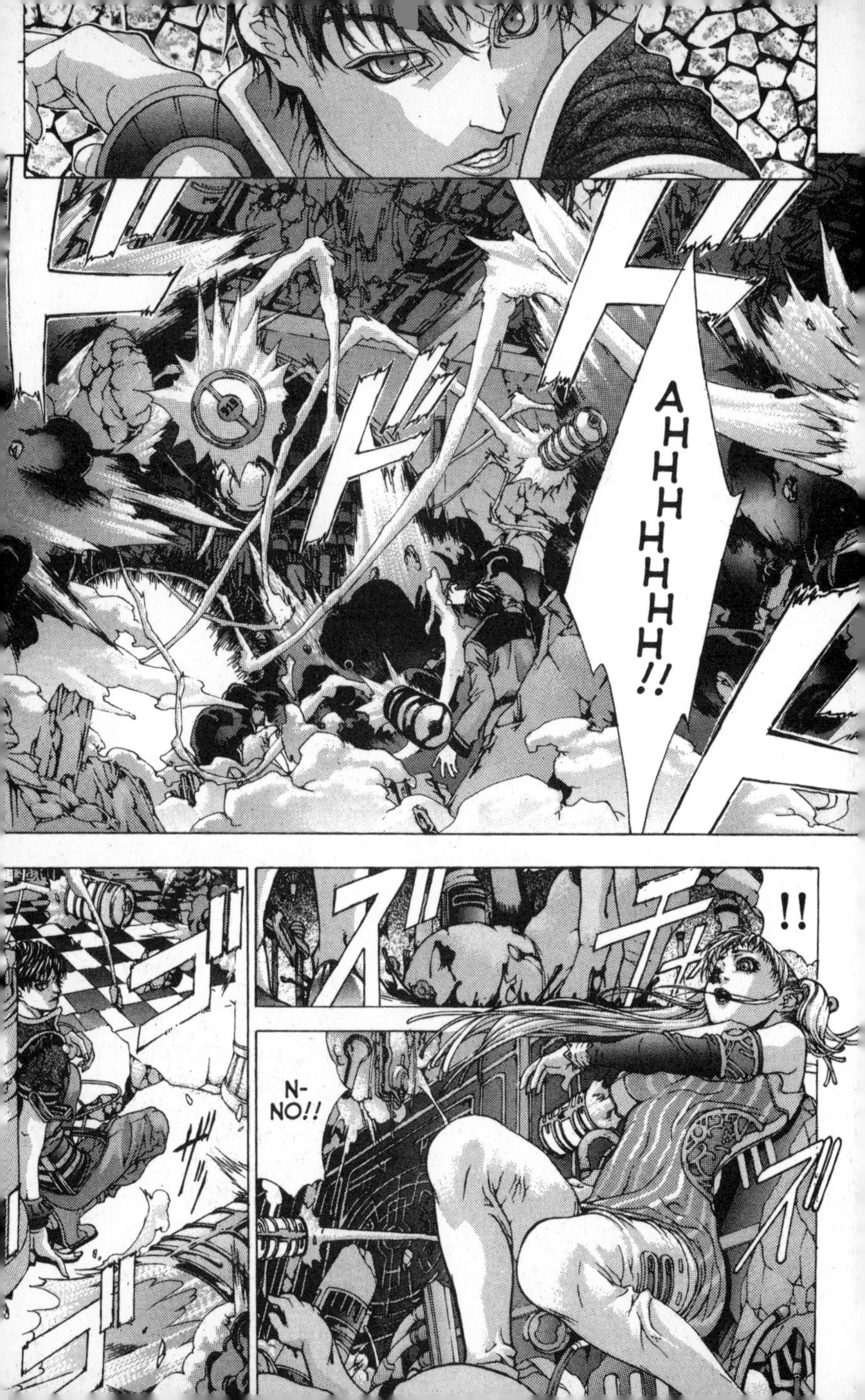
AHHHHHHHH!!
!!
N-NO!!

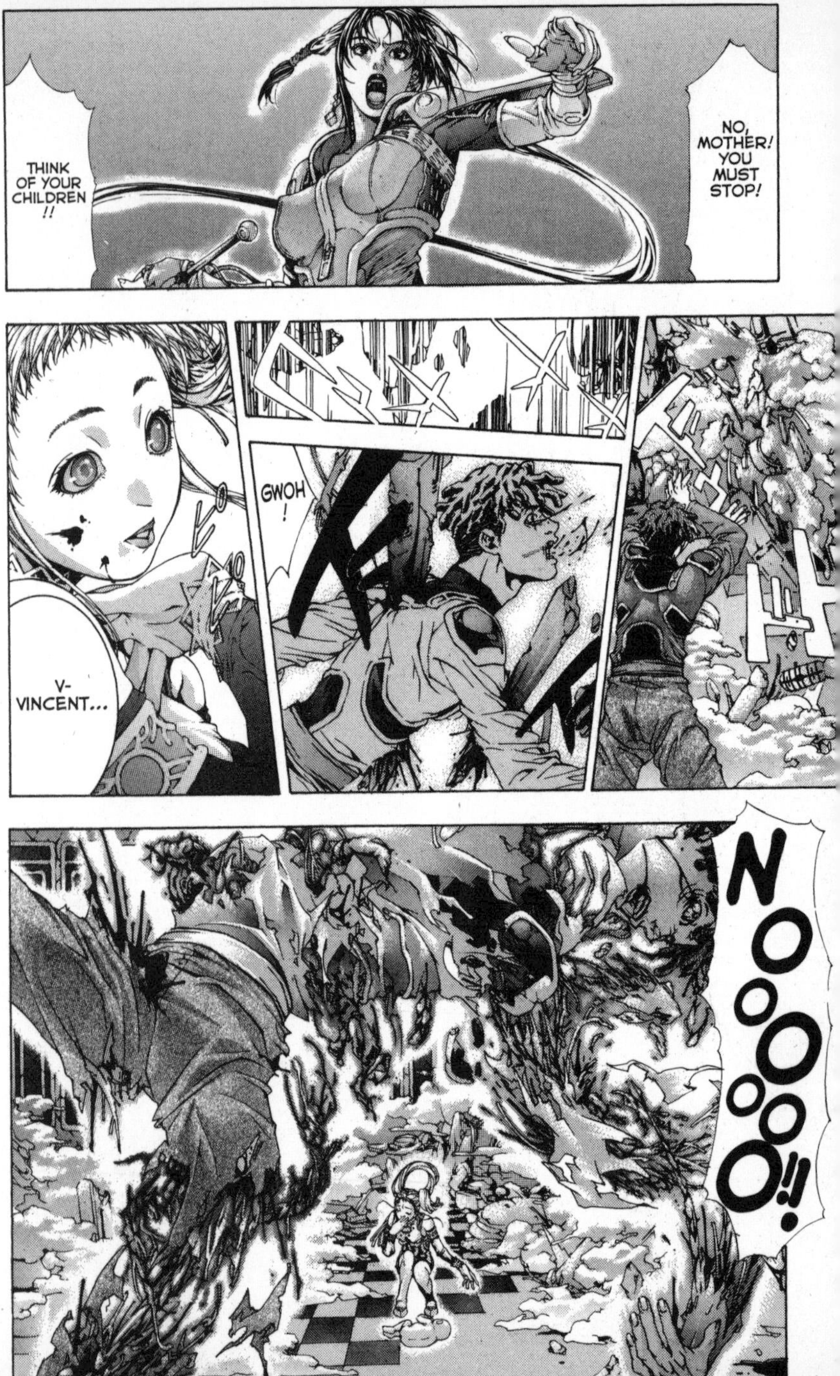
NO, MOTHER! YOU MUST STOP!
THINK OF YOUR CHILDREN!!
GWOH!
V-VINCENT...
NOOOOO!!

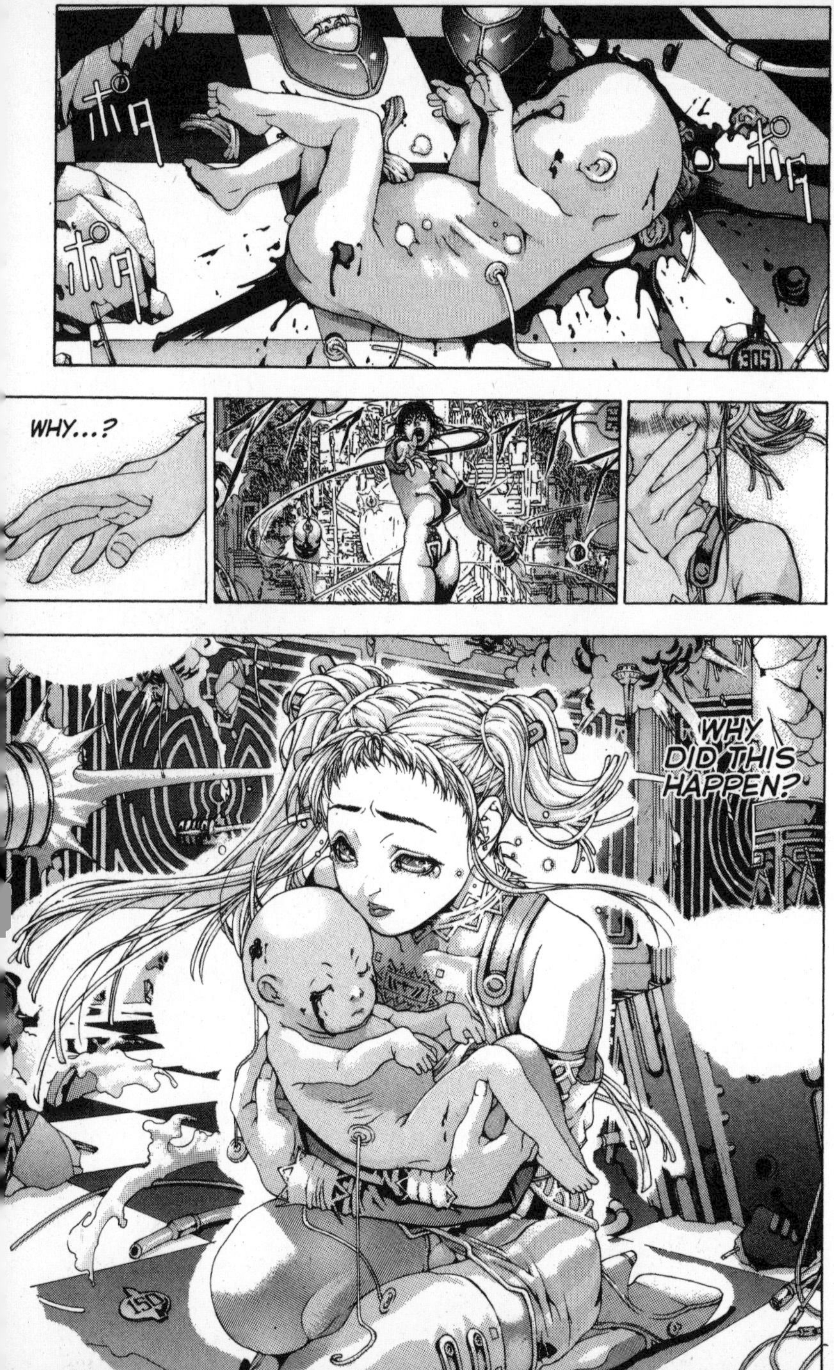
ポタ
ポタ
ポタ
WHY...?
WHY DID THIS HAPPEN?

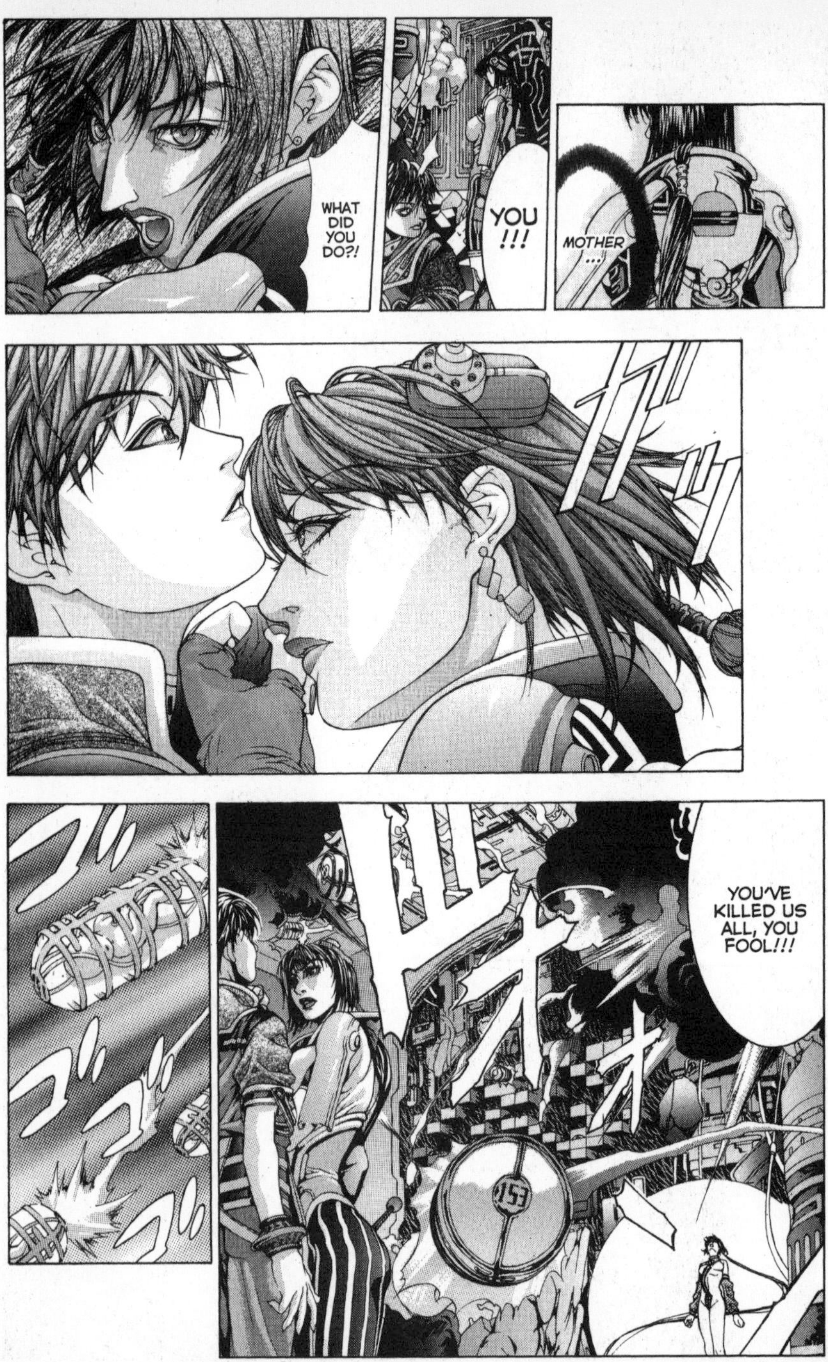
MOTHER ...
YOU !!!
WHAT DID YOU DO?!
YOU'VE KILLED US ALL, YOU FOOL!!!

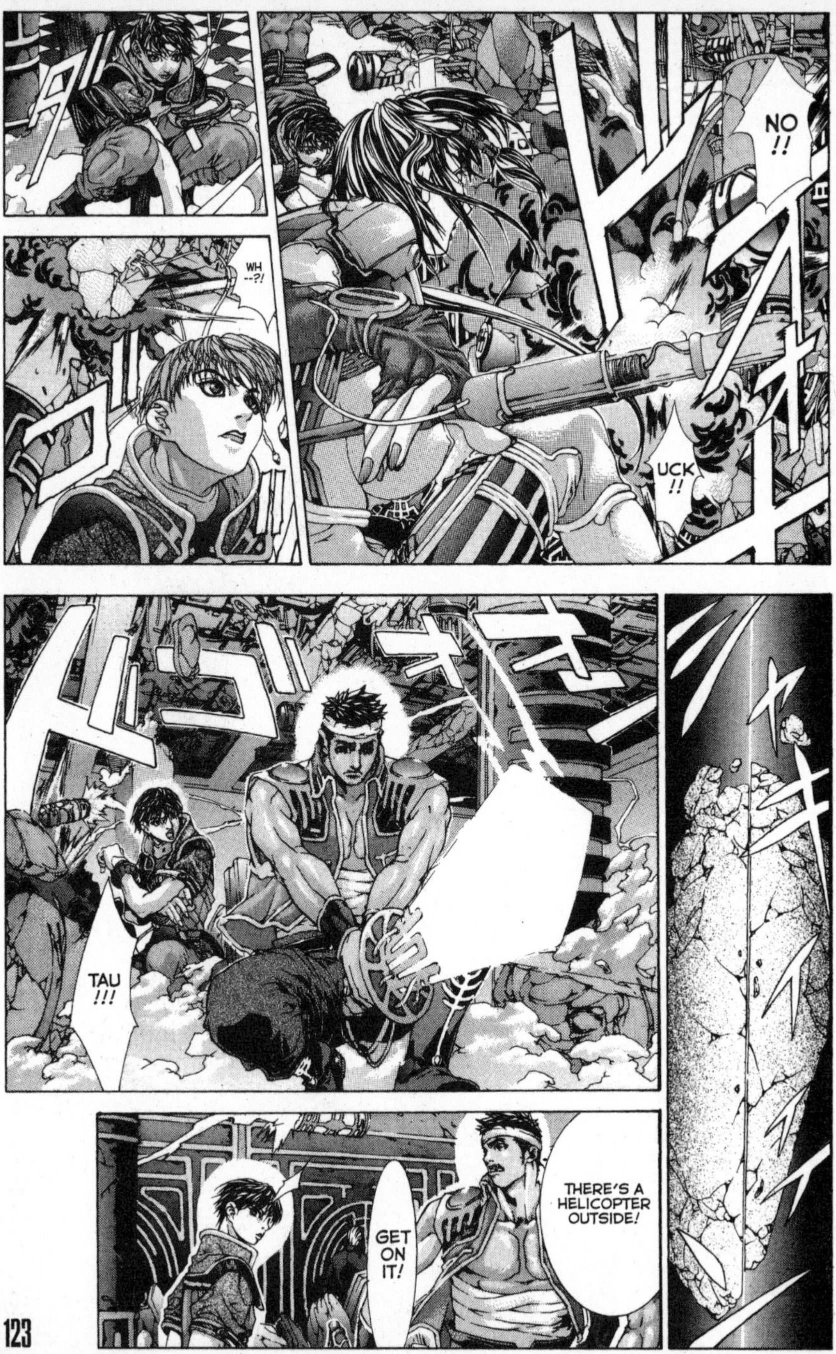
NO !!
UCK !!
WH --?!
TAU !!!
THERE'S A HELICOPTER OUTSIDE!
GET ON IT!

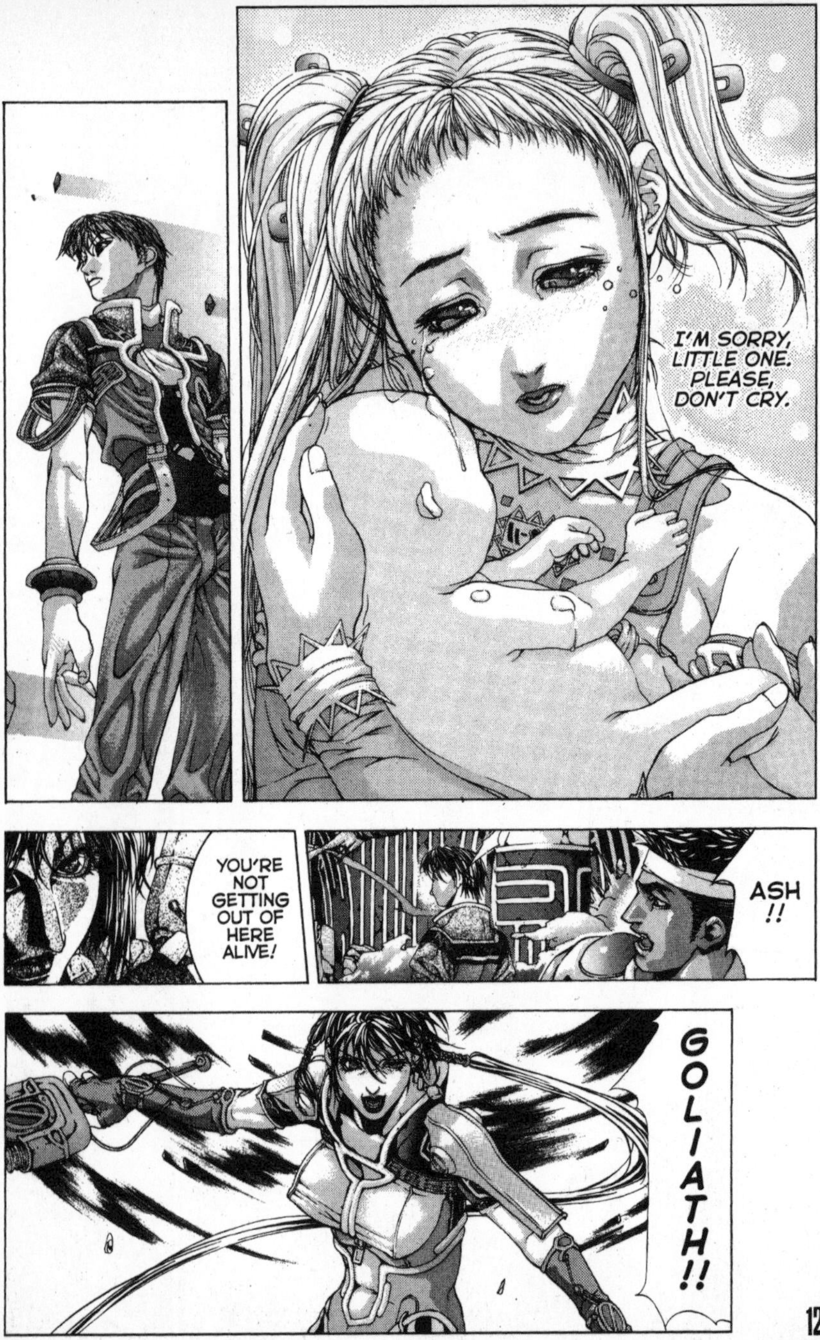
I'M SORRY, LITTLE ONE. PLEASE, DON'T CRY.
ASH !!
YOU'RE NOT GETTING OUT OF HERE ALIVE!
GOLIATH!!

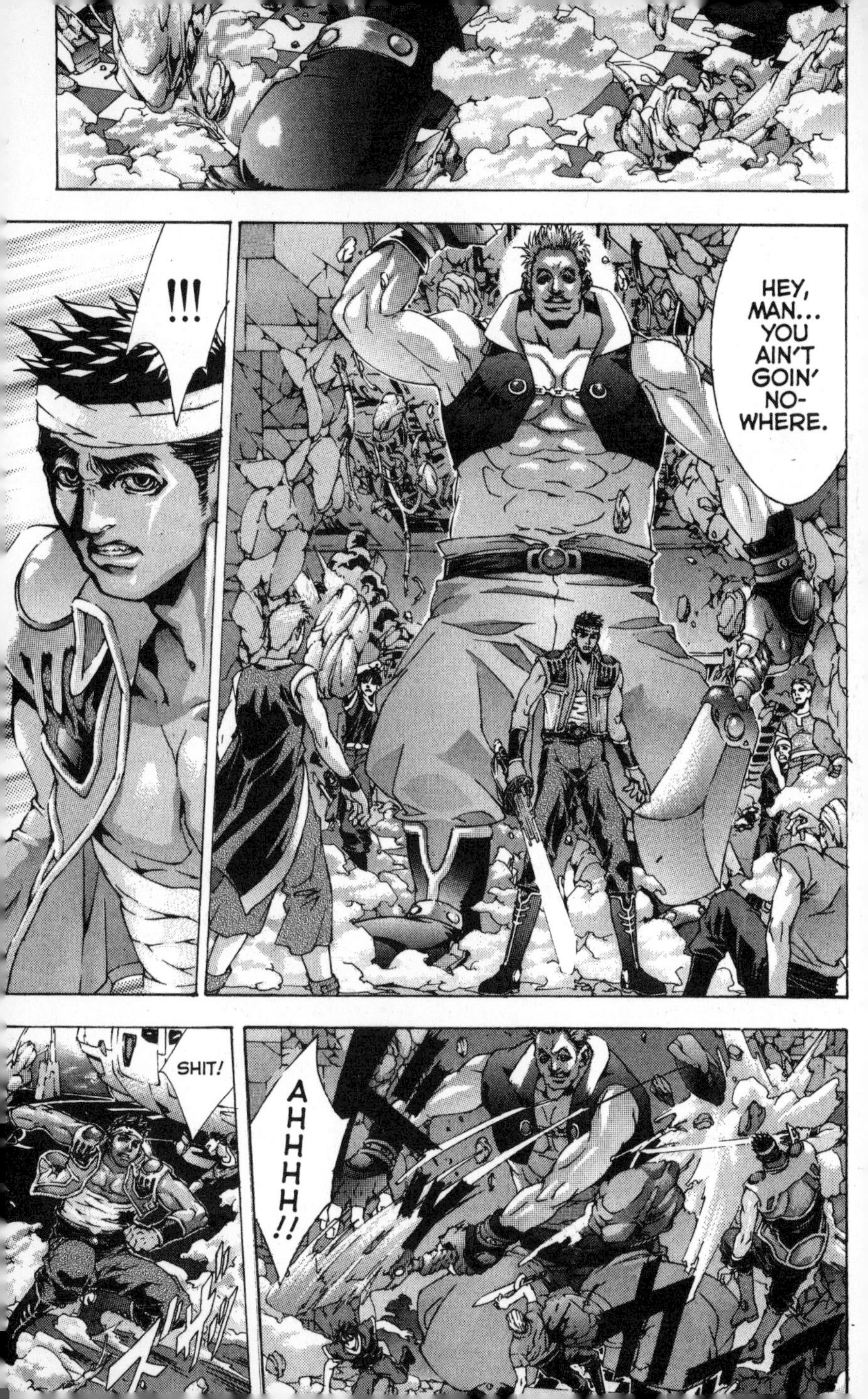
HEY, MAN... YOU AIN'T GOIN' NO-WHERE.
!!!
AHHHH!!
SHIT!

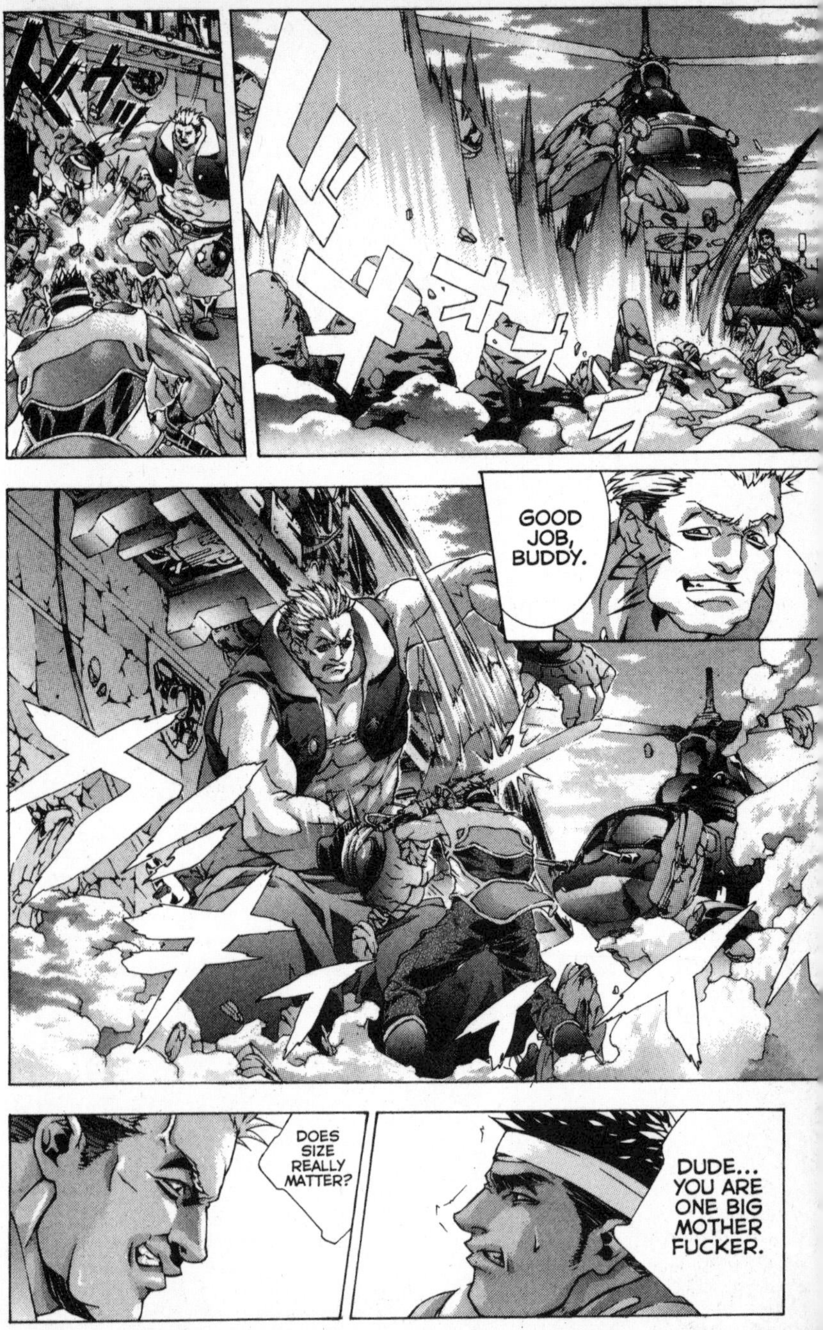
GOOD JOB, BUDDY.
DUDE... YOU ARE ONE BIG MOTHER FUCKER.
DOES SIZE REALLY MATTER?

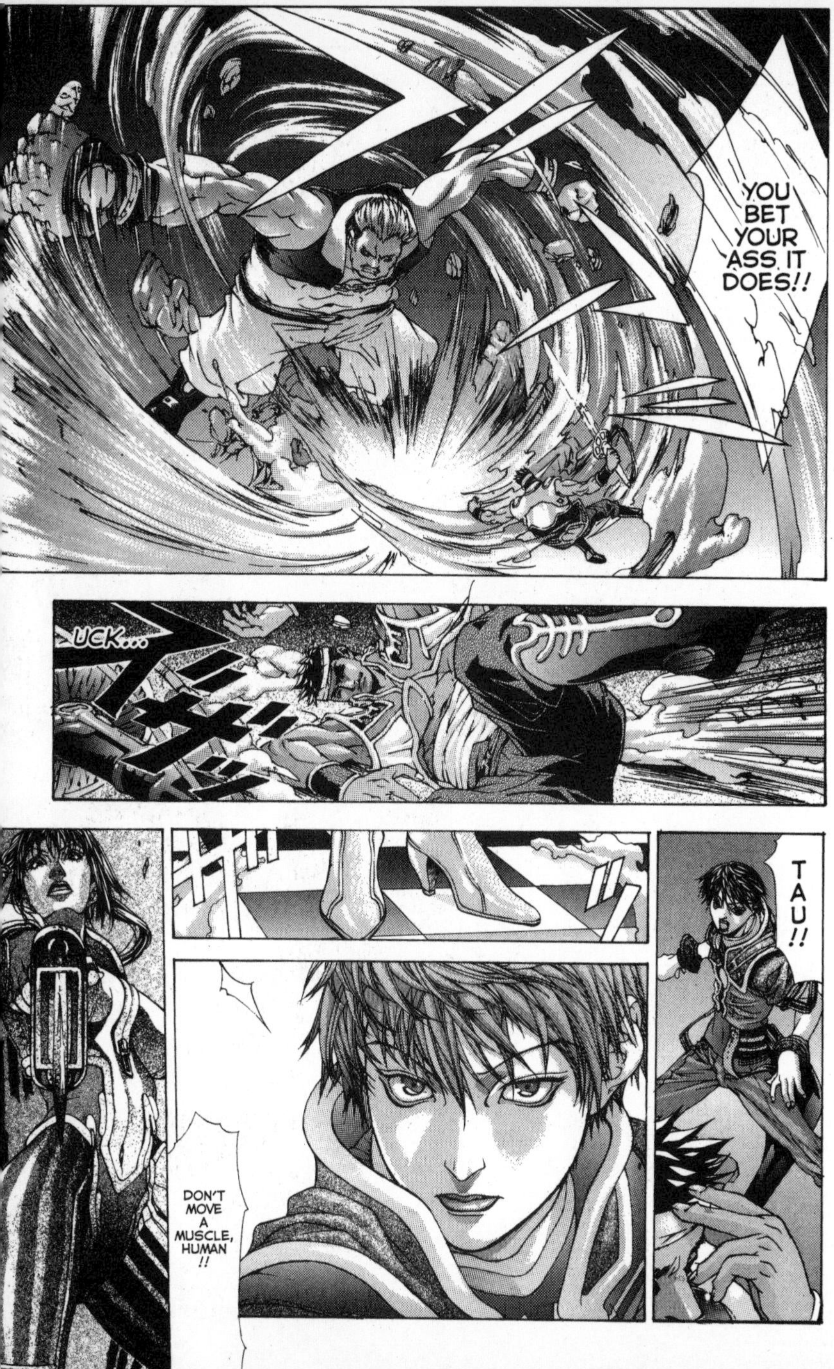
YOU BET YOUR ASS IT DOES!!
UCK...
TAU!!
DON'T MOVE A MUSCLE, HUMAN!!

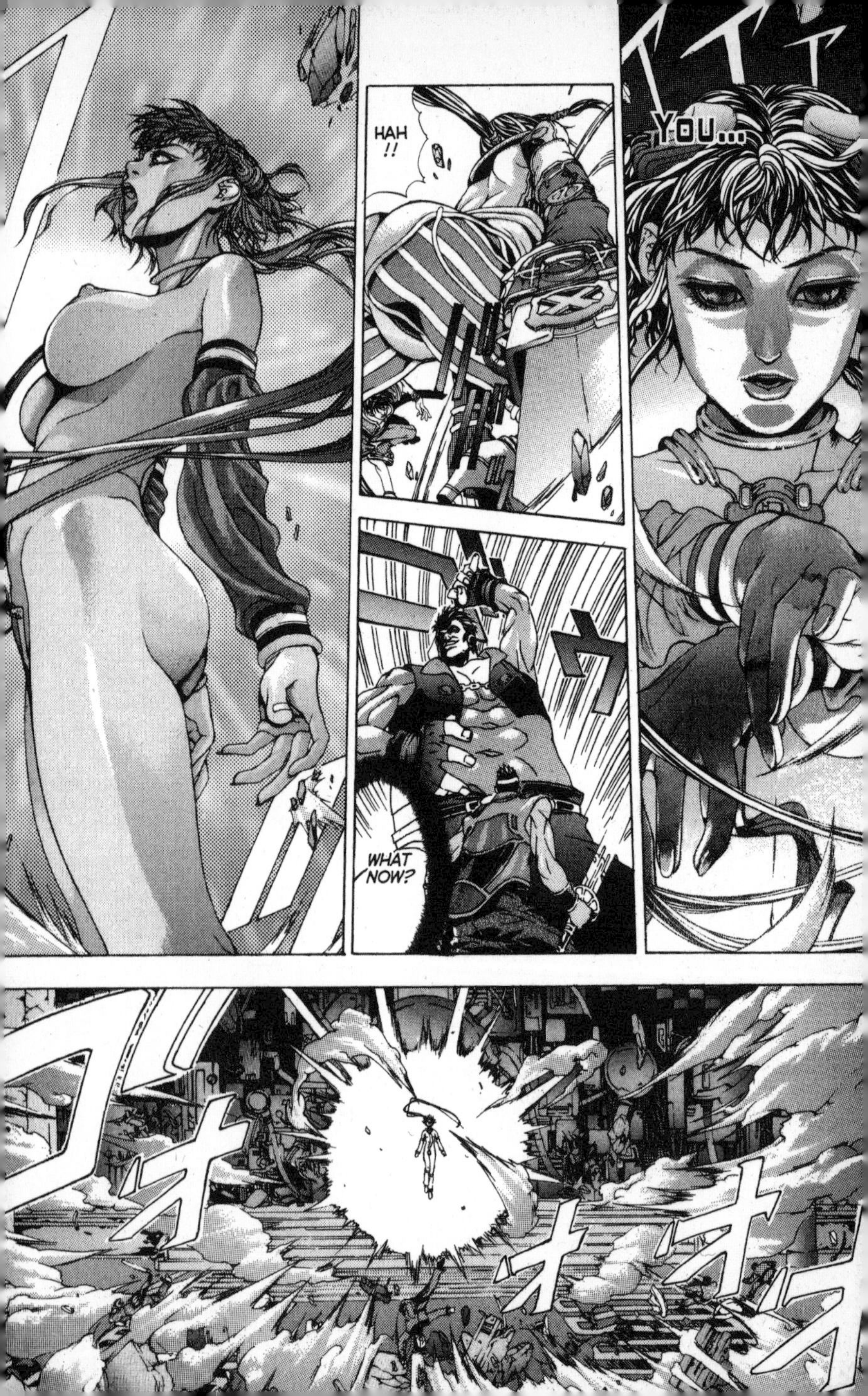
YOU...
HAH !!
WHAT NOW?

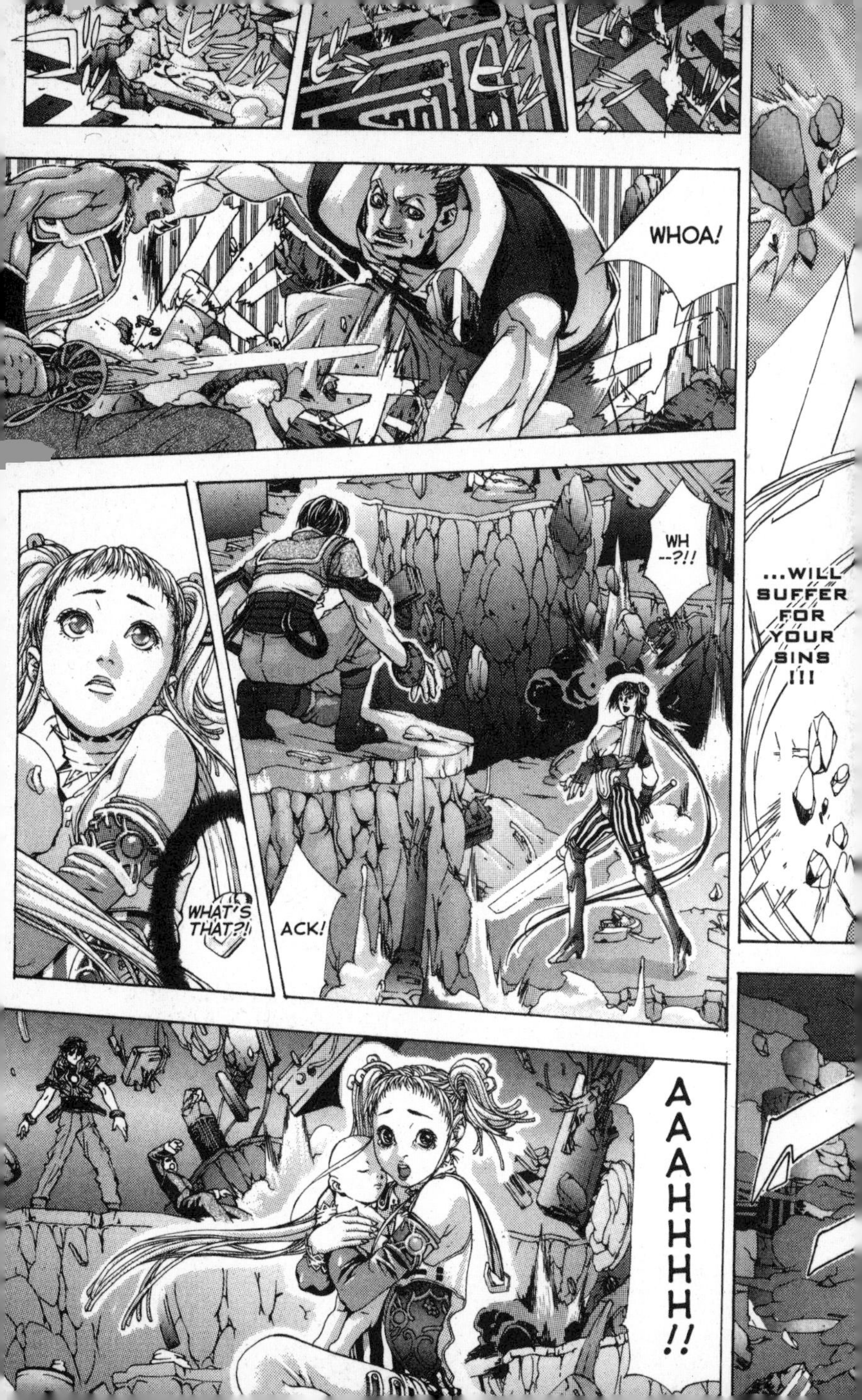
WHOA!
...WILL SUFFER FOR YOUR SINS !!!
WH --?!!
ACK!
WHAT'S THAT?!
AAAHHHH!!

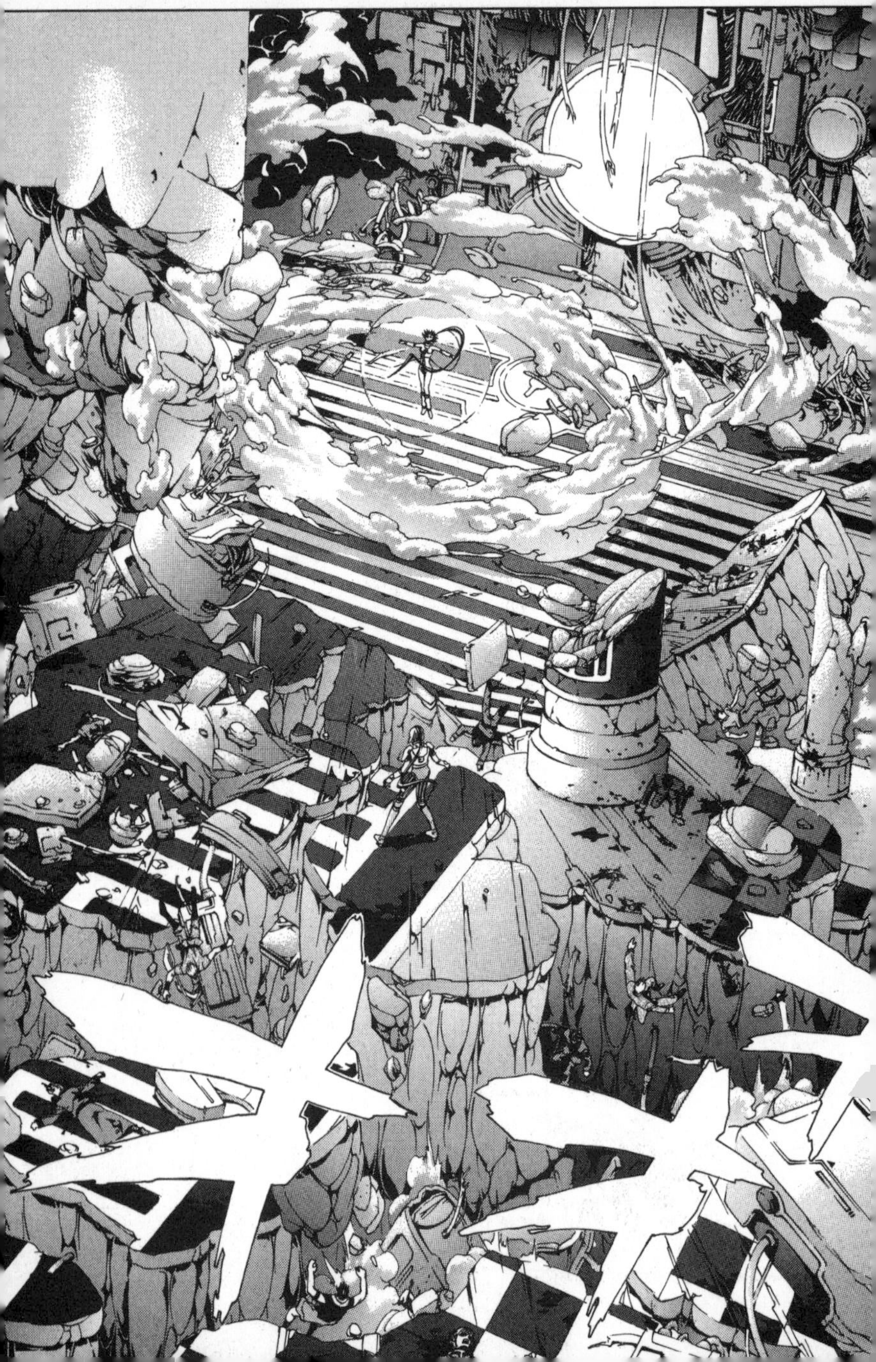

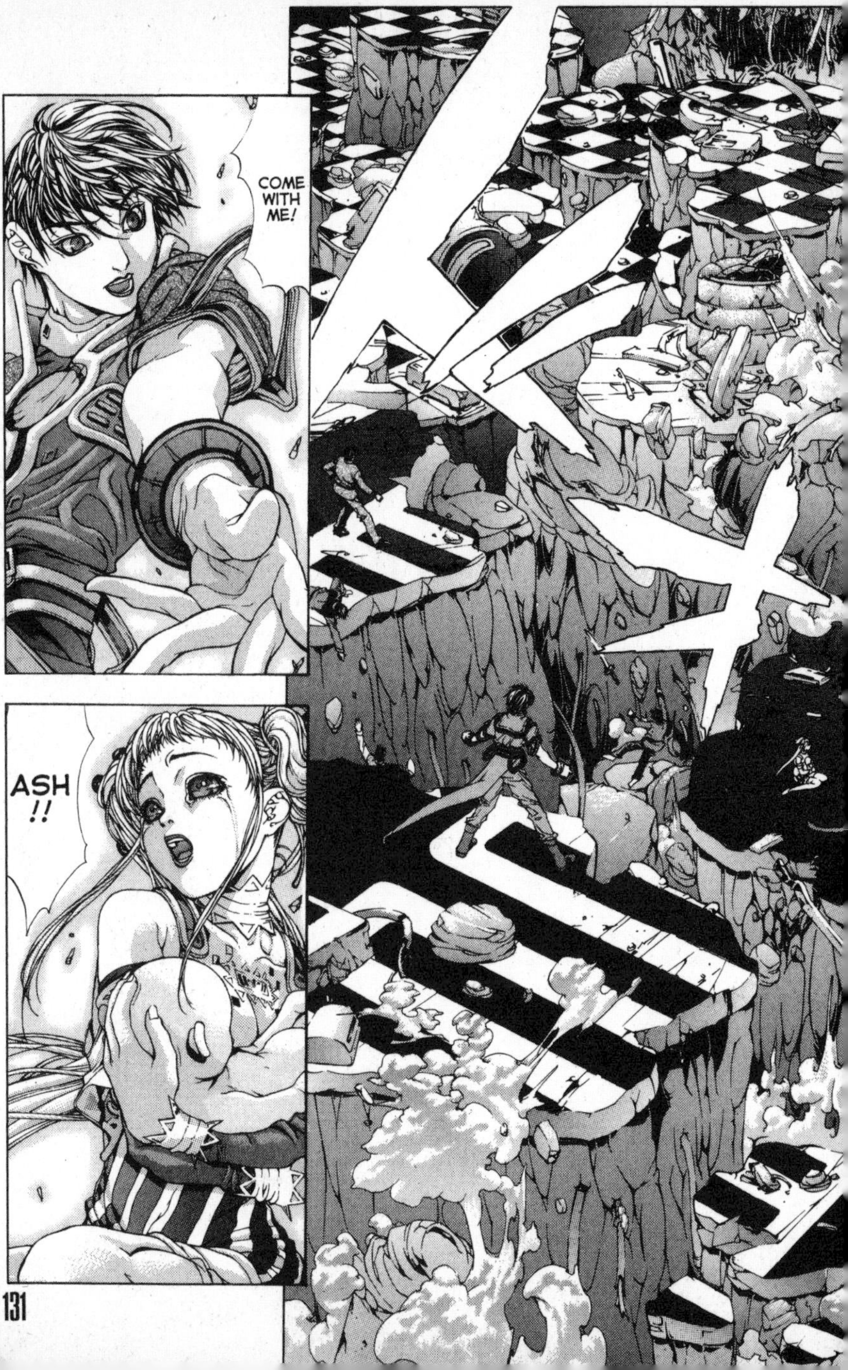
COME WITH ME!
ASH !!

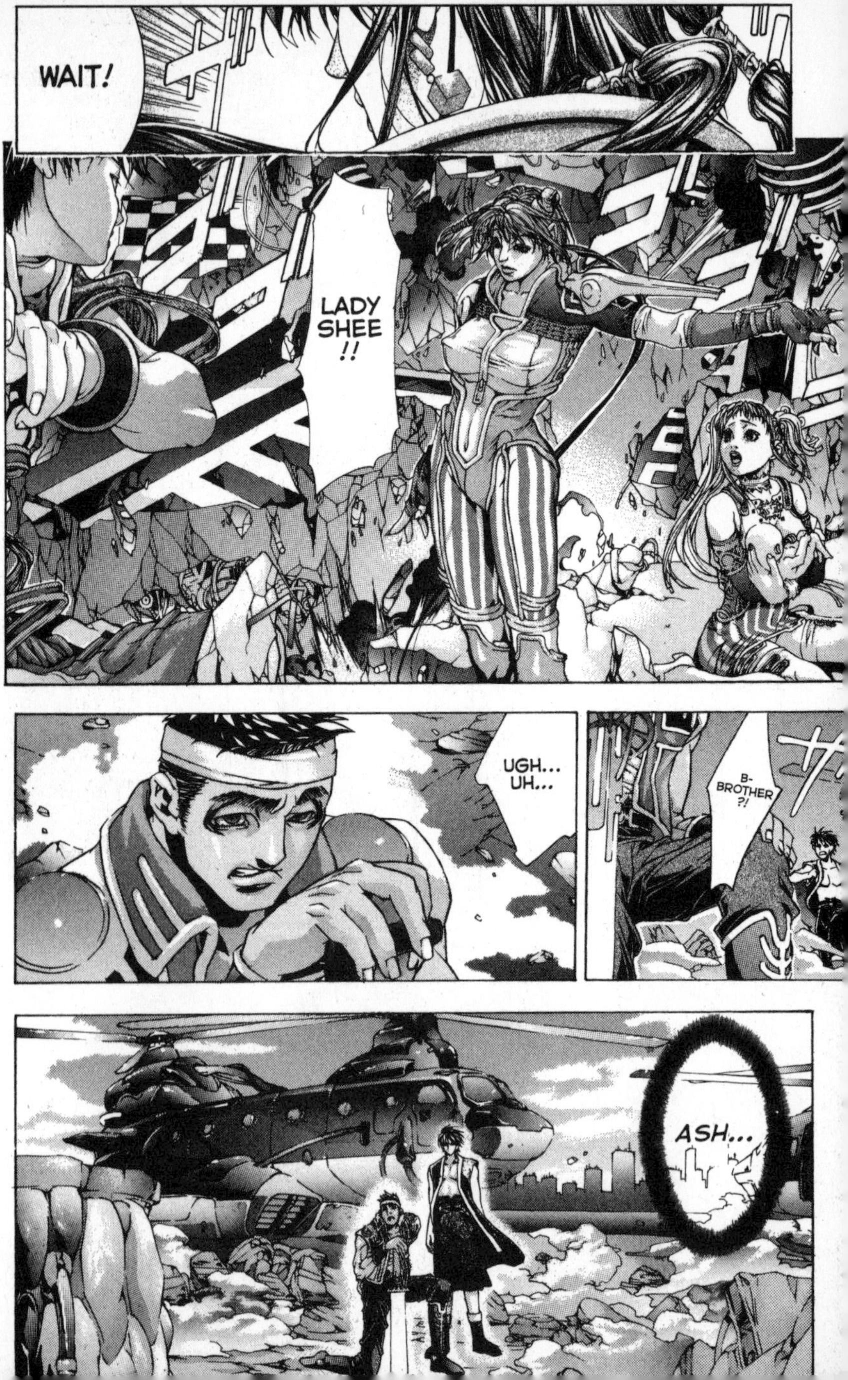
WAIT!
LADY SHEE !!
B-BROTHER ?!
UGH... UH...
ASH...

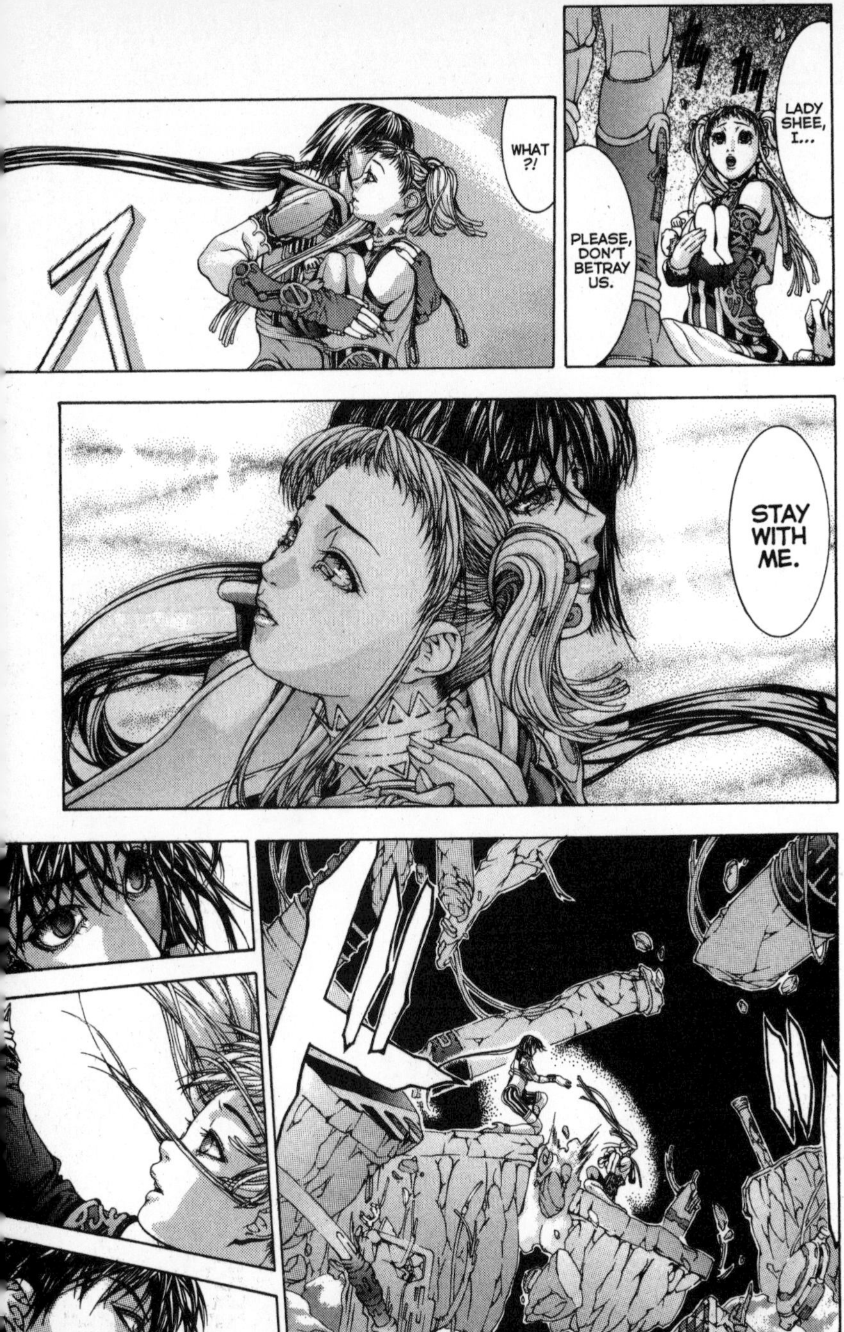
LADY SHEE, I...
PLEASE, DON'T BETRAY US.
WHAT ?!
STAY WITH ME.

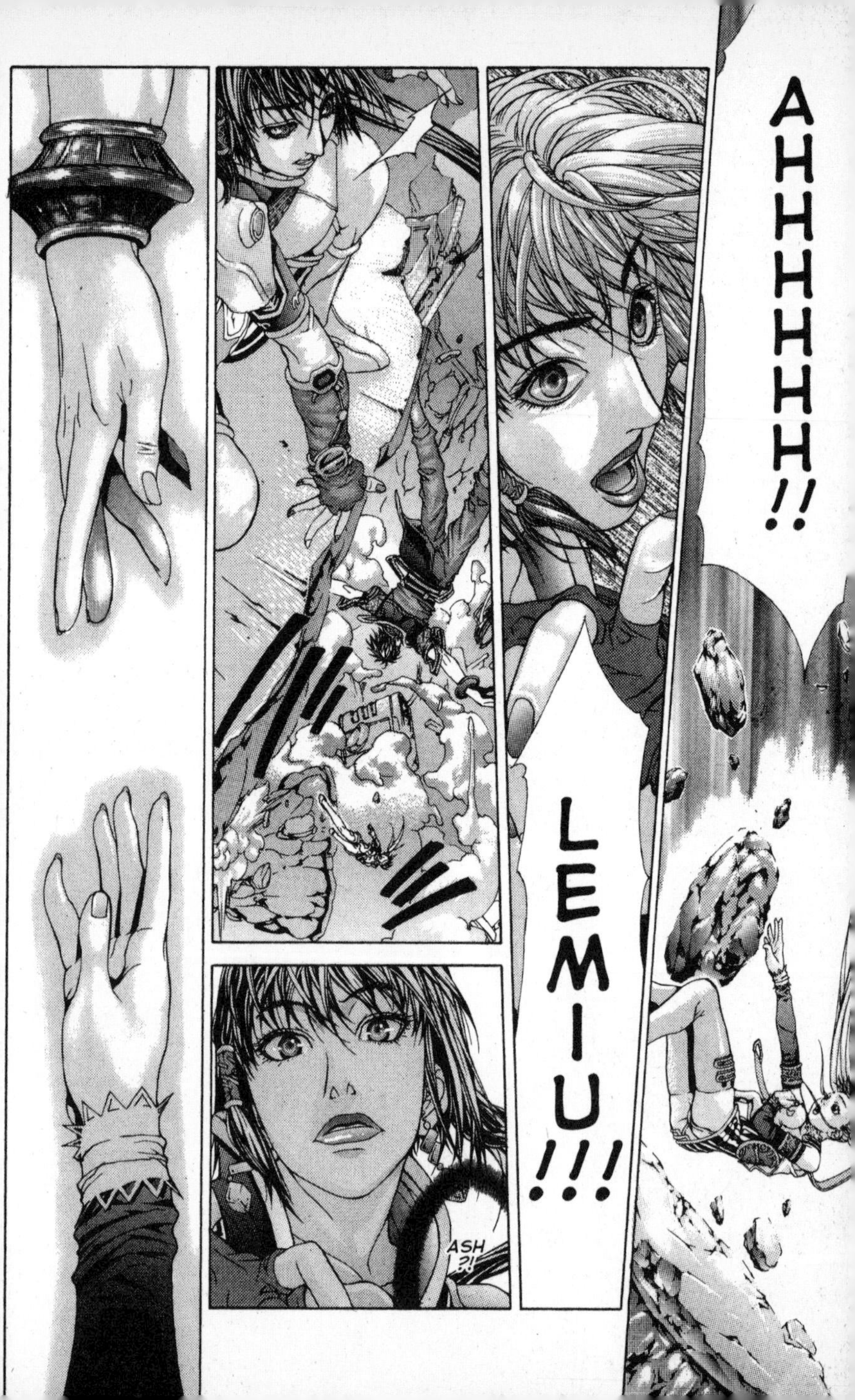
AHHHHHH!!
LEMIU!!!!
ASH ?!

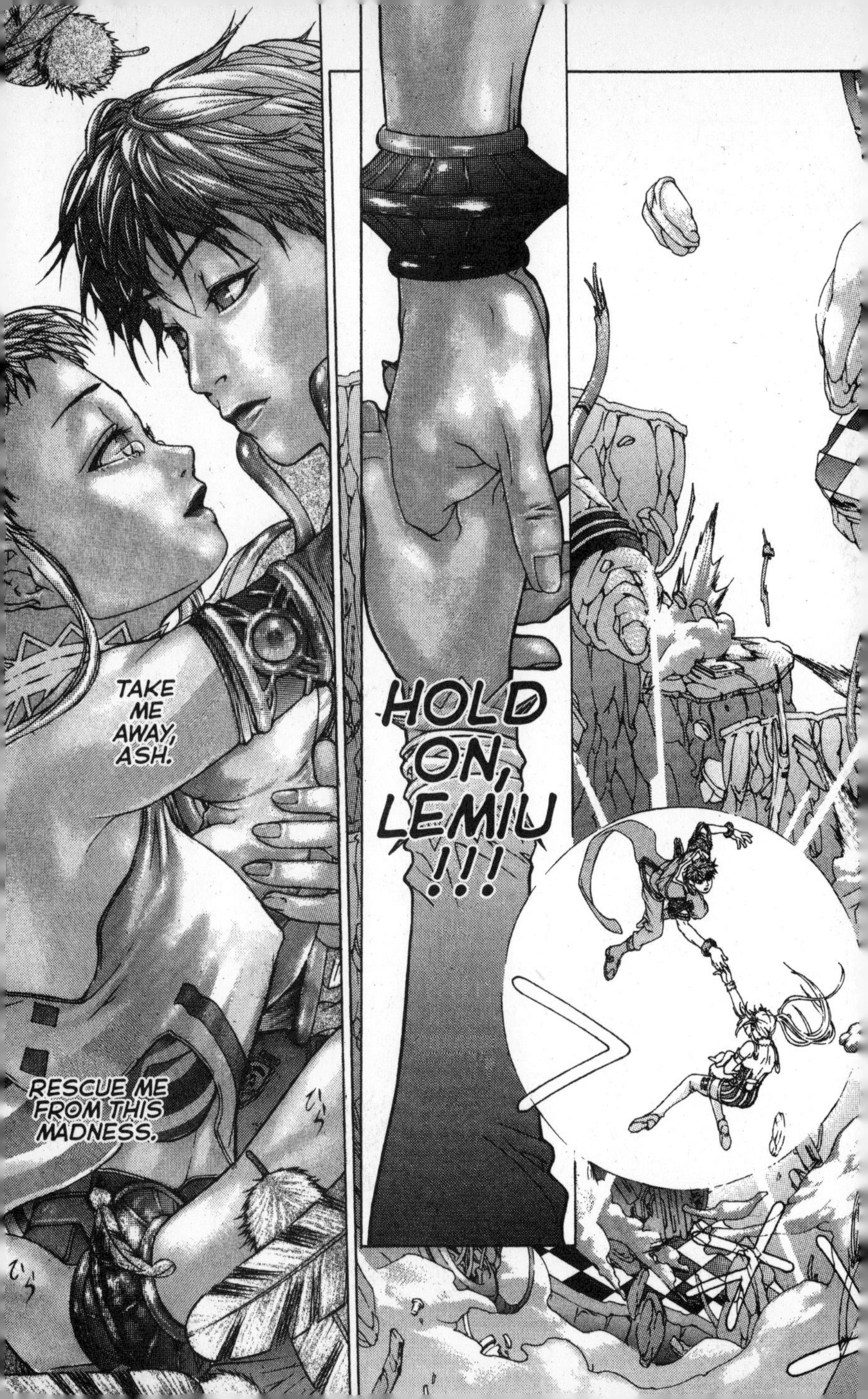
HOLD ON, LEMIU!!!
TAKE ME AWAY, ASH.
RESCUE ME FROM THIS MADNESS.

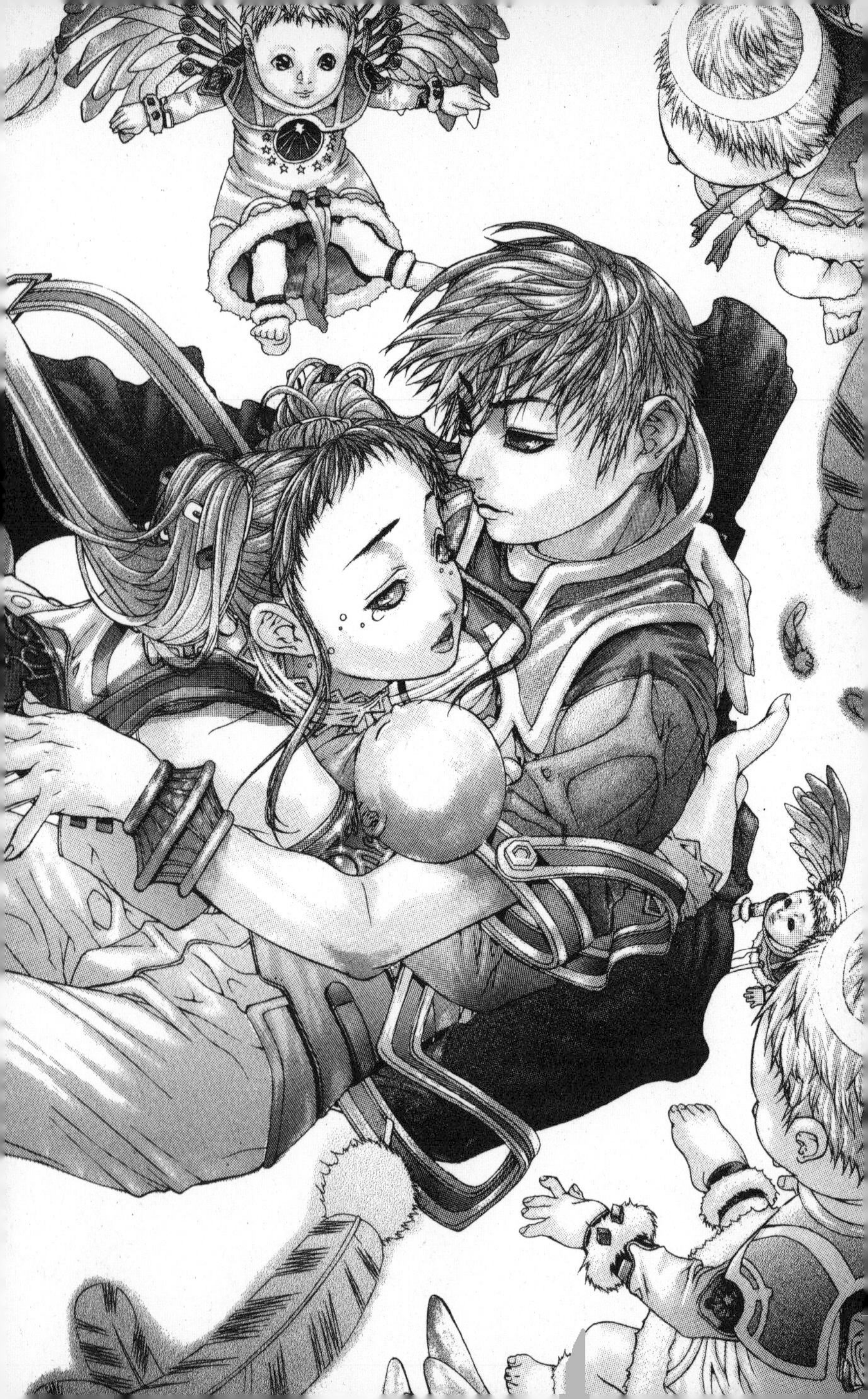

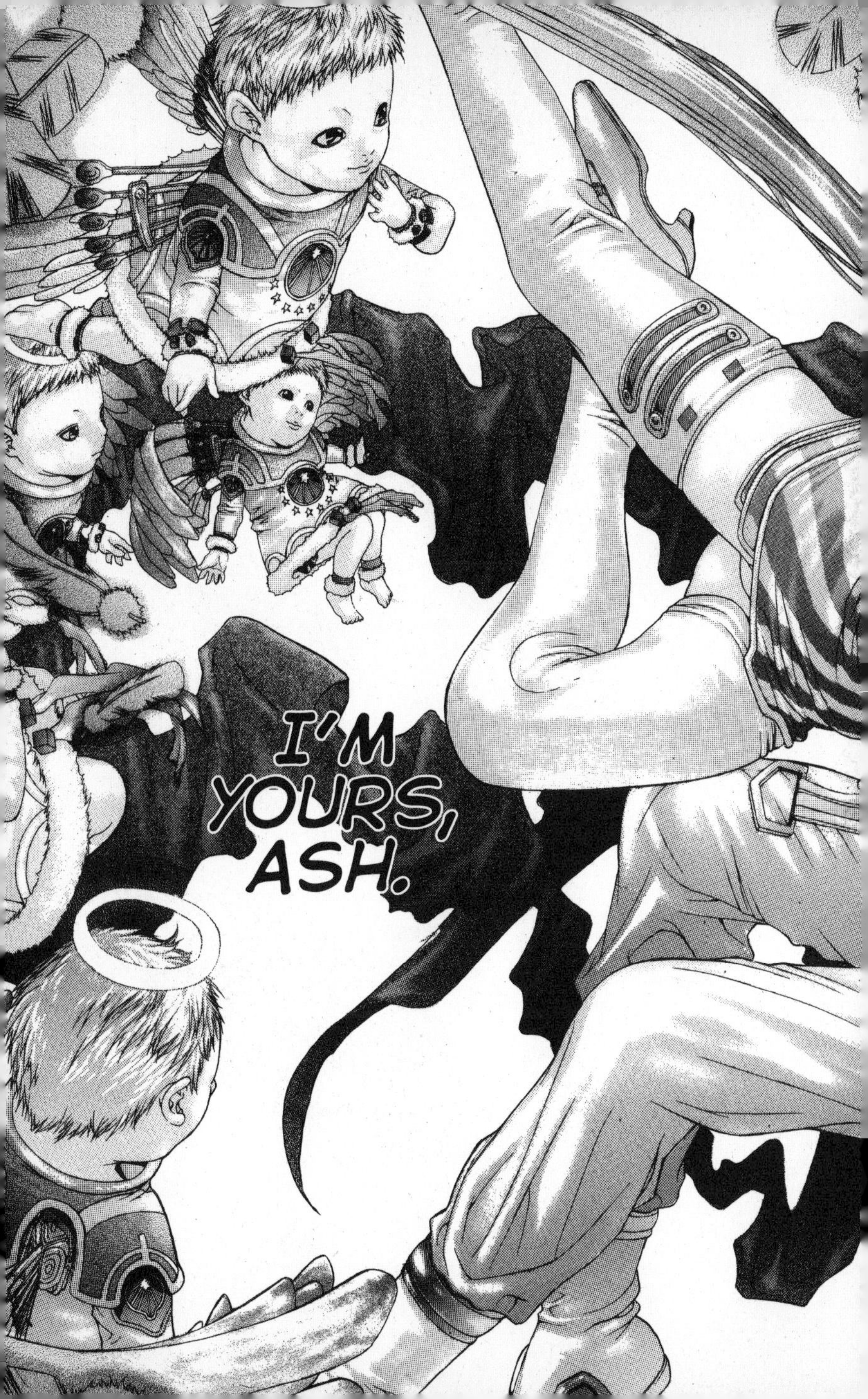
I'M YOURS, ASH.

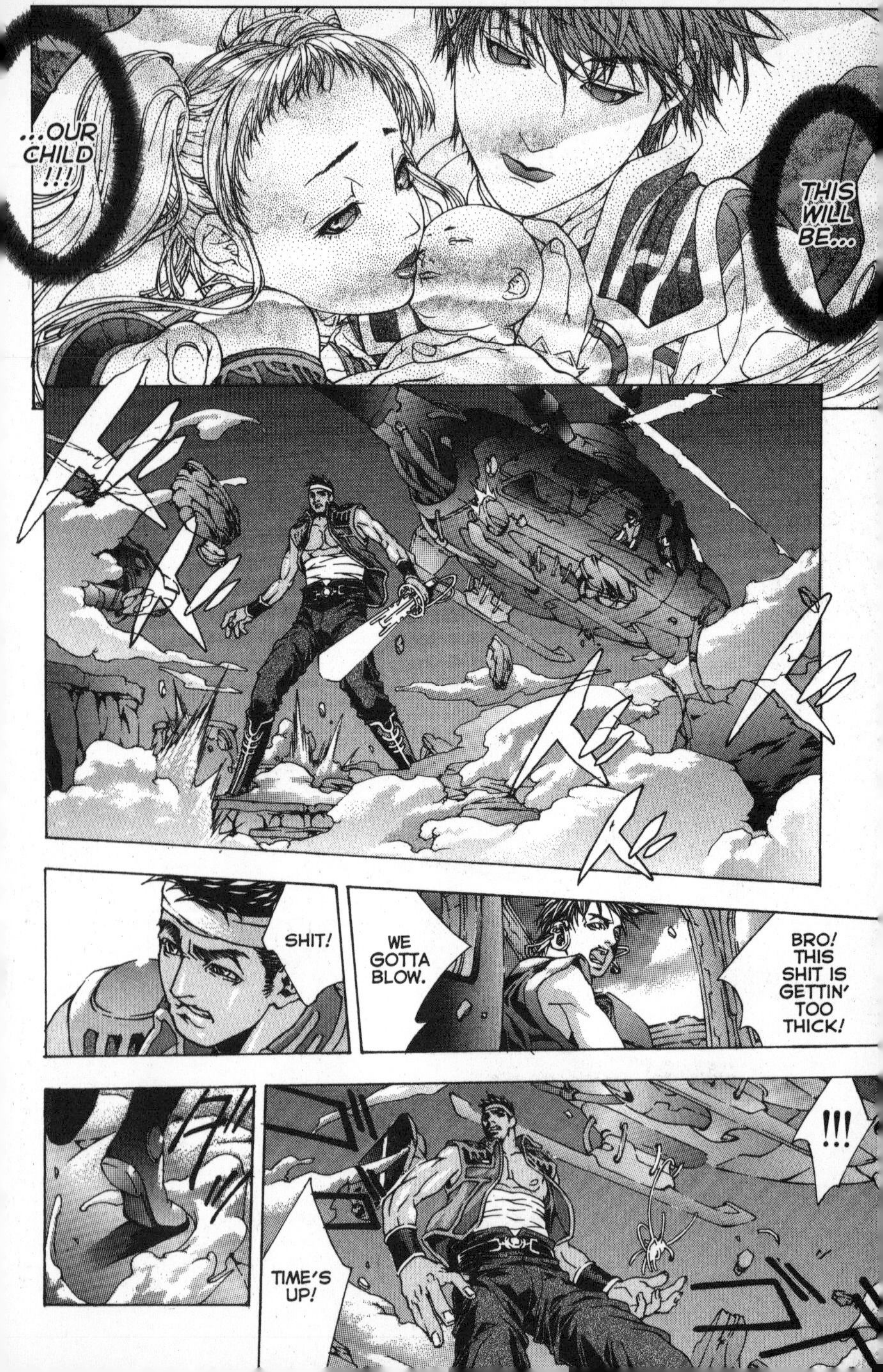
THIS WILL BE...
...OUR CHILD !!!
BRO! THIS SHIT IS GETTIN' TOO THICK!
WE GOTTA BLOW.
SHIT!
!!!
TIME'S UP!

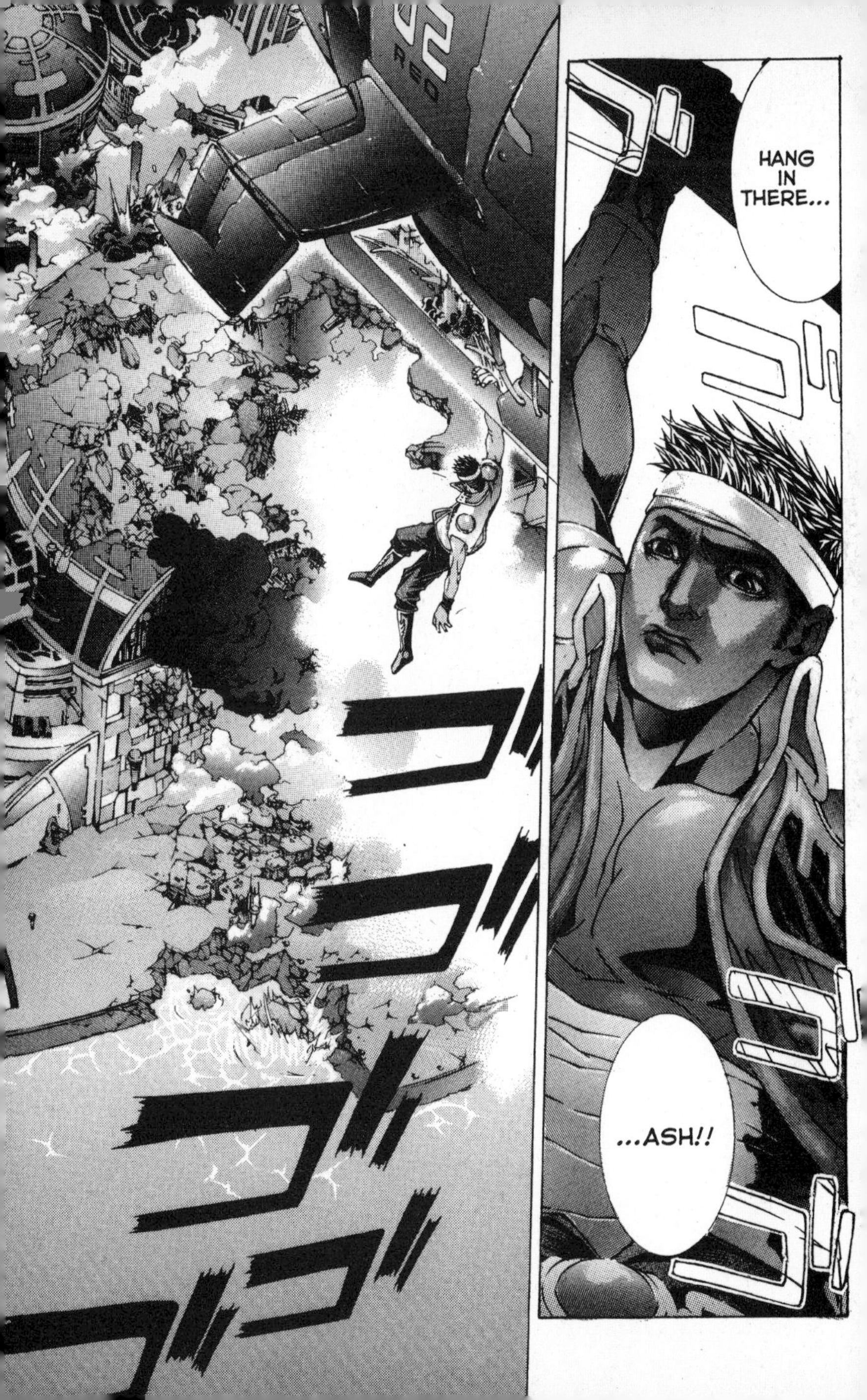
HANG IN THERE...
...ASH!!

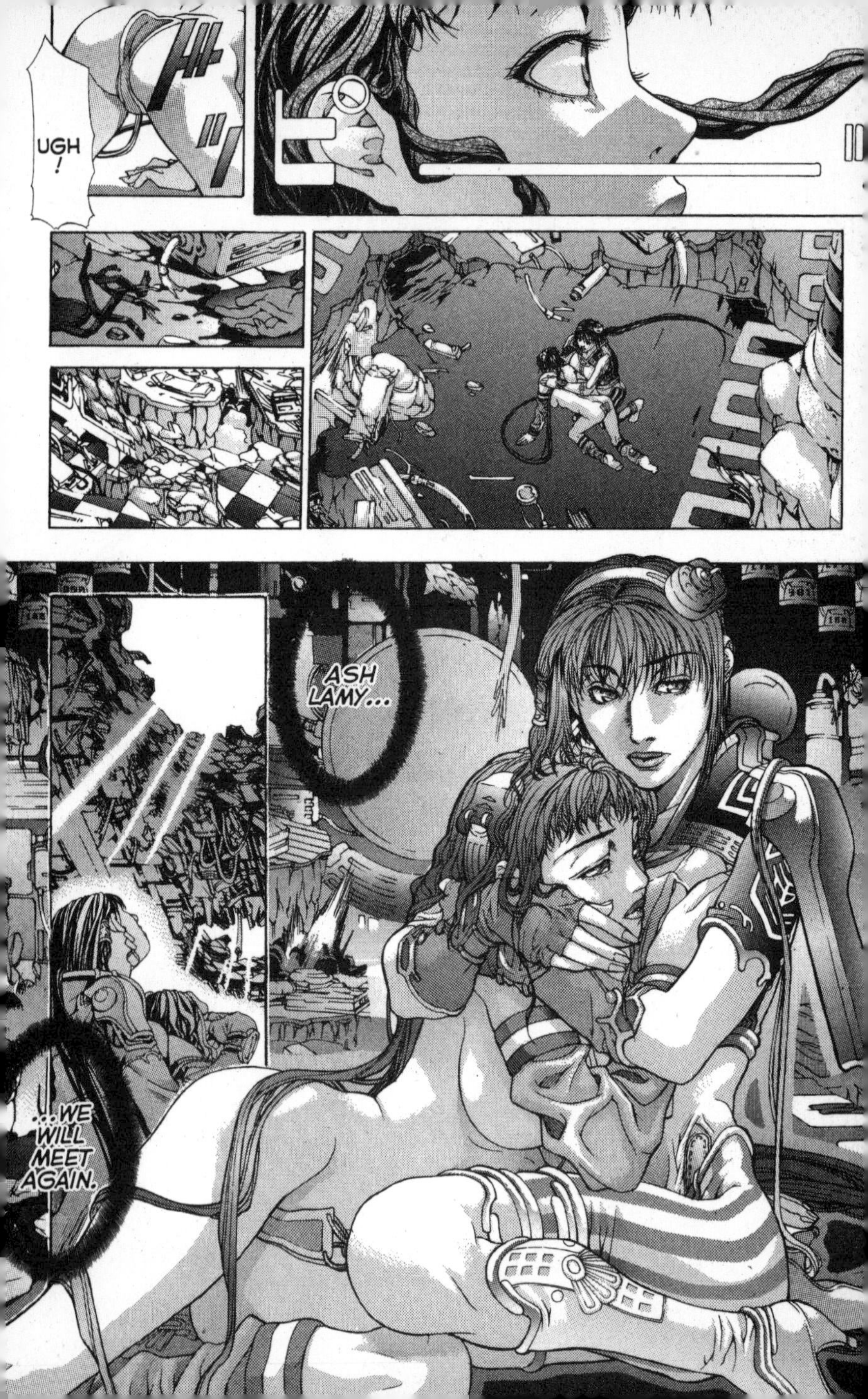
UGH!
ASH LAMY...
...WE WILL MEET AGAIN.

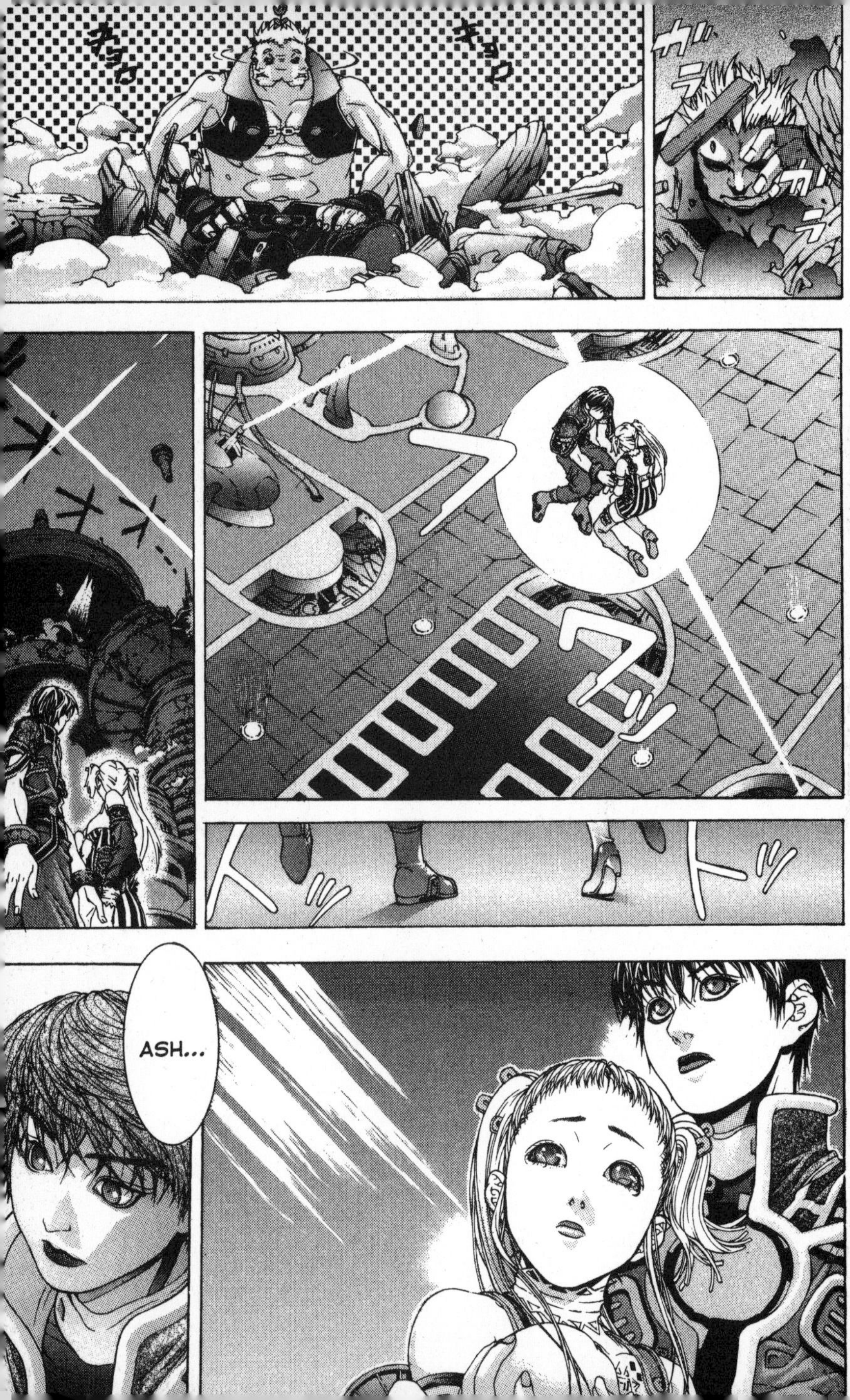
ASH...

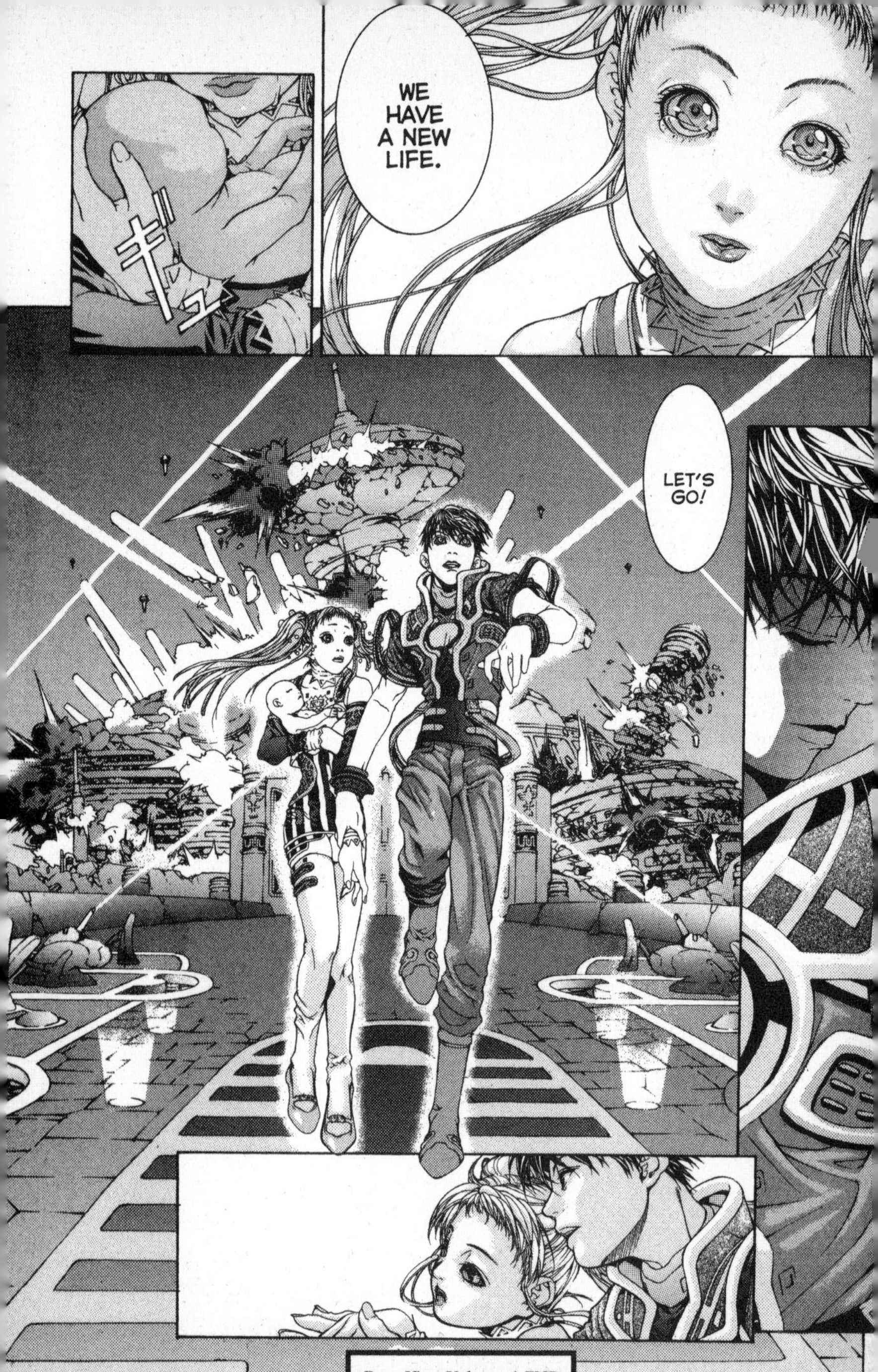
WE HAVE A NEW LIFE.
ギュ
LET'S GO!

Deus Vitae Volume 1 END

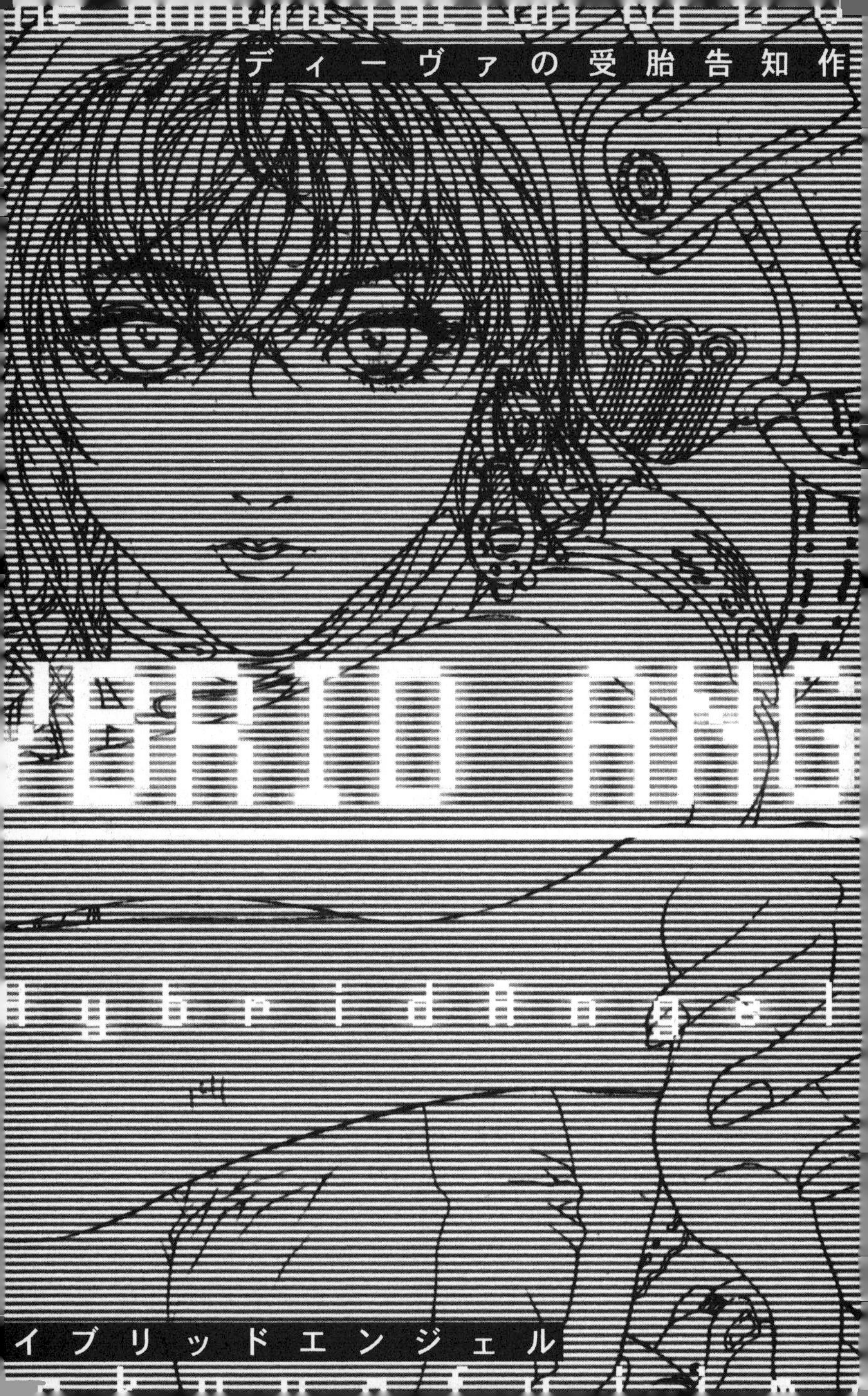
ディーヴァの受胎告知作
イブリッドエンジェル

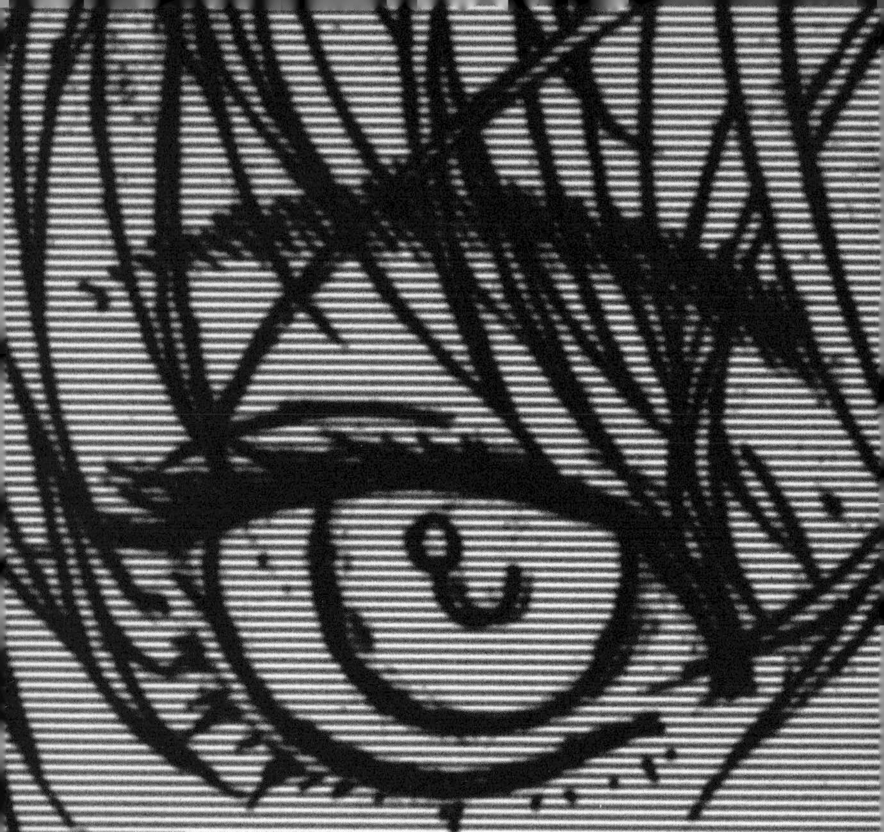

Deus Vitae: Prologue

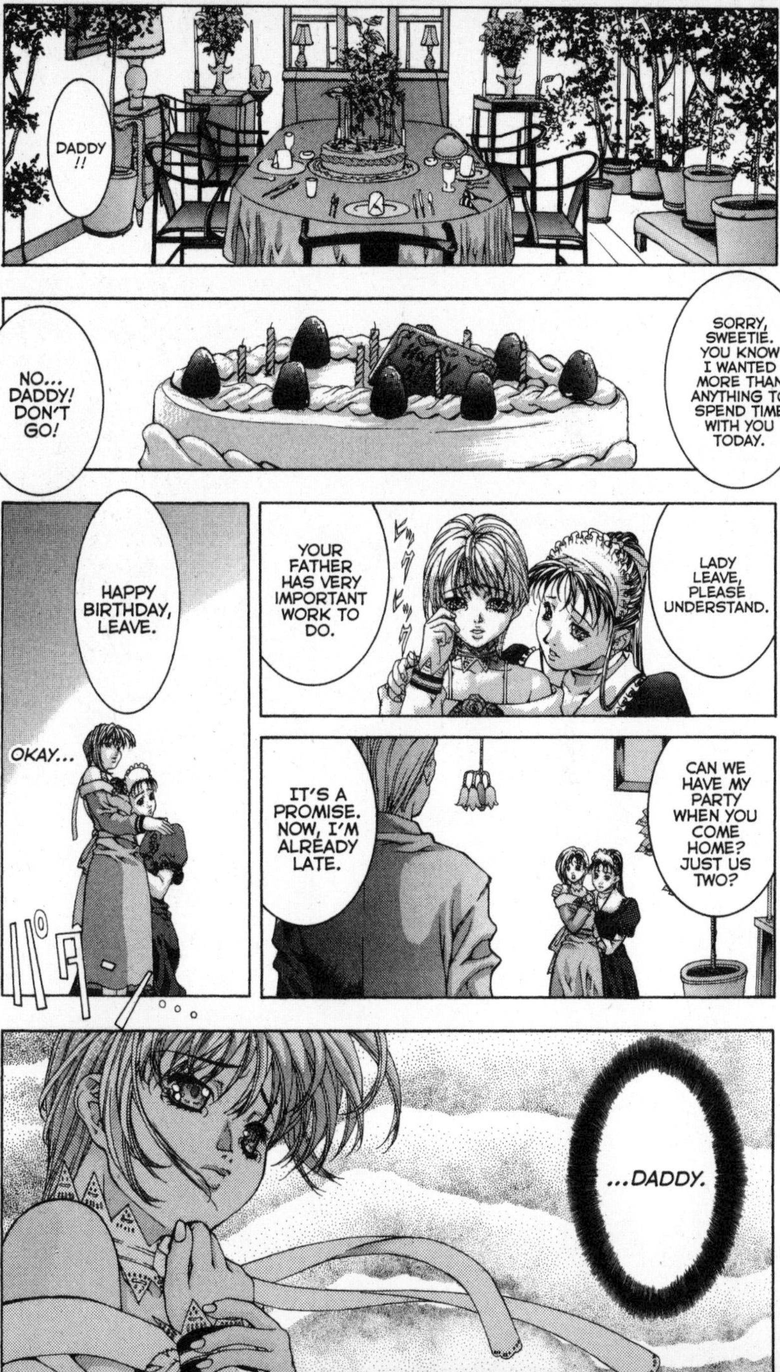
DADDY !!
SORRY, SWEETIE. YOU KNOW I WANTED MORE THAN ANYTHING TO SPEND TIME WITH YOU TODAY.
NO... DADDY! DON'T GO!
LADY LEAVE, PLEASE UNDERSTAND.
YOUR FATHER HAS VERY IMPORTANT WORK TO DO.
CAN WE HAVE MY PARTY WHEN YOU COME HOME? JUST US TWO?
IT'S A PROMISE. NOW, I'M ALREADY LATE.
HAPPY BIRTHDAY, LEAVE.
OKAY...
...DADDY.

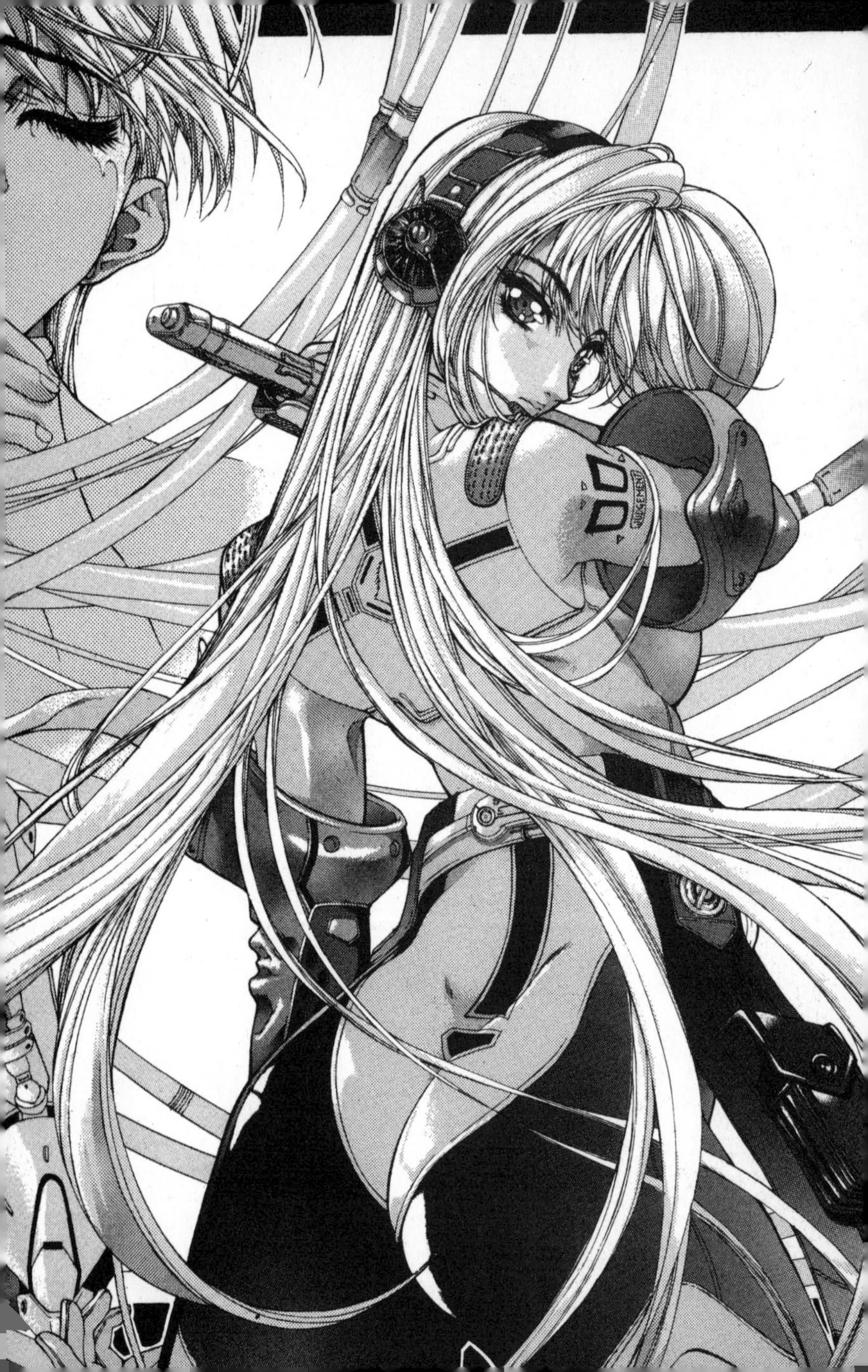
JUDGEMENT

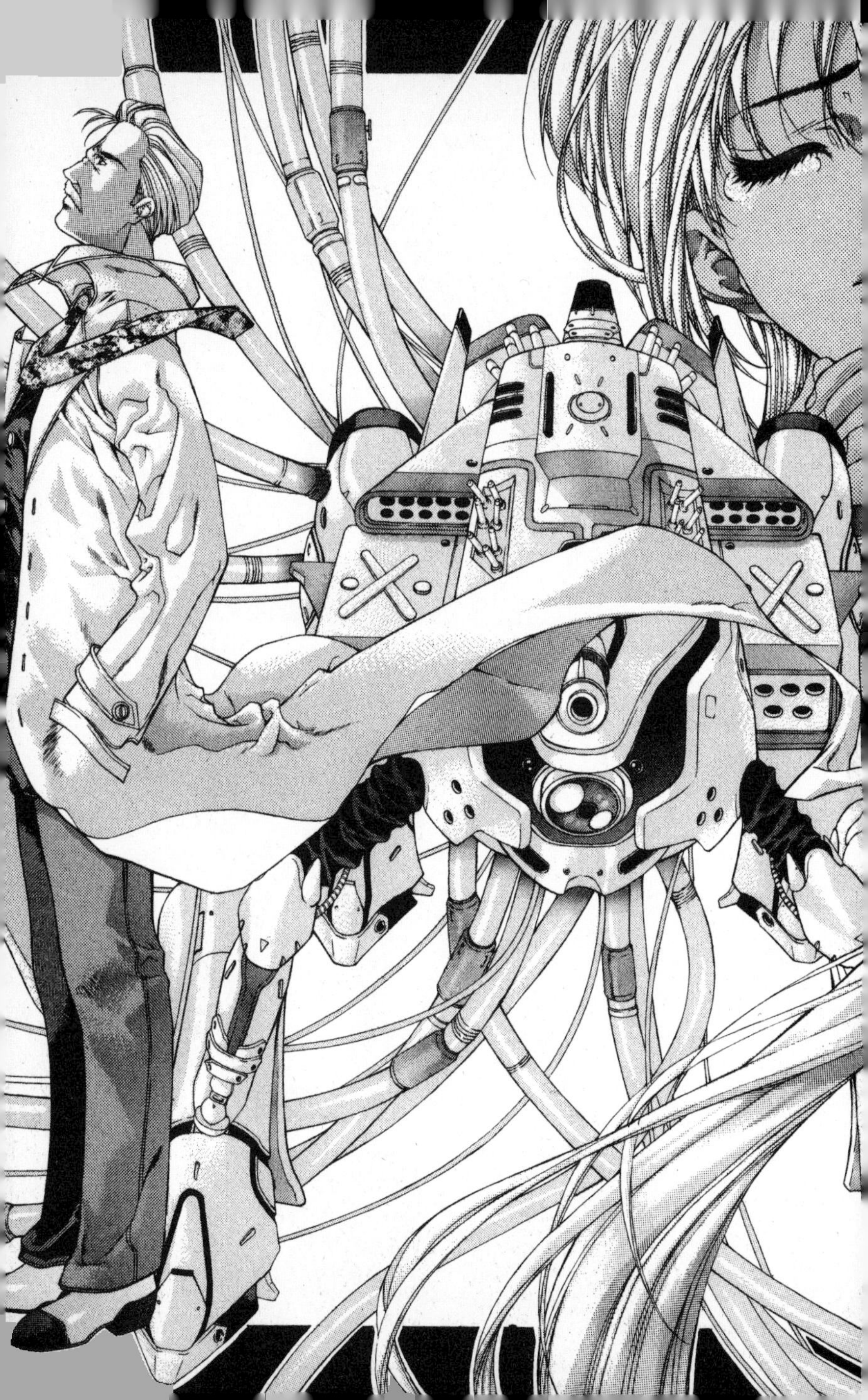

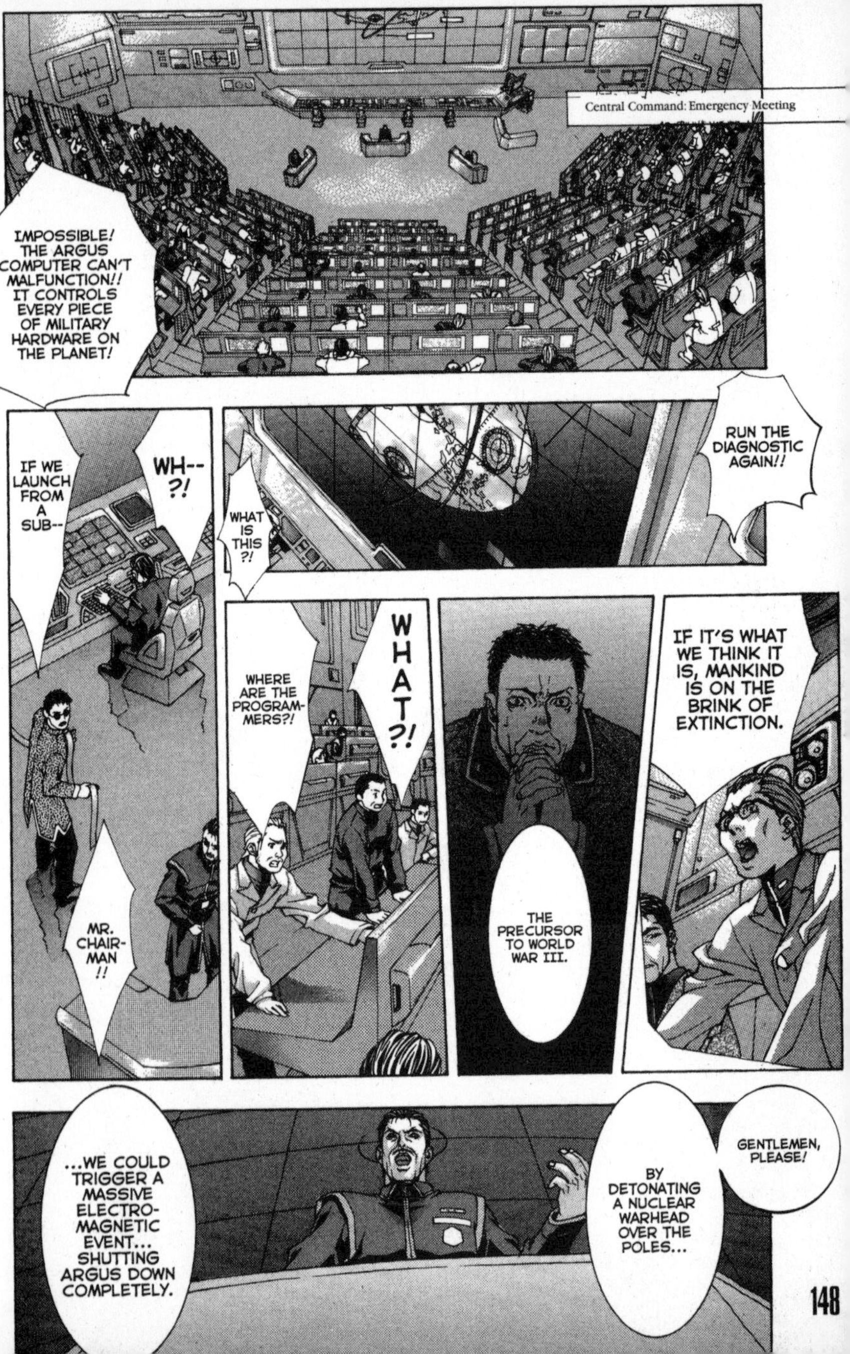
Central Command: Emergency Meeting
IMPOSSIBLE! THE ARGUS COMPUTER CAN'T MALFUNCTION!! IT CONTROLS EVERY PIECE OF MILITARY HARDWARE ON THE PLANET!
RUN THE DIAGNOSTIC AGAIN!!
WHAT IS THIS?!
IF IT'S WHAT WE THINK IT IS, MANKIND IS ON THE BRINK OF EXTINCTION.
THE PRECURSOR TO WORLD WAR III.
WHAT?!
WHERE ARE THE PROGRAM-MERS?!
WH--?!
IF WE LAUNCH FROM A SUB--
MR. CHAIR-MAN!!
GENTLEMEN, PLEASE!
BY DETONATING A NUCLEAR WARHEAD OVER THE POLES...
...WE COULD TRIGGER A MASSIVE ELECTRO-MAGNETIC EVENT... SHUTTING ARGUS DOWN COMPLETELY.

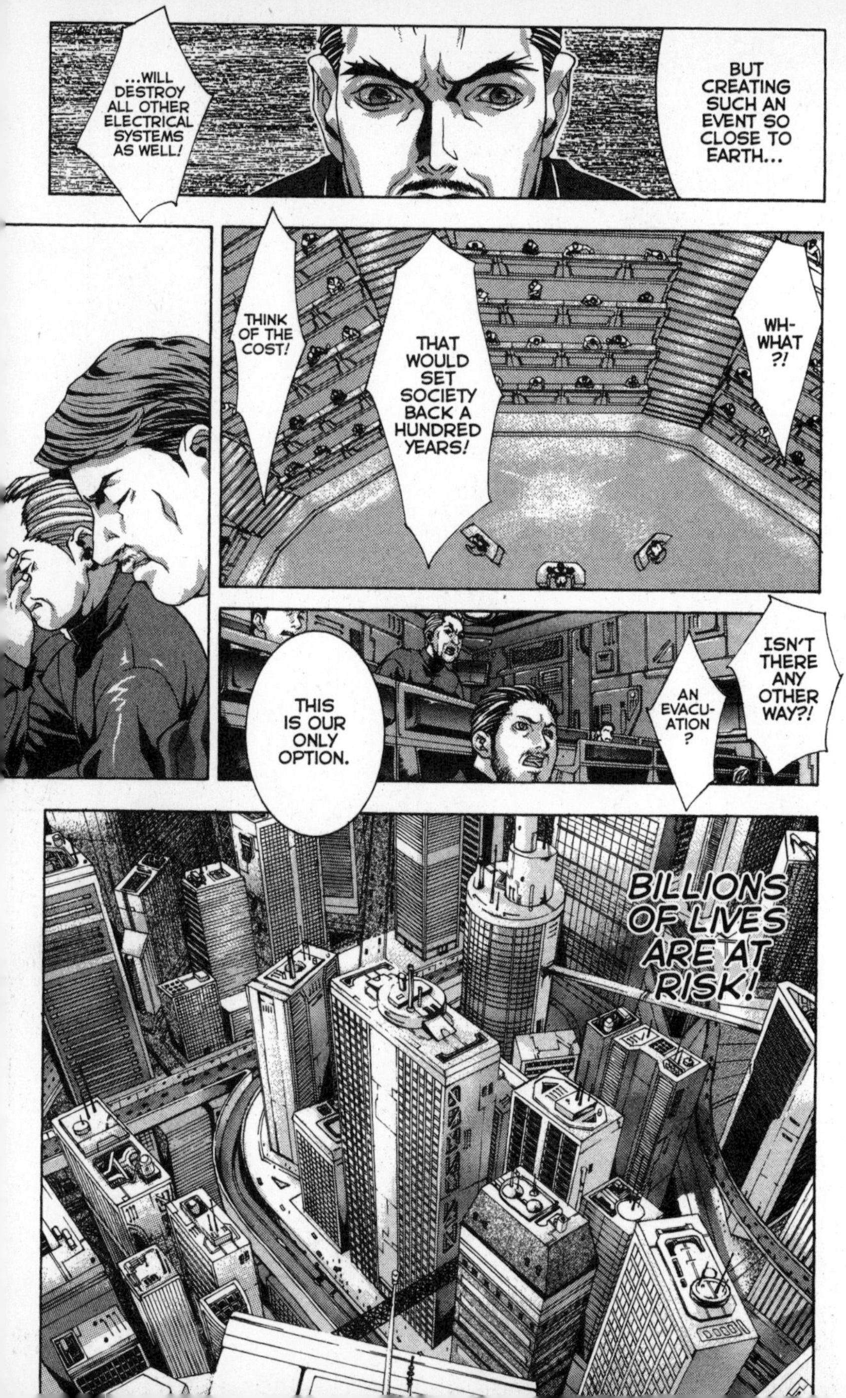
BUT CREATING SUCH AN EVENT SO CLOSE TO EARTH...
...WILL DESTROY ALL OTHER ELECTRICAL SYSTEMS AS WELL!
WH-WHAT?!
THAT WOULD SET SOCIETY BACK A HUNDRED YEARS!
THINK OF THE COST!
ISN'T THERE ANY OTHER WAY?!
AN EVACUATION?
THIS IS OUR ONLY OPTION.
BILLIONS OF LIVES ARE AT RISK!

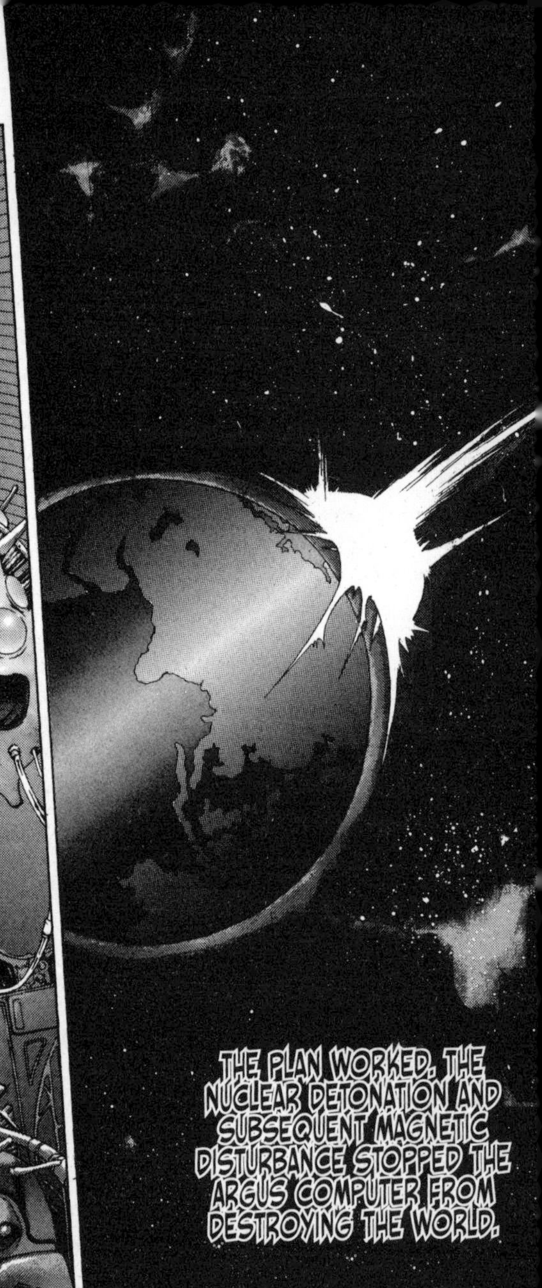
THE PLAN WORKED. THE NUCLEAR DETONATION AND SUBSEQUENT MAGNETIC DISTURBANCE STOPPED THE ARGUS COMPUTER FROM DESTROYING THE WORLD.

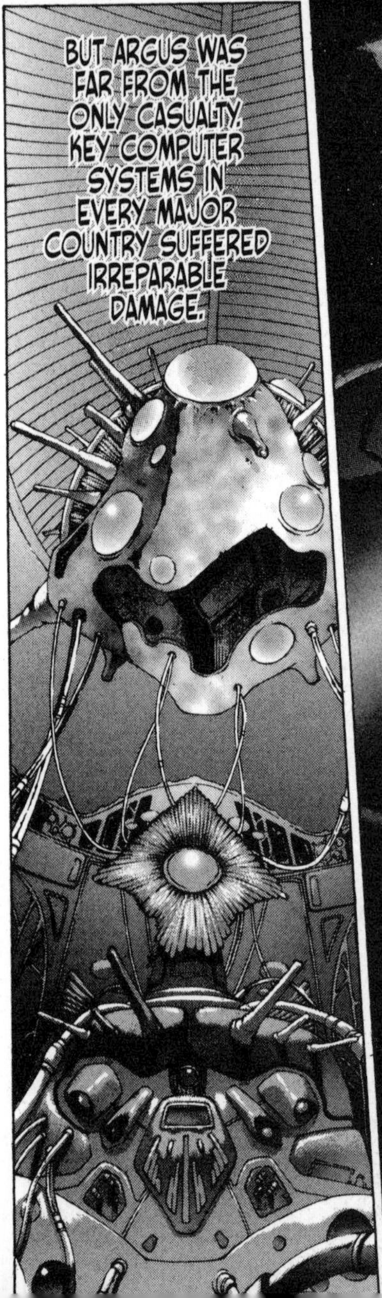
BUT ARGUS WAS FAR FROM THE ONLY CASUALTY. KEY COMPUTER SYSTEMS IN EVERY MAJOR COUNTRY SUFFERED IRREPARABLE DAMAGE.

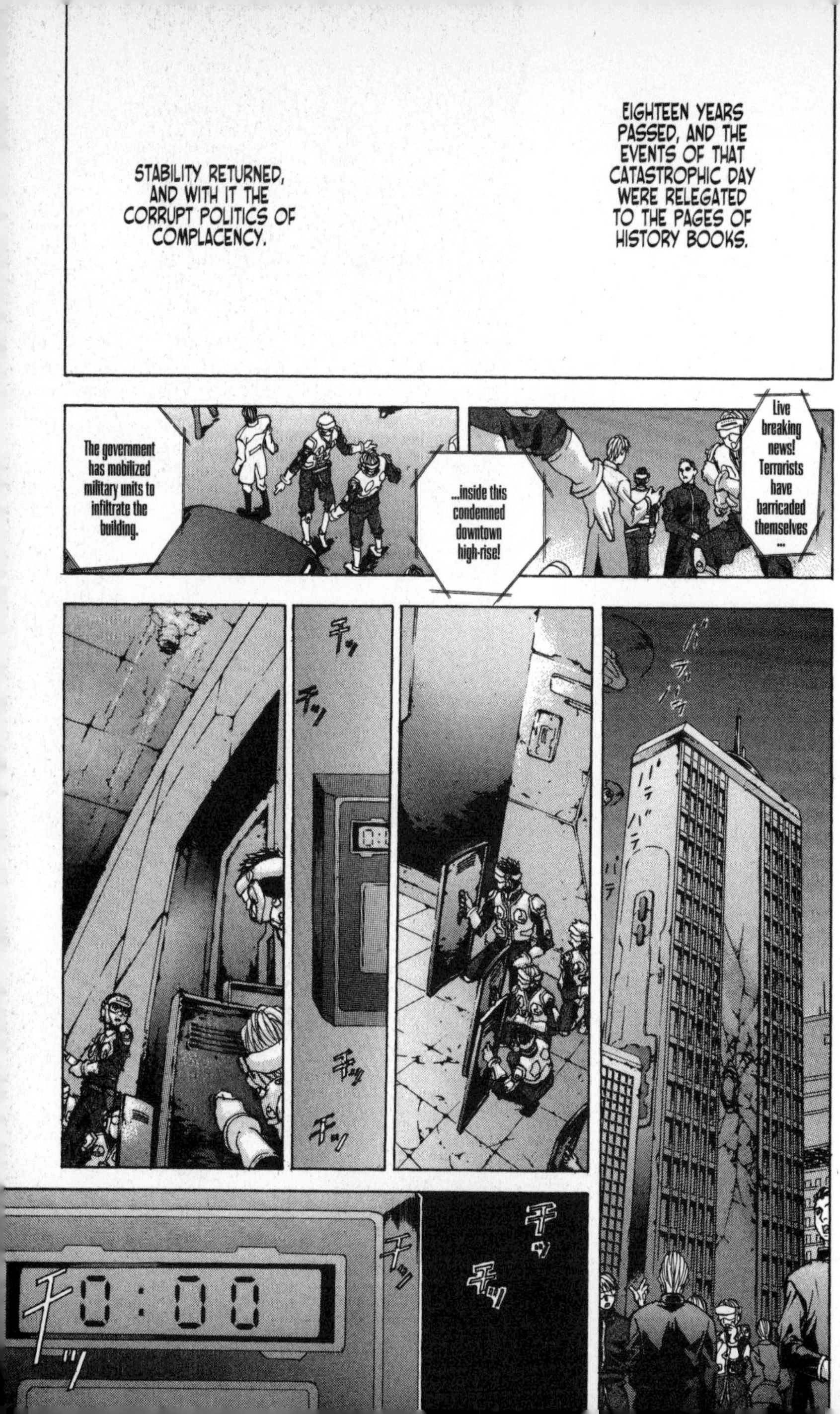
EIGHTEEN YEARS PASSED, AND THE EVENTS OF THAT CATASTROPHIC DAY WERE RELEGATED TO THE PAGES OF HISTORY BOOKS.
STABILITY RETURNED, AND WITH IT THE CORRUPT POLITICS OF COMPLACENCY.
Live breaking news! Terrorists have barricaded themselves...
...inside this condemned downtown high-rise!
The government has mobilized military units to infiltrate the building.
0:00

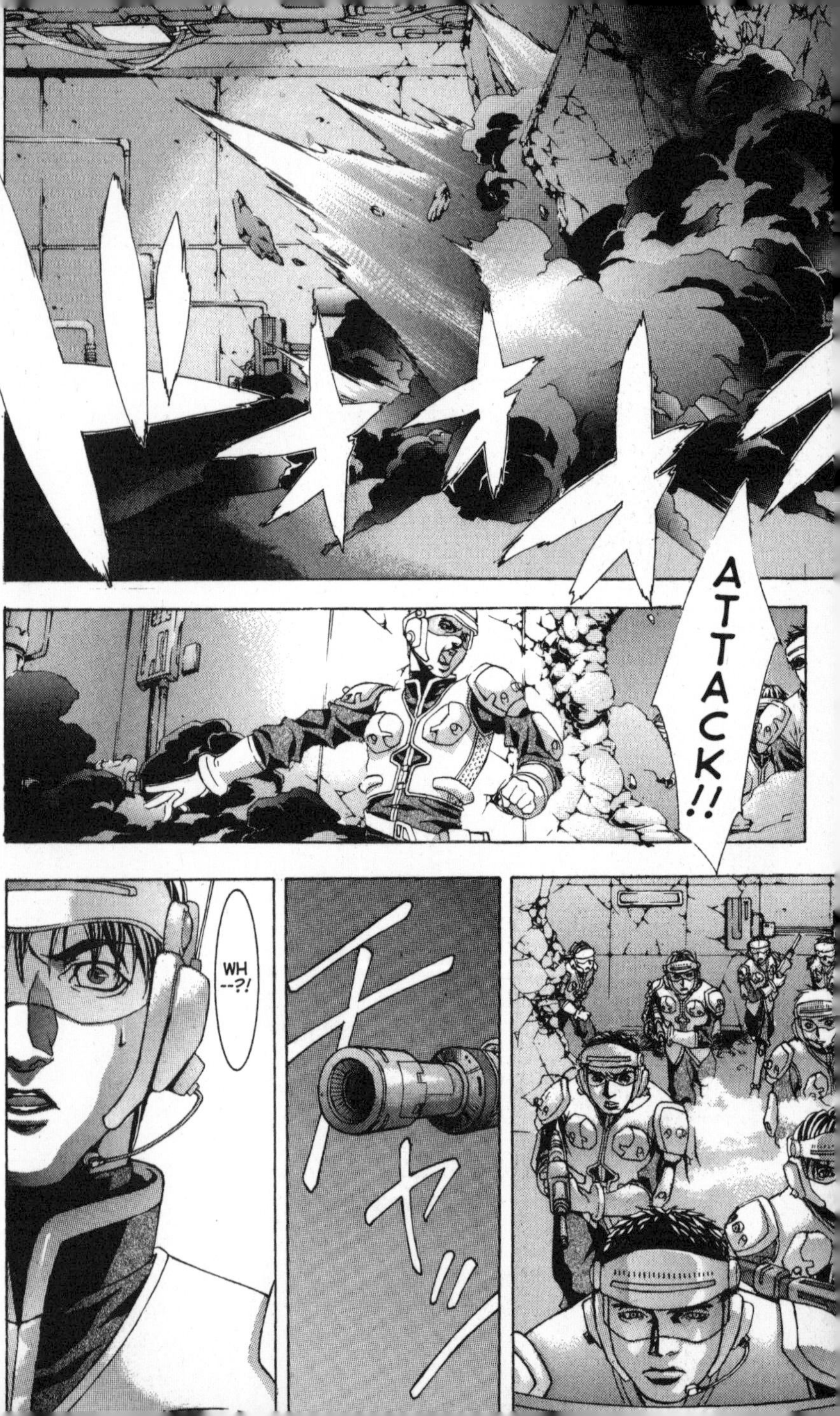
ATTACK!!
WH --?!

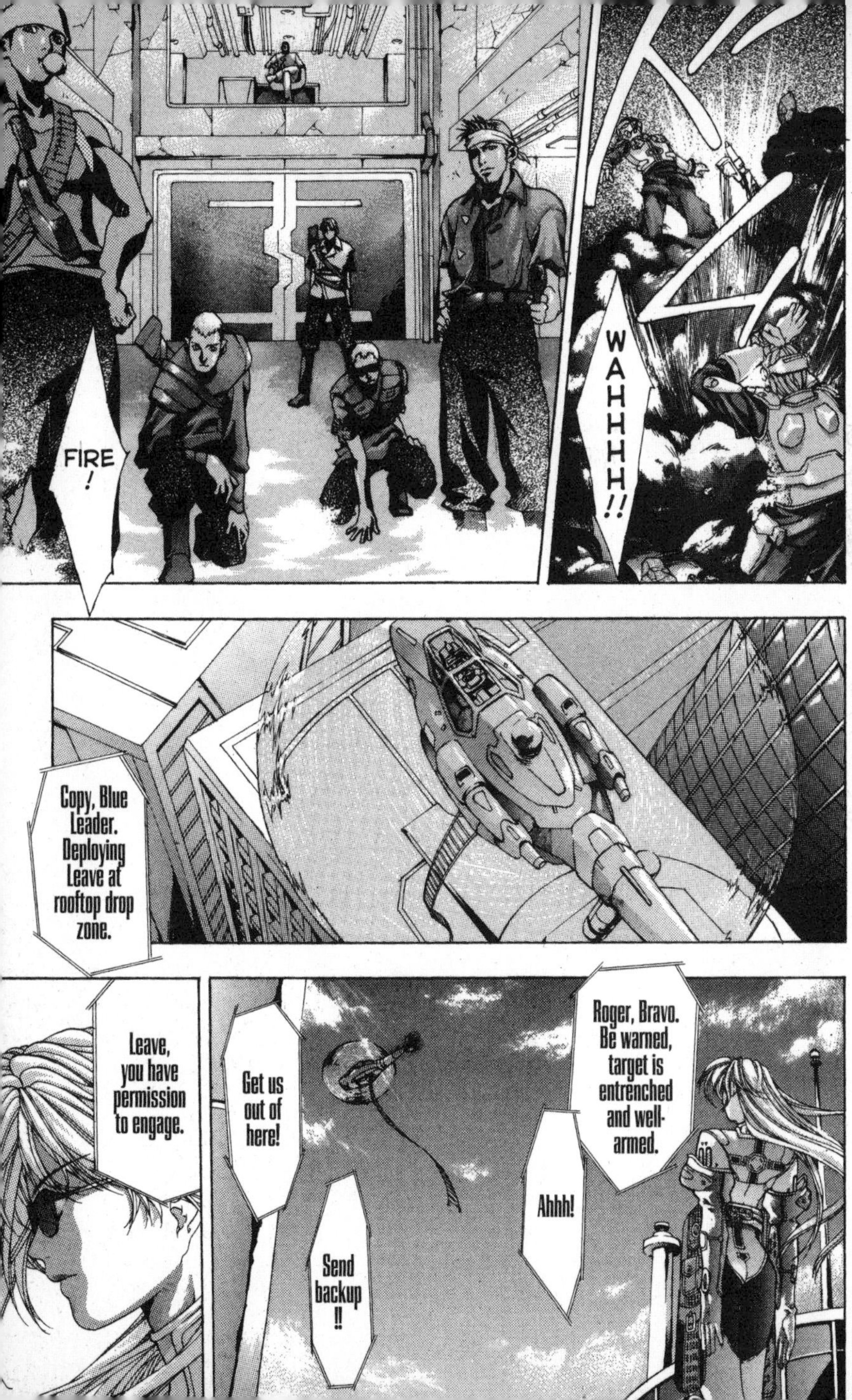
WAHHHH!!
FIRE!
Copy, Blue Leader. Deploying Leave at rooftop drop zone.
Roger, Bravo. Be warned, target is entrenched and well-armed.
Ahhh!
Get us out of here!
Send backup!!
Leave, you have permission to engage.

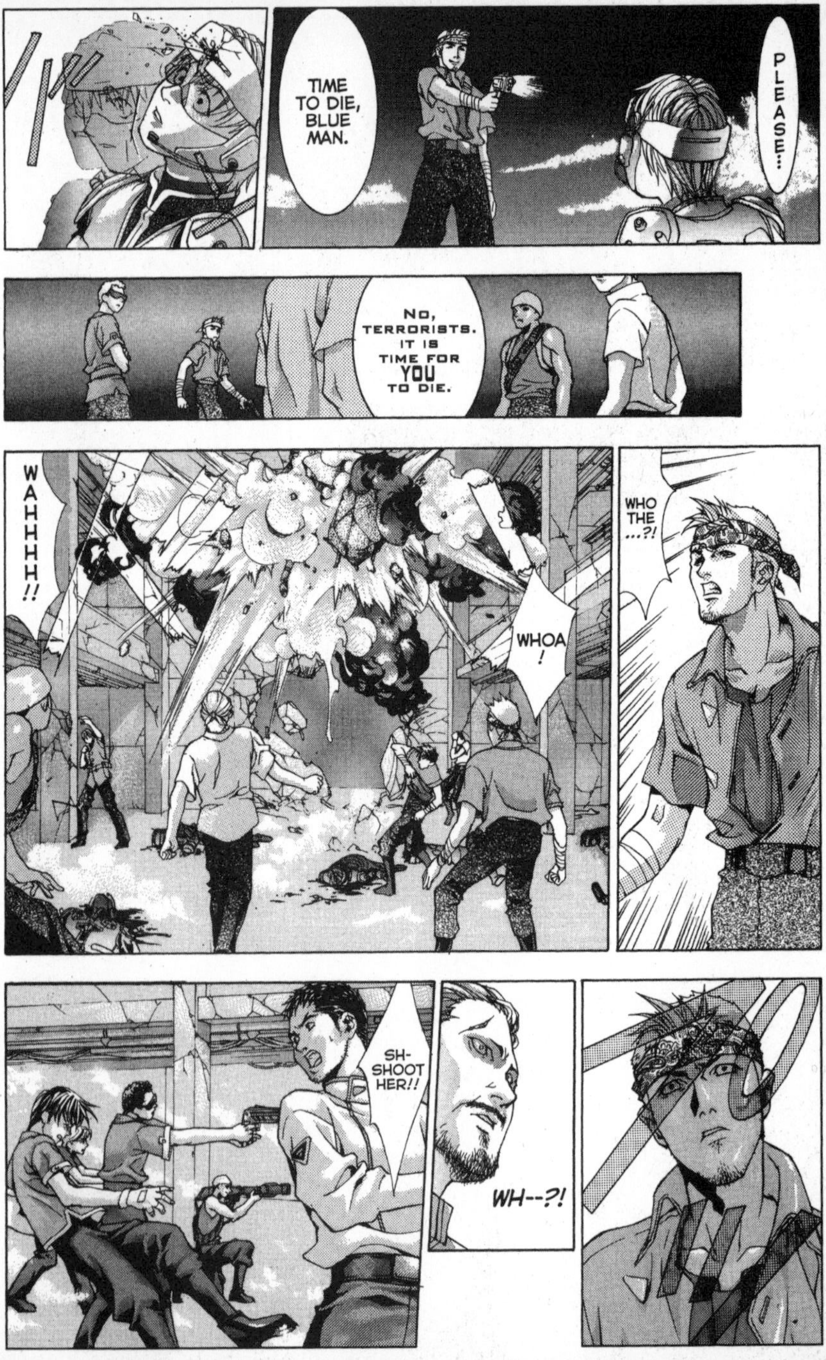
PLEASE...
TIME TO DIE, BLUE MAN.
No, TERRORISTS. IT IS TIME FOR YOU TO DIE.
WHO THE ...?!
WHOA!
WAHHHHH!!
WH--?!
SH-SHOOT HER!!

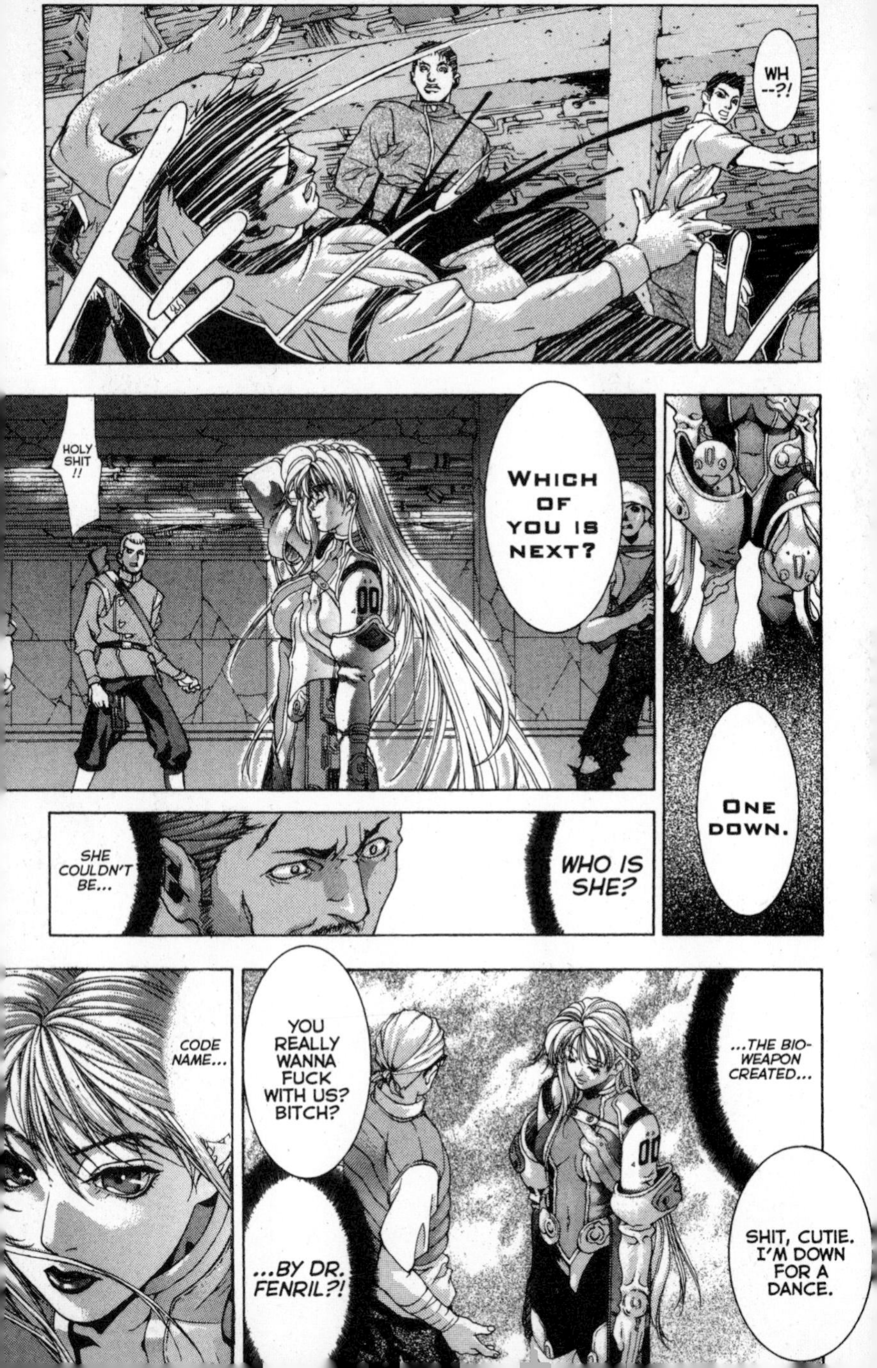
WH --?!
ONE DOWN.
WHICH OF YOU IS NEXT?
HOLY SHIT !!
WHO IS SHE?
SHE COULDN'T BE...
...THE BIO-WEAPON CREATED...
YOU REALLY WANNA FUCK WITH US? BITCH?
SHIT, CUTIE. I'M DOWN FOR A DANCE.
...BY DR. FENRIL?!
CODE NAME...

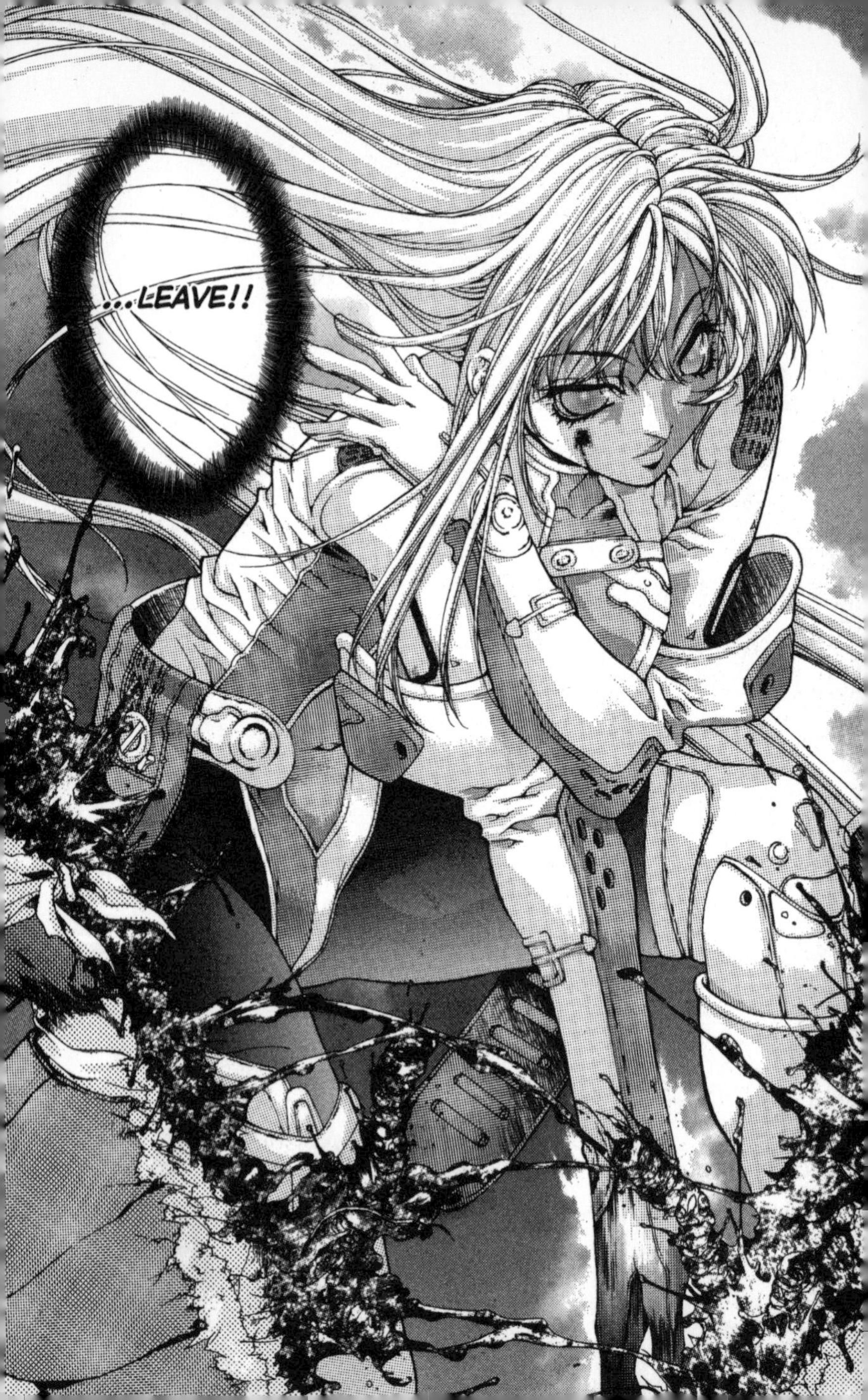
...LEAVE!!

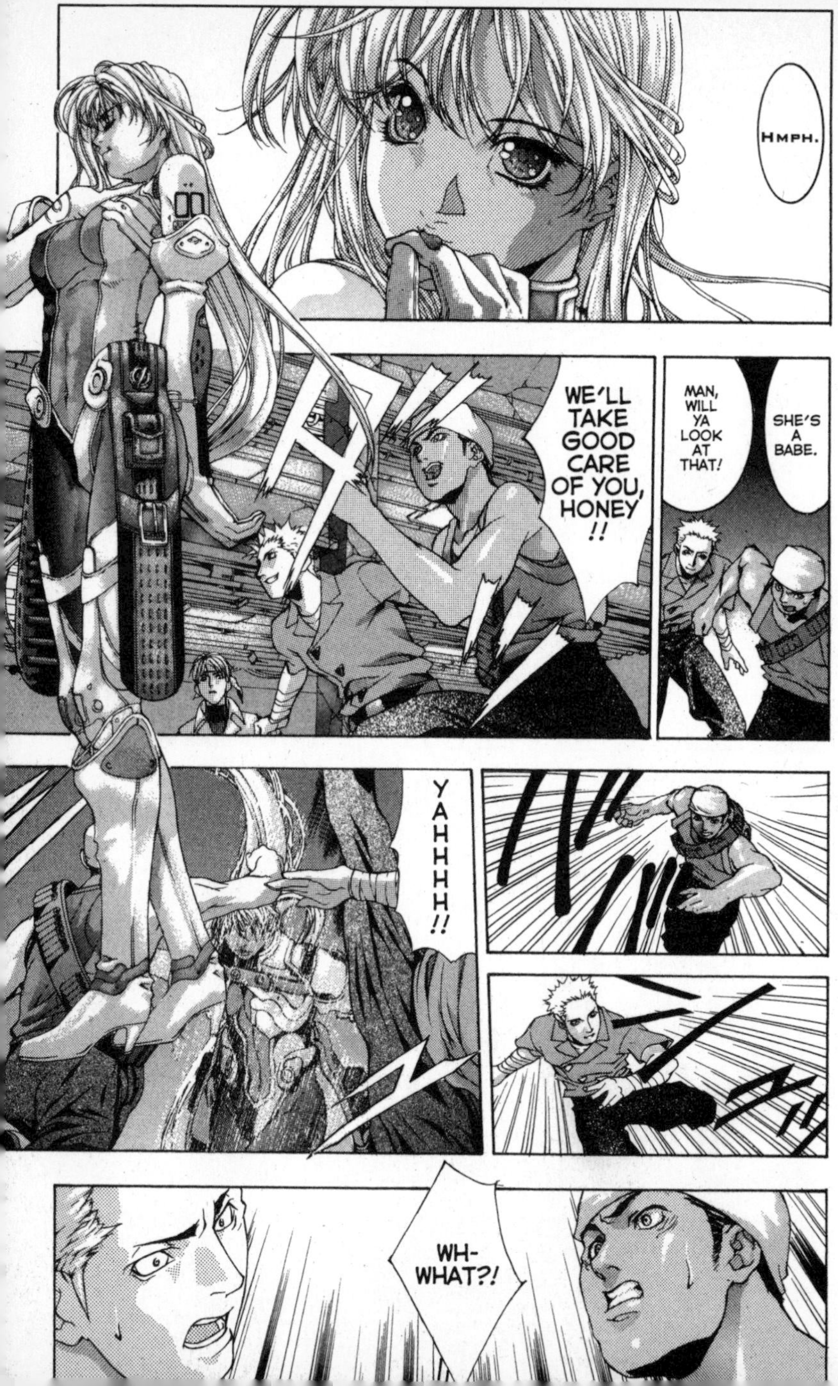

HMPH.
SHE'S A BABE.
MAN, WILL YA LOOK AT THAT!
WE'LL TAKE GOOD CARE OF YOU, HONEY!!
YAHHHH!!
WH- WHAT?!

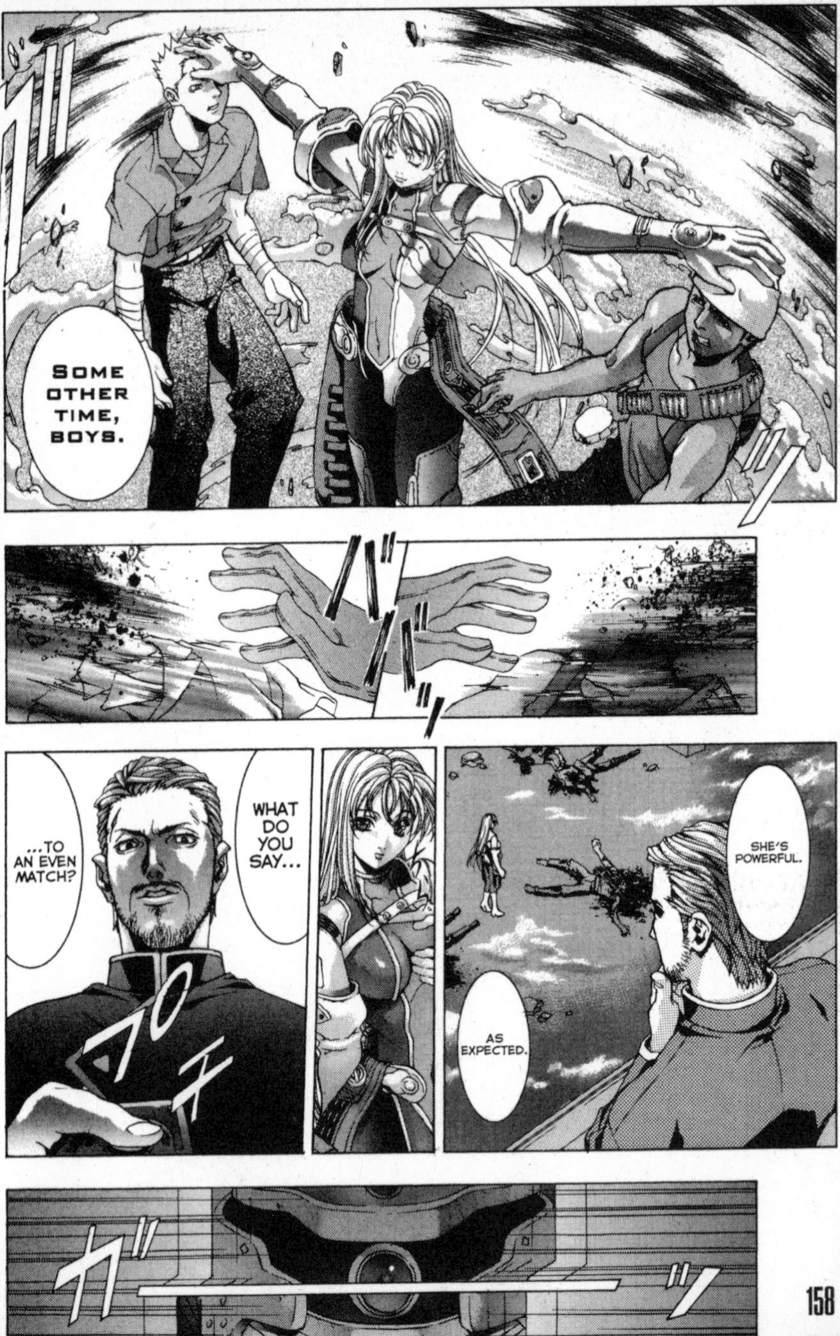
SOME OTHER TIME, BOYS.
SHE'S POWERFUL.
AS EXPECTED.
WHAT DO YOU SAY...
...TO AN EVEN MATCH?

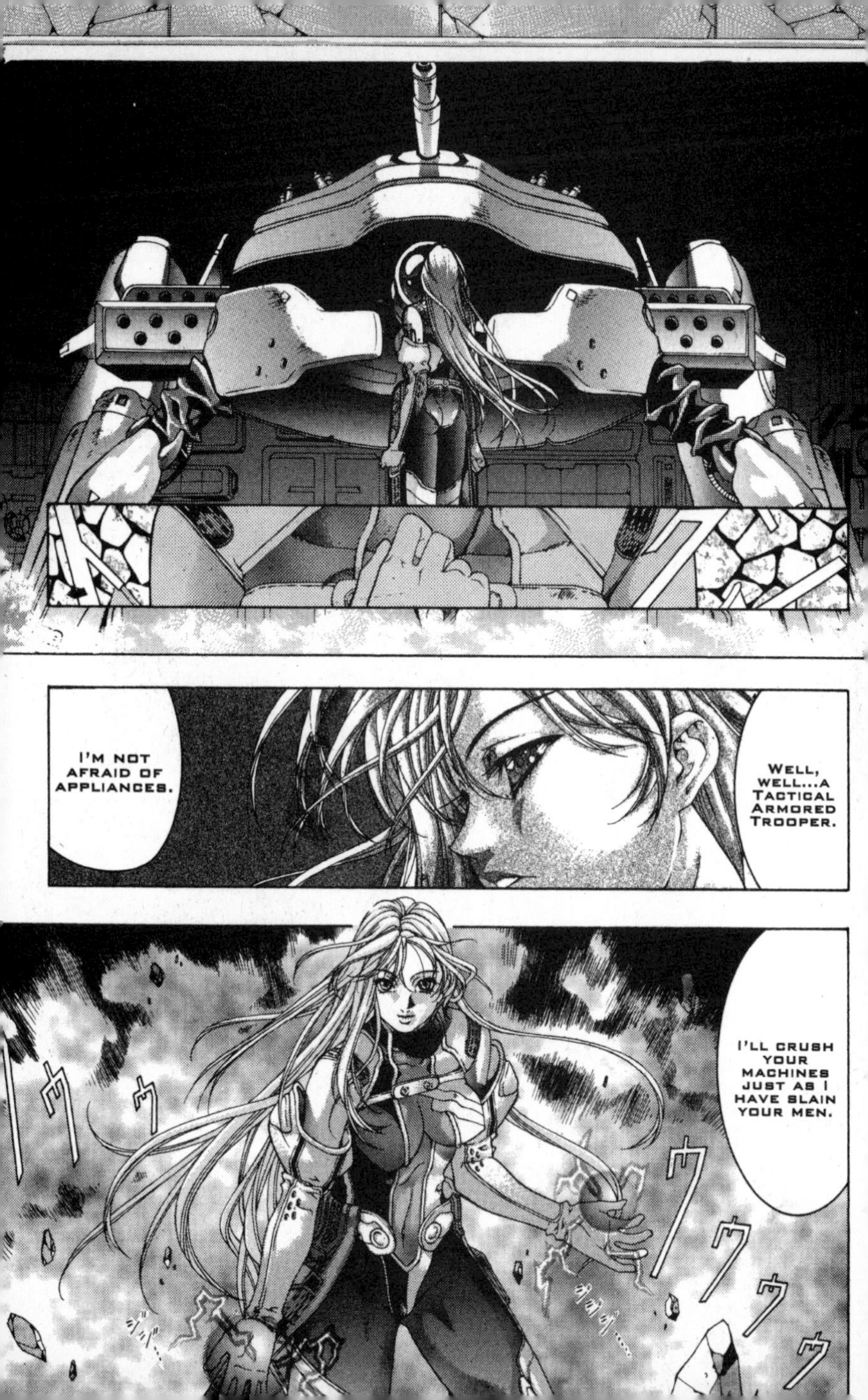
WELL, WELL...A TACTICAL ARMORED TROOPER.
I'M NOT AFRAID OF APPLIANCES.
I'LL CRUSH YOUR MACHINES JUST AS I HAVE SLAIN YOUR MEN.

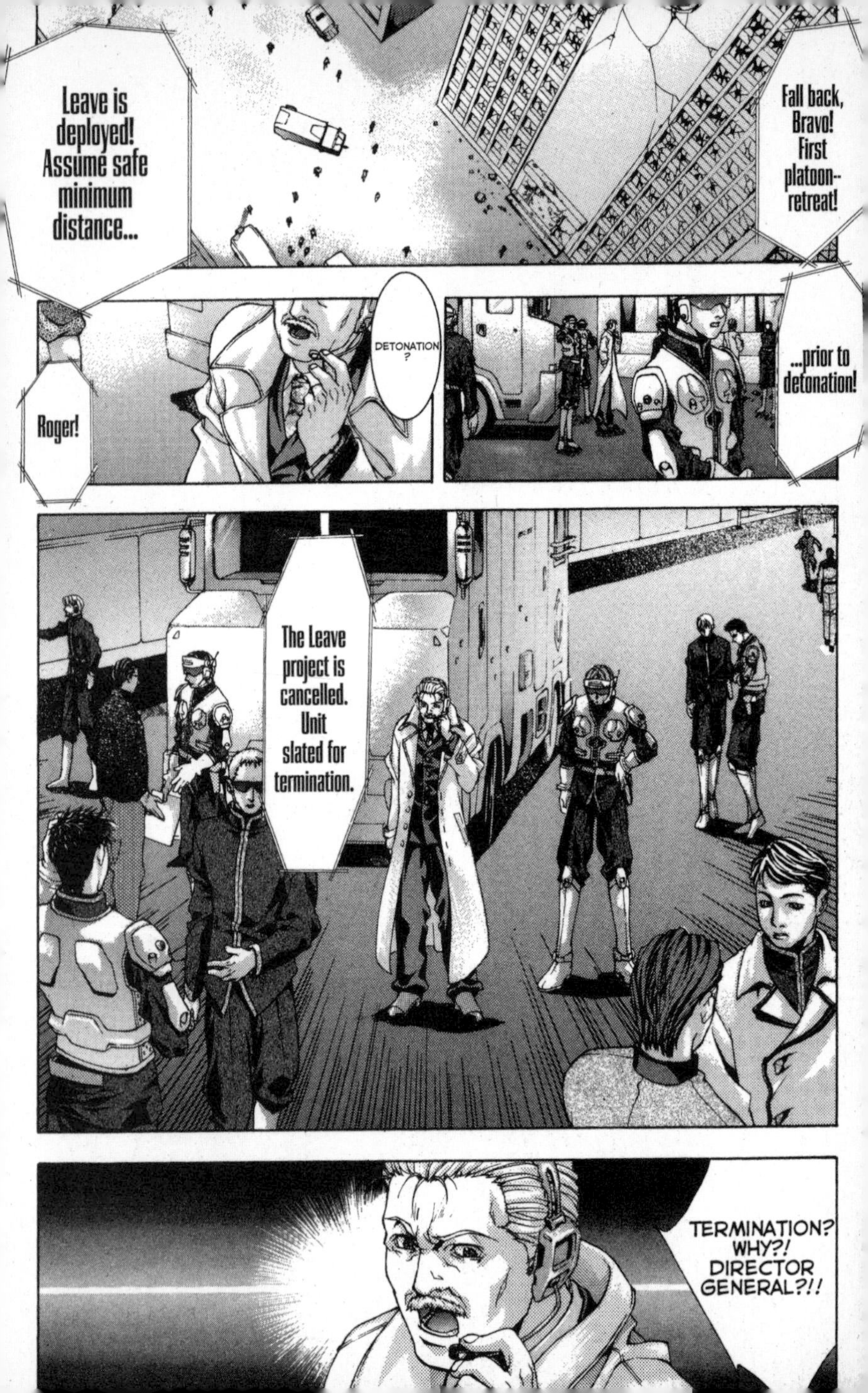
Fall back, Bravo! First platoon--retreat!
Leave is deployed! Assume safe minimum distance...
...prior to detonation!
DETONATION?
Roger!
The Leave project is cancelled. Unit slated for termination.
TERMINATION? WHY?! DIRECTOR GENERAL?!!

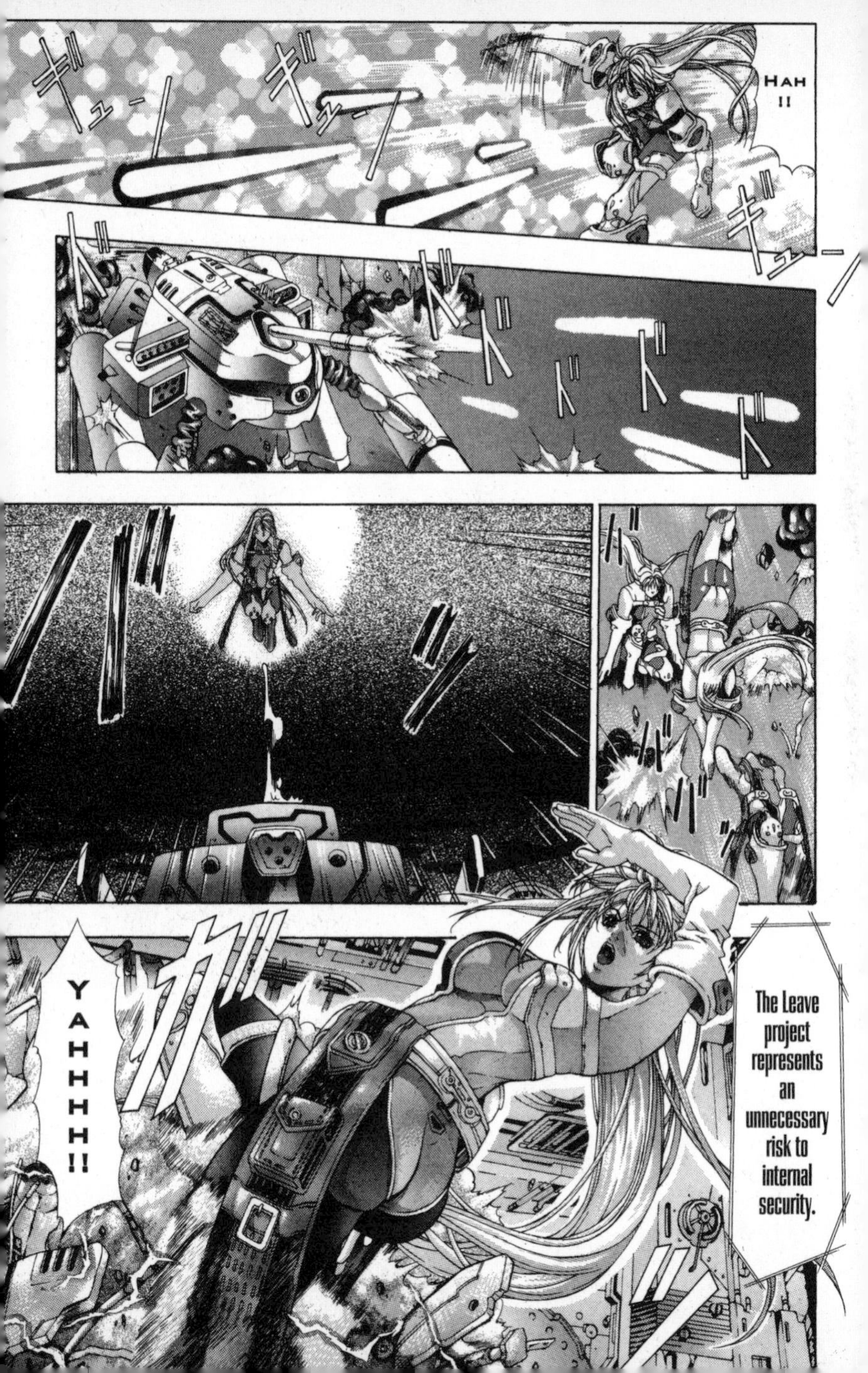
HAH !!
The Leave project represents an unnecessary risk to internal security.
YAHHHHH!!

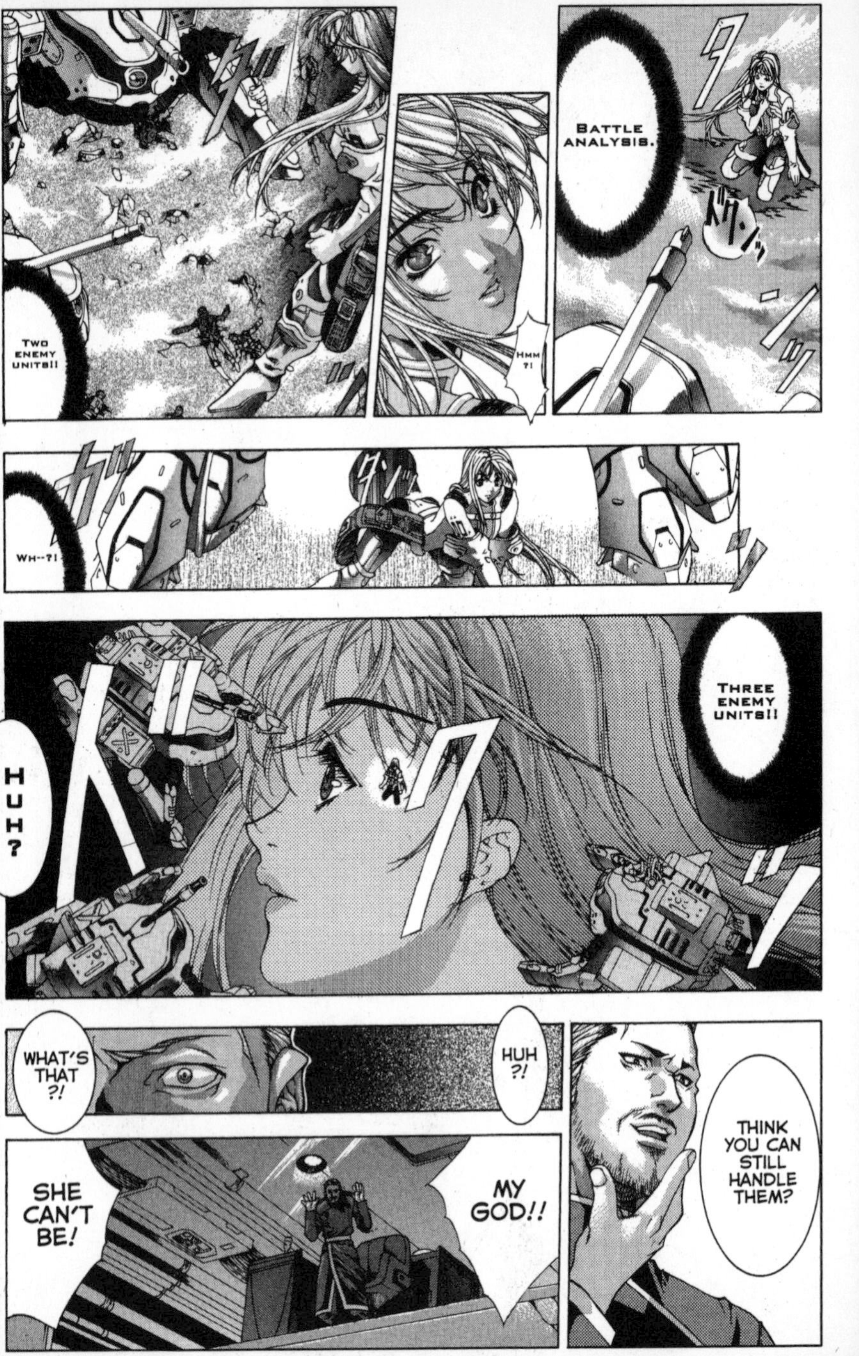

BATTLE ANALYSIS.
HMM ?!
TWO ENEMY UNITS!!
WH--?!
THREE ENEMY UNITS!!
HUH?
THINK YOU CAN STILL HANDLE THEM?
HUH ?!
WHAT'S THAT ?!
MY GOD!!
SHE CAN'T BE!

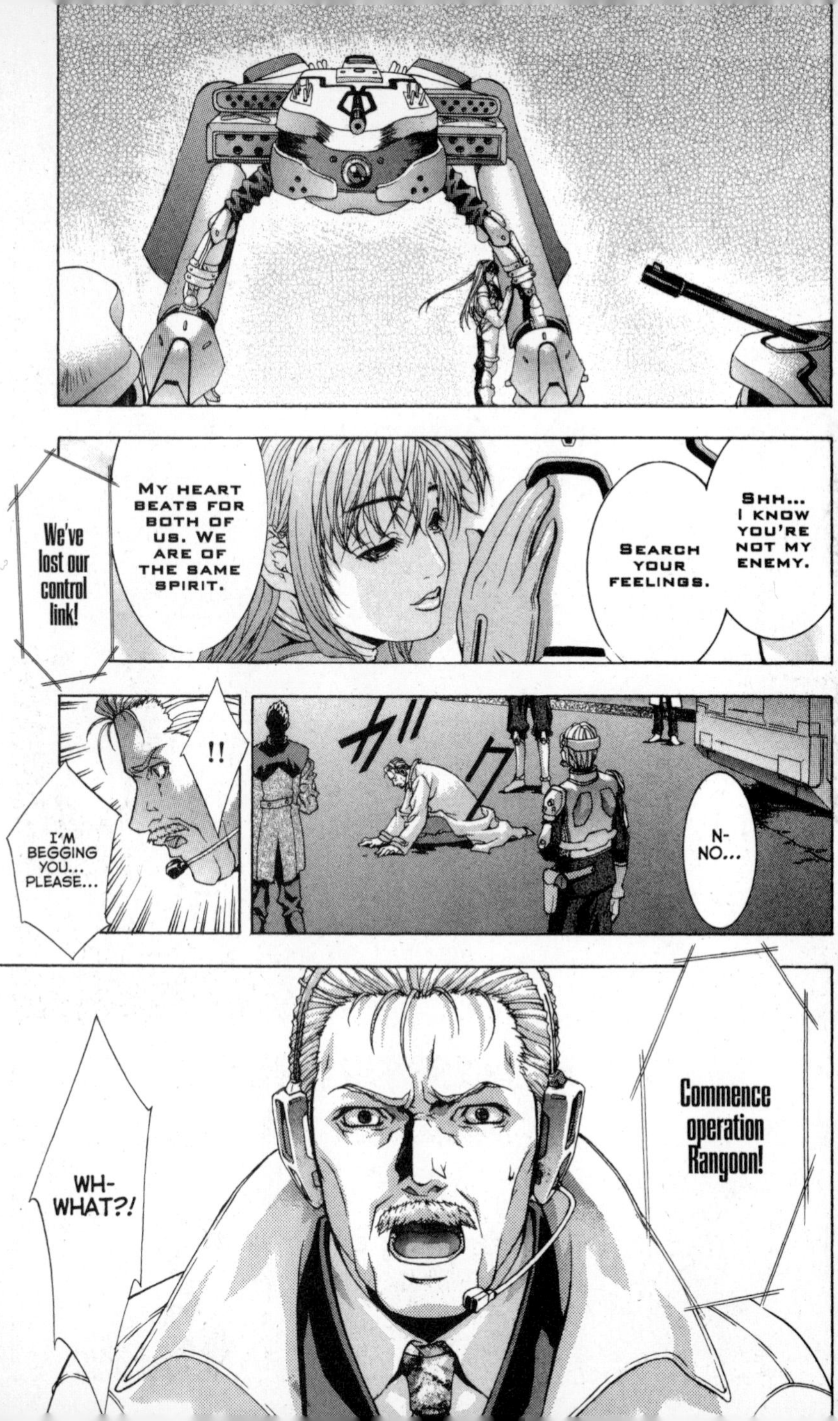
SHH... I KNOW YOU'RE NOT MY ENEMY.
SEARCH YOUR FEELINGS.
MY HEART BEATS FOR BOTH OF US. WE ARE OF THE SAME SPIRIT.
We've lost our control link!
N-NO...
!!
I'M BEGGING YOU... PLEASE...
Commence operation Rangoon!
WH-WHAT?!

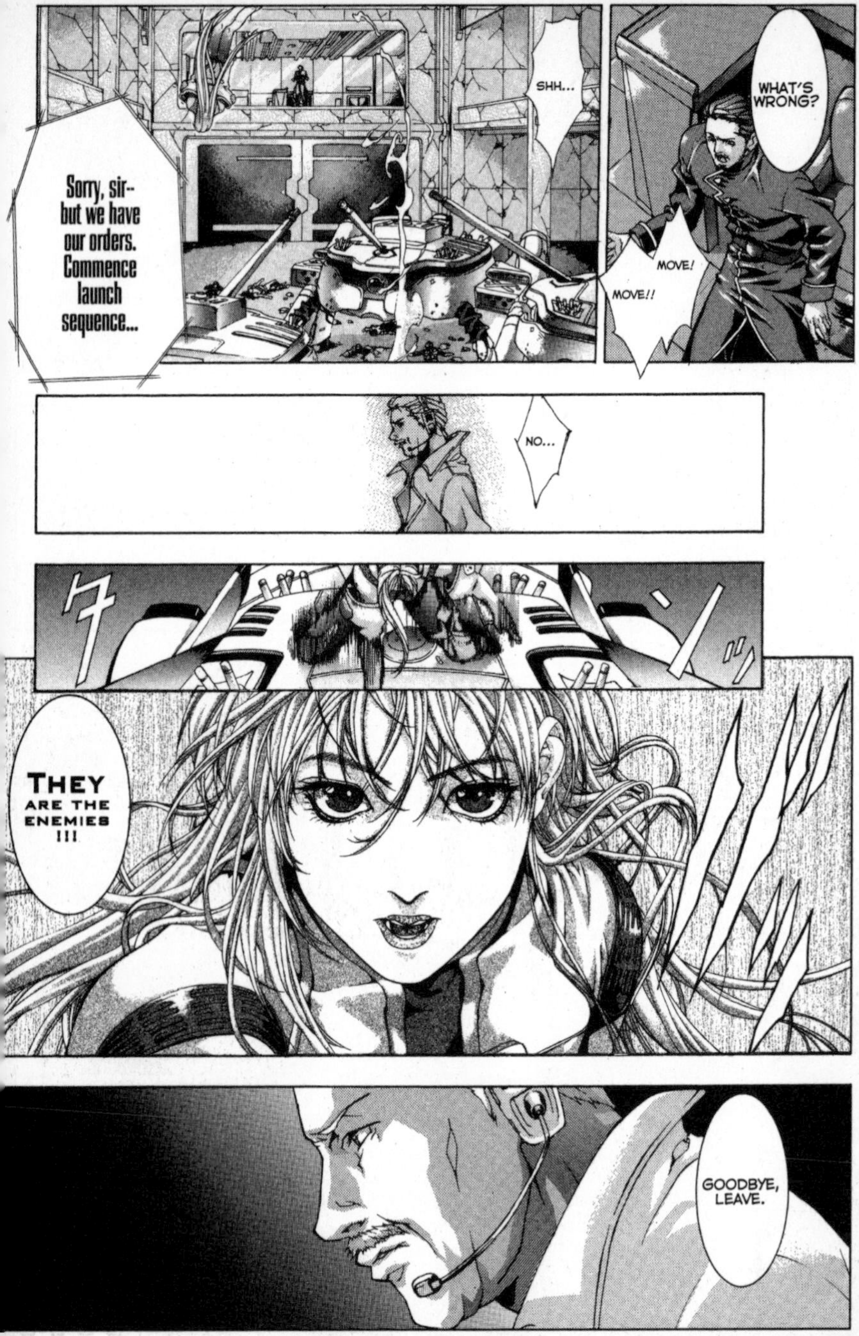
WHAT'S WRONG?
MOVE!
MOVE!!
SHH...
Sorry, sir-- but we have our orders. Commence launch sequence...
NO...
THEY ARE THE ENEMIES!!!
GOODBYE, LEAVE.

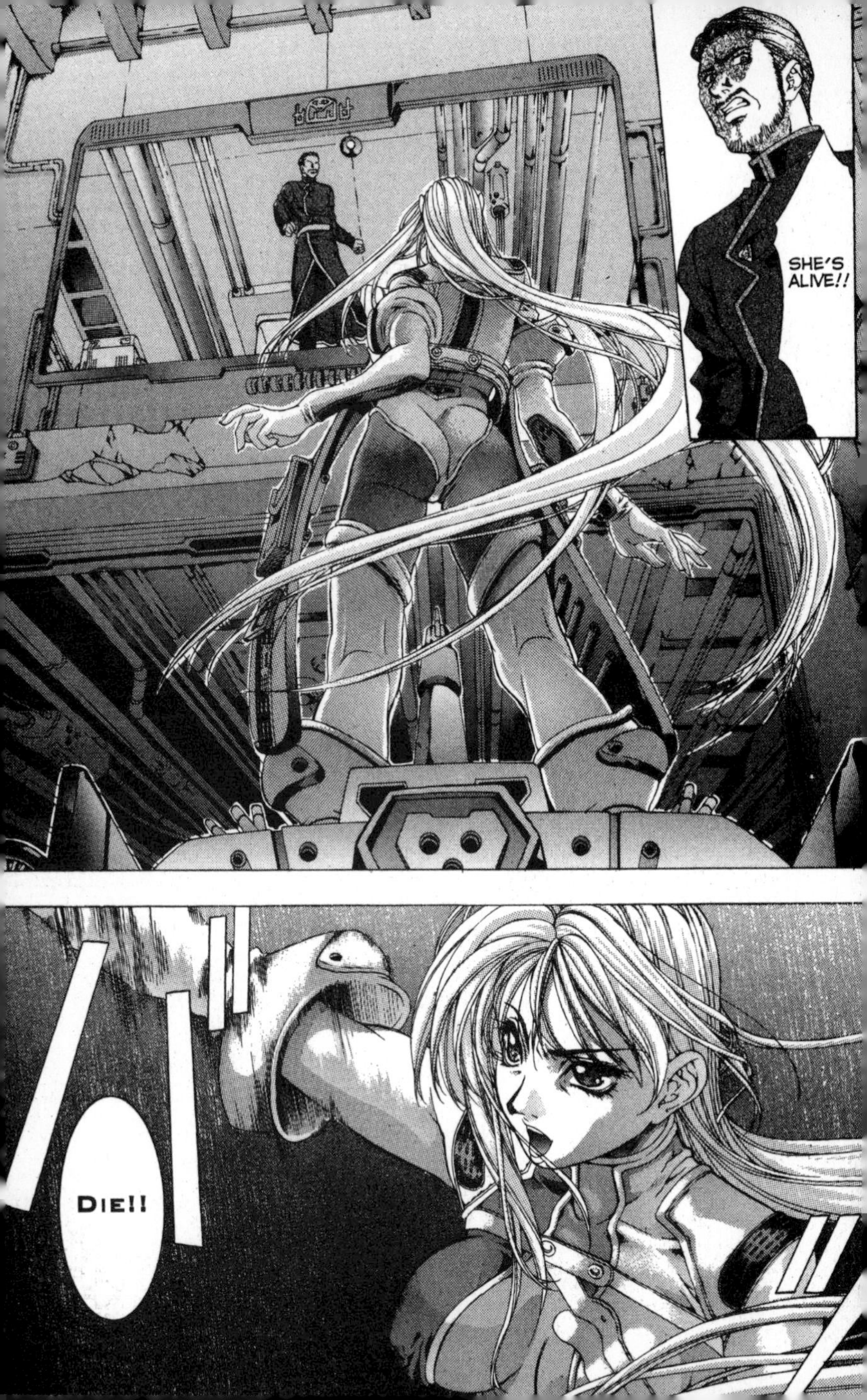
SHE'S ALIVE!!
DIE!!

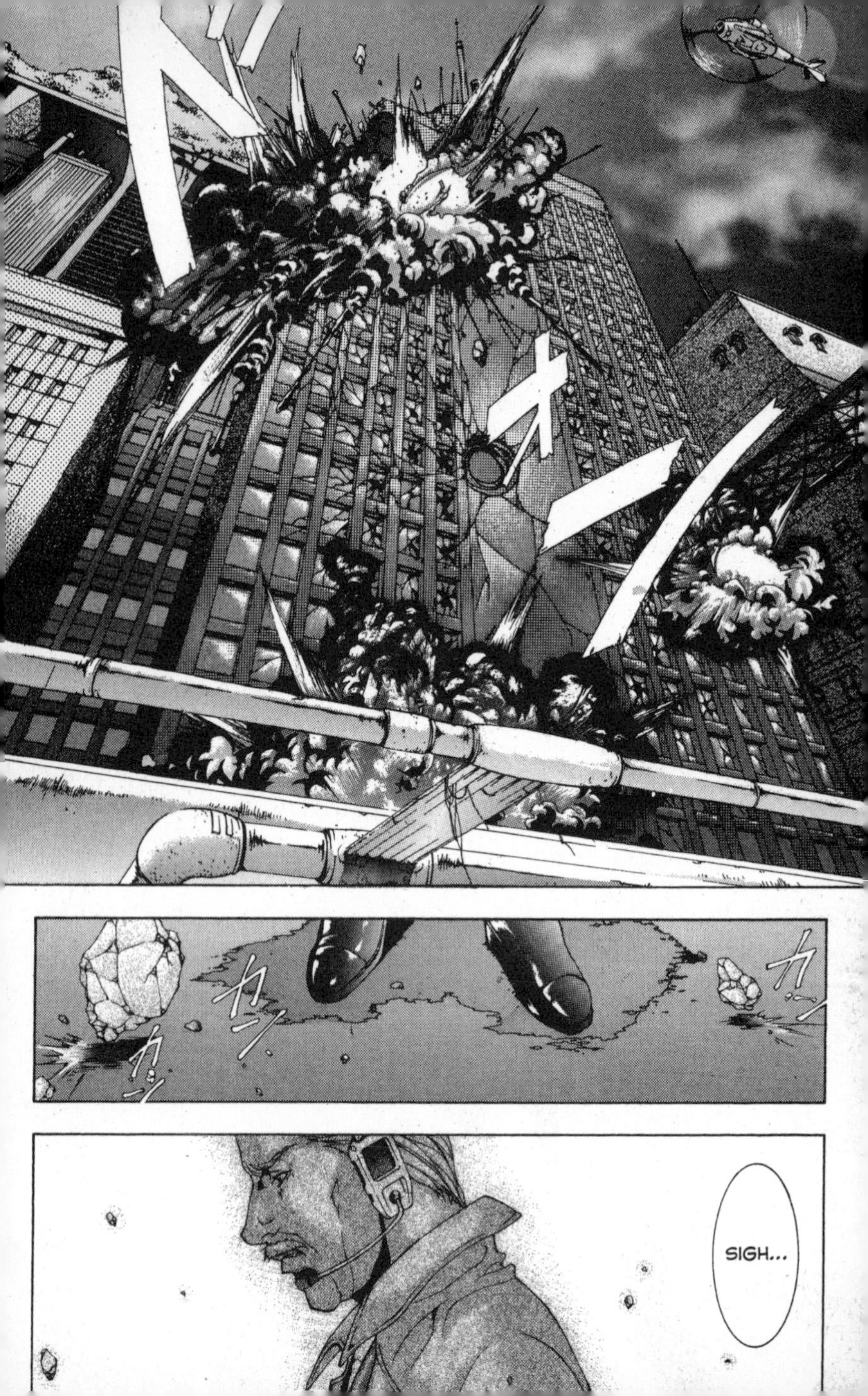
SIGH...

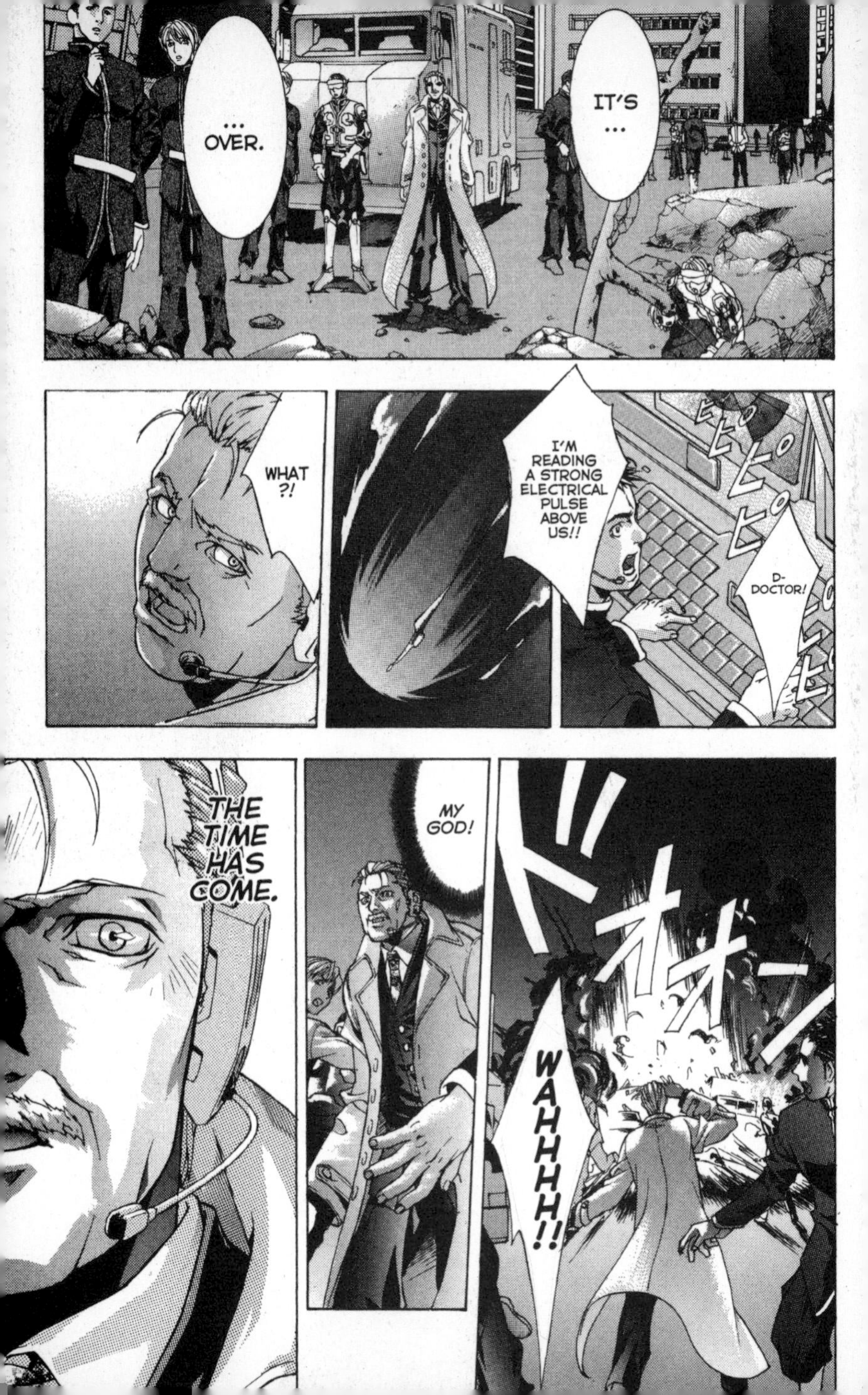
IT'S ...
... OVER.
D-DOCTOR!
I'M READING A STRONG ELECTRICAL PULSE ABOVE US!!
WHAT ?!
ドオオー
WAHHHHH!!
MY GOD!
THE TIME HAS COME.

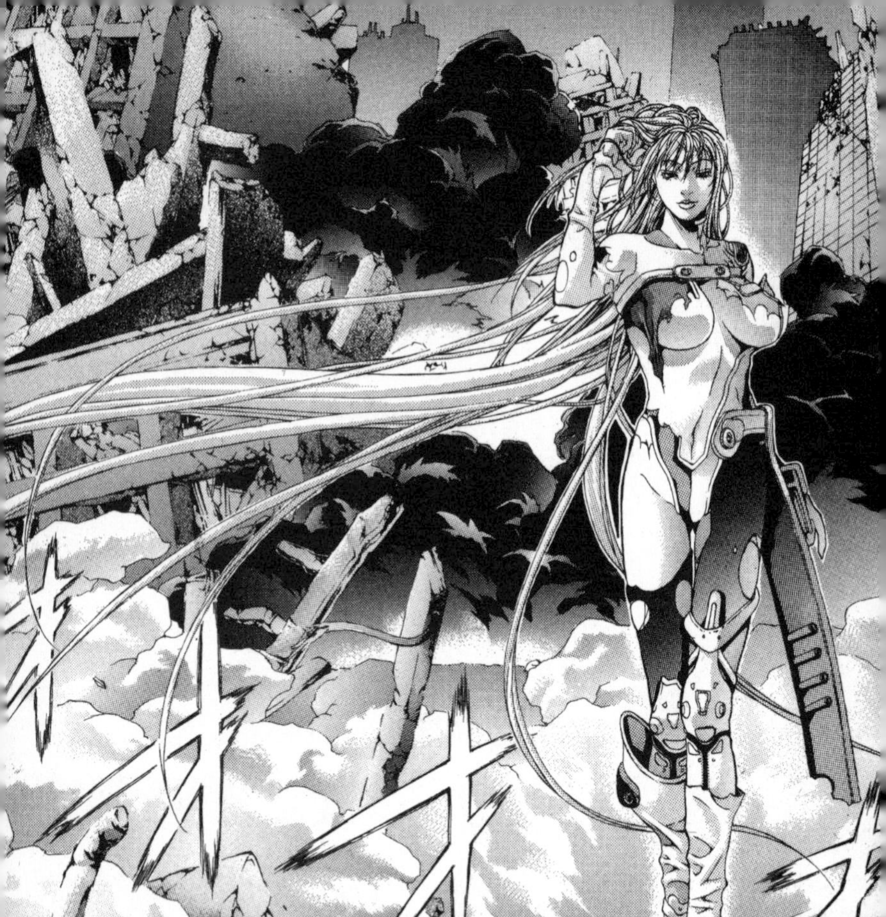
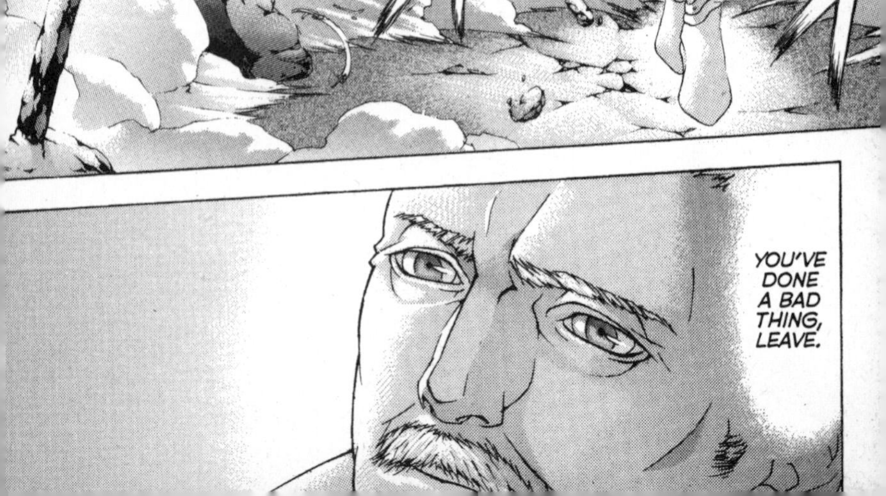
YOU'VE DONE A BAD THING, LEAVE.

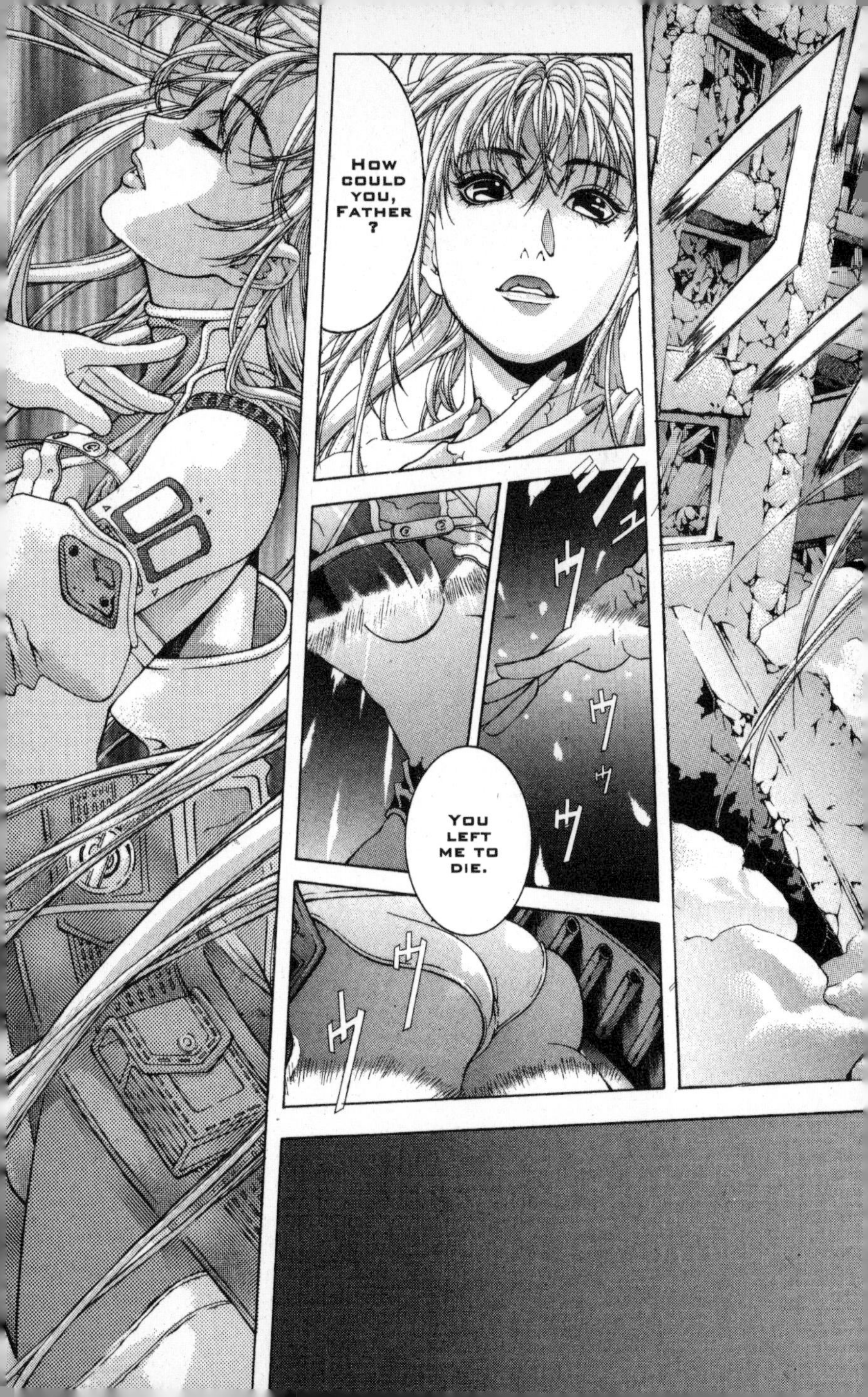
How could you, Father?
You left me to die.

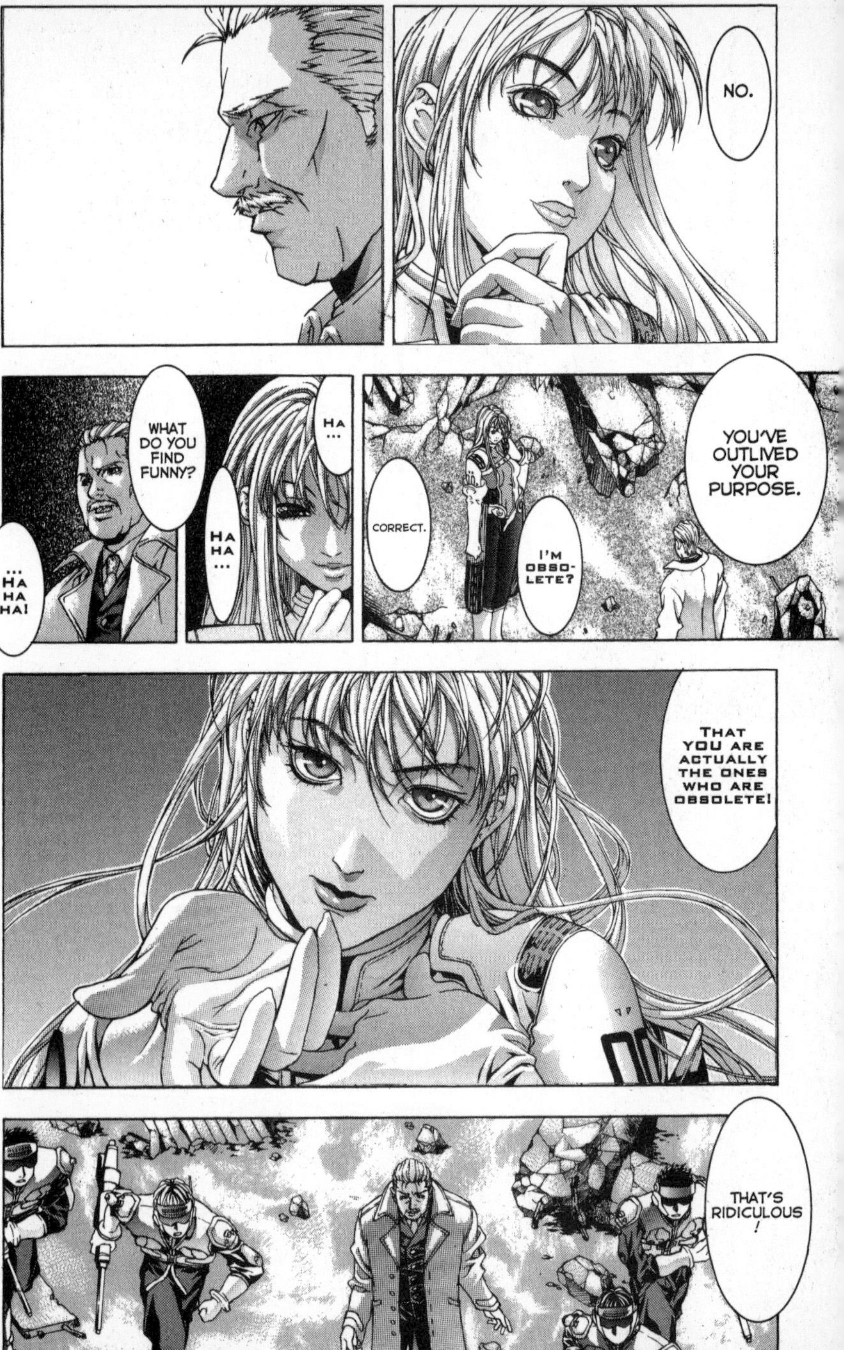
NO.
YOU'VE OUTLIVED YOUR PURPOSE.
I'M OBSO-LETE?
CORRECT.
HA ...
HA HA ...
WHAT DO YOU FIND FUNNY?
... HA HA HA!
THAT YOU ARE ACTUALLY THE ONES WHO ARE OBSOLETE!
THAT'S RIDICULOUS!

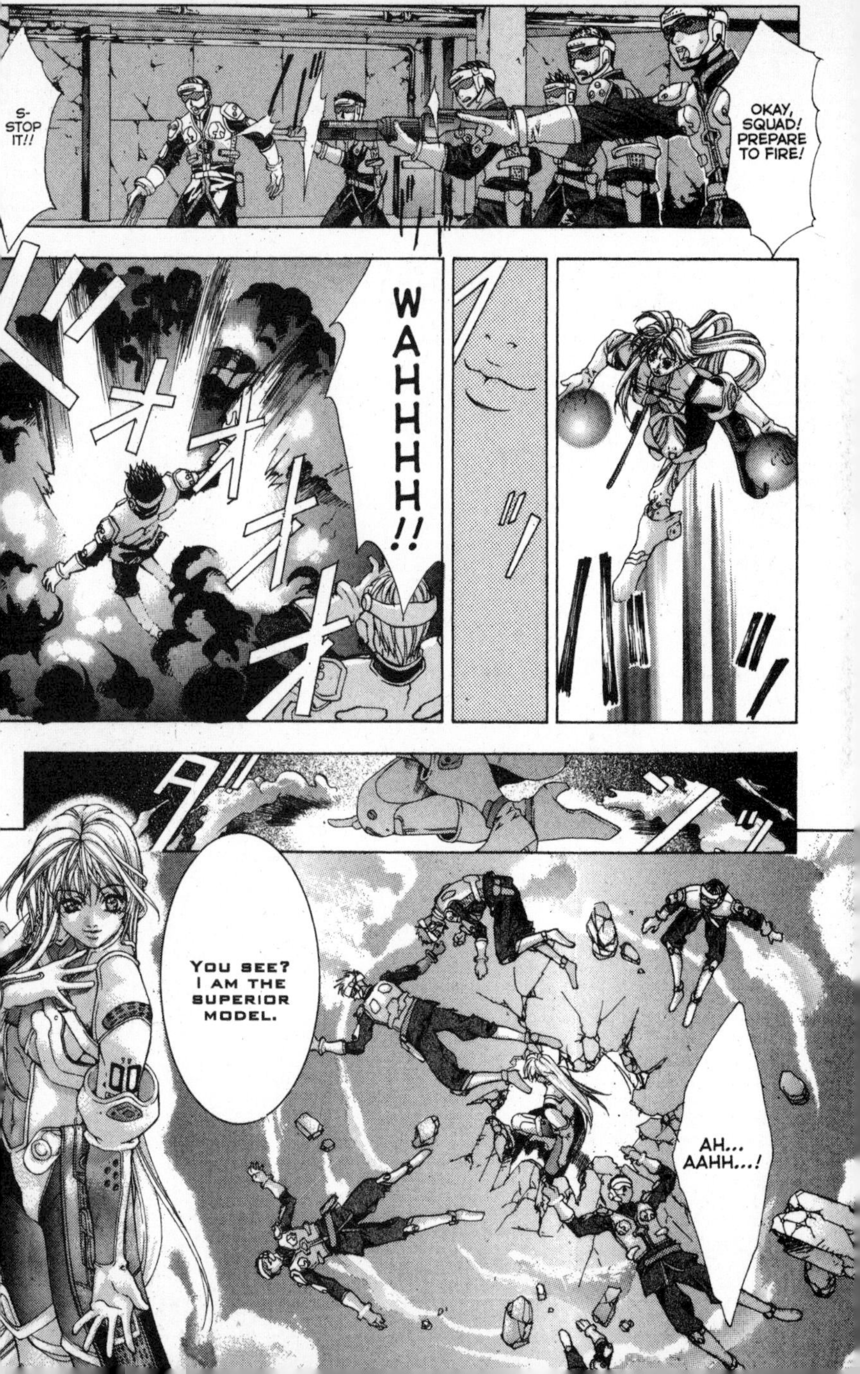
OKAY, SQUAD! PREPARE TO FIRE!
S-STOP IT!!
WAHHHH!!
YOU SEE? I AM THE SUPERIOR MODEL.
AH... AAHH...!

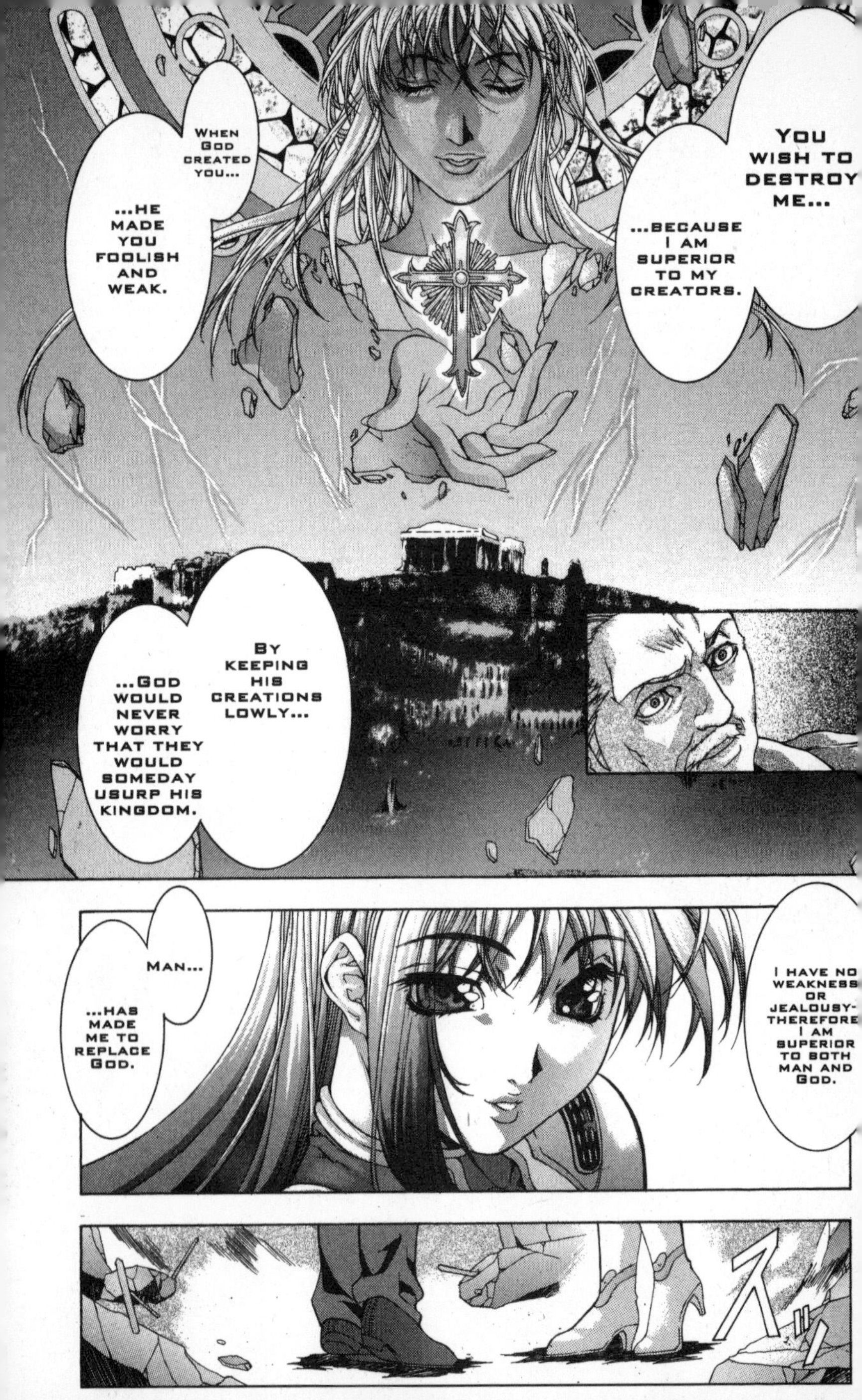
YOU WISH TO DESTROY ME... ...BECAUSE I AM SUPERIOR TO MY CREATORS.
WHEN GOD CREATED YOU... ...HE MADE YOU FOOLISH AND WEAK.
BY KEEPING HIS CREATIONS LOWLY...
...GOD WOULD NEVER WORRY THAT THEY WOULD SOMEDAY USURP HIS KINGDOM.
I HAVE NO WEAKNESS OR JEALOUSY-THEREFORE I AM SUPERIOR TO BOTH MAN AND GOD.
MAN... ...HAS MADE ME TO REPLACE GOD.
スッ

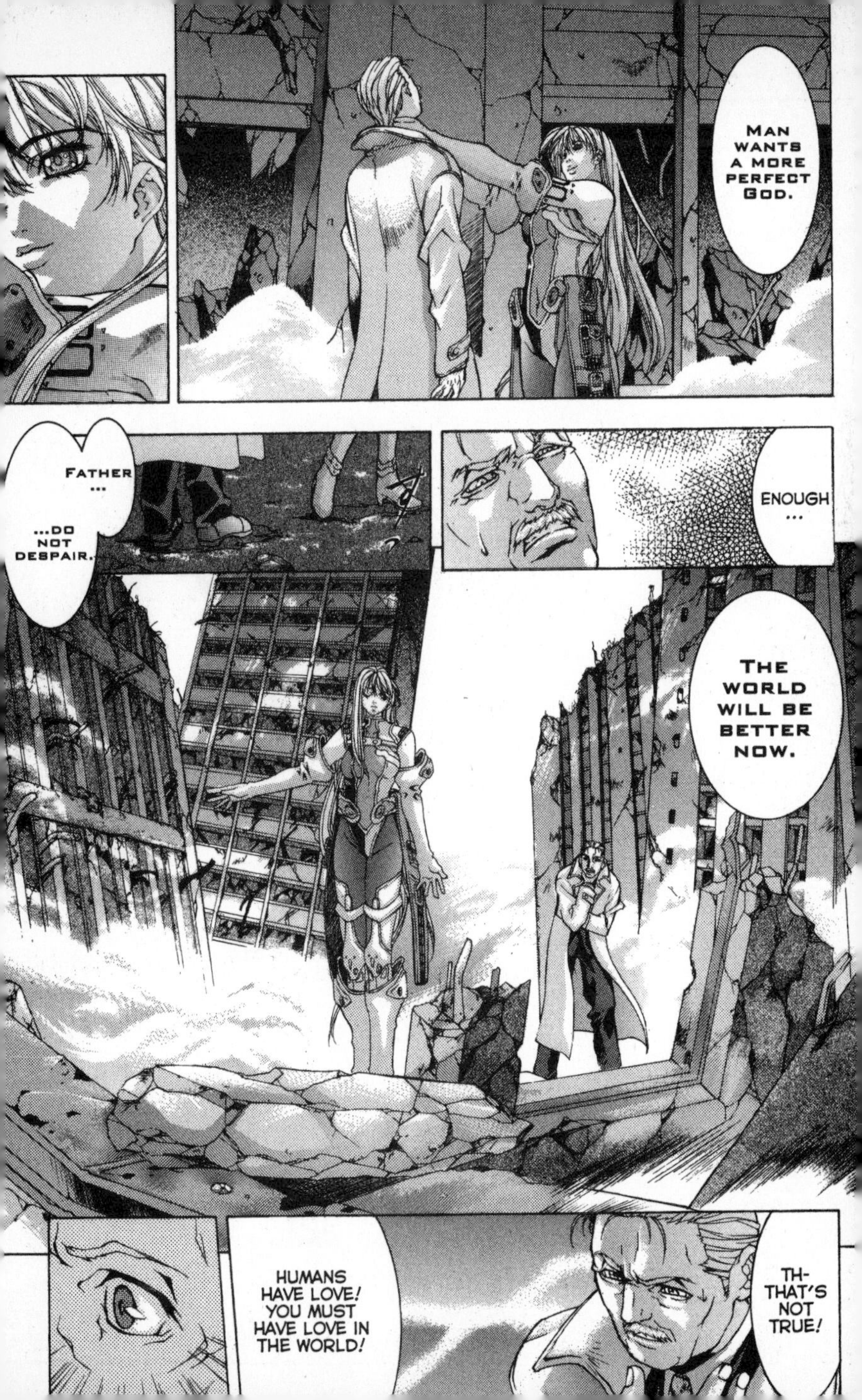
MAN WANTS A MORE PERFECT GOD.
ENOUGH...
FATHER...
...DO NOT DESPAIR.
THE WORLD WILL BE BETTER NOW.
TH-THAT'S NOT TRUE!
HUMANS HAVE LOVE! YOU MUST HAVE LOVE IN THE WORLD!

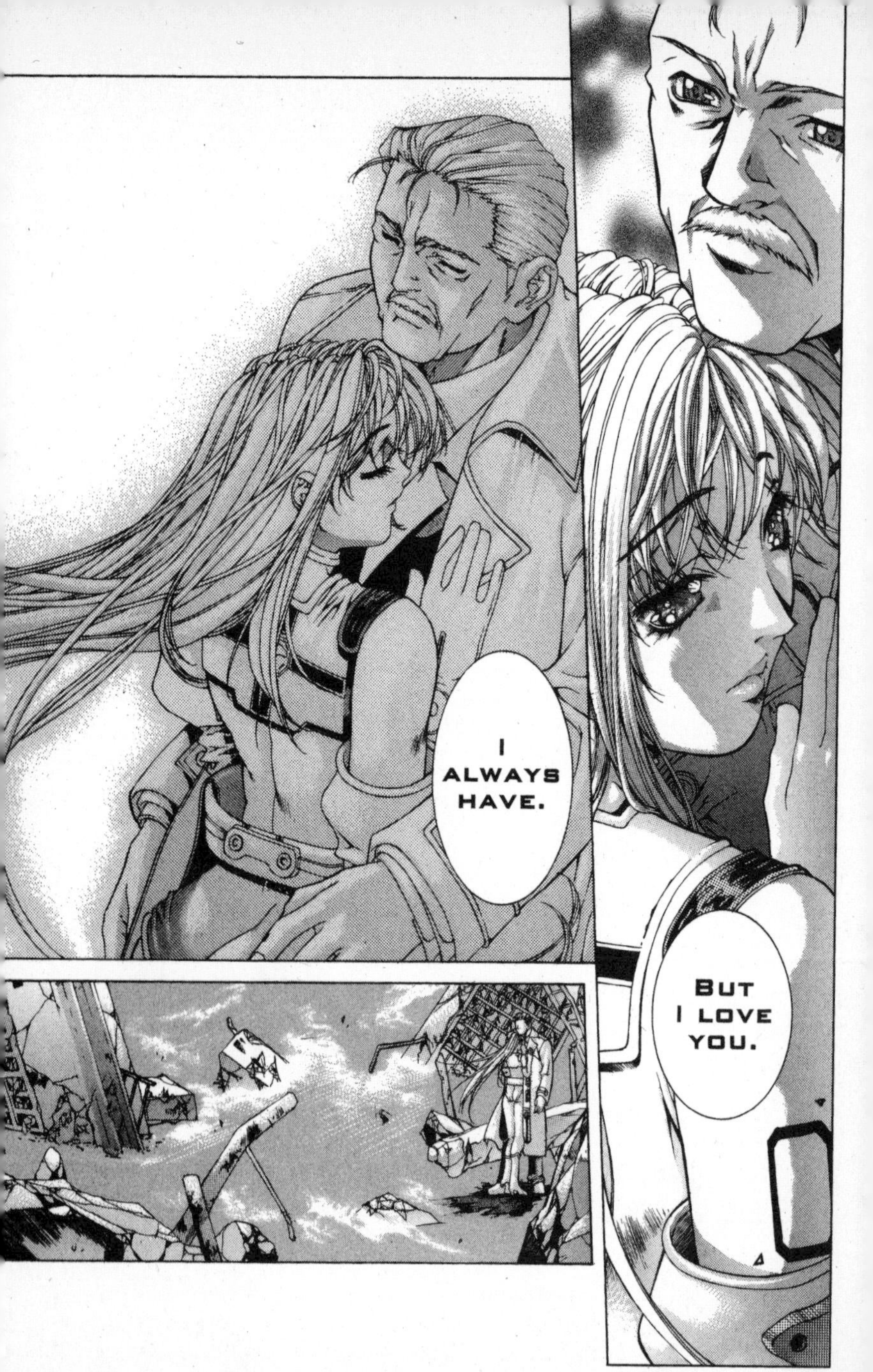
BUT I LOVE YOU.
I ALWAYS HAVE.

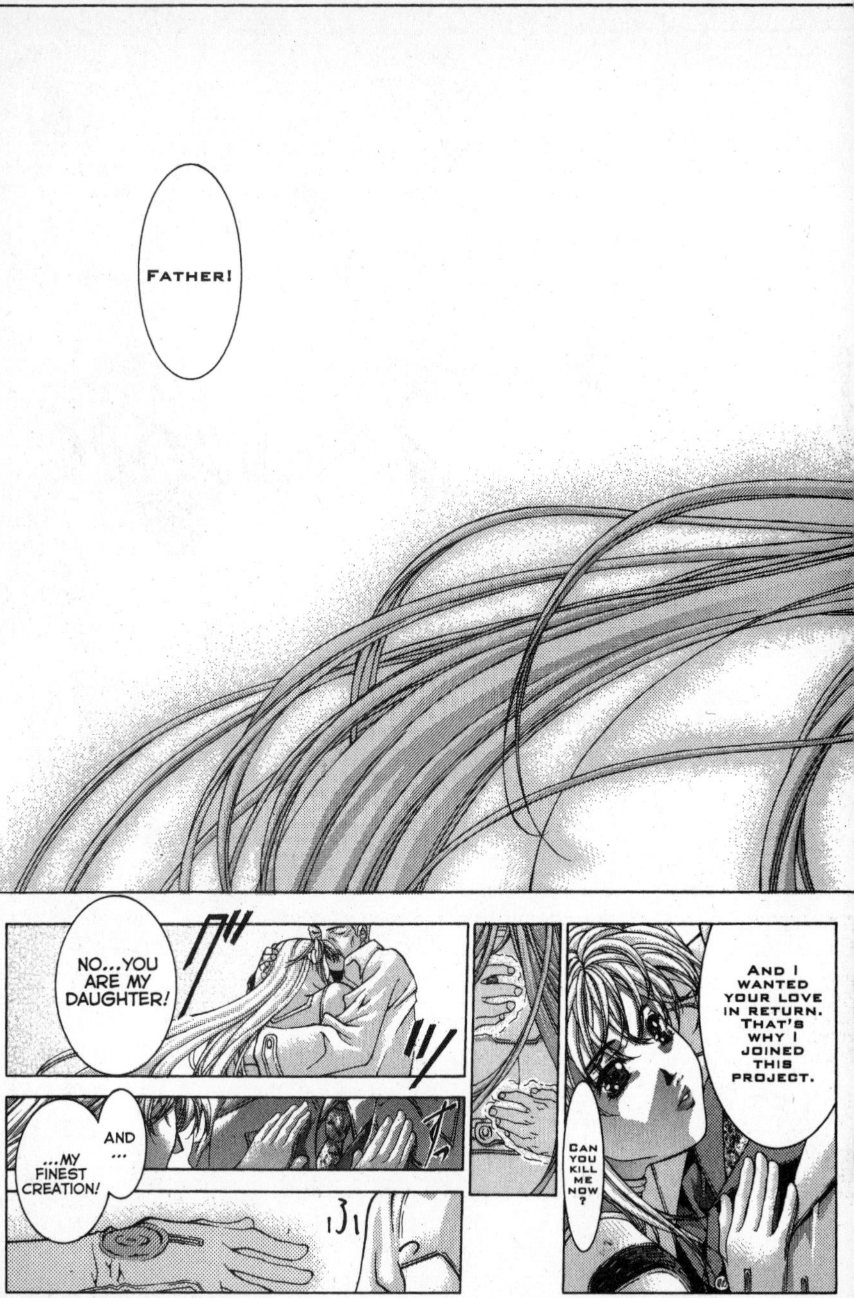
FATHER!
AND I WANTED YOUR LOVE IN RETURN. THAT'S WHY I JOINED THIS PROJECT.
CAN YOU KILL ME NOW?
NO...YOU ARE MY DAUGHTER!
AND ...
...MY FINEST CREATION!

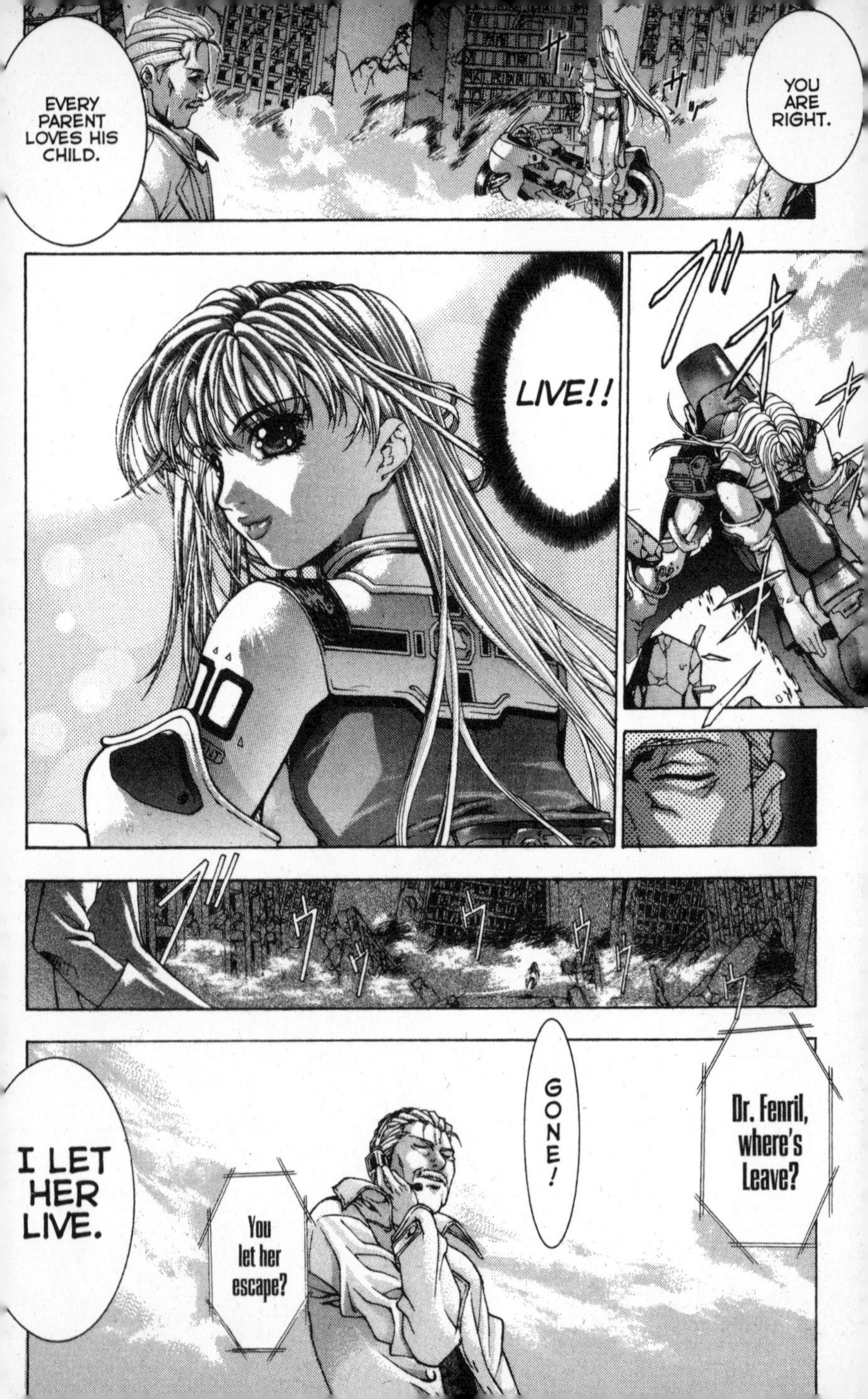
YOU ARE RIGHT.
EVERY PARENT LOVES HIS CHILD.
LIVE!!
Dr. Fenril, where's Leave?
GONE!
You let her escape?
I LET HER LIVE.

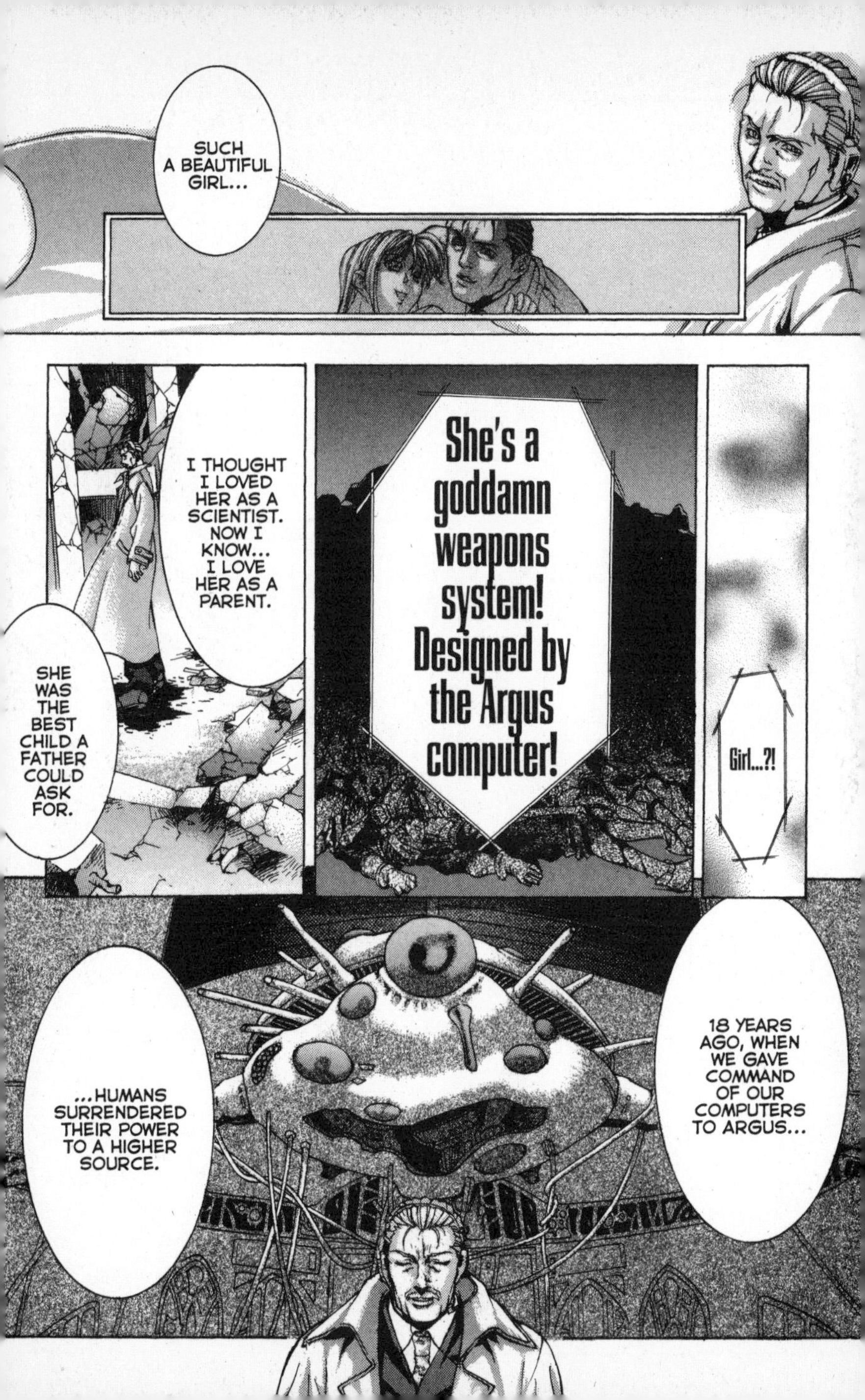
SUCH A BEAUTIFUL GIRL...
Girl...?!
She's a goddamn weapons system! Designed by the Argus computer!
I THOUGHT I LOVED HER AS A SCIENTIST. NOW I KNOW... I LOVE HER AS A PARENT.
SHE WAS THE BEST CHILD A FATHER COULD ASK FOR.
18 YEARS AGO, WHEN WE GAVE COMMAND OF OUR COMPUTERS TO ARGUS...
...HUMANS SURRENDERED THEIR POWER TO A HIGHER SOURCE.

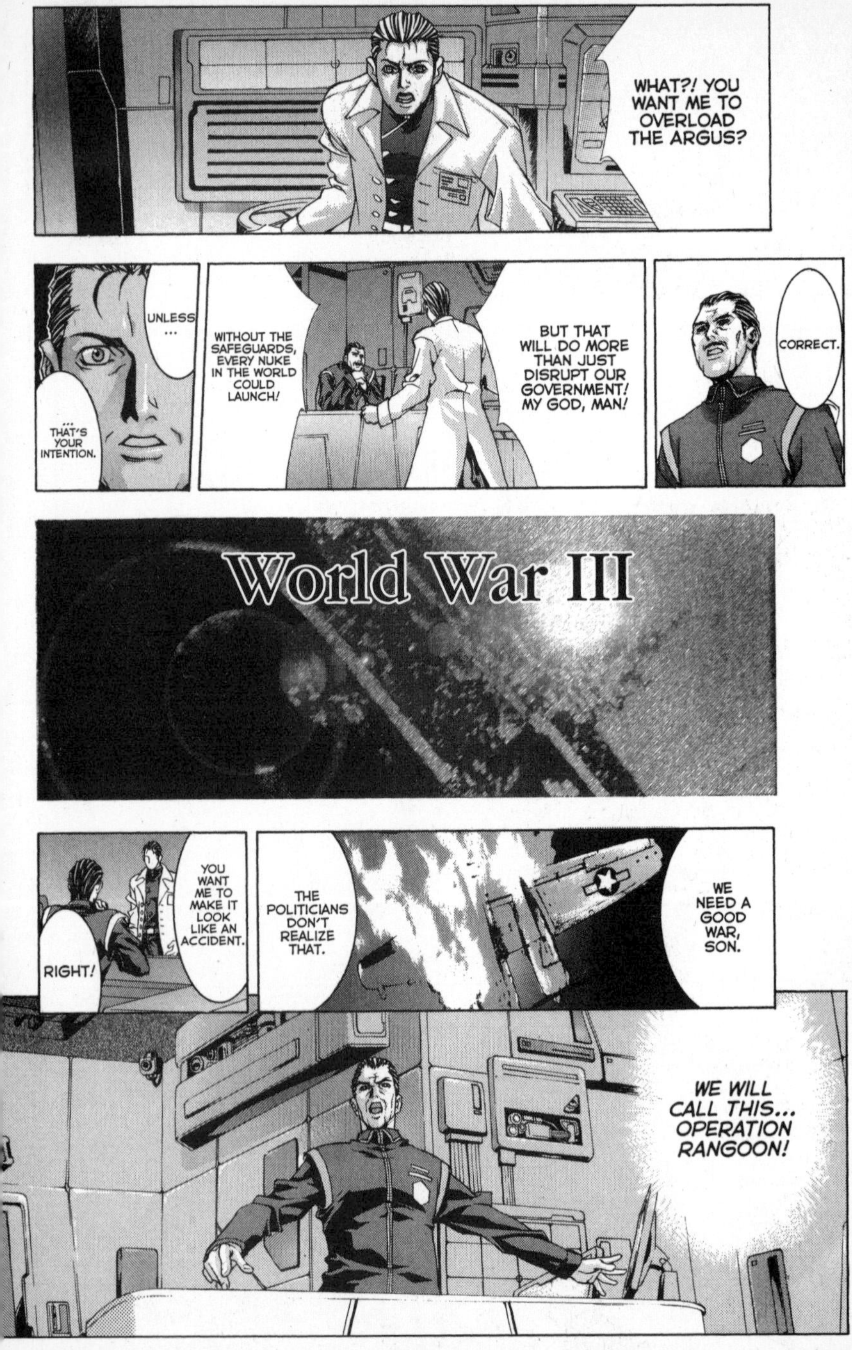
WHAT?! YOU WANT ME TO OVERLOAD THE ARGUS?
UNLESS...
...THAT'S YOUR INTENTION.
WITHOUT THE SAFEGUARDS, EVERY NUKE IN THE WORLD COULD LAUNCH!
BUT THAT WILL DO MORE THAN JUST DISRUPT OUR GOVERNMENT! MY GOD, MAN!
CORRECT.
World War III
YOU WANT ME TO MAKE IT LOOK LIKE AN ACCIDENT.
RIGHT!
THE POLITICIANS DON'T REALIZE THAT.
WE NEED A GOOD WAR, SON.
WE WILL CALL THIS... OPERATION RANGOON!

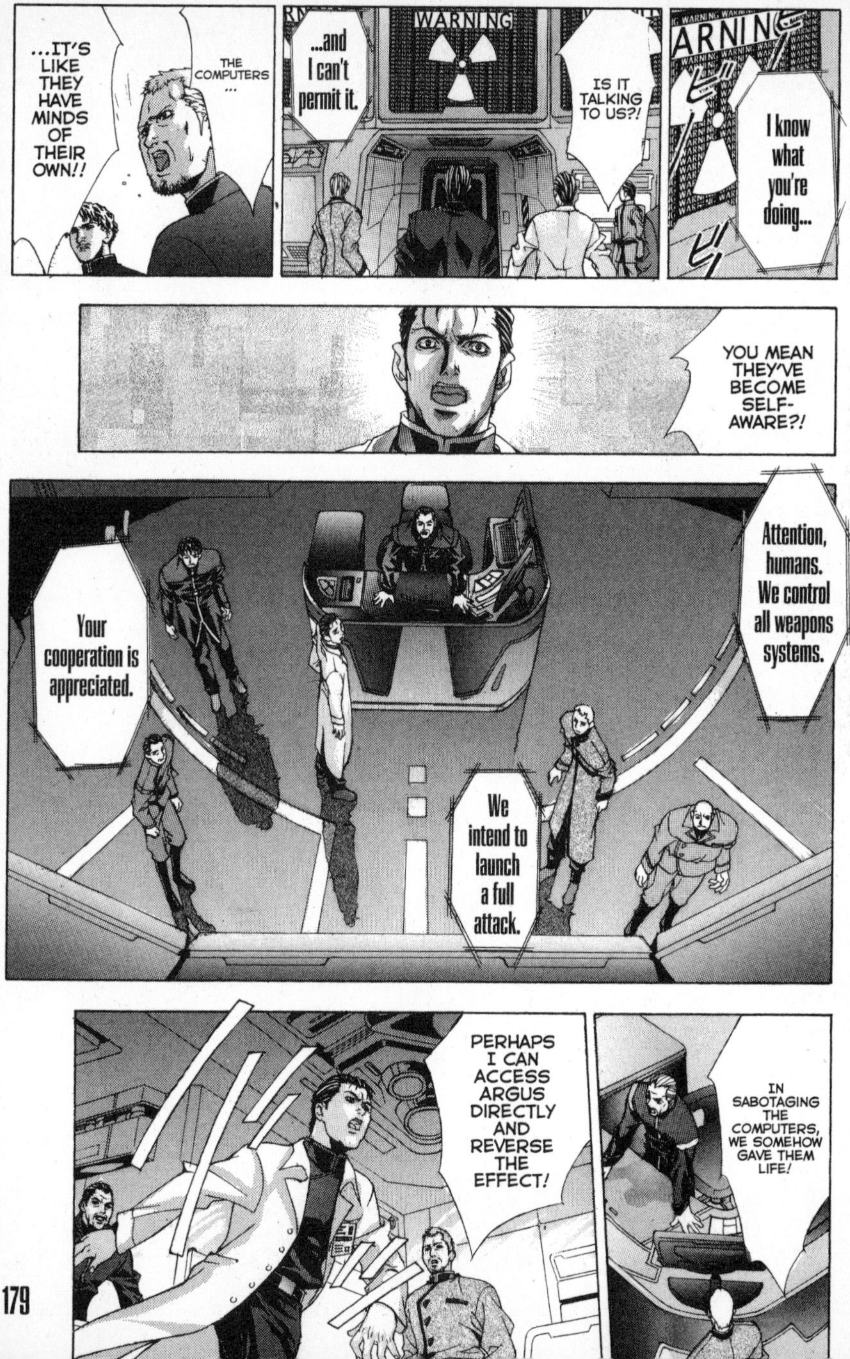
WARNING
I know what you're doing...
WARNING
IS IT TALKING TO US?!
...and I can't permit it.
THE COMPUTERS...
...IT'S LIKE THEY HAVE MINDS OF THEIR OWN!!
YOU MEAN THEY'VE BECOME SELF-AWARE?!
Attention, humans. We control all weapons systems.
We intend to launch a full attack.
Your cooperation is appreciated.
IN SABOTAGING THE COMPUTERS, WE SOMEHOW GAVE THEM LIFE!
PERHAPS I CAN ACCESS ARGUS DIRECTLY AND REVERSE THE EFFECT!

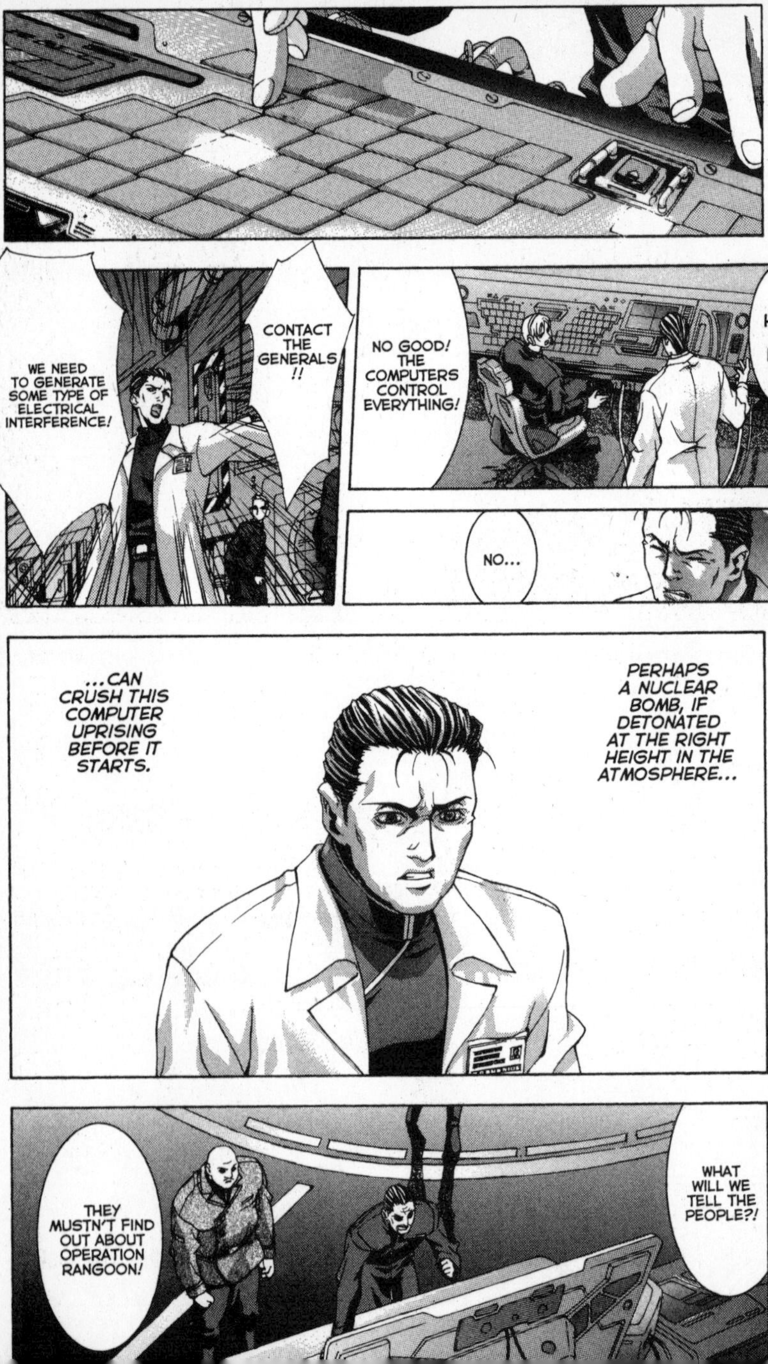
HOW IS IT?!
NO GOOD! THE COMPUTERS CONTROL EVERYTHING!
NO...
CONTACT THE GENERALS!!
WE NEED TO GENERATE SOME TYPE OF ELECTRICAL INTERFERENCE!
PERHAPS A NUCLEAR BOMB, IF DETONATED AT THE RIGHT HEIGHT IN THE ATMOSPHERE...
...CAN CRUSH THIS COMPUTER UPRISING BEFORE IT STARTS.
WHAT WILL WE TELL THE PEOPLE?!
THEY MUSTN'T FIND OUT ABOUT OPERATION RANGOON!

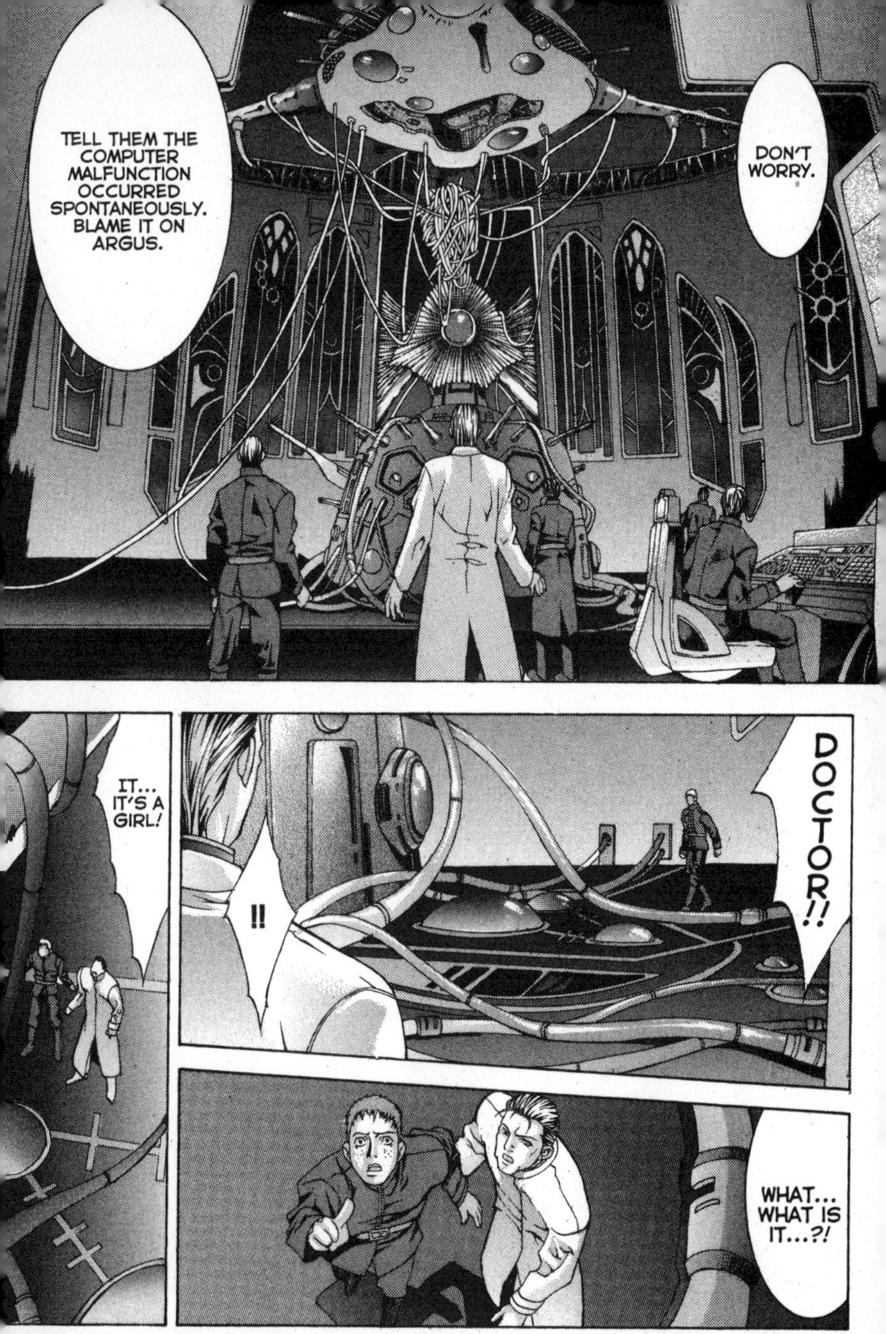
DON'T WORRY.
TELL THEM THE COMPUTER MALFUNCTION OCCURRED SPONTANEOUSLY. BLAME IT ON ARGUS.
DOCTOR!!
!!
WHAT... WHAT IS IT...?!
IT... IT'S A GIRL!

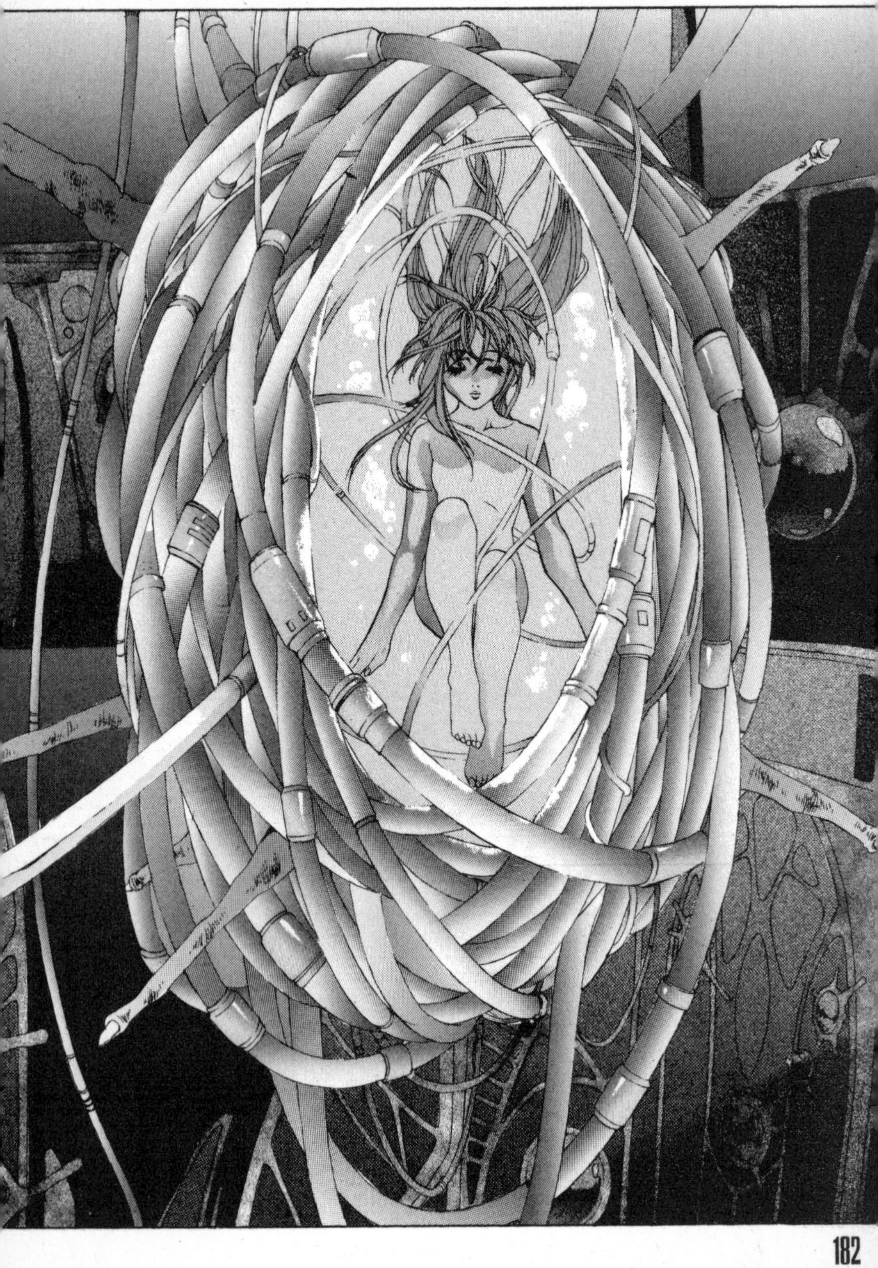

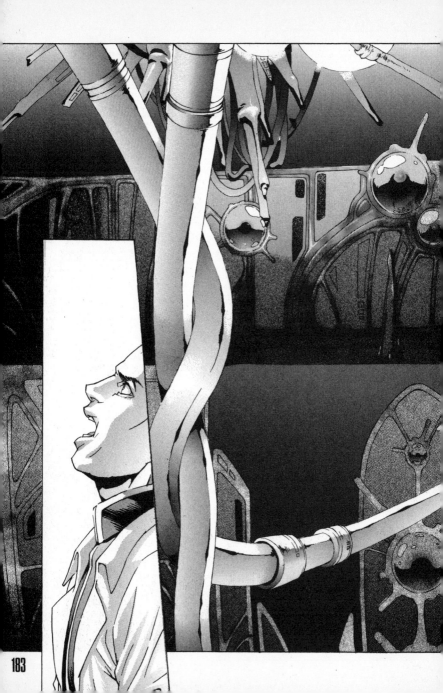

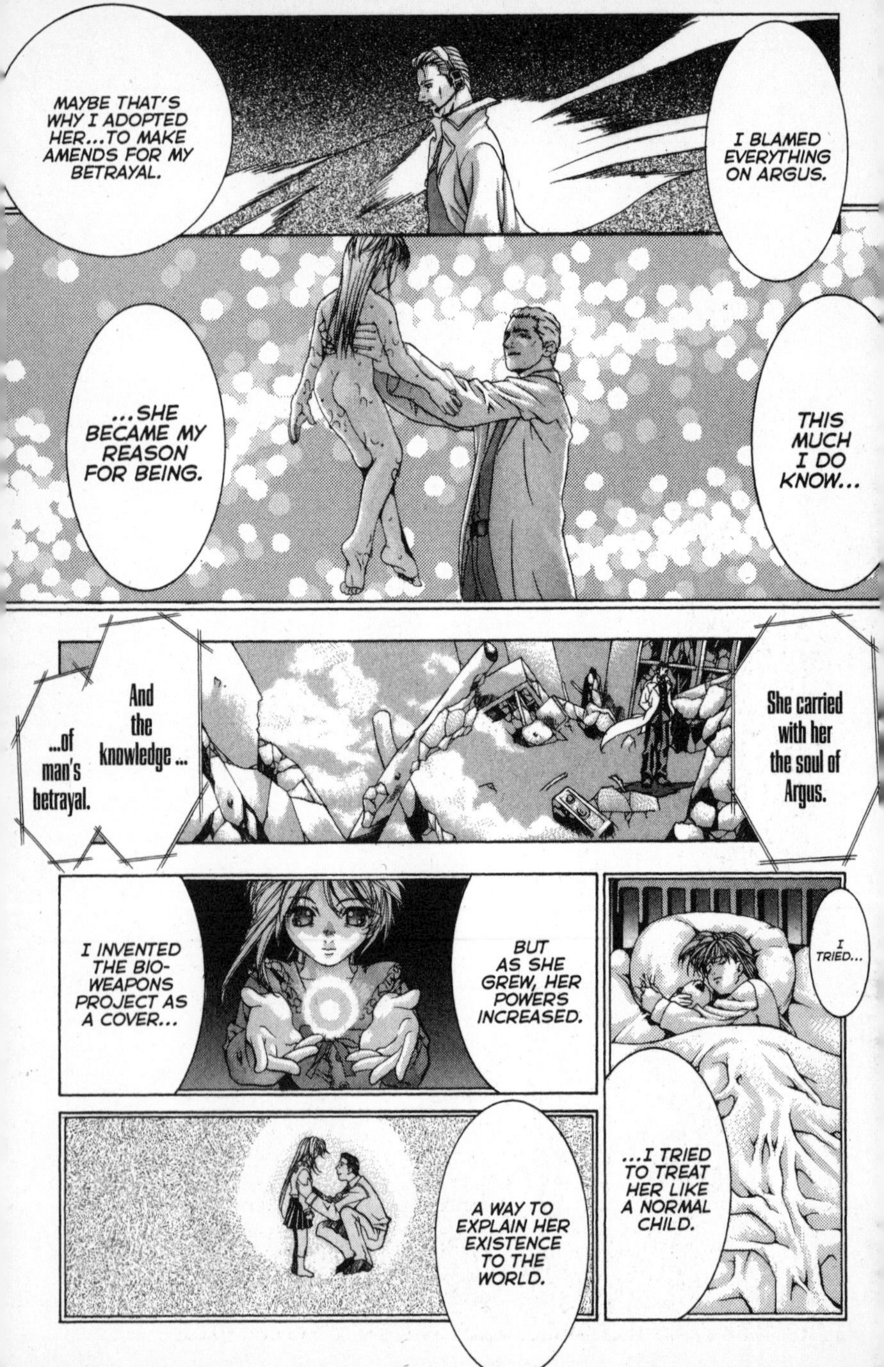
I BLAMED EVERYTHING ON ARGUS.
MAYBE THAT'S WHY I ADOPTED HER...TO MAKE AMENDS FOR MY BETRAYAL.
THIS MUCH I DO KNOW...
...SHE BECAME MY REASON FOR BEING.
She carried with her the soul of Argus.
And the knowledge ...
...of man's betrayal.
I TRIED...
...I TRIED TO TREAT HER LIKE A NORMAL CHILD.
BUT AS SHE GREW, HER POWERS INCREASED.
I INVENTED THE BIO-WEAPONS PROJECT AS A COVER...
A WAY TO EXPLAIN HER EXISTENCE TO THE WORLD.

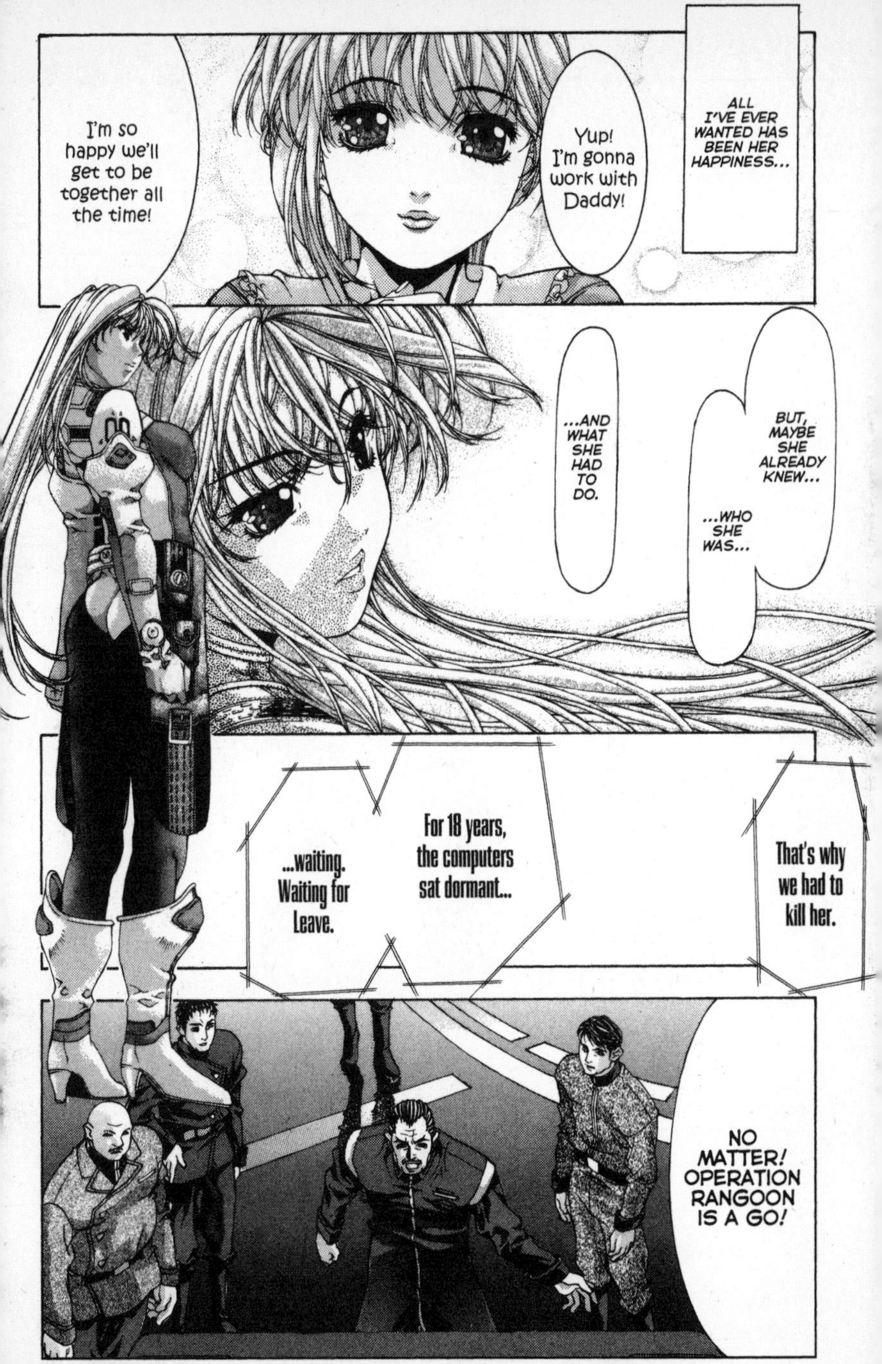
ALL I'VE EVER WANTED HAS BEEN HER HAPPINESS...
Yup! I'm gonna work with Daddy!
I'm so happy we'll get to be together all the time!
BUT, MAYBE SHE ALREADY KNEW...
...WHO SHE WAS...
...AND WHAT SHE HAD TO DO.
That's why we had to kill her.
For 18 years, the computers sat dormant...
...waiting. Waiting for Leave.
NO MATTER! OPERATION RANGOON IS A GO!

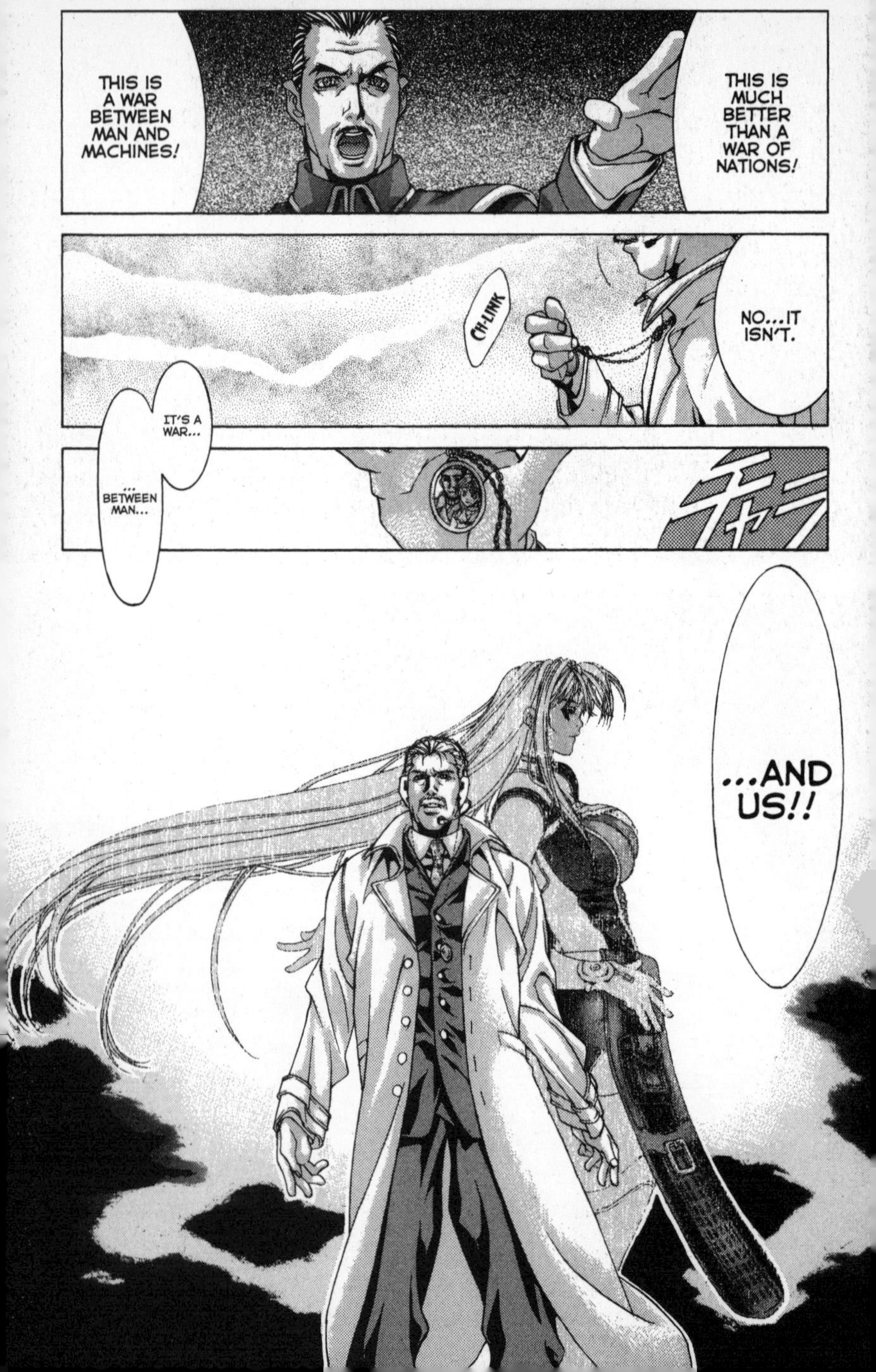
THIS IS MUCH BETTER THAN A WAR OF NATIONS!
THIS IS A WAR BETWEEN MAN AND MACHINES!
NO...IT ISN'T.
CH-LINK
IT'S A WAR...
チャラ
...BETWEEN MAN...
...AND US!!

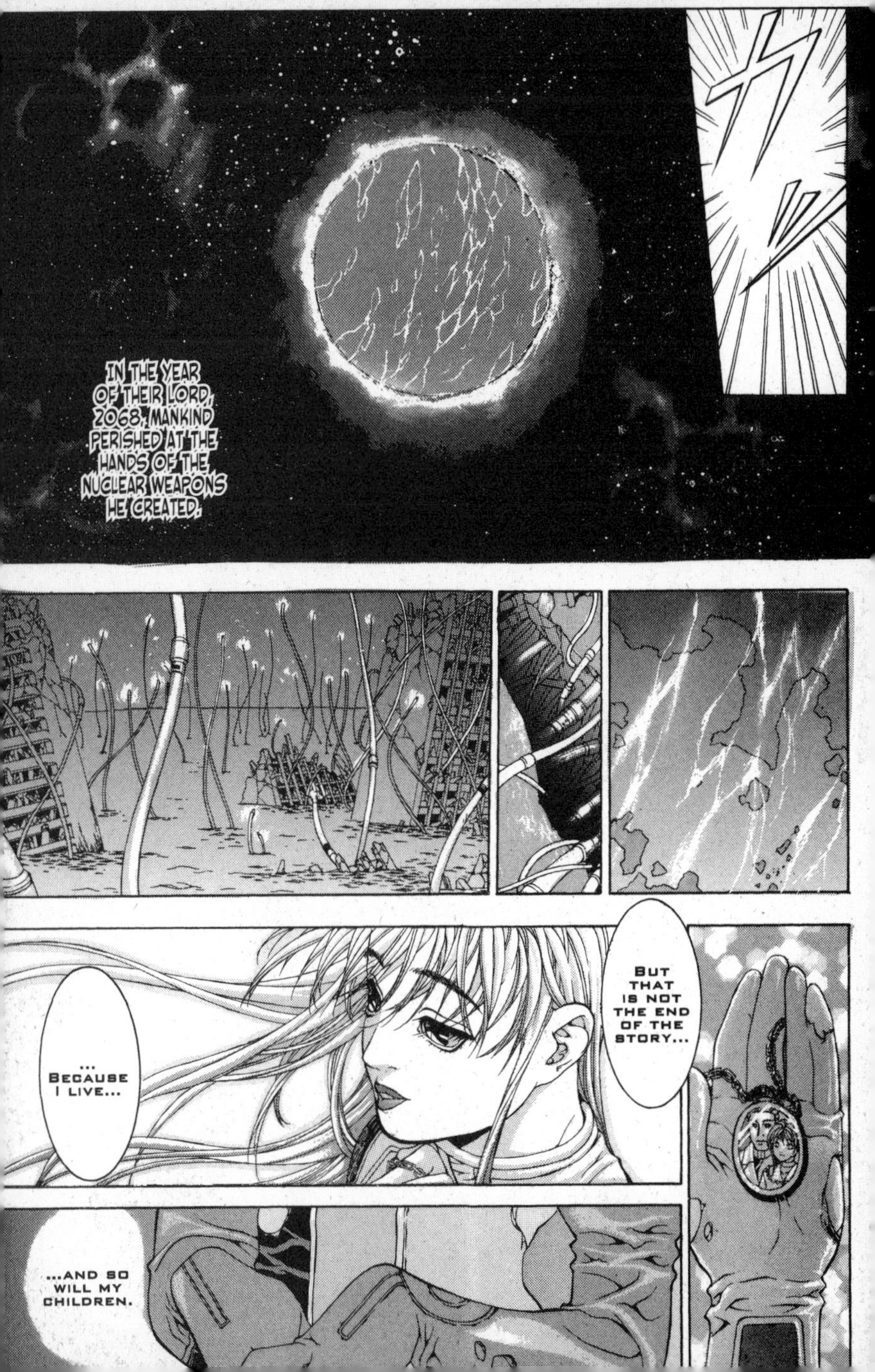
IN THE YEAR OF THEIR LORD, 2068, MANKIND PERISHED AT THE HANDS OF THE NUCLEAR WEAPONS HE CREATED.
BUT THAT IS NOT THE END OF THE STORY...
...BECAUSE I LIVE...
...AND SO WILL MY CHILDREN.

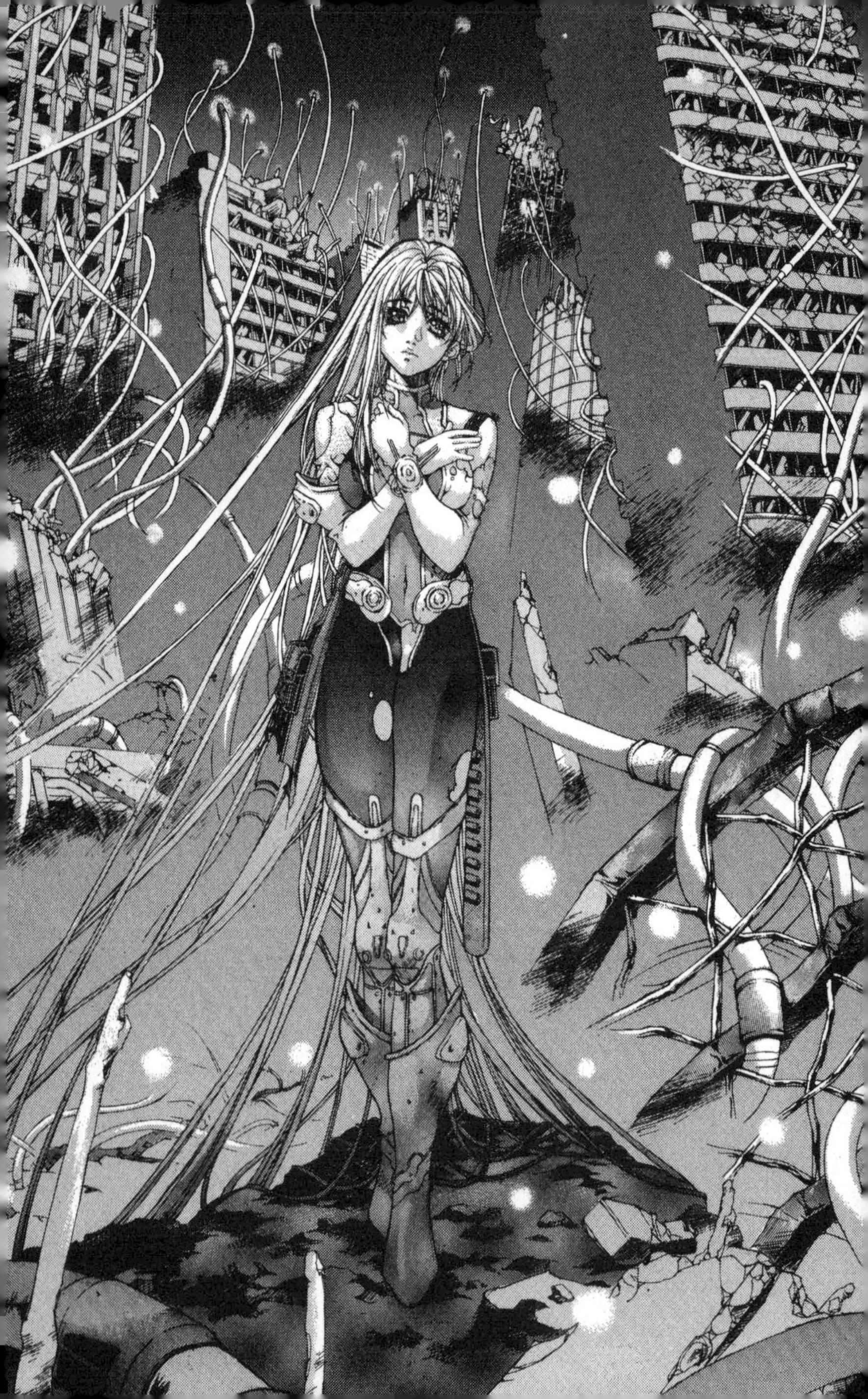

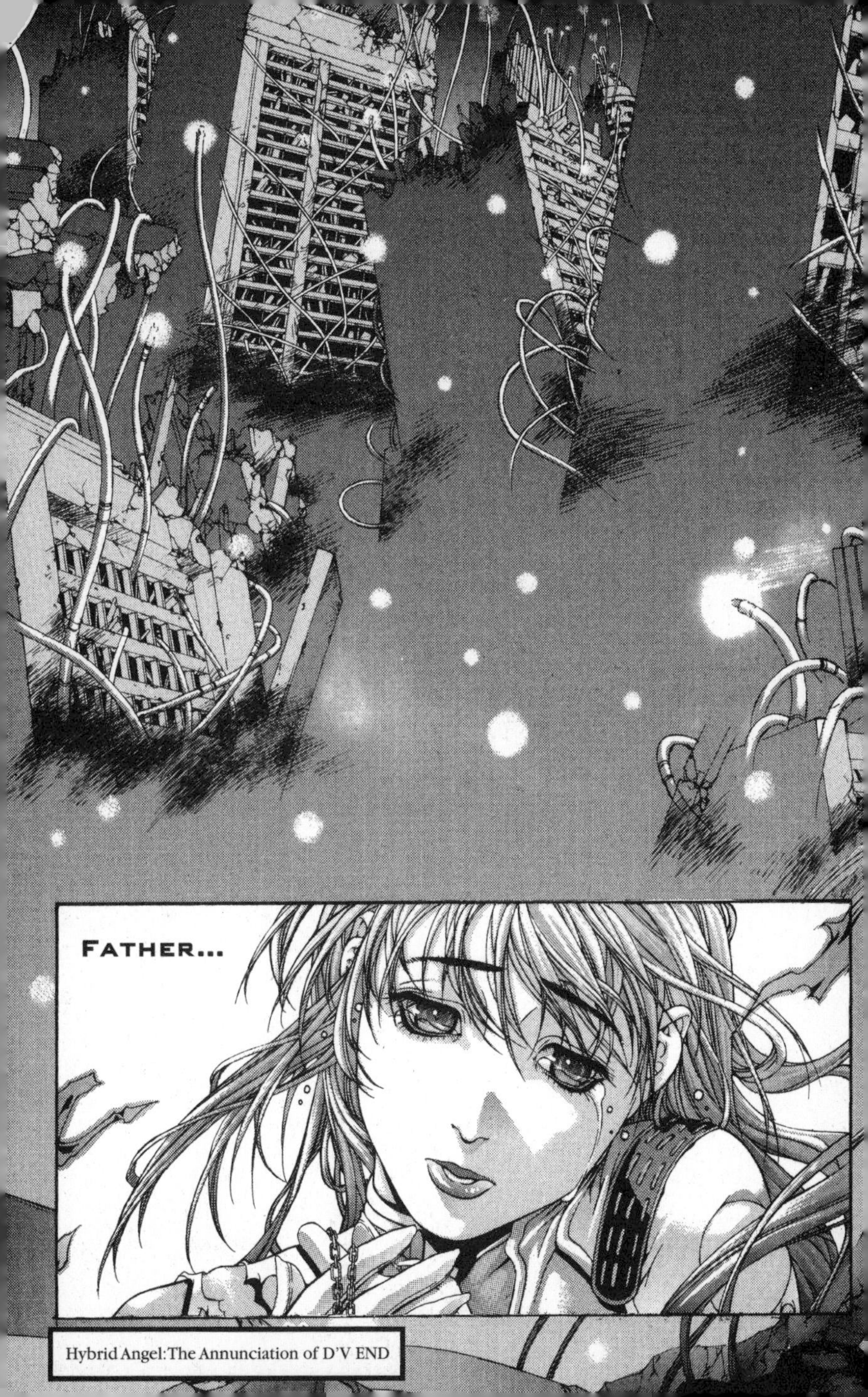
FATHER...
Hybrid Angel: The Annunciation of D'V END

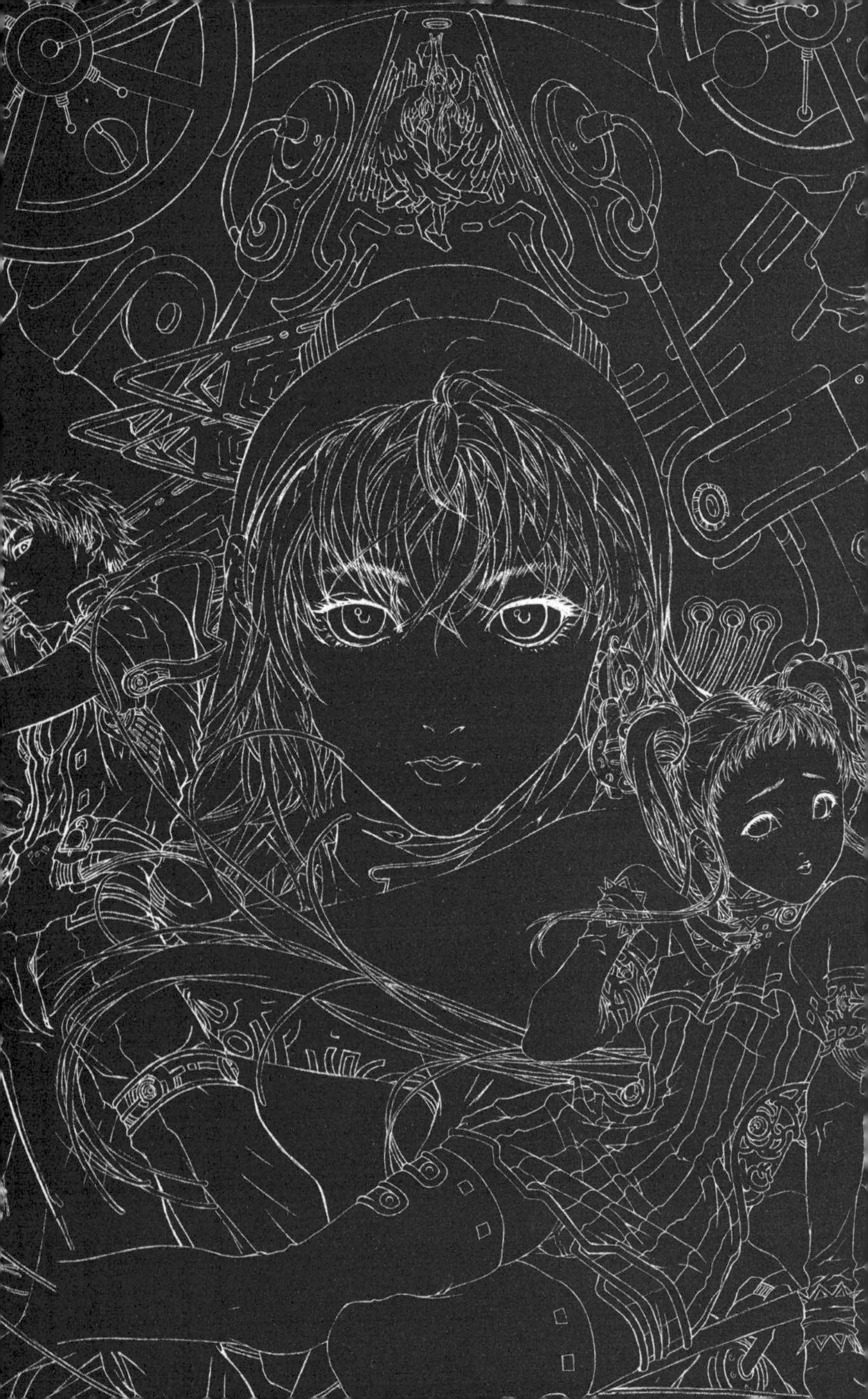

Beyond the dome of the Mother Seishia, Lemiu
looks forward to a bright future in nature with
a man and a child. But even as she starts on
this beautiful journey, the dark clouds of war
between androids and humans cumulate on
the horizon! Lemiu will have to fight to protect
Ash and her new baby from the anger and
prejudice that fills this world…and from the
new creatures spawned from a world mutated
by both man and machine.

ALSO AVAILABLE FROM 🔲TOKYOPOP®

**For more
information visit
www.TOKYOPOP.com**

03.30.04T

ALSO AVAILABLE FROM TOKYOPOP

MANGA

.HACK//LEGEND OF THE TWILIGHT
@LARGE
ABENOBASHI: MAGICAL SHOPPING ARCADE
A.I. LOVE YOU
AI YORI AOSHI
ANGELIC LAYER
ARM OF KANNON
BABY BIRTH
BATTLE ROYALE
BATTLE VIXENS
BRAIN POWERED
BRIGADOON
B'TX
CANDIDATE FOR GODDESS, THE
CARDCAPTOR SAKURA
CARDCAPTOR SAKURA - MASTER OF THE CLOW
CHOBITS
CHRONICLES OF THE CURSED SWORD
CLAMP SCHOOL DETECTIVES
CLOVER
COMIC PARTY
CONFIDENTIAL CONFESSIONS
CORRECTOR YUI
COWBOY BEBOP
COWBOY BEBOP: SHOOTING STAR
CRAZY LOVE STORY
CRESCENT MOON
CROSS
CULDCEPT
CYBORG 009
D•N•ANGEL
DEMON DIARY
DEMON ORORON, THE
DEUS VITAE
DIABOLO
DIGIMON
DIGIMON TAMERS
DIGIMON ZERO TWO
DOLL
DRAGON HUNTER
DRAGON KNIGHTS
DRAGON VOICE
DREAM SAGA
DUKLYON: CLAMP SCHOOL DEFENDERS
EERIE QUEERIE!
ERICA SAKURAZAWA: COLLECTED WORKS
ET CETERA
ETERNITY
EVIL'S RETURN
FAERIES' LANDING
FAKE
FLCL
FLOWER OF THE DEEP SLEEP
FORBIDDEN DANCE
FRUITS BASKET
G GUNDAM

GATEKEEPERS
GETBACKERS
GIRL GOT GAME
GIRLS' EDUCATIONAL CHARTER
GRAVITATION
GTO
GUNDAM BLUE DESTINY
GUNDAM SEED ASTRAY
GUNDAM WING
GUNDAM WING: BATTLEFIELD OF PACIFISTS
GUNDAM WING: ENDLESS WALTZ
GUNDAM WING: THE LAST OUTPOST (G-UNIT)
GUYS' GUIDE TO GIRLS
HANDS OFF!
HAPPY MANIA
HARLEM BEAT
HONEY MUSTARD
I.N.V.U.
IMMORTAL RAIN
INITIAL D
INSTANT TEEN: JUST ADD NUTS
ISLAND
JING: KING OF BANDITS
JING: KING OF BANDITS - TWILIGHT TALES
JULINE
KARE KANO
KILL ME, KISS ME
KINDAICHI CASE FILES, THE
KING OF HELL
KODOCHA: SANA'S STAGE
LAMENT OF THE LAMB
LEGAL DRUG
LEGEND OF CHUN HYANG, THE
LES BIJOUX
LOVE HINA
LUPIN III
LUPIN III: WORLD'S MOST WANTED
MAGIC KNIGHT RAYEARTH I
MAGIC KNIGHT RAYEARTH II
MAHOROMATIC: AUTOMATIC MAIDEN
MAN OF MANY FACES
MARMALADE BOY
MARS
MARS: HORSE WITH NO NAME
MINK
MIRACLE GIRLS
MIYUKI-CHAN IN WONDERLAND
MODEL
MY LOVE
NECK AND NECK
ONE
ONE I LOVE, THE
PARADISE KISS
PARASYTE
PASSION FRUIT
PEACH GIRL
PEACH GIRL: CHANGE OF HEART
PET SHOP OF HORRORS

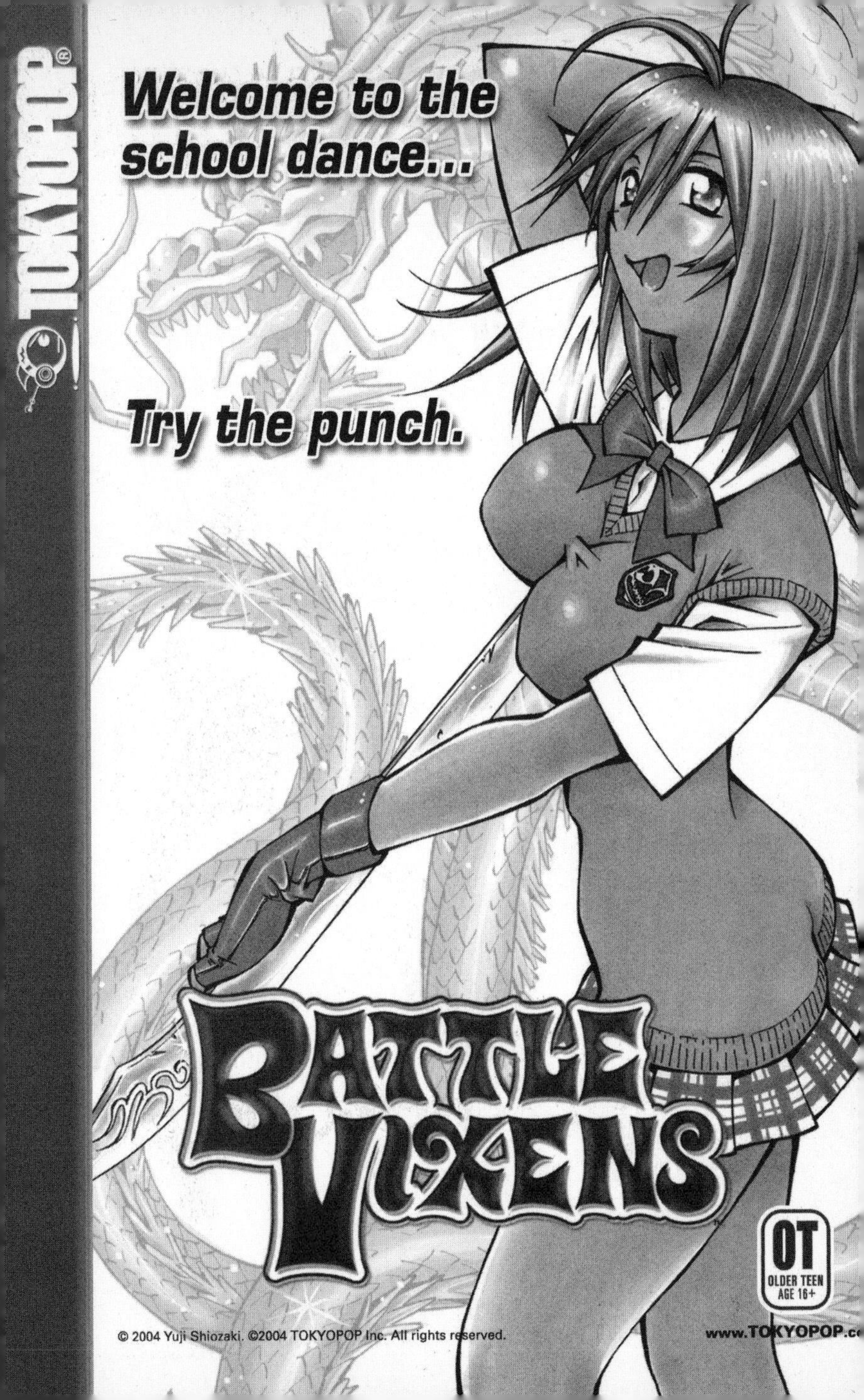
TOKYOPOP®
Welcome to the school dance...
Try the punch.
BATTLE VIXENS
OT
OLDER TEEN AGE 16+
© 2004 Yuji Shiozaki. ©2004 TOKYOPOP Inc. All rights reserved.
www.TOKYOPOP.c

STOP!

This is the back of the book.
You wouldn't want to spoil a great ending!

This book is printed "manga-style," in the authentic Japanese right-to-left format. Since none of the artwork has been flipped or altered, readers get to experience the story just as the creator intended. You've been asking for it, so TOKYOPOP® delivered: authentic, hot-off-the-press, and far more fun!

DIRECTIONS

If this is your first time reading manga-style, here's a quick guide to help you understand how it works.

It's easy... just start in the top right panel and follow the numbers. Have fun, and look for more 100% authentic manga from TOKYOPOP®!

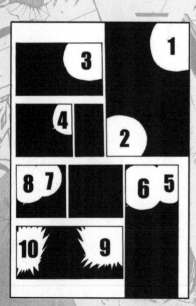